Rising Subjects

Russian and East European Studies

Jonathan Harris, Editor

The 1905 Revolution
and the
Origins of Modern Polish Politics

University of Pittsburgh Press

Published by the University of Pittsburgh Press, Pittsburgh, Pa., 15260
Copyright © 2020, University of Pittsburgh Press
All rights reserved
Manufactured in the United States of America
Printed on acid-free paper
10 9 8 7 6 5 4 3 2 1

Cataloging-in-Publication data is available from the Library of Congress

ISBN 13: 978-0-8229-4612-0
ISBN 10: 0-8229-4612-2

Cover art: Illustration from the cover of the SDKPiL clandestine journal *Czerwony Sztandar* from April 1905. Podlaska Digital Library Collection.
Cover design: Alex Wolfe

For my parents, who kindled my curiosity

Contents

Acknowledgments	ix
Abbreviations	xiii
Note on Translation	xv
Introduction	3
1 Workers and Their Intelligentsia	19
2 Workers and the Public Sphere	40
3 Speech and Action	77
4 Life and Politics	118
5 The Intelligentsia and Its Workers	155
Conclusion	192
Appendix: A Note on Methodology and Sources	211
Notes	217
Selected Bibliography	259
Index	291

Acknowledgments

Historians are lone wolves; sociologists more often work in packs. As I traversed both disciplines, even if I wrote alone I tried to discuss the results with as many people as possible. There is no better way to improve one's own work and to avoid blind alleys. This book is a product of an organic growth, which meanwhile resulted in many additional article-size studies, a research project which allowed me to gather primary sources, and a book in Polish that presented the initial findings for the purposes of this project. Thus many ideas came from consultations, talks, conference interventions, and private conversations that I am unable to recollect in detail, and it would be too cumbersome to list them here anyway. Many ideas presented in this study were suggested by generous commentators, and many resulted from consultations, reviews, or debates around the aforementioned additional products. I was lucky enough to receive generous support from various institutions apart from my irreplaceable alma mater, Central European University (CEU), where during my PhD studies I remained comfortably seated between my main Department of Sociology and Social Anthropology and the Department of History, which graciously accepted my conspicuous presence. Judit Bodnár and Balázs Trencsényi provided ongoing support. Brian Porter-Szűcs and Theodore R. Weeks offered supportive, yet harsh critique and invaluable encouragement to go on with the project.

Additional research was performed thanks to research grants from the Polish National Science Center. The grant contracted as 2012/05/N/HS3/01158 allowed me to gather the vast bulk of my primary sources. I also borrowed some primary sources from a collaborative project contracted as 2011/03/B/HS6/01874, hosted and supervised by Professor Kaja Kaźmierska in the Department of Sociology of Culture at the University of Lodz, Poland. Final work on the book was made possible thanks to generous support by the same institution, contracted as 2017/27/B/HS6/00098 in the Robert Zajonc Institute for Social Studies, University of Warsaw, where I am now continuing to develop my research project, extending it through space and time.

My initial studies of the topic owed much to the faith and support of Kazimierz Kowalewicz at the University of Lodz. Later I often returned there, receiving constant support, understanding, and new ideas from Marek Czyżewski, Andrzej Maciej Kaniowski, and Kaja Kaźmierska. In the meantime, I was hosted as a fellow or guest researcher in many places where numerous people offered me guidance, ideas, and critique: the Eisenberg Institute and the Department of History at the University of Michigan in Ann Arbor (Brian Porter-Szűcs), the re:work Research Center at Humboldt University in Berlin (Andreas Eckert), the Center for Interdisciplinary Polish Studies at the Viadrina University in Frankfurt (Oder), and the Institute for Human Sciences in Vienna. I made final adjustments during my stay at the Center for Advanced Study in Sofia (Diana Mishkova) and at the Center for Historical Research at the Higher School of Economics in St. Petersburg (Alexander Semyonov). The thriving academic environment in all these institutions constantly nourished my thinking and opened many doors to my curiosity and will to read, talk, and write. Librarians in all those universities, archivists from the Polish National Library in Warsaw, and the state archives in Lodz and Warsaw were always supportive of my queries.

In the early years, I was supported by a virtuoso of the archive, who practically taught me how to move there, Kamil Piskała. He recently made a great comeback, offering his disinterested support to track down the much-needed illustrations. In processing the material, Adam Musiałowicz and Izabela Smuga contributed their share. I presented and discussed various chunks of this study as conference presentations, separate articles, and chapters. I am unable to assign any clear priorities or list all meetings, workshops, and conferences, and thus I mention in alphabetic order all those who gave so generously of their time: Agnes Arndt, Volodymyr Artiukh, Jörg Baberowski, Arnd Bauerkämper, Łukasz Biskupski, Eric Blanc, Robert Blobaum, Howard Brick, Kathleen Canning, John Clarke, Marek Czyżewski, Mathieu Desan, Geoff Eley, Jean-Louis Fabiani, Jan Hennings, Stephan Ludwig Hoffman, Jan Ivfersen, Maciej Janowski, Don Kalb, Andrzej Maciej Kaniowski, Webb Keane, Mark Keck-Szajbel, Howard Kimeldorf, Jürgen Kocka, Aleksandra Kowalski, Grzegorz Krzywiec, Peter Linebaugh, Alf Lüdtke, Brendan McGeever, Alexei Miller, Michael Miller, Diana Mishkowa, Daniel Monterescu, Jan-Werner Müller, Vlad Naumescu, Margrit Pernau, Jan Plamper, Gertrud Pickhan, Kamil Piskała, Brian Porter-Szücs, Michał Pospiszyl, Kirill Postoutenko, Harsha Ram, Alfred Rieber, Jürgen

Schmidt, Alexander Semyonov, Marsha Siefert, Ronald Grigor Suny, Keely Stauter-Halsted, George Steinmetz, Willibald Steinmetz, Krystian Szadkowski, Kamil Śmiechowski, Jana Tsoneva, Balazs Vedres, Kathleen Wróblewski, Tomasz Zarycki, and Geneviève Zubrzycki. Last but certainly not least, Paul Barron, Lindsay Curtis, James Hartzell, Sanjay Kumar, David Ridout, and Thomas Rooney helped me at various stages to make my writing understandable. The editors at University of Pittsburgh Press (Peter Kracht, Amy Sherman, and my copy editor, Carolyn Pouncy, among others) welcomed my manuscript with supportive critique and guided me patiently through all stages of the publishing process.

I owe special expressions of gratitude to my parents, who never failed to discuss crucial issues of Polish social and political life and provided essential support in the pivotal moments of my own academic biography.

On all possible levels: academically, intellectually, emotionally and organizationally, this work would not have begun without my former coauthor, discussant, and first reader, Agata Zysiak. Claudia Eggart has since given me fresh insights, renewed faith, and the last push without which this book would not have been finished.

Abbreviations

CKR	Centralny Komitet Robotniczy (Central Workers' Committee)
KPP	Komunistyczna Partia Polski (Polish Communist Party)
KR	Komitet Robotniczy (Workers' Committee)
ŁKR	Łódzki Komitet Robotniczy (Lodz Workers' Committee)
ND	Narodowa Demokracja (National Democracy)
NZR	Narodowy Związek Robotniczy (National Workers' Association)
OKR	Okręgowy Komitet Robotniczy (Regional Workers' Commitee)
PD	Postępowa Demokracja (Progressive Democracy)
PPS	Polska Partia Socjalistyczna (Polish Socialist Party)
PPS-Left	Polska Partia Socjalistyczna Lewica (Polish Socialist Party-Left)
PPS-RF	Polska Partia Socjalistyczna-Frakcja rewolucyjna (Polish Socialist Party-Revolutionary Faction)
PZPR	Polska Zjednoczona Partia Robotnicza (Polish United Workers' Party)
SDKPiL	Socjaldemokracja Królestwa Polskiego i Litwy (Social Democracy of the Kingdom of Poland and Lithuania)
TON	Towarzystwo Oświaty Narodowej (Society for National Education)
WKR	Warszawski Komitet Robotniczy (Warsaw Workers' Committee)
ZG	Zarząd Główny (Heading Committee)

Note on Translations, Place Names, Concepts, and Notes

All translations of Polish sources (primary and secondary) are mine, unless indicated otherwise. As in many histories of the region, place names have different spellings, and the choice is never benign. I decided to use English place names whenever possible: for example, Warsaw and Lodz. Where there is no commonly used English equivalent, the Polish name will be used, because the vast bulk of the sources are in Polish, and the Polish question remains at the center of my focus. Similarly, all names originally spelled in Polish remain so: for example, Feliks Dzierżyński, not Felix Dzherzhinsky.

Also, concepts of identity create difficulties—the description of someone as a "Jew" or a "Pole" in the sources does not necessarily correspond to the current use of these labels, and vice versa. To make things even more difficult, any of these labels convey multiple and mixed affiliations. I try to qualify or clarify these when appropriate. When additional comment on the vernacular wording in the sources is needed I add it in rectangular brackets []. I generally give full bibliographical notation for primary sources (e.g., leaflets or autobiographies) in the endnotes, while a shortened form suffices for secondary literature listed in the bibliography. Detailed information on the notation for particular groups of sources is given in the appendix.

Rising Subjects

Introduction

> His eyes are laughing; his face is glowing; he is carrying almost without any effort a huge timber, throwing it across the street; and as if in triumph he straightens his body. He is truly beautiful at that moment. In his posture, happiness can be read; it can be seen that he has lived to experience something for which he had been waiting for a long time. He was killed on the barricade, and he died happy.
>
> And finally a man of gigantic height and weight approached the podium. His sullen, red face had only one expression: that of dull stupidity. He was ushered onto the podium by a young Jew [żydek—diminutive from żyd, a derogatory expression used among casual antisemites], who introduced him as the one who was supposed to speak in the name of the hungry workers. The fat scoundrel hooted: "Down with Poland, down with the white eagle." . . . The Jew flounced onto the podium in convulsions of wild fury or happiness.

In 1905 new groups of people entered the sparse political scene of Russian Poland. Urban workers came out into the streets in protest, which from striking and picketing led to an urban uprising and the construction of barricades. They also embarked on various forms of public debate such as mass meetings and rallies. The above descriptions are reactions triggered by this unprecedented situation. They are memoirs written by eyewitnesses perceiving the new political practice of workers. Vivid creations of memory in both cases, they reveal important elements of political imagination and emotion. However diametrically opposed, they demonstrate the impact of insurgent democratization on the social imaginary equally well.

The first depiction is about the "politics of the street." Regardless of whether it is an inscription of memory or mere literary imagination, it captures an excitement with the new. It refers to politics forcefully challenging the existing order and the revolutionary zeal of barricade building in June 1905 in Lodz. It is about politics of the street, used to stake claims otherwise illegitimate in palace courtrooms and factory offices. It also registers a pivotal change in the lives of revolutionized workers. It does not stress death but the self-assertion of a person embarking on a struggle bigger than personal involvement, and by this act gaining a form of agency and dignity he had been deprived of for all his previous life.

The second epigraph is a rejection yet refers to a more moderate form of participation—a mass meeting organized by liberals in the building of the Warsaw Philharmonic Concert Hall in November 1905. It describes a semiauthorized rally in a public building with a podium and seats for the participants, where speakers took turns sharing their political ideas, close to even the most moderate idea of what it meant to practice politics. Nevertheless, the picture presented by a noble woman supporting the liberals is a dense composition of all the means usually mobilized to reinforce political difference and exclusion. An anthropological or physiognomic difference separates the rabble and those deemed legitimate to voice their political statements. The orator she depicts is alien not only in respect to class; he also sticks out as a proxy of an ethnic community carefully policed out of the legitimate polity of the Poles. Every detail of his performance renders his claims usurpatory—after all, a "fat scoundrel" cannot righteously represent "hungry workers." It is a "Jew" who ushers in the claimant, ultimately testifying to the foreign and hostile origin of the claim. In a paroxysm of the rabble excited with its own self-acclaimed greatness, even basic emotions, let alone claims, cannot be properly detected. It is not an argument that is uttered but instead "convulsions of wild fury or happiness." It cannot be recognized whether it is this or that, nor does it matter at all amid noise that never does become a voice.

Both depictions touch on the heart of the problem investigated in this study. The invisible limits of participation are made flesh in a vision of heroic self-assertion and a discourse of class contempt embroidered with ethnic accusation. The bearded oldster from the first quote (incidentally, also a Jew) forcefully questions his assigned place, and the popular classes storming the liberal salon from the second quote are doing exactly the same. They demonstrate that politics is a realm with carefully policed limits. They also expose, however, the fact that those limits might be questioned, and sometimes moved. Political action is no less than a redrawing of these limits. This is what happened during the crisis of 1904–1907 in Russian Poland, which is usually called the 1905 Revolution, and indeed might be dubbed "the long 1905." Correspondingly, in undertaking this study I wanted to understand the contentious renegotiation concerning the presence of workers within the public sphere, a communicative space composed of words and practices. Moreover, a large proportion of the urban working class was already female, thus the redrawing of the political also included the gender dimension. All in all, the political sphere was overhauled during the revolution.

The 1905 Revolution in the Russian-controlled Kingdom of Poland was one of the few bottom-up political transformations and general democratizations in Polish history, probably paralleled only by the "first" Solidarity movement in the early 1980s. As the political upsurge ultimately brought about defeat of the popular classes rising for political recognition and economic alleviation, it is not in direct political or social outcomes where one should look for its major significance. The 1905 Revolution introduced a plethora of new issues into the public debate and reconfigured the political field. This insurgent democratization and its corollaries were part and parcel of the broader yet asynchronous transformation of societies and political regimes in modernity. At the same time, it was also an instance of the discontinuous history of plebeian political experience. Therefore, its analysis also addresses broader questions within the historical sociology of the political.

The insurgent democratization set the stage for modern politics in the area and was a tipping point for ongoing developments in the public sphere. It was a change within the conditions that governed the practice of politics; new stakes, new measures, and new lines of division emerged that circumscribed any further actions. Modern mass parties were born, and new political languages appeared, which set the stage for later debates and struggles.[1] Basic divisions, unbridgeable rifts, and mutual perceptions forged in 1905 between parties, ideologies, and social groupings set the tone for the politics of interwar Poland.[2] With the birth of protest culture, labor militancy continued without abating for years afterward.[3] The particular social structure of Polish society and its discursive representation traced the contours of the political sphere in respect to presence and presentation of class.[4] For instance, decades later, the dissident intellectuals in the period of state socialism acknowledged their intellectual indebtedness to and self-conscious imitation of intelligentsia from the turn of the century. They also mimicked earlier tacit assumptions about, and attitudes to, "the people."[5] This was an afterimage of the initial political experience of the Polish twentieth century.

Bearing in mind the significance of this moment, this study explores the change of the public sphere in Russian Poland during the 1905 Revolution. I am interested in how spaces and representations of the political have changed through continuous processes of redefinition and reenactment. I want to understand the circumstances that shaped the nascent modern political practice in respect to the presence of the working class—or for that matter, simply the workers—as a social entity, as a political claimant, and as a discursive construction. To do this, the problem must be disentangled into several interrelated threads, such as those concerning public participation, political discourses, subjective identities and self-definitions, or the relationship between social groups. To ascertain the constellation that precipitated further developments of the Polish political space, I look at the workers' public sphere, the uses of political language, the entanglement of biography and politics, and the image of "the workers" in the press.

Correspondingly, in the first part of this study I scrutinize nascent forms of political education within party milieus, which finally came to the fore in 1905. Strikes, factory constituencies, political street performances, and new forms of public participation constituted nascent forms of the working-class public sphere. Subsequently, I examine the changing regime of political speech (language in action materialized in political proclamations; leaflets and party newspapers distributed among workers). I also ask about new uses and abuses of language, taking political antisemitism as an example of a political device assisting the construction of new political identities and an infrastructure of political exclusion. Afterward, I investigate workers' intellectual pursuits and the relationship between a work-centered life context, militant biography, and political claims. The last section focuses on the political visibility of workers in the press. Here I focus on the interplay of, on the one hand, the acceptance of workers' new "place" and agency and, on the other, pushback from the industrial bourgeoisie, fearful liberals, and nationalists opposing the insurgent democratization.

Insurgent Democratization

"Bloody Sunday" in January 1905, when tsarist soldiers opened fire in St. Petersburg on a crowd carrying icons and portraits of the then-praised tsar, was not only an event triggering the revolutionary process in Russia proper; it also instantly catalyzed outbursts of rioting in the areas at the fringes of the Russian Empire. In Russian Poland, it built on unrest that had been germinating for at least a year, during which dissatisfaction with the economic crisis and conscription for the Russo-Japanese War had already caused people to flock to the squares and confront Russian troops.[6] A complex process consisting of waves of contention and state repression began. It led to uncountable political and economic strikes, to electoral campaigns to the State Duma (a form of advisory parliamentary body introduced in Russia in those days), to street demonstrations that ended in bloodshed. Its pinnacle was a quasi-uprising with street barricades, but on the downside came "fratricidal" struggles between workers.

While the events of 1904–1907 are best known as the Russian Revolution of 1905, a large part of the militant actions, strikes, street fights, and other forms of social unrest actually happened in the urban centers of Russian Poland. Over one-third of strikes in the entire empire happened there, and they were generally more massive than elsewhere, with up to 90 percent of workers striking at least once in 1905. These were not only sporadic outbursts; by 1906 one-fifth of Polish workers had joined a labor union, and a similar proportion had joined a political party.[7] Women accounted for up to one-fifth of those involved.[8] Though the turmoil had a different dynamic outside the cities, the skirmishes also affected the rural population, radicalizing landless peasants and farm workers.[9]

The mass rioting expressed accumulated tensions and dissatisfaction. In the first phase it was a general resistance and refusal of further participation in a system of oppression. Right after the initial general strike of January 1905, the Warsaw governor-general admitted that "workers, having ceased to work, did not make any demands."[10] However, an amorphous refusal gradually changed its character, a certain structure of revolt began to crystallize, and various, alternating sets of demands emerged, along with symbolic points organizing the struggle. Without a doubt, there were social grievances present among peasants-turned-workers migrating to the cities and the impoverished petty craftsmen. The tsarist state was not a liberal dreamland and did not offer much welfare support or political freedoms. What it delivered in abundance, however, was harsh military policing and an ineffective administration, which was widely perceived as foreign and occupational by the local population. Adding insult to injury, factory officials and foremen were often German, and owners were often German or Jewish, while the working population was Polish or Jewish. Such an intersectional regime of domination facilitated an equally complex solidarity of resistance. In an imperial situation characterized by a multiethnic population and unequal access to power, the cultural cauldron was a fertile hotbed for social struggle tightly interwoven with national liberation and ethnic animosities.

When those emotions erupted, every political organization was one step behind. "None of the political parties that would later claim to have organized or initiated the events of 1905 really deserve the credit (or blame) for doing so. It would be better to say that they were poised to take advantage of events that they could neither fully predict nor control," as Brian Porter-Szűcs comments.[11] Nevertheless, membership in all types of political organizations rose rapidly, a process even more striking considering that they were not authorized by the autocratic regime. In fact, any illegal, but for a while hardly clandestine, activity may have led—and often did—to harsh police repression and imprisonment. Nevertheless, political parties grew from tiny cadre organizations run chiefly by the intelligentsia, to mass membership parties, reaching approximately every fifth worker in the Polish Kingdom.[12] Parties and newly emerging labor unions directly mobilized at least 150,000 people, most of them for the very first time.[13] By any definition, it was a unidirectional mobilization. Class-based, internationalist Social Democracy in the Kingdom of Poland and Lithuania (SDKPiL) competed with the more nationally oriented Polish Socialist Party (PPS) and among Jewish workers with the Bund, which aimed to organize Jewish workers throughout the empire. They were soon rivaled by the sheer Polish nationalism of the National Democracy party and its labor branch, the National Workers' Association (NZR).[14] A fierce political struggle between parties competing to build new political identities—be they class, nation, or various combinations of the two—wreaked havoc.

The bid for the new political claimants made real what had been only disputed before.[15] Possible futures for the Polish people had been imagined by party ideologues and writers from intelligentsia milieus. The intelligentsia—with its specific characteristics of an intermediary social position, educational resources, blocked upward mobility, and vocational ethos—played an important role in radical politics and in the elite's response to it. The "masses," however, didn't want to wait for the intelligentsia to lead and educate them, and they went out into the streets. The assumed political community could no longer be postponed or deferred; there was no time left for any visions of a future reconciliation of tensions within it. Political constituencies had to be mobilized and disciplined in the here and now.

Thus the 1905 Revolution is perhaps best understood not as a party bid for power but as a transformation of politics as practice. It was the democratic dimension of mass politics, and not elite party gatherings or even conspiratorial agitation led by the intelligentsia, that circumscribed the contours of the broader social experience of the revolution.[16] Beyond the very top of the political elite, there was a vast group of rank-and-file activists who were at once the producers, the dealers, and the consumers of the era's ideological churn. When the workers spoke and acted, they did so with a conceptual vocabulary inherited from earlier generations of political activists (mostly the intelligentsia). If the distinction between intelligentsia and workers was a crucial nexus of contemporary polemics and action, it may not be reified on the analytical level today. Intellectual history, especially the popular one I embark on, is always produced in the space where the ideas of theorists and full-time activists contact those who are searching for words and phrases that capture their experiences and feelings. Then a feedback loop circles back to the theorists and activists.[17] How precisely that process is characterized is a more difficult question, which I will try address as my arguments unfold.

Even a brief look at the existing historical research overwhelms the reader with the multiplicity of political organizations, labor committees and unions, and associational life that established the cornerstone for modern civil society. The tsarist Manifesto of October 1905, which introduced constitutional reform and abolished preventive censorship, heralded a new era in the kingdom's public sphere. The liberalized law on associations from March 1906 spurred on the development of all types of voluntary organizations, including trade unions. The authorized and underground press flourished, and the number of both commercial and political titles mushroomed. They addressed the unprecedented growth of interest in public matters.[18] The revolution encouraged new social groups, in particular the urban working class, to actively participate in the public sphere. The events, for better and for worse, ushered the Polish Kingdom into the age of modern politics.[19] It was not allowed, however, to remain there.

The revolution failed and was bloodily suppressed, leading to a vast array of social disintegration processes and political repression measures. Elusive political gains on the tsarist state level, such as those gained in the October

Manifesto, were soon canceled after the tsarist regime regained some vigor. In his seminal depiction, Robert Blobaum bemoans the demise of the nascent civil society in these words: "Martial law . . . did much to arrest, if not reverse, the development of civil society. That society . . . perhaps had been brought to a premature blossom by the revolution. Like a warm, early, but also stormy spring, the revolution fostered the sudden budding out of a multitude of associations, societies, and organizations. . . . These bodies, intermediate between state and society . . . were strained, sometimes violently, by their too-rapid growth and by the pressures of popular participation, in unprecedented numbers, by many whose only experience had been that of subjects and not that of citizens."[20]

Inasmuch as tsarist repression was certainly the case, one may wonder what was hidden under the wording of the phrase "pressures of popular participation." Whereas parties and organizations undoubtedly had a lot of trouble managing the sky-rocketing growth in participation, it could hardly have been a key factor in their dispersal and ultimate failure. Similarly, another important voice on the topic, Scott Ury, concludes his outline of the theory of "democracy and its discontents" (the title of his book chapter) with the conclusion that "while democracy may have brought many blessings, it also came with at least one curse that would scar Polish society for generations: political antisemitism."[21] Both authors suggest that the democratic surge imploded under its own weight, as if too heavy to be carried by political newcomers. What remains unnoticed, however, is that it was not the tragedy of popular participation but rather the elite's reaction to it that prevented civil society from "blossoming" and fostered popular anger against "the Jews."[22]

The postrevolutionary regression in civil activities can be explained neither by the unambiguously repressive nature of the tsarist regime, which relentlessly suppressed any emerging civic institutions, nor by the inherent incapacities of the Polish people. The tsarist administration was not the only agent frightened by the emerging self-determination of the people and the democratic surge. A reluctant and later hostile reaction to it was also harbored among propertied strata, growing nationalist milieus, and a significant part of the intelligentsia. The nationalists feared the revolution was carrying a Trojan horse, capable of destroying the true nation. It also questioned the procession of progress as envisioned by the liberal intelligentsia, which was ready to educate the masses but reluctant to accept their political agency. These dual effects triggered by the revolution, democratization and contraction, are important to note when tackling the conundrum of the changing and conflictual public sphere investigated here.

The Conflict Within

The modern transformation of European polities concerned democratization, citizenship, and legitimacy of class-based claims. The expansion of these trends was, however, often followed by contraction, grounded in reaction among particular political agents but also in a broader social countertendency to seek order after the old foundations had been shaken. This dual dynamic influenced the patterns of emerging national public spheres. As Geoff Eley remarks, "the emergence of a bourgeois public was never defined solely by the struggle against absolutism and traditional authority but addressed the problem of popular containment as well. The public sphere was always constituted by conflict."[23] Accommodating the rising working class within the modern polity was one of the more serious challenges that the European political systems of the nineteenth century had to face. At the same time, it drove their democratization on the institutional, social, and imaginary levels, as Eley documents elsewhere.[24] The resulting changes stirred up conflict, and often only an intense social protest was able to tip the scales in favor of political and social democratization.

The limits of the public sphere and of what was considered political was a major stake in this conflict. It defined the realm of the debatable and the set of legitimate claimants. It was the working class who opposed the strongholds of the ancien régime, which had merged with a new bourgeois hegemony often reluctant and fearful of any concessions.[25] Consequently, working-class formation, coherent class action, and labor political identities were crucial factors in the outcome of this confrontation.[26] At the same time, changes in regimes of the public sphere were crucial for the formation of the working class and hence for its recognition as a political actor.[27] In a modified, but not so divergent, sense "every class struggle is a political struggle," as Karl Marx and Friedrich Engels announced in the *Manifesto of the Communist Party*.[28] In this sociopolitical vortex the social question concerning economic well-being was closely intertwined with the acceptance of political citizenship for workers. As the historical sociologist Reinhard Bendix explains:

> The workers organize in order to attain that level of economic reward to which they feel entitled. . . . These practical achievements of trade unions have a

far-reaching effect upon the status of workers as citizens. For through collective bargaining the right to combine is used to assert "basic claims to the elements of social justice." In this way the extension of citizenship to the lower classes is given the very special meaning that as citizens the members of these classes are "entitled" to a certain standard of well-being, in return for which they are only obliged to discharge the ordinary duties of citizenship.[29]

This admission proceeded differently within various national or imperial polities. Often it faced powerful opposition and counterblows executed by the liberal proponents of individual rights. Once opposed to the old autocracies, liberals nevertheless rejected the collective entitlement and political agency of workers, embarking on a "politics of fear," as Marc Mulholland calls it.[30] According to Victoria Bonnell, however, "the two battles—for the civil rights and for the collective rights of labor—had been fought . . . simultaneously in Russia during the 1905 revolution and workers played a leading part in advancing both claims," elsewhere often made sequentially.[31] As a result, the middle strata of the entire empire with all their regional specificities were initially much more saturated with radical ideas and prone to support working-class revolutionary fervor than in Western Europe.[32] The conflict and the class struggle from above came later, not unlike in other instances of European history.[33] The configuration of forces was, however, quite different. It was from within popular constituencies that many actual incentives to reform came. Nevertheless, working-class public activities were not well integrated in the liberal political culture of the scarce but influential bourgeois social order.[34] Thus they faced resistance, conspicuously present on the fringes of the Russian Empire, where seemingly the national question might unify various contenders against the tsarist autocracy.

While the presence of the "foreign autocracy" concealed important tensions within the Polish polity, it did not render them obsolete. Methodological nationalism of any sort is not a good tool to understand this charged reality. Such a research framework still stands strong even if some scholarship has been chipping away at it.[35] The way out is not only to consider the broader imperial situation but to look for fractures within the nation, society, or language-based communicative sphere. The strained negotiation of the working-class presence epitomized the dynamic of democratization and contraction, as well as the internal conflicts and limitations of the forces pitted against old monarchical order. Correspondingly, this study is intended to bring these heterogeneous forces to light and complicate the picture of European democratization and contraction, or revolution and reaction.

The revolution with all its corollaries was a pivotal moment in the transformation of the public sphere in Russian Poland. It underwent a severe transformation encompassing the renegotiation of the age-old nobility's hegemony. Unlike the entrenched landed elites of the ready-made nation states, the Polish elites could not postulate a neat separation from the people or preach their own interests as the embodiment of universal reason. The eighteenth century implosion of the Polish Lithuanian-Commonwealth, leading to the collapse of Polish statehood and the broadly acknowledged "degeneration" of the Polish nobles' political culture, had effectively prevented them from retaking the reins of national leadership. The modern economic transformation and political repression after the January uprising in 1863 further unseated the landed elites from their privileged status, even if some of them remained economically powerful.[36] By the turn of the century, they were put under pressure by the imperial administration and lost credibility among their co-nationals. The industrial bourgeoisie was still scarce and widely perceived as foreign. Members of the urban elite had just begun to assert themselves through philanthropy and could make only a rather weak attempt at social and urban reforms.[37] They were too detached from the state to take the lead, and only later could they get involved in the domestic conflict with new contenders. The self-proclaimed leader of Polish society was the intelligentsia, a particular social strata usually composed of the educated offspring of the gentry and neither a bourgeois intellectual elite nor a professional middle class.[38] Putting into practice their ethos of social service, members of the intelligentsia were quite aware of the fact that in order to think about any national revival, they needed to get the populace on board. The question was under what conditions, in which direction, and how the new crew would behave if confronted with the rough sea of modern politics.[39]

When the benign assumptions about "the people" were challenged, the progressive alliance of the intelligentsia and the populace appeared to be a fragile one. In Russian Poland, state policing was even harsher than in Russia, which prevented any "decent" citizen from conspiring with the militant workers. The same concerned those workers who would be willing to embark on any open conversation with the urban elite. Apart from this, the bourgeoisie had hardly any developed social patterns that workers could imitate and adopt.⁴⁰ Moreover, the state was not a viable addressee of any claims possibly forged in negotiation and supported by other social groups. Had such mediation been possible, the search for support among the progressive bourgeoisie might have boosted the incentives for political moderation.⁴¹ Simultaneously, the "foreign" tsarist regime inhibited any practical political action within the framework of the state and the accompanying modes of reasoning. As a result, a quasi-utopian radicalism and unrealistic views about popular politics nourished debates among the intelligentsia and in the liberal salons. This development further distracted these groups from adopting a political way of thinking,⁴² perhaps much more than in the Western context of earlier opposition against the absolutist state or even in the context of Russia proper under the tsar. All this created a power vacuum under and against the autocratic state. The evacuated space was reoccupied by the industrial working class, which, regardless of its insular presence, defined the situation to a much larger extent than in Russia.⁴³ This trend, however, did not remain unanswered by other social strata, fearful about the overall destabilization of the social order.

Nevertheless, the constellation of the state, labor movement, civil society, and changing social structure renders the case of Russian Poland particularly helpful in exploring patterns of European democratization—especially because, so far, it has typically been overlooked in otherwise well-informed comparisons.⁴⁴ The reason was perhaps its peculiar, intermediary, and sub-state status or the aforementioned binary imagination unanimously pitting autocracy against the democratizing society. The long-inhibited modern transformation combined with uneven yet rapid industrialization made the 1905 Revolution a much more revealing, intensified confrontation than those known elsewhere. Thus it is a "laboratory" shedding light on dynamics and tensions accompanying the emergence of modern mass politics and admitting workers within the assumed political community. The imperial situation of Eastern Europe, additionally marked by the national self-assertion of imperial subjects, supplements the findings regarding the strained negotiations of the working-class presence within the national polities of Western Europe.

At the same time, however, Polish politics in 1905 is worthy of study not because it offers a revealing exception but quite the contrary—a typical case. Unlike the Western bourgeoisie-led models, the Polish path exemplifies the way most of the world actually experienced political modernization. The liminal intelligentsia performed a central role, with elites grabbling with simultaneous devotion to and fear of "the people," not unlike in Central and Southern America, the Mexican Revolution being the most notable example.[45] If in many African or Asian contexts the situation was complicated by the colonial question and racial distinctions, it was not entirely different, with comprador vernacular elites suppressing populist attempts. For this reason, Poland is more in line with global patterns than we often assume, with Western Europe standing apart as the odd case that requires explanation.

A Historically Changing Political Space and the Public Sphere

In historical terms, modern politics was forged as a particular nexus of power and communication within a vortex of state, law, civil society, the public sphere, and other, more tangible institutional forms, such as parliaments or monarchical settings.[46] In part because the problem is viewed from this angle, governments, monarchs, parties, or parliaments and the activities related to these agents attract the bulk of attention in the existing research.[47] My study, in contrast, focuses on more dispersed regimes of class-based political visibility and agency.

Because I aim to investigate the paramount transformation affecting the indirect corollaries of the political regime, I do not deal much with parliament, the legal setting, or the attitude of the state to civil society. Instead, I focus on the public sphere, variably accessible for various social groups, and represent them in a patterned manner. The reason for this is threefold: (1) it is an important under-researched dimension of the emergence of modern politics; (2) in Russian Poland political change affected precisely this aspect, and not so much the state structure; and (3) change was stimulated on the streets and during political mass meetings and not in parliament, for the simple reason that there was none. The State Duma created during the revolution was a place of debate on pan-Russian politics and national autonomy but not on the problem investigated here. My focus, therefore, is the contingent process of reordering and reunifying society in respect to class and nation, through revolutionary dislocation. The fierce struggle that ensued was waged to a large extent within the public sphere.

In particular, I am interested in the transformation of the public sphere by insurgent alternative subspheres, through the introduction of new political practices and modes of participation. Inasmuch as the public sphere is—in the seminal depiction of Jürgen Habermas—the "sphere which mediates between society and state, in which the public organizes itself as the bearer of public opinion," I am interested in how different social groups participated and how public opinion regarding those groups was formed.[48] Usually, the educated, decent, burgher constituencies assuming the mantle of general social representation in the face of the state apparatus have been placed at the center. Here, on the contrary, they are of interest only inasmuch as they evolve in terms of their social composition and react against new contenders making claims from the revolutionary street.

At the same time, the focal point of my interest is the Polish public sphere, seen as a realm of political reasoning, discussion, and practice, "in which political participation is enacted through the medium of talk," to borrow Nancy Fraser's definition.[49] Thus I limit this exploration to Polish-language materials constituting the field of effective discourse and interaction.[50] This decision may appear problematic given a multilingual imperial context and transnational and global academic incentives. This limitation notwithstanding, I do not assert that the polity being envisioned in this sphere had stable borders. On the contrary, the intersection of class and ethnicity was often played out in order to police these borders and secure stabilization of the national body politic. For instance, as it will be revealed below, class-based claims were delegitimized as not appropriately Polish. At the same time, however, class mobilization might acquire undertones of national self-assertion. Class and national elements played out in different proportions within both shop-floor politics and highly nuanced theoretical approaches wavering between "nationalism and Marxism," to borrow Timothy Snyder's wording.[51] The focus on a single language-based communicative space enables me to read such tensions from within and uncover layered cultural imaginaries or a history of particular concepts active in shaping the debate. It gives me a chance to focus on social rifts within the contested polity and the inner struggle defining the public sphere. Unavoidably I present here an incomplete picture of an incredibly complicated situation unfolding in the medium of at least four languages, with Yiddish playing almost as prominent a role as Polish. The origins of the Polish-speaking political sphere, however, are worth studying, because it became dominant throughout this area after 1918. While Yiddish and Polish may have had a similar status before the First World War, their relative weight certainly shifted afterward.

Having said that, I regard this case as particularly revealing when the relationship between the public sphere and the nation state is considered. Modern politics in the Eurocentric sense developed inseparably from the "post-Westphalian" state order. Important in this context is a remark by Chiara Bottici, who notes that "the success of a definition of politics that reduces it to the state is inseparable from the fact that it clearly reflected the change occurring in political life itself: it is because of the emergence of the modern state—a form of political community characterized by the sovereign monopoly over legitimate coercion within territorial boundaries—that people felt the need for a new word."[52] Such an entanglement weighed heavily on the ongoing delimitation of the public sphere, especially given the existence of an external state structure. Within empire states, insurgent national claims were combined with a reappropriation of conceptual and practical inventions regarding politics that initially emerged elsewhere. The political sphere was defined and performed not within the state but to a degree against it. This opposition affected not only patterns of political reasoning and practice in respect to the state but also those concerning contenders from below. For instance, it influenced the shape of Polish nationalism, which "began to hate"—to paraphrase Brian Porter-Szűcs's apt expression—because it was funneled into an ethnic, and not civic, framing.[53] Its later vitriolic ethnic exclusivity was also perpetuated by the particular confrontation with the masses on the revolutionary streets in 1905 and the inability to endorse the state as a principle of order.

Furthermore, the subimperial forging of politics severely affected the potential accommodation of class-based demands. For those excited by new possibilities, and for those frightened by the menace of social turmoil and the fall of old authorities, the revolution was a confrontation with "the masses." The masses, however, were not merely existing groups of people who had never been politicized before; above all, "the masses" (as a concept sometimes coded with differed wording) were a product of a particular regime of political (mis)representation. As Stephan Jonsson notes: "The masses have always been produced through the ways in which certain social agents and aspirations have been represented—politically and intellectually—in modernity. Instead of defining the mass as those without representation, we should investigate the mechanisms whereby any given community represents itself, politically, intellectually, or aesthetically, necessarily produces a remainder, a group of agents and aspirations that cannot be accounted for by the dominant mode of representation."[54]

"Politics in a new key" was also a politics of public representation of the interests that had hitherto been carefully policed out of the public sphere—in part by the tsarist police apparatus, which like its counterpart in every state sought to restrain the turbulent expression of contentious claims, but also by the deliberate exclusion of street politics. Most liberal visions of politics and nostalgic theorizations of the bourgeois public sphere clearly exclude "laws passed under the 'pressure of the street.'" Such laws, according to Habermas, "could hardly be understood any longer as embodying the reasonable consensus of publicly debating private persons."[55] Regardless of the fact that the bourgeois salon itself was never a site of "reason" (in the Enlightenment or liberal sense), it is the logic of representation that sits at the center of the transforming public sphere and determines the targets of exclusion. "The act of representing socially significant passions can be seen as an originary mechanism of politics, as the cause of power—comparable to the distribution of presence and absence, rationality and irrationality, civic agency and subalternity within the public sphere," as Jonsson adds.[56] This "originary mechanism of politics" was activated at a time that may be dubbed a preamble to the age of extremes, when new political ideologies but also uses and abuses of political language gained unprecedented currency and influence in shaping the life of entire populations.[57] It was a time marked by intense testing and contesting of democracy, a crucial oscillation in twentieth-century European politics, as Jan-Werner Müller indicates.[58] On the fringes of the Russian Empire it was more a democratic principle within the social imaginary than democracy as a form of political organization, which was a bone of contention. Nonetheless, the basic principles of division of the body politic forged at the onset were to have long-lasting, often resilient afterlives—including when politics migrated to the loci more typical of a parliamentary nation state. Therefore, how the "presence and absence" of workers and ways of "representing socially significant passions" changed "under the pressure of the street" in this foundational moment is the focus of my interest here.

1

Workers and Their Intelligentsia

> As a young boy I used to look at people playing cards, which was fashionable in those days. I was looking while the elders were playing. And then something changed, more of them gathered to play, but the play did not go on. One disputed about something and we, the youngsters, were often sent away so as not to listen.

T he western fringes of the late tsarist empire were undergoing a serious social transformation. Because of the favorable placement within the imperial, but also global, capitalist economy, isles of industrialization started to sprinkle the map of the region. The accompanying urbanization and the rise of large-scale industrial establishments facilitated the growth of industrial wage labor. In those industrial hubs various ideas started to circulate, with political organizations entering bids for support. Initially modest, those attempts spread, making more and more people aware of ideals taking them beyond their everyday toil, such as socialism, nationalism, or a combination of both. In many cases it was gossip, undefined anxiety, or fascination that emerged rather than any outspoken consciousness, let alone political commitment. The fragment of a biographical testimony quoted above recollects just this undefined feeling.

New ideas and political practices slowly made their way to working-class milieus. Circumscribing the social contexts of working-class life, the composition of industrial labor and its nascent intellectual activities before the rise of mass politics sheds additional light on the subsequent transformation of the public presence of workers during the 1905 upheaval. In general, my view on the revolutionary public is informed by the once thriving cultural histories of revolutionary politics, ritual, and theatralization.[1] However, it also grows out of various forms of structural and social history, which sets the limits for the development of political communication and initially delimits the shape and actions of respective social groupings.[2] Thus I begin with a brief social history of the urban centers of Russian Poland to offer insights into the evolving practices of informal education and politicization before 1905.

Making Proletarians

The history of Eastern Europe is often written in a way that underlines differences between East and West. This strategy of differentiating the history of the eastern peripheries of Europe from its western core centers may be helpful in tackling the general trajectories of vast arrays of dissimilar territories stretching longitudinally from Helsinki to Istanbul. However, it may be a dubious strategy when analyzing the more detailed, spatialized social history of modernity. Multiple differentials embedded in the capitalist transformation of the world triggered uneven developmental processes on different spatial scales, often entangled within connections not necessarily deployed in their direct vicinity. Consequently, rigid geopolitical frameworks and imagined geographies may manifest their limited explanatory capacity in more zoomed-in research. Places enmeshed in transregional commercial networks drew extensively on local resources (land, water, laborers). Simultaneously, they were isolated socially from their direct surroundings precisely by this integration, which prevented any easy classification. Industrial centers of Russian Poland epitomized this pattern because of certain historical entanglements.

The old Polish-Lithuanian Commonwealth finally collapsed in 1795. The state territory was partitioned among three imperial neighbors: Austria, Prussia, and tsarist Russia. These partitions were a turning point in the history of the region, where all elements of European modernity developed under the jurisdiction of imperial states.[3] The agrarian structure of the old Poland, its role as "the first periphery of Europe," and the interests of the landed gentry inhibited urban growth before the collapse of the dilapidated noble republic. Later these factors also remained triggers of long-term path dependency of industrial underdevelopment.[4] As a result, Polish cities and towns at the beginning of the nineteenth century were exceptionally small and rather underdeveloped.

Out of those vast arrays of rural land spotted with neglected towns, this work zooms in on the Russian controlled zone, named at different times Congress Poland, the Kingdom of Poland, and Vistula Land.[5] It was the part most crucial for the subsequent emergence of the Polish nation state, not only because of its geographical centrality and prominent role in the Polish imagination. It had the highest ratio of industrialization and urbanization, which made it more developed than the Prussian part or Galicia (on the northern fringes of Austria-Hungary).[6] Even with the highest pace of growth, however, this development did not happen in a day.

The formation of capitalism proceeded in a specific way, divergent from that which occurred in regions where it had been built over centuries. It was a fragmentary, state-licensed capitalism, in the first phase implemented very quickly from top to bottom by the Polish autonomous government. The intensity of social change was greater than in countries where these processes were more extended in time. In Russian Poland, the change was not evolutionary but revolutionary. Capitalism developed not in existing cities but instead fostered the growth of new urban centers amid old rural realities. A primary accumulation of capital, proletarianization, and a rise of contract labor combined with the rapid development of cities and an internal migration from rural areas (rather than the impoverishment of craftsmen and townsmen, as often occurred in Western Europe).[7] The government took an active part in these processes, slowly loosening the remnants of a second "feudal" regime. The decree of December 1807 formally abolished personal serfdom already during the intermezzo of the Napoleon-backed Duchy of Warsaw. Practically it changed little in the life of peasants apart from facilitating their expropriation from the land.[8] The pivotal event was the January uprising of 1863. As a result, the Polish autonomous government lost its last significant prerogatives, and state-induced early capitalism gave way to a particular form of tsarist, autocratic laissez-faire capitalism.[9] The 1864 agrarian reforms finally ended the long epoch of second serfdom in Poland. The land reform merged with political repressions against landowners and secured peasant support for Russian rule. It also added to the economic collapse of the ineffective kingdom's manorial agriculture, while not necessarily boosting the peasant economy. These measures stimulated migration to cities and facilitated the recruitment of workers and reduction of labor

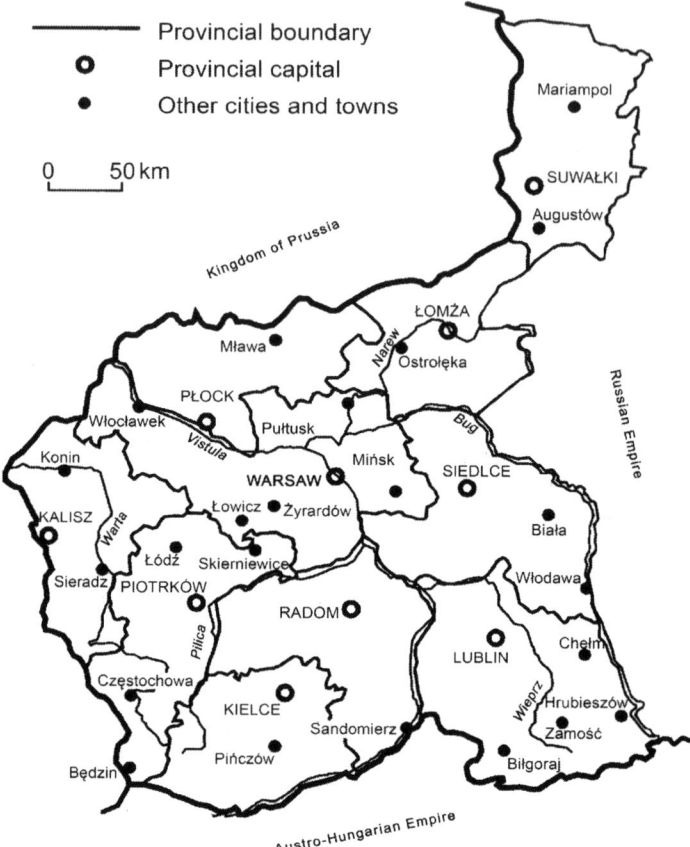

Fig. 1.1. Map of the Kingdom of Poland at the turn of the century. Prepared by Stefan Brajter.

costs. Subsequently, thousands of unemployed peasants, as well as bankrupted nobles, were forced to migrate to cities. The urban areas embarked on the path of rapid industrialization.

Not surprisingly, this period of impressive industrialization dramatically remodeled the existing social structure in the cities. Between 1850 and 1900, a few industrial urban centers flourished, supported by Russian trade protectionism and the booming economy of the empire stimulated by foreign investment.[10] Some of these cities became huge isles of capitalistic modernity, surrounded by rural Polish landscapes. Industrial hubs of Russian Poland were among the huge industrial centers that mushroomed in the nineteenth century across the globe, being positioned in the increasingly porous borderland between the Russian world-empire and European networks of knowledge and technology transfer. Poland thus used to have much more in common with its industrial counterparts farther away than with places directly neighboring it. This does not mean, however, that Polish industrial areas were disconnected from their hinterland. In the 1870s and 1880s the Kingdom of Poland experienced a huge wave of proletarianization and internal migration of peasants or agricultural laborers from rural areas to the emerging industrial centers.[11] However, the technical composition of the working class, a hotbed for further political trajectories, differed in the three major industrial hubs that are at the center of my focus.

Out of the three largest industrial centers of Russian Poland, Warsaw was long-viewed as the capital, even if the reduction in Polish autonomy made it more and more an informal capital. It grew significantly, reaching a half-million inhabitants in 1900 and becoming a vivid Polish-Jewish urban center.[12] It was there that artisanal production and petty industry supplying the meager demand for industrial goods stagnated. The development of industry was gradual, and its results more equally spread and diversified—the mills were of different sizes, there were hardly any large factories, and the profile of industry was highly diversified, delivering multiple industrial goods. The social composition of workers was equally diverse. In Warsaw, former craftsmen were proletarianized, pauperized noble offspring arrived there to look for opportunities (and often failed), and, last but not least, peasants from the region flocked to the city.[13] Thus there were artisan networks there and some elements of early working-class culture.

The Dąbrowa Basin, a mining region on the Southwestern fringe of Russian Poland, also developed relatively gradually, but that was due to other sources of population growth. There had been germs of a mining industry there already, before industrial growth started at full throttle. Its coal output was sent all over the country, and the railway connection with Warsaw from 1848 on integrated local mines and foundries with economic circulation more generally. Here most new laborers arrived from the surrounding villages. For instance, in one of the larger cities of the region, Sosnowiec, the population quadrupled between 1886 and 1897.[14] There was also some population exchange with the already booming mining industry of Germany's Upper Silesia, which stimulated a diffusion of technology, miners' culture, and political repertoires.[15] The Dąbrowa Basin grew "organically" from the rural areas around, drawing from them its labor force but creating an external, invasive body.

In Lodz, soon to become the biggest concentration of the industrial working class, the origin of the labor force was similar. In this case, however, industrialization was much more rampant, soon resulting in the creation of large, vertically integrated textile conglomerates hiring several thousand people each.[16] Before this, Lodz had been a rural backwater town, consisting of only 190 inhabitants and 44 houses in the late eighteenth century.[17] Everything was to change in just a few decades, after the Polish government implemented a special program to stimulate industrial development. It offered a variety of privileges for future investors as well as facilities designed to encourage settlement and investment in selected areas of the kingdom (automatic acquisition of citizenship, free access to building materials, and tax credits).[18] The program proved to be effective enough to stimulate successive waves of immigration—in Lodz, just nine years after its implementation, the population increased from 799 to 4,343 people (from 1821 to 1830). Further increases in population followed very rapidly; the scale was unique in Europe, comparable only with fast-growing, relatively young American cities. From 1850 to 1900 the Lodz population increased by an astonishing 2,006 percent, while London "only" increased by 192 percent, and Manchester, the industrial heart of England, a benchmark for rapid industrial growth, by 557 percent.[19] In just a few decades, this place was transformed from a nondescript village into a city with four hundred thousand inhabitants by 1900.

The nature of the transformation was also marked by the fact that the city was not a developed urban area where the structure of employment and property merely changed; rather, it was a new city built from scratch. The result was the emergence of an unusual industrial city, with its structure totally subordinated to the requirements of production and the market. The single-track growth led to high levels of specialization, and from the 1860s onward more than half of the inhabitants were textile workers.[20] From the 1870s on, there were not enough people around, and the inflow of rural populations intensified. Most of the workers were born in villages, mainly in landless families; the peasant population became the main reservoir for recruiting an urban labor force substituting for proletarianized craftsmen.[21] Up to two-thirds of the population were first-generation migrants, and one-fifth of all workers were single or separated from their families, left in the rural areas.[22] This created a situation where the cost of biological reproduction was

Fig. 1.2. The panorama of Lodz with rural people approaching the industrial giant. Postcard. Courtesy of Łukasz Biskupski.

often externalized to rural areas securing the basic subsistence of workers. Moreover, the specificity of the textile industry and the need for a disciplined labor force facilitated the feminization of labor, which reached a much higher proportion than in other industrial centers.[23]

In all three centers conflicts resulting from class structure were intensified by ethnic and cultural boundaries. For example, in Lodz Polish workers had to face the oppression of Jewish factory owners or German foremen, supported by a tsarist regime equally foreign to them. At other times, though, such workers collaborated with Jewish or German proletarians against exploitation by their own countrymen. The proportion of Polish post-peasant populations grew, outnumbering Jewish and German inhabitants, who nevertheless remained a significant part of the city dwellers. By the turn of the century in Lodz the proportion of Poles (according to language classification) reached 46 percent, while Germans made up to 21 percent, and the Jewish population 29 percent.[24] At the same time, however, 43 percent of factory owners were of German descent, 47 percent were Jewish, and only a tiny minority (even smaller in the textile industry) was of different background, which included Polish.[25] The social structure was characterized by a small

Workers and Their Intelligentsia • 25

presence of intelligentsia and a strong, almost binary class polarization.[26] For instance, Jews composed by no means only the upper strata; while 36 percent of male Jews in Lodz were active in commerce (a large part as petty shopkeepers or middlemen), 45 percent were active in craftsmanship and industry (25 percent for women). These were obviously not only factory owners but also artisans, workers, and urban poor.[27] In sum, the city was characterized by a rapidly proletarianized, multiethnic, feminized working class with few organic leaders or established class-based cultural milieus.

Although the social structure in Warsaw was less polarized—with a larger proportion of intelligentsia, craftsmen, and skilled workers—the ethnic composition was also highly complex. In 1897 the census data indicate almost 58 percent of the population was Catholic, with 35 percent Jewish and only 3 percent Evangelical Christians.[28] Religious affiliation does not correspond neatly to nationality (mainly because of the Catholic Germans), but in Warsaw it did not matter that much because of the relatively low number of Germans and a degree of Polonization higher than in Lodz. Similarly, a larger chunk of the Jewish population was entirely Polish-speaking and affiliated themselves with Polish culture. Jews were also overrepresented among the owners of factories and craftsmen but not so much among factory workers, as in Lodz.[29]

In these circumstances the influx of migrants to the swelling urban centers did not trigger a larger drive toward cultural invigoration or political involvement.[30] The rhythm of industrial work was only incidentally punctuated by social protests. In 1861 Lodz witnessed a Luddite-style riot of impoverished weavers who attacked one of the first mechanized mills and attempted to destroy the steam engine.[31] In 1883 in Żyrardów a strike of female textile workers indignant about the sexual misconduct of foremen and declining piece wages erupted. It was, however, only in 1892 when the first large wave of strikes and street fights happened in Lodz. A spontaneous strike after May Day and a parallel anti-Jewish pogrom in the neighboring slum district, Bałuty, were the first events that triggered a broader debate. While emerging socialist circles, for the first time, saw the potential for mass action, the bourgeoisie and intelligentsia were frightened by the growing problem of an almost destitute industrial working class. It was also the first time when the tsarist administration felt obliged to react in a way other than short-term street policing, and some concessions for the aspiring Polish-speaking skilled workers were made.[32] In 1892 there were still no stock repertoires of contention, and workers, when gathered, spontaneously attempted to elect their own king.[33]

This situation was about to change, however. Initially as a weak undercurrent, later as a massive movement, the educational situation also began to evolve.

Not surprisingly, there were few opportunities to pursue an education. The school system was extremely limited due to the general educational policies of the tsarist empire, made worse by the repressive measures taken against Russian Poland. Only a few children of working-class background were able to attend school at all, and they emerged barely literate.[34] Up to the age of twelve, children rarely worked for wages. As a result, it was sometimes possible to send one's offspring to the "official" school. Schooling was, however, usually limited to three years and highly ineffective. Combined classes, where already trained children were used to teach younger pupils instead of proceeding along their own educational path, did not help the educational goals, but it was some form of school nonetheless.[35] It was, moreover, a widespread conviction among "the adults" that some schooling would do no harm. Alternatively, at least some families were able and willing to send a child (more rarely subsequent ones) to an unofficial private tutor—a student or pauperized intelligentsia member—for "private lessons," usually with a couple of other children in a conspiratorially rented room.[36] These pockets of educational opportunity often ended abruptly, which only triggered a further will to learn among some of the more intellectually vigorous working-class children and adolescents.

Similarly, Polish workers had extremely limited opportunities for professional mobility. Even in large industrial hubs positions in vocational training were rare.[37] In cities like Lodz, the founding of more modern professional schools with larger teaching capacities was a major theme in local reform discourses expressed in the press and by more outspoken public opinion.[38] The situation was not much better in industrial plants, where high-ranking staff were often "imported" along with technology from abroad or recruited from the generally more affluent and better-educated German population (especially in Lodz and the Dąbrowa Basin). In this context, it is no wonder that any form of party-orchestrated education or alternative forms of mastery and upward mobility within the party structure was attractive to people striving for more fulfilling lives.

Learning the Revolution

More ambitious young workers were eager to participate in alternative forms of education. Those youngsters who were lucky enough encountered an educational circle. Such circles—focused on reading, training, or transferring general knowledge—were a local mutation of the "Sunday school" movement and a relatively broad phenomenon at the turn of the century.[39] Concurrently, informal educational practices took hold in Russian Poland. Here, however, they were not only informal but illegal, since any educational activity required endorsement of the appropriate tsarist office, and any gatherings of this kind might be subjected to punitive measures. This repression notwithstanding, new forms of underground education emerged, and libraries and reading rooms supplemented discussion and educational circles.[40] In many cases, it was only there that the workers learned to read, as one of the voluntary intelligentsia teachers remarked: "The boys often could not read, and when, during my first visit there, I pointed out the need to learn, they were excited. I read them a brochure with scientific content, and with happiness I registered that almost every one of them receives every sentence with burning eyes. In a very short time I noticed that everybody could already read to some extent. I had results, and I was very happy that the circle was growing."[41] This was a typical communicative situation in which transfer of knowledge and stimulation through reading were initiated by the intelligentsia. Here one may guess that, in addition, most probably "the boys" were doing their best to keep up with the expectations of the young lady from the intelligentsia—an important external authority and an upper-class female—assessing their pursuits. Initially, almost all the circles were organized by radical intelligentsia of different ideological shades but with a common commitment to educate "Polish people." It was the milieu of a post-positivist intelligentsia putting into practice the idea of working with "the people" and "for the people" that was the main driving force behind those activities. Thus the practice of lecture and discussion circles was part and parcel of the intelligentsia's ethos of social service and enlightening mission "among the people," which put into practice ideas of "organic work."[42] As a result, it was often tainted with paternalism and prescribed a vision of future popular classes' identities and politics.

This paternalism notwithstanding, circles for workers were organized differently in respect to the structure of hierarchy than intelligentsia ones. Even if the transfer of knowledge was more vertical, with an intelligentsia speaker and working-class listeners, they were less hierarchical. There were no permanent charismatic leaders as in intelligentsia-only circles.[43] In the circles for workers, speakers changed according to the topic, and rarely was there a deeper spiritual or intellectual agenda. Unlike circles set aside for gymnasium youth, which concentrated more on debating "illegal" topics, ideas, or books, the circles for workers were occupied more with general knowledge. Initially it was the basics of science, preliminary topics in history or geography, or propaedeutic for the social sciences that was more attractive to workers.[44] Circles for workers were rather alternative "universities" with lectures, classes, and discussions within which more "advanced" workers often had their say. In this way agency within the circle might be distributed irrespectively of the more one-dimensional transfer of readymade knowledge. Later intellectual communication was also more equal, as ranks of intellectually sound and experienced workers grew steadily.

These workers, after having developed their interests in general educational content, later willingly accepted the parties' ideological offerings. The class on social science, if led by party members and committed socialists, could be used for agitation purposes as well.[45] In times of clandestine, illicit activity, underground educational circles were one of the few available forms appropriate for political proselytism. Nevertheless, political agitation had to be tightly interwoven with educational content. Conversely, general social knowledge was built on a backbone of militant concepts and popularized theories of the forefathers of socialism. Gradually, however, this political message came to the fore. Along with the development of political parties and growing ideological polarization of the intelligentsia, such educational activities were penetrated by an explicitly political agenda, be it socialism's class liberation or Polish nationalism's rebirth of the nation.[46] The politicization of educational content progressed in parallel in socialist circles with more and more general educational activities organized by the parties' members or sympathizers, and within nationalist milieus, with the growing reach of the Society for National Education (Towarzystwo Oświaty Narodowej—TON). Subsequently, more party politics came in, and limits separating general lectures from party meetings tended to be blurred. The circles began to be an explicitly politicized activity. Therefore, a short overview of party politics is presented here.

The political scene was highly fractured, and the level of antagonism between the parties was growing. One party, Social Democracy in the Kingdom of Poland and Lithuania (Socjaldemokracja Królestwa Polskiego i Litwy, SDKPiL), had founded its program, strategy, and agitation on class as the basic frame of reference and affiliation and on labor unity as the main identity, overcoming or even annulling the national one.[47] It was engaged in a common struggle alongside the Russian proletariat for class goals and internationalist socialism, sublating the nation state based on exploitation, which was to be an efficient and appealing strategy. The seed for the party was initially a splinter group, opposed since 1893 to the "nationalist" taint of the Polish Socialist Party (Polska Partia Socjalistyczna, PPS). This second group indeed tried to combine class struggle with claims for national independence and treated a sovereign Polish state as reconcilable with socialism. The labor struggle was from this perspective a means of regaining independence, and independence offered a way toward socialism. Particular writers differed, however, in respect to the proportions of the two.[48] Such an inherent tension was a reason for the forthcoming split in 1906, which had its main cause in the divergence of class and national claims in the party's political agenda.[49] More to the right, the circles connected with the National Democracy party and later its labor branch, the National Workers Union (Narodowy Związek Robotniczy—NZR, created in June 1905), took the nation as the basic form of affiliation. In the given circumstances, they abandoned any insurrectionary hopes and concentrated on the struggle for political and cultural autonomy and the right to use Polish in different spheres of life. The superiority accorded to national unity meant the abandonment of economic claims or class demands that might affect "Polish" industry. That equaled subordination to factory owners or landlords.[50]

A slightly separate story concerns Jewish politics, which is not directly addressed in this study, although in the biggest industrial centers up to one-third of workers were Jews. In a word, the association that championed the mobilization of this group was doubtlessly the Bund, probably the best organized of all socialist parties before 1905. The Bund's ideological offer included class politics but simultaneously affirmed Jewish identity. The Bund approached its supporters usually in their everyday language—Yiddish—and fostered the nonterritorial cultural autonomy of the Jews within the possibly democratized Russian state.[51] Although Zionism was already its competitor, among workers in Russian Poland it was not very influential.[52] At the same time, the PPS mobilized Polish-speaking Jews, and the SDKPiL promised an internationalist abolition of nationality for all. I explore further the changing party landscape and the intensifying mutual antagonisms in chapter 3. Here suffice it to say that despite this differentiation, all these milieus built corollary associations and stimulated workers' intellectual activities.

Party-sponsored activities were composed of several concentric "spheres" of involvement. The politically active working class was not homogenous, and the level of involvement was much diversified. There were groups of sympathizers and regular participants in various lecture and discussion circles. Even if tighter groups of regular participants were not exceptionally large before revolutionary upheaval, they were quite influential as leaders of workers' public opinion. The broader circle, dubbed by one of the PPS agitators as "the readers" (*czytacy*), were regular receivers of party publications and distributed brochures and books.[53] However, the leaflets that had the biggest print runs reached beyond any party structure. This created a structured readership (far more limited before the revolution than during it), composed of interested workers and those who first approached the leaflets by accident. Even if they were not supporters of any party or were adherents of a different ideology, they nevertheless participated in a shared community of language and to some extent a certain emotional community. As readers they were confronted with new languages describing the world, different from their everyday or professional vocabulary. The leaflets were often the only texts the workers read, but they were later vividly commented on, debated, and reread aloud. In this way, party propaganda also stimulated general readership. The leaflets thus had a broad impact on readers.

It was not easy, however, to increase the number of receivers. In the reality of the tsarist state, executing additional repressive means in the rebellious multinational borderlands, such forms of political propaganda soon approached structural limitations. Further massive political education and political participation of workers was hardly possible in conditions of illegality and police repression.[54] Forms of nascent civil society could emerge in tsarist Russia before 1905, as revisionist scholarship on Russian autocracy has demonstrated. It was, however, in the major cities of Russia proper and only among highly ranked elites where those margins could be created.[55] It required a revolution to change these conditions.

The situation indeed changed during the revolutionary upheaval of 1905. Certain forms of action became legal or at least tacitly accepted due to a moderate liberalization of the tsarist regime or just its incapacity to police every contentious activity at will. This category included labor unions, more open debate on social issues in the press, and a mushrooming number of associations, to name only a few. The upsurge of political militancy paved the way for a vivid protest culture. The secret educational circles or agitation meetings had prepared the participants to act more publicly once circumstances made such activities possible. Along with the revolutionary mobilization those workers trained in, reasoning and speaking were often important pillars of more open agitation and political claims made public. At the same time, large new groups joined the political cauldron of the revolution, and public participation became an unprecedented mass experience.

The revolutionary upsurge from January 1905 on surprised almost everybody, from the tsarist administration to the leadership of the socialist parties to the rank and file party circles and, last but not least, to hitherto rarely politically active workers. Socialist militants from the PPS self-defense militias confronted the tsarist police in November 1904 during the demonstration on Grzybowski Square in Warsaw. This clash radicalized urban workers but did not spark a mass movement to stand against the tsarist autocracy.[56] The atmosphere was tense because of the ongoing Russo-Japanese War and related conscription, strongly opposed by the Polish population. As a result, even before the direct outbursts of rioting and massive strikes began, a feeling of anxiety spread; a mixture of longing, revived expectations, curiosity, and awe. To quote one young man who lived through it: "In the year 1904 and into 1905 there was something out of joint, there was something strange in the air, because in houses of the working people, and on the fields and everywhere, one could meet people greatly intrigued by something. . . . One could hear 'socialism' often, and I was excited. My mother told me often about socialists, who they were, that they wanted people to be equal, to remove exploitation. Father told me to be quiet."[57] Indeed, after years the socialist underground education had done its job. Yet socialist milieus remained underground, and the narrow cadre organizations were hardly capable of stirring massive unrest out of hand. Nevertheless, there already must have been widespread awareness of mysterious groups openly opposing the tsarist power apparatus and questioning existing factory relationships. There was also a slow growth in general claims to a recognition of personal dignity on purely human grounds, registrable in the petitions received by various tsarist and factory administrations.[58] It was perhaps a poignant feeling for workers hardly participating in open political or contentious activity before. Something was in the air.

That something exploded in January 1905. A spark initiating mass resistance was lit by the events of "Bloody Sunday" in St. Petersburg, which became a catalyst for the general strike of January 1905. Almost the entire

Fig. 1.3. A strike in Poznański's factory in Lodz after the announcement of the great lockout. Collection of Museum of Independence Tradition in Lodz.

city of Lodz came to a stop, and waves of protest swept against disoriented policemen in Warsaw and other cities. Paroxysms of rioting hit with huge force, combining a class strike, a national awakening, an economic opposition to growing deprivation, and a general refusal to endure the harsh regime, all at once. It was, perhaps above all, an ultimate demand for recognition of the basic human dignity of each worker, as well as for the right to give voice to his or her own situation. The very issue of who was a political subject became a basic stake of politics. The main significance of the strike was precisely the proletarians' claim to legitimacy. After the first general strike of January 1905 the Warsaw governor-general admitted that initially "workers, having ceased to work, did not state any claims."[59] It was a political event par excellence, not an expression of particular demands.

This *political* dimension of strike was successful. The pages of various memoirs written by members of the intelligentsia or party activists are filled with descriptions of calm and dignified behavior by workers who were appropriating the streets for marches seemingly without any strict purpose. They encouraged other workers to join and urged those sitting in cafes to cease the consumption of luxuries "while workers are striking."[60] The fact that with workers off the job the entire city ceased to function had a profound effect on everybody around. It very directly reshuffled the social imaginary, bringing forth a group which had not occupied a prominent place before. Stanisław Brzozowski, a Polish philosopher then sympathetic to the socialist cause, was thrilled by events in the "city of blood and toil" (Lodz). He reoriented his entire philosophical project so as to recognize the paramount significance of work in the world.[61] In one of his essays he expressed the point bluntly: "Besides the proletariat the present crisis did not reveal any other life form capable of development and purposeful action."[62] Similar statements also sounded among the bourgeois public, which still believed in a more general liberalization of the tsarist regime. For instance, one of the textile moguls of Lodz claimed in an interview that even "some factory owners revealed a revolutionary mood, which in 1905 encompassed also the bourgeois," because they "thought that they supported a liberation movement, bringing an attractive future for all."[63] In a word, the workers gained an unprecedented political legitimacy.

Such a bid for pure political legitimacy did not correspond to any prior expectations. The size and "spontaneity" of the first strikes surprised and astonished all political factions. One of the local SDKPiL activists wrote in

Fig. 1.4. The cover of the satirical magazine *Kolce* from December 1905. Initially the bourgeois public was full of hope about the general liberalization of the tsarist regime. Here a proletarian (very similar to the one usually depicted on PPS propaganda material, although disguised in the traditional Cracow pants) is slashing the dragon of "bureaucracy." Polish National Library Digital Collection.

his memoirs: "To what degree did our party in Lodz direct this strike? Very little.... The strike commenced without any proclamations..., was spontaneous, and organizations were completely surprised by this enormous revolutionary blow."[64] This situation changed when a complex interaction began between party agitators and workers. Initially, parties were not controlling strike mobilization at all. The initial general strike, being a work stoppage and seizure of urban space, gave birth to different contentious activities. Well-organized party structures capable of agitation and communication between factories, branches, and cities emerged only later.[65] The scattered groups of workers parading the cities and calling other crews to join them ceased to be a typical sight during the strike. Strikes were more synchronized with activities of the party structures able to coordinate expressions of dissatisfaction in different factories. This does not mean, however, that they were able to control them entirely or launch them at will. The parties, nevertheless, set the tone for strikes. They pushed certain topics or inspired forms of expression for grievances.

As a result, the form and content of striking activity bifurcated. Waves of single-factory strikes followed—aiming to fight for better wages, shorter working hours, and better work conditions. At the same time, more all-encompassing strikes were organized under slogans less connected with the workplace. Workers struck to demonstrate sympathy for the general proletarian cause (May 1), solidarity with Russian workers (strikes supporting the Moscow uprising in December 1905), or dissatisfaction with the reforms of the tsarist autocracy (strikes against the Duma projects and election).[66] Social and political demands perpetuated different forms of protest.

However, one cannot artificially separate the economic and political dimensions of the strike movement. While the first general strike was not specifically economic in nature, claims for better working conditions soon arose, and the actual situation in the factories in respect to wages and working hours improved.[67] The tsarist administration hoped that addressing economic grievances would calm the general upheaval and put pressure on factory moguls to compromise as a part of emergency policing. Local economic strikes mushroomed after this initial success. This led to important gains, which created conditions for further action. Only with additional resources (e.g., time, moderate increase of income) was it possible to develop political and cultural activities. Even seemingly trivial shop-floor negotiations, when successful, boosted workers' self-assertion and capabilities for further action.

Nevertheless, the specialization of strikes bore witness to at least two important processes. Workers began to consciously strive for social and economic gains, cooperating closely between both factories and departments within a single factory. For instance, when only one department crucial for the production process ceased to operate, the practical bargaining power was exactly the same as if the entire factory came to a stop. Other workers, however, were not deprived of their wages. At the same time, large, general political protests signified the rise of a broader feeling of solidarity or a certain form of imagined class community, populated by all the workers of the industry branch, the country, or even the entire Russian Empire.[68] This dimension was especially tangible in the general strikes encompassing all of Russian Poland (January 1905 and October–November 1905), or those only slightly smaller (May 1905, January 1906, May 1906), and the solidarity strikes with Russian workers (January 1905, December 1905).[69] The strikers must have felt at least some connection with their distant comrades. Not only did a sense of contemporaneity of different events and struggles emerge but also an "imagined community" binding different workers who did not personally know one another. Strikes also established a broader repertoire of contention characterized by "cosmopolitanism, autonomy and modularity,"[70] typical of modern protest forms. Their intended goals reached beyond the immediate here and now and became coordinated attempts aimed at a future, general political transformation, requiring systematic step-by step efforts.[71] Mobilization for such strikes, with abstract aims deferred in time, also testifies to a growing ability to comprehend the individual situation or problems within one factory from a broader perspective of the general political and economic situation and a corresponding will to protest for a general change.

Such developments, however, do not indicate that strikes were merely orchestrated from above by party structures. Often party functionaries tried to resonate with the emotions generated on the street and in the factory and therefore called for strikes at the right moment, after detecting a already heated atmosphere among the workers. Party committees were also able to benefit from economic strikes even if it had not been party agitators who called for them.[72] Such successes contributed enormously to their prestige and subsequent influence as political entities capable of organizing "the masses." Subsequently, as party structures developed into mass organizations with effective printing industries and distribution mechanisms, they were often capable of calling a strike for political or even tactical reasons and, conversely, of calming revolutionary moods in moments when they considered such sentiments inappropriate.[73] However, that was not always the case, and dynamics of mass protests sometimes had greater influence. Moreover, socialist parties were not always able to cooperate, so strike dynamics became an important factor in the interparty struggle. In this sense, calling for and against a strike might be regarded as a trial of a given party's organizational capacity and the fidelity of its adherents. When it succeeded, such a strike became a powerful weapon against opponents. Yet such conduct effectively prevented the creation of a common socialist or workers cause—muddying the waters, inducing conflict, giving rise to ambiguity, and undermining the still precarious authority of the parties among the working class. Nevertheless, any successful strike was a transformative experience for its participants.

The strike itself was often combined with a very direct struggle for recognition of the dignity of the workers and the need to renegotiate factory relationships. Not only did the strikers openly put on trial the exhaustive power of the owner to dictate all the conditions, but they also explicitly questioned practices of hierarchical communication. For example, violence from foremen and their power to arbitrarily punish workers was one of the main bones of contention. Foremen who were exceptionally tyrannical were simply thrown out of the factories. This practice was combined with a kind of retributive humiliation. According to reports, offenders were carried away on wheelbarrows and dumped in some place which usually was not too clean.[74] In labor-management negotiations it was often easier to agree on financial conditions than on personal issues. Workers often stubbornly resisted bringing a hated foreman back to the factory, fearing that any promise of improved behavior would not last for long.

From Industrialization to Revolution

In conditions of relatively rapid proletarianization, political activity was often the first entry to the world of letters and public participation. Various studies on labor movements and proletarian mobilization—regardless of whether they concern strikes, cultural activity, or class consciousness—point out the role of existing proletarian, usually post-artisanal culture and established social ties in facilitating the emergence of resistance and public demands for greater democracy.[75] Russian Poland, however, with the single exception of Warsaw, had neither lower-class urban networks nor well-established artisanal cultures constituting a hotbed for contentious politics of various kinds.

In Russian Poland it was the other way around—political mobilization and intensive work by political parties stimulated intellectual activities and the emergence of the proletarian public. Such was the role of self-education circles in the early phase of working-class politicization. Later, during the 1905 upheaval, strikes were an important form of public activity in the factory and on the streets. They included engaging in forms of direct communication (as within the strike and factory committees), negotiating political opinions and strategies, participating in public performances (displaying banners or announcements), and undertaking complex public activities such as speeches or debates. These were the crucial dimensions of a new mode of working-class public presence.

2

Workers and the Public Sphere

> The working class . . . won elementary human rights, gained awareness of their power. . . . Till recently, the person and dignity of the worker was not in any way protected against harm. . . . Now it is different! The worker has forced everybody to respect his personal dignity, one already takes his person seriously, his will dictates the conditions of work.

The public presence of workers changed during the massive unrest commonly known as the 1905 Revolution. The fragment quoted above is certainly an overenthusiastic statement of an activist who was involved in pushing this change forward. Its author was a tireless organizer of early labor unions. Being educated as an electrical engineer, Bernard Szapiro was involved in PPS-Left union organizing. Certainly, the expressive tone is also intended for performative purposes; it encourages working-class readers to take what allegedly belongs to them and to force intelligentsia readers to accept this change. It may not be the direct evidence of the change actually happening, but it testifies to what was at stake. Even if the suggested empowerment of workers and their subjectification as "the working class" were not yet accomplished, they were underway to such an extent that readers might take this expression as a meaningful call for action. Similar calls did not go unanswered, and newly forged labor unions, made to some limited extent lawful within the tsarist legal framework in 1906, indeed reshuffled the situation for workplace bargaining. It was, however, only one dimension of a more general transformation of the political. This transformation concerned opportunities to argue, participate, and last but not least, to just be in public as workers. It meant renegotiation of the workers' "place" in various domains, from relationships in the factory to the regime of speech. The change encompassed the emergence of a public sphere populated by workers, either as a separate space of articulation or as a conditionally accepted part of a more general public. And indeed, such a working-class public sphere was put into practice during the 1905–1907 upheaval.

Admittedly, the revolutionary public sphere was by no means limited to workers. The political mobilization, from excitement to hatred and fear, affected the vast strata of urban society. Nevertheless, it was a public sphere of the street, factory hall, "reclaimed" theater: not of a burgher salon or a party gathering. The relationship between those spaces and the people who usually populated them changed. According to Geoff Eley, the public sphere is "the structured setting where cultural and ideological contest or negotiation among the variety of publics takes place."[1] Without a doubt, the revolutionary proliferation of public, politicized action reconfigured the structure of this setting, making it possible for the broader "ideological contest or negotiation" to emerge. Despite the multiple identifications of the participants during protests, they nevertheless shared a place within a highly politicized yet common public sphere of revolutionary politics. Their class backgrounds may also have differed. It was an unprecedented moment of collision of classes, when people were acting together but also against each other. This plurality notwithstanding, the massive participation of new groups of people, mainly urban laborers of various kinds (not limited to the working class in any strict sense), made the pendulum swing heavily in the direction of the proletarian public sphere.

By this term I do not mean just the working-class public or even a counter-public opposed to the long established, elite patterns of participation or bourgeois interests. Those characteristics did apply, but what is more important is the capacity to incorporate and transform forms of public participation in a way directly affecting the participants and their political potentials. In this vein, the peculiarities of the proletarian public were investigated by Oskar Negt and Alexander Kluge in their research on plural and oppositional public spheres.[2] Disagreeing with Habermas's classic approach,[3] the authors scrutinized forms of publics, different from a liberal salon. While historically many forms of counter-public emerged, creating a launchpad for contentious politics and an alternative for the bourgeois public sphere, only some of them fostered the processes of learning and created social situations where habits concerning public performance were broken. In a nutshell, Negt and Kluge's proletarian public sphere does not refer to actual organizational forms but to the emergent practice of public questioning of the most fundamental assumptions about the participants of the situation. To borrow another theoretical parlance, Negt and Kluge try to describe acts of "polemicization of the commonplace."[4] A wildcat strike, factory occupation, or collective autodidacticism transforms the place of workers, not only within the hierarchical social edifice but also in respect to their customary leadership of the union or the party.

While interested in acts of performative redrawing of political boundaries, Negt and Kluge nevertheless consider public spheres as strictly related to subjective experiences, embedded in the class-specific context of life. This argument applies not only as a materialist critique of the bourgeois public sphere; it also concerns the proletarian public sphere. In this case, however, the experiential hotbed for participation is simultaneously and reflexively reconfigured by various forms of public activity. This dialectical interrelation is crucial to comprehend the actual transformation spurred on by the proletarian public sphere. The transformation affects both the participants and the political space they enter. Here I am interested chiefly in political practices sitting between these two dimensions, constituting the presence of participants within the political. These practices were also mediating between the old sedimented culture and a new insurgent one. In the same vein, practices constituting the proletarian public sphere indicate that it is not a failed, derivative, or imitative form of the bourgeois public sphere but an alternative pattern of turning problems into debatable issues.[5] It has its own genealogy and principles of organization, but its developments are entangled in a dialectical relationship with the dominant forms of political articulation.

A similar approach was successfully applied to historical material by scholars such as Günther Lottes, who broadly documented the emerging alternative "plebeian" public of the English Jacobins.[6] It was an actual attempt to question the monopoly of the burgher public or even a parallel plebeian constituency, fostering new forms of political expressions on the verge of modernity. English radicals forged practices different from those of premodern unrest, grounding them in broad literacy and informed participation performed in clubs, within corresponding societies and in open air rallies.[7] It was not always possible, however, to create horizontal patterns of negotiation and decision making not interrupted by violence and turmoil. What is even more important is the fact that to prove successful, such a sphere had to constantly embrace a dialectics of contention and cooptation in respect to the dominant form of public participation—for instance, by petitioning Parliament.

Similarly, in most European contexts, from its very beginning the emerging bourgeois public approached alternative forms of plebeian constituencies. These constituencies were later suppressed and foreclosed, a process often repeated in later historiography and favoring the visibility of bourgeois publics.[8] In the case investigated here, the new challengers of mass politics abruptly entered a scene where only nascent and highly specific forms of elite public were developed.[9] This was because of the historical lineages of the Polish noble republic and later tsarist autocracy inhibiting other paths. Initially the distance and exclusion applied to illiterate working-class contenders may have been less fictitious than those against the plebeian public or artisanal radicals elsewhere. Correspondingly, the dynamics of inclusion, cooptation, and marginalization is detectable in the very different context of the emerging Polish public sphere during the revolution.

For instance, workers' intellectual pursuits were heavily indebted to, and stimulated by, the radical intelligentsia. It was a particular social strata, endemic in Eastern Europe, neither a bourgeois intellectual elite nor a middle class composed of professionals more common in Western European societies.[10] In the Polish case, it was mainly (but not exclusively) composed of the offspring of the gentry, who looked for new opportunities in urban settings after they could no longer sustain the lifestyle of the noble manor.[11] As a result, they formed an underspecified "sphere of society" with some education.[12] Yet they perpetuated, and were burdened by, a specific "ethos": a calling to social service combined with a certain "missionary" zeal and condescension toward "the people" inherited from their noble culture.[13] The intelligentsia both meddled and mediated between publics. It provided an informal education for workers and developed most party politics.[14] As a result, the emerging working class was initially captivated by radical intelligentsia politics, much different from the aristocratic or bourgeois salon. Nevertheless, the working-class public soon started to follow a more independent path with its own political practices and alternative ways of debating and making political claims. Even then, however, claims uttered within the proletarian public sphere were fueled by political languages acquired from outside and directed toward the general public. Their success was conditional on external recognition. Also, on a personal level, workers were often forced to leave their class background behind to establish a political life. They often embarked on political practice precisely to free themselves of the shackles of a work-centered existence. Nevertheless, these entanglements did not abolish the potential for transformation inherent in workers' political presence, which is the topic of this chapter.

Being in Public

The urban public sphere of the prerevolutionary Polish Kingdom did not leave much space for a working-class presence. Intense military policing of the autocratic state limited, if not prevented, any political expression concerning class relationships and the "national question." Party activity of any kind was illegal and diligently policed with multiple measures directed against various rebellious subjects, from "owners" of socialist leaflets to editors at national press outlets. Workers populated the streets while rushing to work and going back home, but they were hardly considered as legitimate users of the urban space.[15] Factory relationships were highly hierarchical and possibilities for negotiation scarce. Reasoning was not tolerated. "The entrepreneur considered himself a chosen one, at whom the subordinates were obliged to look with reverence and obligation," reported one of the Warsaw left-liberal titles soon after the shock of the revolution.[16] All means were used to keep workers in their place. Concurrently, workers themselves were burdened with harsh living conditions, subdued within the tsarist-capitalist configuration of power, and still too disorganized to launch an alternative public sphere grounded in workers' values, habits, and life contexts. The problems were also not openly debated by external observers. Undoubtedly, harsh preventive censorship severely limited any debate on social, let alone political issues.[17] "This situation has completely changed," the author of the aforementioned article resolutely announced during the most turbulent month of strikes and street fights in the middle of 1905.[18] After the initial outburst of resistance workers started to organize themselves and be organized by emissaries of political parties.

Soon after the strikes began, the workers began to form "strike committees," which were gradually transformed into semilegal and more structured factory committees. This was an important means to negotiate with the management and constituted first bodies of collective bargaining at a time when labor unions were still entirely illegal. Moreover, it was also an essential platform for workers' emerging political will. Within this framework factory crews were for the first time able to elect their representatives and simultaneously were forced to negotiate different interests, opinions, and strategies among themselves.[19] Similarly, strike activity was not limited to simply bringing work to a stop. The rallies, marches, and mass meetings accompanying strikes were a manifestation of the workers' presence in the public sphere and important forms of public participation. In times of revolutionary upheaval, mass meetings (*masówki*) were organized almost everywhere, and streets turned into displays of political ideals and collective emotions. One of the militants recalled: "Lawful posters appeared for the very first time. They announced rallies organized by socialist parties. Two weeks of civic freedoms given by the tsarat [a contemporary word for the Russian autocracy] suffocated by the revolution were greatly utilized by socialist parties. . . . There were rallies in theater halls . . . , in factory halls, . . . and many other [venues] with many thousands of participants. There were also discussion rallies where the programs of the PPS and the SDKPiL were thoroughly discussed."[20] These rallies contributed significantly to the politicization of participants and funneled their enthusiasm into mass entry of political parties. Another author of a memoir remembered that "from the very first freedom days in 1905 I joined the PPS, I participated in almost all demonstrations and rallies, and I distributed party literature."[21] Politics entered streets that, regardless of the police and military repression, became vivid spaces bustling with speeches, polemics, and visual expressions of political commitment. On the days of mass strikes, workers left factories and, often wearing elegant Sunday attire, marched from one factory to another proudly displaying their socialist insignia in public.[22] The practical aim was to encourage others to join the strike. However, the implicit rationale of acquiring political visibility and staging ideological commitments was probably even more important. Such expressionist manifestations reconstructed the public domain on yet another level.

These actions questioned class-based partition of bodies and practices in public. Manifestations and rallies, especially at the beginning of the revolution, had an inclusive character, encompassing a vast palette of social milieus. Therefore, they directly fostered encounters and collisions of bodies in the urban public space. They were acts aimed at staging a transclass body politic on the streets. Thus revolution simultaneously intensified the urban

Fig. 2.1. Workers gathering on the streets of Lodz. Collection of Museum of Independence Tradition in Lodz.

predicament—in Judit Bodnar's wording, "the tension between the physical proximity and moral remoteness of city dwellers"—and temporarily overcame it.[23] After the announcement of the October Manifesto, when the tsar, under the pressure of strikes and riots, granted the people basic political freedoms, euphoric moods proliferated. In Lodz, Warsaw, and other cities of the Polish Kingdom, crowds flocked to main streets and squares to manifest their enthusiasm and put their new freedoms into practice.[24] Moreover, numerous political gatherings took place in private flats, and people met and debated in various auditoriums. Speakers and listeners included not only local intelligentsia and bourgeoisie but also workers.[25] The material and class composition of public participation changed: workers speaking publicly and being listened to had never until then been common.

It is probably hard to report on the atmosphere of those days in scholarship. Instead of making the attempt, let me extensively quote a contemporary writer, Józef Dąbrowski [aka Grabiec], former member of the PPS, here writing as a secretary of the Warsaw newspaper *Kurier Codzienny* (loosely associated with the PPS). Regardless of, or perhaps because of, its effusive style, it gets much closer to the atmosphere of those days. It contains a mixture of expectation and excitement already tainted by ambiguity. It also bears witness to the high level of pluralization and almost uncontrolled multiplication of political identities. Certainly not least, it demonstrates the intermingling of various, hitherto separated class milieus.

> Demonstrations on the streets. . . . Police and patrols powerless . . . on the corner of Sienna and Marszałkowska a march comes, pupils [*sztuba*], workers, girls . . . I recognize the banners of the "Proletarians" [PPS Proletariat was a small fraction of the socialist movement programmatically situated between the "main" PPS and SDKPiL]. There is a handful of them, they sing squeakily, "To the barricades!" "[Na barykady!," one of the more popular socialist songs] . . . The police and an army squad approaches. Apparently against the proletarians. "To hell with them!" They passed . . . I go farther. Suddenly I hear shouts behind me—Are they already fighting [or] aren't they? I turn around instinctively and I am dumbfounded . . . the "Proletariatians" roar "Long live," "Hurrah," and carry the policemen in the air. By the banner nailed to a wooden pole like a church pennon, on the shoulders of "the people" a fat constable is sending kisses with his hand, like [Helena] Bogorska [famous singer and actress]; the workers greet the soldiers . . . The devil takes me . . . The pavement splits.[26]

The memoir continues to present the ecstatic experience of the forthcoming days already tainted with ambiguity regarding the rivaling political forces and "the masses" acting:

> Dusk. Warsaw looks unprecedentedly exceptional . . . Streets are full [of people], there is no sign of the police. Crowds dressed elegantly, illumination, dominated by red lampoons. Hum. From every side "the Red" ["The Red Banner"—*Czerwony Sztandar*—one of the revolutionary songs]. We are constantly passing workers' marches . . . We approached a great scene . . . the march comes, red banners, red lampoons, they sing "the Red." It seems like it's a revolution . . . Suddenly around the corner a dozen hussars arrive . . . Obviously, according to their habit "powstancy kochajoncy ubirajut, kak zajoncy" [in Polonized, phonetic Russian, roughly: the lovely insurgents flee like hares]. Some more nervous revolutionaries escape in panic, and they bump into us. We call for order—by mercilessly hitting them with our walking sticks on their heads, ordering them to stop and go back [to the demonstration]. Finally, the attempt is successful. The march splits [to let the hussars go]. The hussars are riding

through . . . Near the red banner—they salute. This was not like that ever before! The crowd becomes enthusiastic. On Marszałkowska Street at about eight o'clock—I hear for the first time "Poland Is Not Yet Lost" ["Jeszcze Polska nie zginęła!," incipit of a patriotic song about fighting for national independence, the future anthem of the Polish Republic]. A dozen or so adolescents, holding hands, walk in the middle [of the street]. Apparently, the Kilińszczycy [members of an association named after Jan Kiliński, a popular patriotic hero from an artisan background active in the Kościuszko uprising of 1794] attempt to organize a march. . . . On Nowy Świat Street I see a march composed of craftsmen and women. The power of tertiaries [*tercjarki*, female members of a religious association], various hens. A lot of serious foremen. Over the crowd there is a giant white banner waving. And a song is heard: "Who entrusts himself to his Lord's safekeeping" ["Kto się w opiekę"—a religious hymn]. The Christian democracy movement was able to organize a march on the spot. There are about two thousand of them. . . . A moment breeds people, or at least street speakers. Today it seems that the same has happened with people as with the apostles on Pentecost. An epidemic oratory is ruling the day. On every corner there are speakers—they are giving orations—either from a window or from the lamppost or standing on a chair carried out from the concierge['s room], or they are carried on their neighbors' shoulders. They rant and rave about the tsarat, the bourgeois, the bondage . . . the orations are heard in Polish, Russian, Jewish [Yiddish].[27]

This vivid political culture filled a certain lacuna left by older communal networks often torn apart by migration to cities and new forms of industrial labor. On the one hand, new practices mediated experiences of urban life and allowed for the articulation of grievances that were looming large.[28] On the other hand, many earlier cultural forms of rural origin were maintained by new urban dwellers. Socialists utilized many elements of religious imagery and rhetoric, without invoking any direct connection with the allegedly "religious" or "eschatological" qualities of their ideology.[29] Such overlaps were grounded in a certain intransigence of cultural forms and repertoires.[30] Thus a politicized open-air festivity (*majówka*) resembled in many respects a village party with food, singing, and dancing. One of the participants remembered: "When spring came, lecture circles usually moved with their activities. . . . There were presentations, declamations going on. . . . After lectures, a meal, and finally dances, in the evening a 'march' was

Fig. 2.2. The cover of the satirical magazine *Mucha* from October 1905, illustrating the pluralization but also the antagonization of the public sphere after the publication of the October Manifesto. Polish National Library Digital Collection.

organized. . . . One hung a red lining or a handkerchief on a walking stick, it was carried on the front and imitated a banner; as the 'march' went on, the participants of the meeting (*majówkowicze*) sang . . . of course singing unbearably out of tune and tailoring the melody to their own musical tastes and abilities."[31] The nationalists, in turn, were not engaged in conspicuous dancing or unruly singing. They cultivated the national body through a more explicit hierarchy and discipline: "Excursions enjoyed great popularity; [they] were organized during the summer months in the Wawer woods, where in the fresh air lectures were heard, political discussions took place, and gymnastics performed, under the leadership of Stefan Dziewulski."[32]

Regardless of these differences, in both contexts political and intellectual activities played an important role during such evenings. As one proletarian agitator remembers, "during those gatherings there used to be one or two hundred people or more. There was always music, and one danced and played. But the most paramount element were the agitation speeches."[33] In this way, political message was transferred through cultural practice. Simultaneously, the cultural practice performed in public redrew the political limits.

Just as past cultural forms helped carry political agitation, they also shaped new repertoires of contention. A political demonstration with singing and banners bears much resemblance to a Corpus Christi procession or other church rituals. Even the melodic structure of songs popular among militant workers is relatively similar to the church hymns with their contemplative pomposity and repetitiveness.[34] Doubtlessly, the tradition of public funerals attended by crowds of political allies of the dead was important because it was one of the few relatively legitimate forms of public gatherings under tsarism. However, it was also the most established form of expressing emotions in public and joining with others of similar sentiment. It was important to build forms of public participation familiar to the participants and not create unnecessary exclusion.

To ensure a broad impact, the new public domain of workers had to be inclusive. In a familiar atmosphere workers did not feel inadequate, as they would in many transplanted forms of the bourgeois public sphere, which maintained gentle mechanisms of exclusion such as speech mannerisms or a required dress code. For instance, it was not recommended to wear exquisite clothes to workers' gatherings; neat and modest working attire was encouraged instead. The goal was not only to save money for strike funds but also to discourage any implicit rivalry in elegance, which would repel some more modest or poor comrades.³⁵ While performing in public before others, workers often wore Sunday clothes and elegant hats. By this performance they assumed the mantle of citizenship in new circumstances. Among themselves, however, they often aimed for a neat but low-profile appearance to emphasize their dignity as workers.

In sum, all these forms of presence on streets and squares ushered people into the public realm. It made them visible among themselves and to others. The workers noticed how numerous they were, and so did the urban elites. During the rallies and meetings, bodies of different classes and habits could rub shoulders. People might accustom themselves to one another, learn and talk, but also openly quarrel. Political speeches of different breeds mushroomed, exposing listeners to new, contentious, and conflicted political ideas. Such plurality also concerned languages, cultures, and ethnicities, where "orations Polish, Russian, Jewish" were heard. These changes did not pass without notice, and many were frightened by new contenders undermining the social order. The presence of many languages caused resistance. Suddenly, those hitherto regarded as illegitimate, or just foreign, also demanded the right to conspicuous presence in the streets, so far empty because of repression but considered Polish by the decent citizens of the nation. Those groups greeted, with some relief, intensified tsarist policing aimed yet again to push the unwanted elements out of sight.

As tsarist repressive measures increased, workers were not always able to demonstrate in the streets. Being deprived of the right of civil presence in the political and spatial dimensions simultaneously, they politicized spaces of production. Being reduced to the sphere of production and rendered invisible beyond it, they creatively modified the space assigned to them. They reappropriated many seemingly antipublic spaces of production and thus reclaimed them for public purposes, so that they could become places of open discussion and contact with political ideas. Factories became public spheres. While still embedded in the context of production, they nevertheless began to be commonly perceived as spaces of political expression as well.³⁶ One of the creators of those politicized spaces recalled: "The [political] work became massive. Still illegal, it became somehow semipublic. In factories mass meetings were held with the party emissaries; discussions were organized. Hundreds of people participated in these gatherings. Factory organizations were growing fast and massively."³⁷ There workers gained autonomy. They built a space governed by their own rules, (usually) free of police supervision but also free of the internalized gaze of other social classes, which might have disciplined public practices to force them to comply to the tacit laws of the bourgeois public sphere. Those spaces of political activity were eagerly protected against the inroads of any foreign elements in order to maintain those precious pockets of freedom, which were so hard to get.[38] The awareness of this tension appeared in the biographical testimonies of those involved:

> The repressions were present above all on the streets, leaving factories and mines alone. Almost all organizational life moved there. Meetings and discussion rallies were organized in the factories. The training of defense squads took place there, and weapons were kept on the spot. It was a form of exterritoriality. Even if many of those factories were under special supervision of the police or army squads, even if police and soldiers were constantly in guardrooms and toilets, they rarely entered departments and workshops, because they felt foreign and unsafe there. Traitors were still rare.[39]

As a result, factory spaces were turned into relatively independent proletarian public spheres. There the issues concerning workers' lives were hotly debated in public. Mass political meetings mushroomed with mobile agitators proselytizing ideas close to their hearts, party representatives giving political orations, and finally workers debating among themselves, making sense of this vivid inflow of political content. Announced political programs were used as means to explain the world around them and relate the everyday experiences to broader social processes. Those debates supplemented work activity or just replaced everyday toil, as they typically happened during strikes. These mass gatherings and discussions created new communicative circuits and public contexts not previously known to the workers who were mobilized politically for the first time in such large numbers. In those spaces they acquired political knowledge and a certain public ethos of participation.

Similarly, private rituals, present from time to time in factory spaces, now gained political significance. Even personal holidays were saturated with political content, leading to a tight interweaving of private and public domains, as one worker recalled:

> When I entered the guardroom I was surrounded [by people], lifted up on hands and carried to the other room on the second floor, while at the time "the Red" was sung. After I had been carried into the room like an idol, I saw

an exceptional decoration made of plants and flowers. My weaving workshop was especially distinguished; it was flooded with greens and flowers, and on the top of the machine [there were] three shuttles and the factory banner with the inscription "Long live the SDKPiL" and "Down with the tsarat." I was so perplexed that I several times tried to move the workshop to start it, not realizing that the regulator was tied with a string, which meant [that I had to] ransom myself.[40]

In such situations workers were able to assume a kind of self-definition normally not available to them at the workplace. They were no longer subsumed under hierarchical forms of communication, if not direct bondage. Instead they could be socialized into a world of equals debating with each other.[41] This realm was regulated by certain tacit rules and explicit regulations, which secured the right to equal expression, promoted self-control, and funneled the untamed energies of wannabe speakers. They were not always effective, and increasing political antagonism again allowed aggression if not violence to sneak into the proletarian public sphere. In general, however, moderate factory constitutionalism—epitomized in autonomous decisions about the organization of debate, strike policies, discipline of petty thieves, and the like—offered a significant opportunity to decide about the collective and learn to act in public.[42] In those rapidly proliferating spaces, workers found episodic experience of public sociality, which would be so important later when creating more long-lived workers' associations in other contexts.

Moreover, staging the proletarian political meeting in a way that stimulated debate gave the participants a share in the political community. An identity could be reconstructed: for instance, as a respectful speaker capable of convincing others of his arguments. In factory meetings, articulation of a political utterance also demanded an ability to convince others of a particular line of argument. Talented speakers sprang up, being able to build a special form of authority out of their political zeal and argumentative wit. One of the autobiographers remembered his brother who became an emerging oration-star: "[He] used to often speak at mass meetings and workers' gatherings. He was outstandingly smart. His logic and arguments made him a bogeyman for the PPS people [the brother was SDKPiL member]. Because they had spotted him at the assemblies organized by the PPS, they were frightened by his speeches. In discussion he backed them into a corner, so they often attempted to throw him out by force, and if they were not able to do so, they interrupted assemblies."[43] This fragment demonstrates that rank-and-file workers also participated in the speaking culture and were encouraged to learn how to speak and argue effectively.[44] Being a successful speaker must have been an important component of the brother's identity, as he was remembered precisely for this trait. This was a viable alternative way of building personal dignity posited against the workplace. Moreover, it was also a modern experience of fracturing the self and introducing alternative domains of meaning or social roles and respective identities, which by itself offered new spaces of freedom.[45] After all, a political debate was an exciting experience not known before, not to mention an attractive alternative to everyday factory or workshop work. The context of political debate was highly pluralized, which stimulated the development of polemical abilities and rendered effective speakers even more desirable. Thus the plurality of roles within the proletarian life context was supplemented by the plurality of political positions.

Plural Commitments and Democratic Surplus

After the initial agitation of novices, when political identities might be forged from scratch, it soon appeared that there were more challengers to win the support of individual workers. This change resulted in the development of highly polemical and reflexive mobilization strategies taking into consideration the existence of opponents. This evolution had its correlation in forms of the public sphere and the experiences of its participants. Changes in practices of agitation, public performance, and oral culture followed. The waters got muddied as the political competition between parties intensified. With new possibilities for agitation and the massive inflow of members, parties started to openly compete for more adherents. Limited competition and polemics were already common before the revolutionary upsurge. Only after it, however, did socialist milieus turn from cadre, conspiratorial organizations into massive political parties, and nationalists began to agitate urban workers much more intensively. The nationalist leaders noticed the potential and dangers ushered in by mass urbanization and the rise of the working class relatively late, so by the time they threw their hats in the ring, the competition was already high.

Before 1905 policy differences were muted—limited in in socialist journals primarily to who better epitomized the true socialist ideals. The bone of contention was, unsurprisingly, the national question but also the alliance with the Russian proletariat and the chances of democratizing the Russian Empire through such a common struggle.[46]

In late 1905 the entire mode of communication changed. The political press broadened its definition of potential means of ideological presentation in agitational texts. Instead of merely informing readers about the predicaments of capitalism under tsarism and explaining the world while employing a particular ideological vocabulary, the parties openly questioned their rivals in self-reflexive polemics. This change paved the way for more advanced political rhetoric and complex arguments using various forms of inter-discourse. Journals and leaflets often used quotations, indirect references, irony, or sarcasm to distance themselves from competitive presentations or simply to mock them. For instance, when nationalist writers suggested that a tsarist official was murdered because he was hostile to socialism, the PPS writers struck back by ridiculing such claims and ironically suggesting that other tsarist officials must then be clearly supportive of socialism, as indicated by the title of the article: "Skałon Is a Socialist Sympathizer and Margrafskij is a National Democrat" (Skałon sympatykiem socjalistów, Margrafskij narodowym demokratą).[47] More advanced analyses of political support and opponents' strategies also appeared: to delegitimize national democratic attempts to address different social classes with opposing interests, for example. Collating contradictory elements of the national democratic program, *Czerwony Sztandar* presented an elaborated analysis of class-based interests and positions.[48] This shift in tone urged Rosa Luxemburg to note in one of her letters that "it's no longer possible to present a positive party program in an agitational form. . . . Now while writing the article . . . one must address not only the PPS but also the ND and the PD and even the conciliatory party. One has to consider their every move."[49]

On the other side of the political spectrum, nationalist texts, although initially issued from a minority position, were designed to gradually undermine the dominant position, as a frontal attack might discourage convinced readers. Later, as the balance of power changed, they switched to more direct insults against their opponents. Socialist texts, in turn, moved from the mode of "enlightening presentation," just explaining the world, to more argumentative, point-to-point polemics between socialist parties and ironic strategies against the inroads of nationalist propaganda. Such strategies did not always simplify workers' choices; it was no longer enough to embrace socialism as such. One agitated worker recalled the puzzle:

Fig. 2.3. The cover of the SDKPiL clandestine journal *Czerwony Sztandar* from April 1905. This was the only underground publication printed in color, and the banner on the vignette was indeed red (dark gray here). Podlaska Digital Library Collection.

And then a fresh surprise approached me, [the agitator] started to explain to me the difference between the PPS and SD [SDKPiL], from which [explanation] I did not understand anything. So, I tell him that I do not want to have anything to do with those who expel the Russians [*moskali*, a derogatory term used deliberately by the narrator to mimic and mock the language of the PPS hostile to Russians in general].... So, I ask him: but *Sprawa Robotnicza* [the SDKPiL journal], what is this? Ah! This is SD. So, I will be in SD![50]

Apparently, the readers of proclamations or people listening to political orations were confronted with a complex, polemical discursive setting, which forced them to face the plural political field. Because of the competition between parties, entangled political processes, and the launching of new institutions, workers entered pluralist and protodemocratic contexts. To put it another way, everybody had to confront the possibility of adhering to other political positions or narratives. This was far from an obvious experience for the political debutants desperately trying to make sense of the situation: "After every speech, workers argued for a long time, which sometimes resulted in a fight. Then I was astonished why one group quarreled with another, and why speakers threw each other out of the soap box [that served as an improvised rostrum]. But the revolution has done its job and I began to understand what's going on. Soon I noticed that in our factory there are three party organizations: Social Democracy of the Polish Kingdom and Lithuania, Polish Socialist Party, the National Democracy party."[51] Workers had to reconceptualize their own commitments, turning them from a simple "awakening"—from passivity into a conscious choice. This choice needed to be grounded and justified, not only in front of others but above all the tribunal of their own selves, now among the politically differentiated peers demanding more conscious commitment. This might create a tough emotional puzzle: "Not a single night was for me sleepless because of two feelings fighting in my heart and not leaving me calm. After a three-month-long struggle between nationalism and internationalism I was convinced that in socialist movement there is no place for separate nationalist parties."[52] In some cases, the ultimate choice was later narrativized as a formalized story of ideological maturation. It occurred, for instance, in standardized depictions of Bolshevik ideological peregrinations documented in many Soviet files. It is, of course, hard to assess to what extent it was a practice already forged in prior communication and thus a genuine form of expressing the committed political self.⁵³ One of the SDKPiL militants, writing in Moscow in the 1930s, recollected:

> This year [1905] was a pathbreaking one for me. My concepts were entirely crystallized. Being on the services of this and that and yet another party I had an opportunity to get familiar with their programs. At the beginning I did not care that much about the programmatic differences, what was important for me was just the fact of the direct participation in the revolutionary movement. I was, however, dissatisfied with the nationalistic taint in the PPS and Bund; on the contrary, the slogan of international struggle of the proletariat was close to me. I understood that my only place is in the SDKPiL.⁵⁴

Such a retrospective depiction does not mean that people were thoughtfully aligning with one party or another according to some form of deliberative choice. They talk about the party platform and recite the party-based arguments in retrospect. However, they also confirm in their narratives that the way to make sense of their own decisions was unavoidably embedded in the plural political context. It stimulated self-reflection, even if only after the political affiliation was already an accomplished fact.

Once convinced, the workers needed to be capable of defending their commitments publicly. To do this, their political intellect had to be freed from the direction of the intelligentsia or party control. They had to forge an independent political self, defensible in confrontation. Agitation and educational strategies changed accordingly. It was not enough to offer a simple way to comprehend the world; it had to be compared, criticized, and exposed to potential counterarguments. A consciously "proletarianized" SDKPiL agitator, Stanislaw Pestkowski, who approached the proletarian milieu as his own new class of choice, recollected the new communicative circuit on the agitation circle he had led: "Facing such strong activists I organized an agitators' school. We used to gather on Sundays in a group of about thirty people. The classes lasted three to four hours. I used to give a topic a week in advance, dissecting it into separate theses. The classes were conducted according to the discussion method; I spoke only at the very end. This school enjoyed great popularity."⁵⁵ The situation was further complicated by the diverging and evolving strategies of the main parties with respect to the most hotly debated topics. For instance, in the first months after the tsar announced plans for the Duma and elections were organized, socialist parties unanimously boycotted it as politically bogus. A lot of ink was spilled to convince workers that they would not gain anything from this staged liberalization. At the same time, however, much was done to explain how democratic institutions work to provide evidence that this Duma could not be considered as one of them. Later, the strategy changed, and one by one socialist parties realized what gains the nationalists enjoyed, capitalizing on the chance to agitate around the ballot. The National Democratic movement was able to offer a tangible feeling of agency to working-class voters. For the first time they had a chance to express their preferences, even if they had little impact on the actual electoral outcome. All this produced massive information campaigns clarifying the strategies of parties or explaining the logic of political institutions. Although not all the recipients were able to make much sense of it, there were some who left the political battlefield rhetorically and politically educated.[56] The lack of democracy contributed to the rise of knowledge about it, as the ideal of democracy was used as a point of reference to debunk tsarist electoral policies. A similar conundrum concerned the emerging labor unions, with some parties having decided to tacitly influence legal, nonpartisan unions and others launching illegal, party-controlled organizations more independent of police supervision.[57] Although all these controversies stimulated the growth of political knowledge, they also induced conflict.

While one may observe the gathering of storm clouds throughout the "long" months of 1905, only after the nationalists forcibly entered their bid for influence among urban workers did the hurricane burst forth. The heated atmosphere aroused political emotions that needed to be tamed. Even before the intraclass political conflict escalated, the PPS responded to the rising tension during factory mass meetings. The party propaganda attempted to proselytize moderation and the culture of debate.[58] While the temperature of debates between socialist parties rose, the polemics remained harsh but *verbal*. The conflict with the nationalists, however, resulted in regular (and lethal) street battles. Fierce fights, increasing waves of aggression, and mutual acts of revenge occurred equally on both sides of the conflict, often out of the control of the parties' headquarters from mid-1906 on. Only after several attempts to calm things down at a party level did a bottom-up initiative of the shop-floor militants lead the sides to the negotiation table in April 1907.[59] This ended the atrocities, leaving a highly conflicted political landscape behind. Apparently, while democracy and pluralism may have brought many blessings, they also led to brutal conflict between the parties.

Making Claims for Citizenship

All those acts and practices constituted transgressions of limits of the legitimate. They broadened the realm of what among workers was considered "practicable" as forms of public and political participation. Those who had been feared before now had to at least recognize the significant power of workers as a threat to be dealt with. Those who had not taken workers into consideration as claimants and essentially equal people now recognized in them a real, active factor, if not an interlocutor to engage in political communication. The change was enthusiastically documented (and to some extent proclaimed in performative register) by its ardent supporters such as the labor union organizer Bernard Szapiro quoted in the opening paragraph of this chapter. For the workers the world around was reconfigured, and police, burghers, and the bourgeoisie looked at them differently.

Sometimes, such an altered gaze was forced on tsarist functionaries, when workers temporarily took the upper hand in the streets. During processions with banners, policemen or factory administrators who were passing by were often forced to praise the socialist insignia (for example, by taking off a hat), or even to walk ahead of the procession, personally holding the banner.[60] Tsarist gendarmes were pushed aside to the pavement; they had to make way for groups of workers, whereas policemen were simply insulted and driven away.[61] The revolution also led to a changing relationship between bodies, as was demonstrated above in a different context. However crude such forms of reclaimed citizenship may seem, they nevertheless testify that workers became aware of their new visibility, if not their overall position or place in society.[62] This quotation shows one example: "I was wondering, how it works—a handful of people are gathered and mister commissar, the lord of life and death of those people, entered the room white as a sheet, throwing a wobbly, and said: 'excuse me, I came only on official business.' What a power, this is the value of the associated man. For the first time I was struck by this fact."[63] The tsarist administrative apparatus, probably least inclined to stimulate change by its announcement, also registered the differences. Some of the fearful reports of its officials are catalogs of attempts to question the borders of political visibility and the delimited realm of action. One outraged tsarist official described events in Sosnowiec:

The newcomers declared that now there is freedom of the press and that they can print whatever they like; they simultaneously shouted "Long live social democracy!" After having printed the proclamation, the crowd went away. That day, from the early morning on boys and adults walked around the city and without any restraint gave away various proclamations, also to military officers. . . . In the building of the Winter Theater, when the audience had gathered for the performance, a young worker entered the scene and having read the tsarist manifesto, he threw it on the ground, began to trample it, and said that it was not a constitution but a cheat. After that he started to explain to the audience the nature of the constitution from the social democratic party's point of view.[64]

What could be said and done did change. It affected not only, and not primarily, the relationship between the tsarist administration and populations under its jurisdiction.[65] Above all, the relationships between classes and milieus enclosed in single communicative spaces, such as national areas or substates on the fringes of the Russian Empire, changed. To put it another way, the revolution affected "Polish society" (which obviously did not necessarily consist of ethnic "Poles," still a dubious category in those days) even more than the confrontation between the "Poles" and the external imperial power. This collision of classes and the possibility of a productive political encounter in a single space—for instance, at a political rally in a theater—was also recognized by the bourgeois press. While the more conservative journalists would eventually condescend or fear the workers' presence, in the beginning these encounters were greeted enthusiastically. A journalist's account from a rally organized by the Warsaw technicians' association left little doubt in this regard: "This is the rally of Polish thought. On the scene a committee of the technicians' association—on the chairs and in the lodges—all of the states! In the first rows, the heroes of the new era: the workers! Hail to them, priority for them!"[66] This mode of political participation was not previously known to those marching or debating. It must have deeply reorganized the notion of who they were in relation to other social groupings.[67] It was a form of political subjectification, simultaneously creating new forms of self and recognized places of political utterance, where workers took part in the emerging public sphere *as* workers. For instance, they were recognized as essentially equal by intelligentsia members of the socialist party structures, as recalled in some memoirs.[68] This in itself provided implicit evidence of recognition for their importance and dignity.

Fig. 2.4. The results of the demolition of a brothel in Warsaw, one form of "popular justice" during the revolutionary unrest. Polish National Library Digital Collection, DŻS XII 8b.

Moreover, workers could participate in regular elections, or at least they could consciously decide not to do so. Although the initial plans for the Duma did not allow workers to vote and excluded national minorities (including the Poles and Jews of Russian Poland), under pressure from the street the October Manifesto issued by Nicholas II in 1905 promised more generous suffrage.[69] Along with this tactical liberalization confirmed by a Duma decree on December 24, 1905, some institutions known from parliamentary systems were introduced, even if in forms often resembling their own caricatures.[70] The voting statute largely disadvantaged the lower classes, allowing only workers from big factories (in the factory curia) or official tenants (in the urban curia) to vote. Moreover, it assigned to these votes very mediated and limited, almost nonexistent power. It nevertheless was a significant act of empowerment for many people who had never before been able to participate in electoral politics of any kind. As a result, the very fact of being able to vote and witnessing an entire electoral campaign with meetings, speeches, and a huge dose of explaining what it was all about provided an unexpected new recognition for workers as political subjects.[71] The State Duma appeared more like fiction than any type of legislative power and even in its meek form was soon dissolved. This triggered bitter debates but allowed less and less for belief in any real political leverage via the ballot. Nevertheless, subsequent elections provided genuine inclusion for workers, offering them a certain form of participation and citizenship in the national body politic, now turned into an electoral agent.

It was the National Democracy party that used this opportunity to boost its support in a most effective way. The party from the onset opted to take part in the election and soon launched a powerful agitation machine. This was to a significant extent a source of national democratic success and subsequent rise to the status of a most significant political player.[72] The ongoing agitation was largely based on dubious political practices, such as kindling antisemitism and exacerbating antagonism between ethnicities (which became increasingly significant sources of hostility) and supporters of different political agendas.[73] This dimension, however, was also an important pillar in successful national democratic mobilization.

If by any standard Russian Poland underwent a transition to democracy, the elements of protodemocratic public culture also emerged and affected both genders.[74] People attempted to recraft their attitudes to themselves and others. They began to claim a certain form of citizenship. The new citizenship in many aspects encompassed female workers, even if this dimension did not leave a tangible signature in the sources. Although the sociality of the labor union, the solidarity of the shop floor, and the heroism of the street fight enshrined "male" militancy, the movement was not entirely exclusive in respect to gender.

The history of Russian populist radicalism confirms the early inroads of female militants into radical milieus.[75] In Russian Poland as well it was mostly women from the intelligentsia who got involved in politics. Some of them made spectacular political careers, and a significant number of women played leading roles in the socialist movement.[76] Only later did female comrades from the working class become part and parcel of the revolutionary effort.[77] At the turn of the twentieth century in Russian Poland, the share of female workers was already significant.[78] As female workers were employed in bigger mills, they were also mobilized during the revolution despite the initial reluctance and barriers imposed by traditional female roles. As a result, at the apex of the revolutionary surge women made up to one-sixth, and in some districts up to two-fifths of socialist party members in Lodz, where the labor force was the most feminized.[79] Those women were active participants in conspiracies, organized the distribution of party publications, and took

Towarzysze i Towarzyszki!

Ogłoszono manifest carski. Car obiecuje, że prawa konstytucyjne rozszerzone.

Manifest carski — to nowe oszustwo! Wczoraj manifest ogłoszono — a jednocześnie kozacy porąbali naszych towarzyszy na torze kolejowym w Sielcach.

Taki był początek carskiej konstytucji w naszym Zagłębiu!

Manifest cara nie spełnia głównych naszych żądań!

Żądamy zwołania sejmu ludowego w Warszawie, opartego na podstawie powszechnego, równego, bezpośredniego i tajnego głosowania!

Żądamy natychmiastowego uwolnienia uwięzionych towarzyszy, zniesienia stanu wojennego, wolności obywatelskich!

Car naszych żądań spełnić nie chce!

Precz więc z carem i carskim rządem zbójeckim! Rewolucja zmusiła carat do drobnych ustępstw — i tylko drogą najostrzejszej walki rewolucyjnej dojdziemy do celu.

Dość ucisku! Dość nędzy i upodlenia!

Precz z samowładnym rządem! Niech żyje rewolucja!

Niech żyje socjalizm! Niech żyje sejm ludowy w Warszawie!

Dąbrowa, dnia 1 Listopada 1905 r.

Okręgowy Komitet Robotniczy Zagłębia Dąbrowskiego Polskiej Partji Socjalistycznej.

Fig. 2.5. A typical layout of a political leaflet, this one published by the PPS in the Dąbrowa Basin after the announcement of the October Manifesto. Note the opening call addressing both genders. Polish National Library Digital Collection.

part in demonstrations and street fights. This last activity left a sad imprint on the registers of people killed during the revolt. For instance, one-fifth of the people officially listed dead after the June uprising of 1905 in Lodz were women, which testifies to their active involvement.[80] While the nationalists saw women as guardians of nationhood at home, socialism was not a male-only issue anymore.[81] Against the backdrop of traditional postpeasant culture, male heroism, and practical exclusion of women from the public sphere, any female activity was a significant sign of change.

Women took this step and entered the proletarian public sphere, but not without friction. The place of women changed during the revolution, for women themselves and their male counterparts alike. Paradoxically, the redefinition may have started with the hierarchical gender relationship. For instance, a factory foreman, not always a sworn enemy, might ask a young female worker to distribute some leaflets, which might later lead to more serious involvement in socialism.[82] The content of the distributed leaflets also encouraged women to join the movement. Many proclamations started with an opening phrase addressing the comrades but also in female form: comradess. The PPS even issued a special journal for female workers, *Robotnica* ("workeress," female worker), unfortunately published only once. This official and dignified address doubtlessly made a huge impression if we consider the impact on male workers, proud of being somehow recognized as equal partners in conversation or exchange. Apparently, even for women from an intelligentsia background recognition as equals was a serious issue. One of the young adepts of socialism admitted: "[Some important party member] addressed me as 'comradess.' It impressed me a lot, I was only seventeen then."[83] All in all, such self-assertion was even more powerful for women comrades, as it changed not only their class position but also the gendered dimension of it.

The relationships between socialist militants and their wives tended to be tense enough to trigger official statements in socialist journals. The local correspondence circulating among PPS militants gives insight into the practical obstacles of the distribution of the party journal that were caused by family life. Not surprisingly, it was not safe to read *Robotnik*; for anyone caught with a copy, severe police persecution was guaranteed. Nevertheless:

> In Pabianice [small town near Lodz] they get from us forty to sixty copies, and they are read, according to local estimations, by four to five hundred people.

We were told in secret that if anybody burns the issue after having read it, "there are people there who will punish him," thus the respect for our papers is enormous; funny scenes accompany this: some worker brought a copy of *Robotnik* home from the factory, his wife understood what it was, so she abruptly attacked him so as to take the paper and burn it. The worker was not eager to give it back, testifying that he values his life. As she insisted, he took it out and wandered around until he found somebody else who took the baton.[84]

In those days the wife was expected to take care of the home. Avoiding the risk of arrest, unemployment, and often irreversible poverty was a perfectly rational survival strategy. The resulting resistance of female family members to male political involvement was a serious issue.[85] "Family issues" were not limited to female opposition to politics. Young female workers involved in socialism encountered resistance from their fathers and brothers. Male family members tried to prevent women from political and public involvement, in addition to themselves sometimes having different political commitments.[86] However, the common political involvement of fathers and brothers propelled political conversation into the working-class chamber. The intensity of social contacts also increased, sweeping women out of the home's limited life context.[87] The same fathers and brothers might support new politicized interests of women, but even if they themselves were involved, they might be equally inclined to deliberately limit women's access to "male-only" issues. The key to successful political mobilization lay in the hearth, and conversely, politics severely reconstructed family relationships.

A seemingly grassroots campaign was launched to address this hotly disputed topic in *Robotnik*. It explicitly questioned the rigidity of the public-private division, diagnosing the obstacles it created for socialist politics. Husbands were used to treating socialism as a male-only issue and often excluded women from their political business, simultaneously preventing them from participation. Not surprisingly, this not only limited female participation but also backfired, as those were the wives who resisted their husbands' long-term involvement. Thus the paper criticized the exclusion of women from the public sphere by ordering them to take care of "the pots and children but not mess with men's business." In response, one of the supposed female readers postulated in a letter published in the paper that wives should be better informed and allowed to take part in their husbands' political activities, that papers and proclamations should be read aloud and

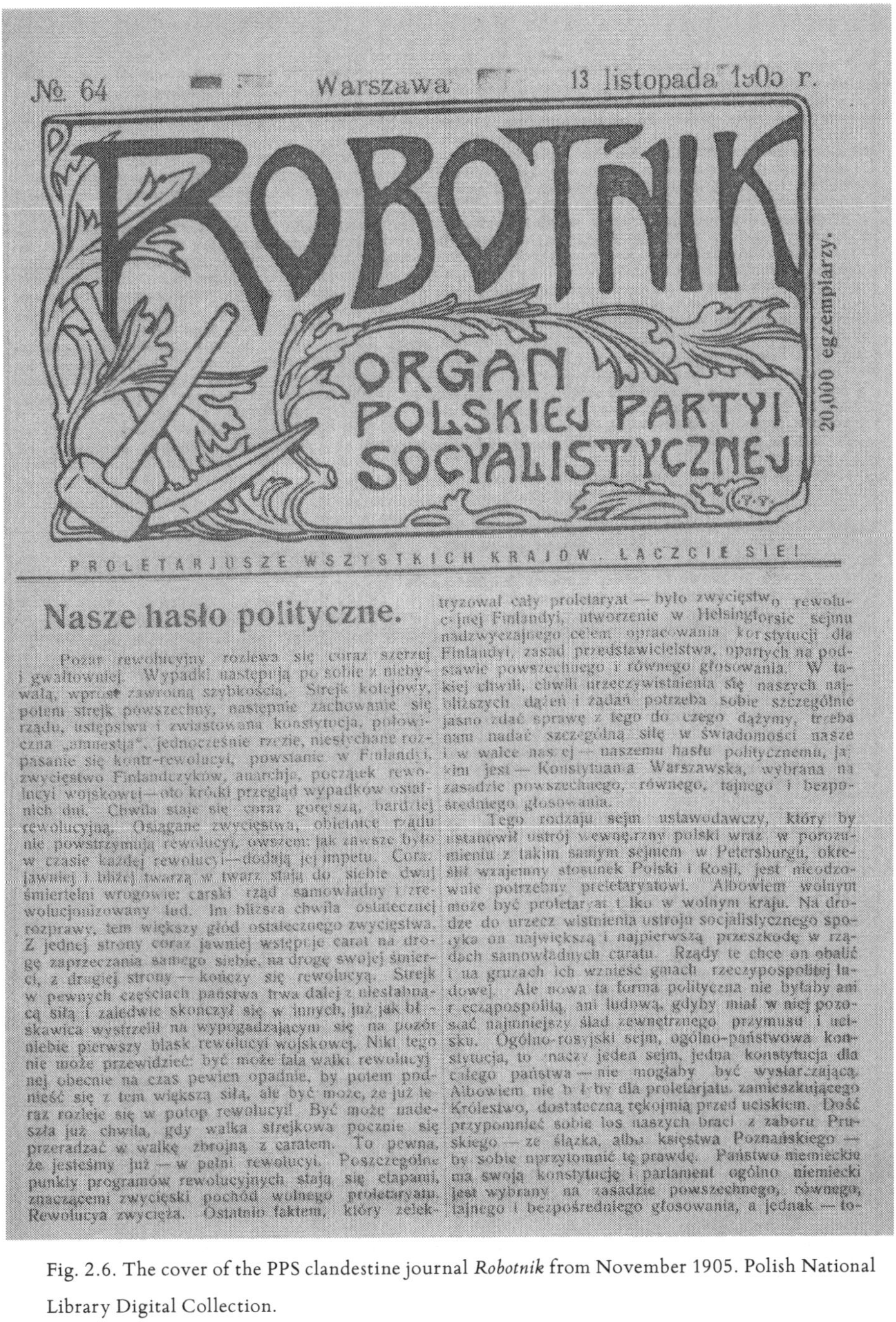

№ 64 Warszawa 13 listopada 1905 r.

ROBOTNIK

ORGAN POLSKIEJ PARTYI SOCYALISTYCZNEJ

20,000 egzemplarzy.

PROLETARJUSZE WSZYSTKICH KRAJÓW, ŁĄCZCIE SIĘ!

Nasze hasło polityczne.

Fig. 2.6. The cover of the PPS clandestine journal *Robotnik* from November 1905. Polish National Library Digital Collection.

discussed at home (an important issue because women were much more often illiterate), and that the party should be more involved in organizing female political life by preparing dedicated gatherings and lectures that were more women-friendly and focused on female issues.[88] Such a letter was also an important gesture in publicizing the female voice—after all, it was published in a paper held in high esteem among comrades.

This course of action agreed with the party line, which openly declared that their program was directed "to all the oppressed and exploited, regardless of differences of religion, language, or sex."[89] The same article called for the full inclusion of women in the public domain and argued that they could develop intellectually and politically as well as men if the circumstances were favorable. It is no coincidence that it was the PPS that most vividly addressed the women's question within socialism. This party responded most comprehensively to the complex social composition of the Polish Kingdom, and the mixture of national and class demands.[90] The PPS was sensitive to multiple regimes of oppression and its members built a nascent theory of intersectionality, supporting its actual socialist universalism. This sensitivity contributed to the recognition of the place of women in the socialist movement. Not everybody, however, was happy with the changes and inclusion of workers, women, or Jews in the public domain.

Enemies of Democratization

The mass movement looming large was greeted with ambivalence. Workers' protests destabilized the existing social order. The feeling that "something is out of joint" also affected groups other than workers. As argued above, the scale of the movement and its rebellious dynamics were a surprise to socialist parties. The National Democrats, in turn, complained that they were unprepared for activities in the urban environment on this scale, even if they had already developed a functional network of institutions.[91] No wonder the revolution was a shock for the positivist intelligentsia and the liberals, who were having a hard time accommodating themselves to the new mode of politics. Commercial elites as well were not too enthusiastic, for obvious reasons.[92] Some of these groups were eager to criticize the revolution and condemn its disruptive potential. Apart from the general opposition, however, on a micro level an explicit and unmediated presence of workers within the political sphere also provoked resistance. This resistance also appeared among people and milieus generally supportive toward populist politics, if not involved in fanning the flames of social turmoil. New people appearing in spaces where they had not been welcome triggered outrage among those who felt that they were the legitimate occupiers of those spaces. The ultimate evidence of the operation of power is resistance, as the Foucauldian dictum says.[93] To paraphrase, one testimony to the breach of political boundaries is resistance from the border guards.

The guardians of order feared its disruption, even if they had been staunch opponents of the tsarist state. Although at first the contingency and openness themselves caused concern, hopes for a better future remained intact. Commentators from the intelligentsia often spoke of chaos posing danger but also creating possibilities. "Warsaw looks like 'the first day of Genesis.' Total chaos everywhere and in everything. On almost every street there are already speeches, party banners, and songs," noted Władysław Reymont, an honored Polish writer, a distanced observer rather than a partisan of any particular cause.[94] More conservative commentators did not maintain this finesse of analysis and soon began to condemn "anarchy" out of hand.[95] In the case of conservatives, it was simply a feeling of undermined hierarchy that perpetuated this condemnation.[96] The National Democrats were also worried, but what bothered them most were the inroads made by political ideals other than nationalism. Nevertheless, by fighting revolutionary "anarchy," they successfully managed fears of a destabilized society and profited heavily from general weariness with the revolutionary unrest.[97] Within liberal milieus, in turn, fears of the new regime in the public sphere assumed the form of policing unwanted elements. Although the liberals supported the revolution in the beginning, they later lost faith in the possibility of liberalizing the state system. As a result, they ceased to accept new forms of politics not always fully aligned with their own ideals.[98] This evolution can be traced in self-reflective comments from the main figure of Polish liberalism, Aleksander Świętochowski. On the eve of the new year of 1906, he felt obliged to summarize the ups and downs of his political agenda in the turbulent year of 1905. Among other tribulations, he recalled one of the political rallies he participated in:

> We enter the philharmonic hall packed with people, with hearts full of joy and merry hope, . . . but we did not manage to open our mouths before we were greeted with some hellish fanfare—wild howls, screams, maledictions . . . Finally we were allowed to speak. Even though none of us uttered any bad words,

which would not be a praise for freedom and warm-hearted greeting for the people, after every speech screams and maledictions burst out again. Eventually we were deprived of voice completely and people started to burst onto the lectern, they cursed everybody and everything apart from themselves: . . . the government, bureaucracy, tyrants, bourgeoisie, liberals, patriots, democrats of all sorts, and above all the progressive ones, who were the hosts of this gathering [Progressive Democracy was the name of the liberal party].[99]

This depiction could be read almost as a synecdoche of the entire liberal confrontation with the emotions of the populace. It captures the clash between expectations and reality, salon politics and a mass rally. What mediates between them and helps Świętochowski make sense of the clash is contempt for the rabble, who are not grateful for everything the progressives have done for them. The problem with the revolutionary rabble was not, however, limited to its class composition.

The ethnic composition of the people acting in public was also unacceptable to some commentators. Such a reaction is clearly visible, for instance, in the epigraph to my introduction. It demonstrates how various measures could be used to delegitimize the presence of Jews in the same liberal political rally from November 1905 described by Świętochowski. At the same time, the language used there undermines the credentials of the working-class speakers, who were allegedly no more than liaisons for Jewish interests. When workers entered the public sphere, they were sometimes depicted in a way similar to that in the epigraph: "ushered onto the podium by a young Jew." The stories about "the Jew flouncing on the podium in convulsions of wild fury or happiness" and just a while later "lunging on the banner with the white eagle" and "throwing it on the ground" as expressions of antinational feelings are almost a part of the genre.[100] The clichés mobilized here are cultural tokens expressing much more than a simple description of a political rally. They might be applied in various circumstances to rallies or political speeches with a multiethnic working-class public. The situation in which "the orations were heard in Polish, Russian, Jewish" (as in the "decade of freedom" recalled above) or Polish and Jewish workers protested together carrying socialist banners in different languages during funerals and demonstrations in Lodz in May and June 1905, were not rare. Tsarist officials noted this fact with some astonishment.[101] Many political activists were, however, uneasy about such instances, even if they did not endorse antisemitism per se.

Michał Sokolnicki, a member of the intelligentsia and a leader of the right-wing faction of the PPS, must have strolled Warsaw in October 1905 in a similar manner as Józef Dąbrowski, quoted above. Even if he was associated nominally with the same party, his writing on the decade of freedom in Warsaw reveals much more ambiguity and suspicion toward the protesters: "I realized that the actual people have not much in common with this imagined [version], which was given to us by old insurrectionary, emigrational, and democratic ideology, and which was inherited by the Marxist worldview imported to us from Germany. In the people there were indeed elements of work, heroism, and sacrifice, but under the surface, capable of solidarity and sacrifice, there was only dark ignorance; poverty acted from within without restraint, and this huge mass was lacking any idea, just because nobody had introduced it there before."[102] Sokolnicki did not consider the political agenda of the protesters as an idea of sorts and stopped a step before suggesting outright that the real problem was their ethnic composition. His bitter political enemy Stanisław Kozicki, the "official" chronicler of the National Democracy party, while writing about the same events, was much more outspoken in his revulsion against the multiethnic crowd. In his writing, the delegitimization of the working-class presence through ethnic hatred reached its zenith. In the official history of the National Democracy party he described popular participation using "chthonic" expressions referring to the uncontrollable and inhuman forces crawling out of the depths. "Then everything that was hidden underground bubbled up. Above all the true face of the socialist movement was revealed. The streets of Warsaw were full of crowds, which did not have a Polish character. He who has seen this conquest of the Warsaw street by foreign elements will never ever forget the feeling of awe that must have overcome him."[103] Additional meanings behind these insinuations may be revealed by comparison with the parallel fragment in Kozicki's unpublished memoirs. In this more private document, Kozicki added more figurative expressions and contexts revealing deeper reasons for his fears. In the memoirs the source of his shock is clearly the political presence of people who are not entitled to it. The "decade of freedom" was one such traumatic experience, which redirected the intellectual trajectories of the National Democracy party, because these unwanted groups (non-nationalist workers, Jews) assumed active political subjectivity as soon as channels of political expression were unblocked.[104] They were not only fruits of "epidemic oratory"—or as Kozicki himself wrote, "random speakers"—but above all politicized, working-class Jews.[105] Had they remained passive "Jews in gabardines," they would have been acceptable. As soon as the "foreign crowds" claimed a right to political expression, however, it provoked a reaction from "national Warsaw":

> Then the crowds flocked onto the streets, but they were crowds composed of people *not visible in the downtown* every day . . . , the *Jewish crowd* appeared, they were not, however, Jews in gabardines, known to Warsaw and not hated. There were members of the socialist Bund and other Jewish associations, Jews who came in most cases from Russia, with Russian customs, willingly speaking Russian, referring with the *highest aversion to the Poles*. It was revealed in speeches, often given in Russian by *random speakers*, in shouts, in a hostile attitude to the Polish population, which initially being intimidated left streets free for these foreign crowds . . . . We were all just overwhelmed by how the streets of *our city* looked, we realized for ourselves that our position as the Polish population is seriously endangered. Marches with red banners and revolutionary songs . . . appeared. *National Warsaw was not visible* at all.[106]

This quote is a masterpiece of something that one can call a "racialization" of political difference. It contains a myriad of discursive strategies aimed at securing the stable position of National Democrats as embodying the national interest. There is a metonymic sliding between national and nationalist and between the nation and the National Democracy party. The same applies to the enemies; the working-class protest and above all the socialists are unanimously associated with Jews. What triggered the anger of the nationalist chronicler was the fact that the public space was occupied by those who were not entitled to be there (i.e., Jews) or those who could enter the public domain only when guided by proper leaders, who would "introduce there [proper] ideas" (i.e., workers).[107] Those unwelcome groups shocked the national elites with their very presence, and adding insult to injury, they made political claims ("shouts"). According to this mode of reasoning, every political force opposing "national Warsaw," itself clearly represented only by the National Democrats, was immediately not only a political opponent of the nationalist party but a grave danger to the Polish nation and its ethnic purity.[108] Whenever this force was composed of people not entitled to political presence for some reason, then it was described almost as an inhuman, chthonic, quasi-natural force that must be resisted by any means available.

It is important to note in this context how the nexus of ethnicity and class was mobilized to delegitimize political opponents. Rising political antisemitism is not at the center of my focus, and it is widely documented in existing scholarship.[109] However, it helps explain an intersectional position of revolutionary contenders such as Jewish workers, workers allegedly led by the Jews, or socialists considered to be serving Jewish interests.[110] In the discourses mobilized against popular participation during and after the revolution, this nexus was very important, as it tended to rule out rival political ideas. The fact that popular contention or redistribution was delegitimized as un-Polish and foreign not only secured the triumphs of the political right; it also relocated political conflict onto terrain much more destructive to democracy, since political practice was grounded in assumptions about shared civic community.

Furthermore, the reconstruction of politics faced resistance because of other dimensions of new claimants' identities. As I mentioned above, the revolution ushered women into the public sphere. Not surprisingly, their arrival attracted the attention of less progressive forces. The condemnation of new participants had, therefore, a fully intersectional character. Misogyny went hand in hand with vitriolic antisemitism in service of the opponents of revolutionary democratization.[111] The chief antisemite, Jan Jeleński, was for a long time a marginal figure not taken too seriously by nearly any of the political formations.[112] During and after the revolution, however, his statements gained more publicity, and the language he used entered into mainstream debates.[113] It was no longer a scandal to claim that "In a society with little political consciousness, perhaps like any other, suddenly a great number of politicians appears—politicians of various estates, various sex, and . . . age! Whoever is alive and can utter sounds of speech is politicking, and at famous rallies persons foreign to us and degenerated hold sway— such as Estera Golde [female physician and activist of the PPS-Left of Jewish origin), frighteningly shallow, mindless, and shortsighted."[114] While the publications of Jeleński and his followers assumed the most extreme form (i.e., exorcising the "masons, Jews, and socialists—the perfectly matched trio aiming at the destruction of Christian societies"), similar utterances ceased to be a rarity.[115] They came in many variants—condemning biologically degenerated workers, Jewish enemies of Polishness, or foreign socialists—and they appeared in the writings of prominent literary figures and those previously known to hold a progressive worldview.[116] The merger of class hatred and antisemitism became a long-lasting amalgam among the Polish public.

In sum, the revolution changed the political scene not only in respect to the presence of popular contention in the public sphere but also in the spurring on of vicious forms of resistance against it. Modern political languages maturing in the revolutionary public sphere not only accommodated democratization but also harbored antisemitism. Antisemitism was a powerful means of modern democratic mobilization. As Scott Ury comments, "while democracy may have brought many blessings, it also came with at least one curse that would scar Polish society for generations: political antisemitism."[117] The rise of political antisemitism came *neither* from the elites (as an antirevolutionary reaction) *nor* from the masses (as the supposed bubbling up of eternal hatreds and prejudices). Instead, it was generated and cultivated in the space between, with agency widely distributed among people of varying class positions. At the same time, however, even if mastered in unison by national democratic mobilization, elite and popular antisemitisms had different morphologies and dynamics.

Apart from stirring mass support among some urban populations, antisemitism might paralyze working class protest in the multiethnic industrial hubs, as happened farther east, where popular pogroms wreaked havoc.[118] In the Polish case it was above all helpful in delegitimizing workers among the higher echelons of the Polish public. That did not happen, however, chiefly because of the already antisemitic masses entering the scene, as the liberal-conservative argument about masses causing the degeneration of politics would suggest. The reason was the broad antisemitic panic of the elites fearing the masses. Although fear directed at the masses was not caused by their perceived antisemitism, elite antisemitism might result in the masses being described as Jewish-ridden and thus illegitimate.

A New Sociality

The emerging forms of the proletarian public sphere during the revolution were an important backdrop against which the transformation of politics occurred. Confrontation with this complex political setting was an important school of politics for participating workers. It was also a form of general education, allowing those who participated to develop broader interests and an active attitude to the world around them while exchanging information about the social reality they were part of. The change in workers' intellectual pursuits was profound enough to be noticed by the internal committees of the parties and was put under public scrutiny in official announcements such as political leaflets. For instance, the PPS-Left delivered quite unambiguous information to their readers.

> Past tiny gatherings, hidden circles, or lectures are redundant today—on the one hand because one can make everything publicly in relevant existing organizations thanks to the revolution, [while] on the other hand the mass dimension of the movement does not allow us yet to dedicate all our efforts to shaping and bringing up individuals. Previously it was the party that assumed the role of the teacher-nurturer. Nowadays maybe even she [the party] should be satisfied with awakening and maintaining the masses' striving for education and culture, show them the way and the means to satisfy those needs either in existing educational institutions, saturated with the democratic spirit, progress, and love for free, independent knowledge or in the self-education institutions created by the workers themselves.[119]

The picture of this transformation emerging from my research does not indicate the parties' intention to resign from circle-style work in favor of stricter control of the mass worker. Parties were still interested in bringing up independent agitators capable of autodidacticism and did not limit the will to acquire general knowledge and discuss. The need for effective political action put pressure even earlier on Russian Social Democracy, leading to the birth of the Leninist centralized party doctrine.[120] In the sources I investigated, both documentation of the socialist parties and militants' memories registered possibilities for new modes of action but not so much a drive to control the intellectual pursuits of members.

An interest in controlling the intellectual life of the masses was, however, revealed among the intelligentsia milieus dedicated to maintaining social calm. Many of them were not ready to accept forms of political participation that did not comply with their expectations. To describe and manage the situation, they used various rhetorical strategies condemning workers, especially those supporting other political ideas. The intelligentsia, however, also clearly noticed the changes in political practice. The same applies to educational associations already then controlled by the National Democracy party, a political force explicitly hostile to the revolutionary upsurge. The report of Polish School Motherland (Polska Macież Szkolna, a national-democratic educational organization created based on TON) admitted that "the readership among the people grew unprecedentedly in recent years because of the interest in political events."[121] While acknowledging the change, the political Right also undertook active measures to restrain popular participation.

This resistance notwithstanding, revolutionary public spheres created multiple opportunities for reasoning and speaking freely across boundaries between those who were supposed to speak and those who were supposed to listen. It was also a step away from the previous hierarchical knowledge transmission of educational circles stimulated by intelligentsia speakers. Despite initially being top-down, alternative education managed to trigger the will for public adventures of newborn men of letters. They transmitted information to other recipients while short-circuiting the hierarchical order of knowledge. Those political-educational milieus were places where all the political publications were digested. Reading material was vividly discussed and transformed among recipients, autonomously and often against the "official" authorial intention of the enlightened writers. Therefore, it is crucial to understand the forms of public before examining political discourse of leaflets and brochures in detail.

Experiences in reading were supplemented by the experience of the street. Engaging in public performance and assuming a visible place in the urban public sphere empowered people in contact with the tsarist police and the higher echelons of society. When pushed out of the streets, public participation proliferated within factories; spaces of production turned into hubs of agitation and debate. In all those places a protodemocratic culture emerged, with workers negotiating their action in emerging factory constituencies and debating, if not fighting, with political opponents among their fellow workers. In every one of these practices workers crossed the boundaries imposed by social order, hierarchical relationships, and their own limitations; together they composed the emergent proletarian public sphere of revolutionary politics. The rhetorical means used in this emerging public sphere and, more generally, the changing role of language are examined in the next chapter.

3

Speech and Action

> Often [the leaflets] were found in the aisles of workers' houses or directly in flats, inserted in chinks of not so tight doors or stuck on walls, fences, or telegraph poles, in factories on machines, in workers' lockers for clothes and tools. The youth read those propaganda materials willingly, passionately, almost openly discussing [them].

In many memoirs left by workers, as in this quotation, leaflets were the main point of contact with political ideas. In police reports, leaflets were singled out as having a particular power to excite revolutionary spirit on the streets, and they were the most common evidence mentioned in court records and archives of the secret police, the Okhrana, to prove the guilt of recently arrested suspects. Their production was seen as a significant success, and those who printed them were the most venerated heroes. There was something exceptional in those sheets of paper, which made them so important to everyone involved. As material evidence of political processes, they offer insights into political languages in action.

In the tsarist empire, the revolution marked the rise of politics in a new key, as Carl Schorske called it. Although he initially meant the transformation of parliamentarian politics in the age of mass parties and the introduction of a new political dynamic, the label remains relevant for the context investigated here. The old, aristocratic mode of engaging in politics was no longer carefully questioned by bourgeois liberalism but smashed by politics gauged to move "the masses."[1] The revolution fostered the emergence of mass politics when new groups of people were massively mobilized and parties grew in number, making them no longer salon conversation clubs or conspiratorial circles.[2] In Russian Poland, however, in contrast to Austro-Hungary, it was not the parliament that focused attention and spurred mobilization. Even if the Duma triggered numerous debates and electoral campaigning was intense, it was not the place where the parties forged their constituencies and vice versa. The new parliament was too much of a smokescreen for a persistent autocracy; the empire was too fractured nationally, which molded separate public spheres; and the representation of lower echelons of society and more radical political forces was too weak to spur a real debate. As a result, political programs meticulously honed at party rallies years before were now put into practice on the revolutionary street.[3] There they confronted rising emotions, collective action, and antagonistic competition, which could be tamed only by effective agitation.

The main source preserving the contours of political communication are party journals, brochures, and, above all, the more elusive political leaflets—their number, regularity, and evolution over time give a broader overview of change during the revolution. First of all, these material vehicles of political agitation carried not only worldviews or, simply speaking, ideologies. Exposition on this basic level is needed to comprehend the complexity of the political field. However, detailed reading also reveals other dimensions. Forms of addressing the reader and polity, tacitly assumed in the language of the leaflets, traced the contours of emerging and changing identities beyond simple adherence to this or that political program. Second, the language of leaflets reconfigured the domain of the speakable and the doable.[4] As acts of speech uttered within a dense communicative context of the revolutionary street and factory, the leaflets encouraged action and presented its particular forms as possible and significant. They cast recipients as positioned in a given way in respect to their social surroundings and circumscribed the regimes of possible activity. Third, the leaflets make it possible to view politics as a field of forces and track its reconfiguration over time. The 1905–1907 escalation bore witness to how words gained power to mobilize people.

Leaflets, Proclamations, and Reading Publics

Within the emerging public sphere *for* workers, which was also more and more the public sphere *of* workers, patterns of contact with the written word varied. The oldest forms were brochures or booklets that were several dozen pages long. They were read among still-narrow circles of agitated workers before the revolution and later remained the source of political knowledge for those already versed in the basics of a given ideology. They were reasonably priced, distributed among close adherents, and used for more focused, personal agitation.[5] Another category consisted of party-published periodicals, which were also popular among those already convinced.[6] Brochures, and to some extent party journals, were read among socialist circles and workers aspiring to them, studied in silence or recited in small groups, later contemplated, before finally resonating in public meetings. Larger books were laboriously studied in dimly lit basements and prison cells or popularized during illegal discussion circles. The main reading material, however, to which workers were exposed was political leaflets.

These single-page leaflets were the most readily available material distributed secretly in the factories and streets and used broadly to encourage and bring in new supporters. They were also used for current communication between party organizations and workers.[7] As an important pillar of printed socialist agitation, they undoubtedly contributed much to the politicization of workers and their general reading activity. Indirect evidence of their influence can be interpolated from the vast fragmentary data of titles and copies published.[8] The popularity of leaflets fostered their standardization, and soon they formed a genre of sorts with a typical layout and structure. As the "party technique" was quite well developed, the leaflets were almost always printed—in different techniques and quality but certainly not handwritten.

The opening line was a direct address to the recipients. An exposition of the situation followed, and the leaflet continued with a political analysis, party-sponsored solution, and ideological commentary in varying proportions. The text was closed by a call to action, or if that was conspicuously impossible, by some indication of a future triumph. There was almost always a signature of the organization that issued the publication, usually at the end, augmented with specification of a party committee (central, or local from a particular city). As a political genre, the leaflets were well embedded in oral agitational culture. Their content deliberately mimicked a political oration with its direct address to the reader and accompanying battle cries. On the other side of the communication circuit, the oral-written distinction also tended to be blurred because the leaflets were often read aloud and discussed. While leaflets were "loose" flyers distributed broadly in all possible places,

Fig. 3.1. A typical SDKPiL leaflet. Polish National Library Digital Collection.

the same content was often used in proclamations: larger sheets of paper stuck somewhere to be displayed until some policeman removed them.

These publications were the material substrata of the beginnings of mass politics in Russian Poland. Written and created by parties, they quickly became crucial in politicizing the relatively narrow circles of workers that existed before the revolution. Although in retrospect one may observe the gathering of storm clouds at a much earlier time, it was the revolutionary upsurge that caused the volcano to erupt. A proclamation found in the early morning, when the factory whistle signaled the beginning of work, was often the first step in political initiation.[9] These impromptu readings encouraged workers to further explore options and consequently to become party members.[10] Furthermore, these leaflets shaped the polemical zeal of contrasting party programs, and not infrequently they were a decisive factor leading someone to switch party affiliations.[11]

Leaflets were the basic message carrier in communications between parties and their supporters; for instance, they were used to spread information about the party's policies, calls for strikes, and political programs. They also provided spaces for polemics with other political narratives, thus constituting the substrate of the emerging proletarian public sphere.[12] Consequently, even people who were not direct supporters of any party or represented a different political faction were exposed to the language of leaflets. The ideological messages presented there were performative texts, actively interacting with their readers on the streets and shop floors.[13] Reference to the efficiency of this mobilization allows one to investigate the ideological shifts, built identities, and exclusionary logic inherently present in a serious reconfiguration of the political field. Let us now examine how the process unfolded.

Against the Old World

Soon after the initial January general strike spread, workers parading through cities and raiding factories to put a stop to any remaining production found, or were given, party leaflets. Without a doubt, socialist parties were not controlling the tumultuous events, but they tried hard to do so. According to their current capacities, they immediately printed leaflets informing the workers of what had happened in St. Petersburg, and later in Lodz and Warsaw, and called for further action. The initial enthusiasm notwithstanding, an important challenge for the new political forces mobilizing the masses was to undermine the current government's grip on the people's imagination.

As is widely documented in the literature on tsarist Russia, support for the tsar among peasants was not uncommon, although not necessarily because of any "naive monarchism."[14] In Russian Poland the foreign character of tsarist rule impeded its legitimization among the elite, which had an established concept of legitimacy. However, the centuries of class oppression carried out by the Polish nobles and the very fact that it was finally the tsar who had given land to the peasants and abolished the remnants of second serfdom enabled the Russians to claim a certain legitimacy among the peasants "over the heads" of the Polish elite. These attitudes to some extent also existed among the urban working class, whose members were usually of peasant origin. In 1905 workers still sent (or planned to send) petitions to the Russian administration in the vain hope that it would support, or at least protect, the workers against the local bourgeoisie.[15] Because of this latent attachment, the political parties were eager to convince the workers of the savage and hostile nature of the tsar and the illegitimacy of the entire autocratic tsarist regime. However, they had first to convince the peasants and workers that the concept of legitimacy was something that they should care about before the parties could delegitimize tsarist rule as tyrannical and foreign (or both).

Consequently, the delegitimization of tsarist rule and the dissolution of its sacral authority was enacted mainly by contesting the very concept of the tsar. Above all, protesters had to be convinced that the system intent on crushing their uprising was weak (giving incentives for further unrest), even if they already entertained no doubts concerning the legitimacy of tsarist rule. Tsardom, usually embodied in the very term "tsar," was put in the crossfire of libelous accusations and verbal humiliations.

Bloody Sunday in St. Petersburg provided an effective platform for this purpose. What the Russian workers experienced outside the Winter Palace easily demonstrated that expressions of loyalty to the tsar would not prevent the repressive apparatus from bloodily suppressing all demands. Moreover, hostility against the tsar was the main point of reference unifying the heterogeneous demands that characterized the first phase of the revolutionary upsurge.[16] The most common phrases (according to lexicometric analysis) pointed to the criminal character of the regime, depicting the tsar as a directly involved villain stained with workers' blood and emphasizing the despotic, autocratic, invasive, and foreign genesis of tsarist rule (*zbrodniczy rząd carski, rząd morderców, rząd samowładny, rząd despotyczny, krwawy car, despotyzm carski, rząd krwawego cara, rząd najezdniczy*).[17] This critique was strengthened by presenting the flaws and weaknesses of the tsarist regime, an approach later used to demonstrate the feasibility of political struggle and the chances for a successful overthrow of the existing order.

As the revolutionary tide rose, open calls for the overthrow of tsarist rule on the way to creating a new society were issued with increasing frequency. Recipients might read that "Our worst enemy and severest oppressor—the Muscovite tsarat—is already staggering under the pressure of the revolutionary movement, and its downfall is inevitable."[18] Likewise, "the tsarat is weakening, so we have to bash the walls of the invader with huge hammers till on the debris we can build our better lot."[19] Later, as tsarist repressions became more severe and the situation began to be framed as an outright struggle, the rhetoric was even more hostile: the tsarat was "a mad dog dying in a sea of blood," which "dies as a monster, . . . suffocated with a knee to its chest and fist in its eye"![20] References discrediting the tsar and tsarat constitute the most common topic in the printed party materials. Over half of all leaflets and proclamations contain such a critique, as though the automatic association of the tsar with the worst things imaginable was a main pillar of change. Nonetheless, the old order of legitimacy and the autocratic political edifice were crushed, something that workers on the streets confirmed in a very direct way. Surprisingly, such antistate keywords were dominant not only for the PPS but also SDKPiL, with its program targeting capitalist exploitation. The fact that the rhetorical field was initially organized around the idea of *tsarist* oppression handicapped SDKPiL from the start. People's conception of the enemy and corresponding mobilization were more along PPS party lines. An already intense campaign to define the new, turbulent reality sped up.

The presence of language in the new political forms was tangible. The revolution was an event ushering new groups into the public eye and introducing them to a new type of sociopolitical language. Singular concepts carrying complex but also contested meanings were important pillars of agitation and made it possible to comprehend the surrounding world in a new way. Concepts became an active determinant of historical change shaping perceptions and actions of historical actors when deployed in discourses spurring on the mass political mobilization of new groups of people.[21] Massive distribution of political leaflets, often the first point of contact with systematic written discourse and political ideas, intensified this dimension among the workers of Russian Poland. In debate and action they were motivated by concepts such as revolution or socialism, which then underwent significant changes when confronted with the new political reality.

One of the most widely discussed concepts of modern times—revolution—played a far from obvious role. The idea and concept of a revolution and a revolutionary had been widely entrenched in socialist discourse for years and were backbone concepts in socialist writings in Polish virtually from their first significant appearance in the late 1870s and 1880s.[22] As a result, these concepts were used relatively often in printed materials before 1905. However, revolution meant a profound, general change of the social order to come, instead of concrete, material events and actions in which one could participate. Consequently, the word "revolution" was, in the vast majority of cases, supplemented with an abstract adjective, forming collocations such as "social revolution" or "people's revolution."

Like many modern concepts, this one is saturated with a temporal and normative surplus—it prognosticates a desired future rather than describes any empirical chain of events.[23] Correspondingly, socialist discourse contained the already singularized concept of a revolution composed of ideo-typical characteristics coagulating into a collective singular. Thus the content of events withered away, yielding to the general idea of the revolution as an act that included not only a seizure of power or reversal of roles between masters and slaves but the universal emancipation of all people. This conceptual content was emphatically rearticulated in the context of 1905 to give meaning to unprecedented social and political events.

Surprisingly quickly after Bloody Sunday the concept of revolution started to be used descriptively in reference to current events. Already on January 23, SDKPiL proclaimed: "Workers! On Sunday, January 22, a revolution broke out in Petersburg."[24] This declaration created a coherent view of the previous day's events as part of a revolution. Soon the concept of the revolution, with all the semantic burdens it carried, served as an unambiguous articulation of various heterogeneous struggles and dispersed acts of resistance.[25] General strikes, peasant struggles, school strikes, and the much diversified context throughout the Russian Empire were combined into one coherent narrative about an epochal event—a revolution—in which all the people involved would participate.

Such an act of linguistic baptism was, at the outset, problematic.[26] The articulation of a set of events and the act of naming them retroactively created a coherent entity with definite characteristics, which enabled further mobilization. Bloody Sunday, and locally the January general strike, became a cornerstone of the future revolutionary identity. A crucial step in this process was introducing a coherent and common term to describe all the heterogeneity of struggle. Furthermore, the retained temporal and normative saturation of the concept of revolution allowed participants to see and interpret their activity in specific meaningful categories, offering them a sense of belonging and a common fate, supplementing the political identities induced in those days. However, the detailed meanings saturating the concept of the revolution were diversified and contestable.

The concept assumed different shapes to correspond to different political identities, visions of the historical process, and envisioned community, becoming part of the "structure of theoretical thinking" of particular parties.[27] Whereas SDKPiL and the left wing of the PPS envisioned revolution as a teleologically and normatively understood action leading to a definite but general social transformation (a view that came closest to the preceding socialist understanding of the term), the core of the PPS imagined revolution as a military confrontation with a foreign army, paralleling the main goal of the party—the struggle for socialist independence. In contrast, in the discourse of the NZR the revolution was at best a descriptive term referring to disorder in the Polish Kingdom.

Moreover, the NZR materials provide clear evidence of the contestable nature of the term "revolution" in those days. For the nationalists it included a derogatory component: that of an undesired, dangerous social transformation menacing Poland if the socialists put their insane ideas into practice.[28] The nationalists were deeply aware of the performative significance of the concept bringing the new revolutionary movement into life. For this reason, they not only contested the legitimacy of the term and the feasibility or even reality of the revolution but rejected these ideas outright: "A great slogan of revolution was thrown at you. This slogan kindled your hearts and minds, and a noble anger and grief against our eternal oppressor—the tsar—encompassed you. Unexpectedly you all stood up to fight, exposing your defenseless breasts to the shots of vicious Muscovite soldiers."[29] Besides reducing the revolution to a "thrown slogan," the NZR openly declared it to be fictitious and false. The party stated, for instance, that "a general revolution is a deliberate lie of the socialists. It is nonexistent, and it will never come, because there are no conscious forces among the Muscovite people."[30]

Thus the NZR clearly opposed calling the occurring events by the unifying and meaning-giving name of "revolution."

The term "revolution" functioned as the negative pole in the polarized discourse of the National Democracy party, converging with chaos and anarchy,[31] associated with the hostile interests of the socialists and Jews in seducing benign Polish workers. In their view, the "Polish worker in the name of Jewish and Muscovite interests, in the name of a fictitious revolution," could only cause his or her own misfortune.[32] Similarly, the nationalists bent over backward to affiliate the concept of socialism with dubious practices of anarchy and even declared it a sort of Jewish conspiracy against the Poles. Even within socialist milieus, however, the concept of socialism was far from unanimous.

The concept of socialism was ushered in gradually, with growing presence during the unfolding of the revolutionary process. This corresponds with the rise and fall of socialist parties, which initially followed one step behind the mass movement, trying to tune in to its contention and later seizing much more influence and gathering numerous adherents before losing support once more because of the nationalist countermobilization. The spelling changed accordingly. At the beginning there is a larger presence of the older form (*socyalizm*), allegedly more "foreign" and perhaps with some "aristocratic" flavor. It remained prominent among political enemies eager to stress its alien character—unfitting and dangerous in Polish circumstances. Among the socialists themselves it gave way to a Polonized form (*socjalizm*), which gradually predominated.[33]

"Socialism," in the discourse of (socialist) leaflets, functions as an umbrella term, a conceptual token signifying a set of meanings and values, referring to such values as solidarity, freedom, and lack of exploitation. Thus "socialism began to gather under its banner the entire, large proletarian family, unifying all the suffering, all willing to get rid of the yoke of bondage."[34] When this happens, "the idea of brotherhood, freedom, and equality will triumph—the idea of socialism."[35] Socialism here is a normatively and temporally saturated concept, conveying both a set of values and the future state of society. It seems that party writers either assumed that the readers already knew what socialism was all about (a highly problematic assumption indeed), or else they just wanted to provide a universally appealing signifier, to which many could adhere without going into detail. As a result, the leaflets were an immediate means of communication, grounded in the existing knowledge of the readers. It is not the case, however, that socialism functioned like this in all the materials, due to a lack of precision or general impossibility to define it. It was quite accurately and extensively defined and explained in larger brochures, which circulated in a much different way.[36]

It was in the leaflets, however, where concepts or meanings important in shaping a general socialist worldview were disseminated. In the days of highest enthusiasm, sometimes the poetic imagination overcame rhetorical sobriety. The fragment below is highly indicative of the bombastic style, sometimes resembling a religious sermon merged with a call to battle, that can be found in the materials of both socialist parties. The example embodies the mixture of religious and enlightenment metaphors deployed to carry the idea and banner of socialism, which made a long-lasting imprint on readers. At the same time, the example is dense enough to include an occidental geopolitical imagination and a whole set of meanings coding the opposite poles of the desired socialist freedom and the tsarist yoke.

> The western wind—this was the large gust of the proletarian idea, the workers' struggle for freedom, for socialism, which having flown over all directions of the world and everywhere having awakened millions of the laboring and the exploited to a new life, reached from the West to the enormous, frosty graveyard of the Tsarat [tsarist lands], and started to blow and blow till it fanned the sparkle of light in the heads and the flame of riot in the hearts among a broad mass of the laboring and exploited, till they were resurrected and went to break the ages-long icy cascade of the Tsarat.[37]

Obviously, the reading material introducing socialism was not always so melodramatic. A broader analysis exposes a revealing bifurcation. In most socialist leaflets (as in the above quotation) socialism is a general and vague term, an object of adherence. All socialist parties ritually end their proclamations with the slogan "long live socialism" (or something similar). Both the PPS (later two factions) and SDKPiL frequently used expressions such as "under the banner of socialism" and "the idea of socialism." More detailed reading, however, reveals that what was meant by the concept of socialism might differ significantly. Where a broader context is available, one can recognize two sets of meanings. The first defined socialism as a set of political ideas or just as a movement, something one could adhere to, participate in, and so on. This definition is more in line with the contemporary dictionary meaning and common use in earlier literature, both polemical and socialist.[38] In the second set, however, socialism might be understood as a future state of affairs, a world without exploitation that one can long and fight for, something that will come in the future as a system of social organization.

The most interesting point, though, is that both sets of meanings were distributed between the socialist parties in a nonrandom way. Whereas the PPS consequently deployed the first meaning, associating itself with socialism as a movement and encouraging workers to join, SDKPiL much more often used the time-saturated concept of socialism as a future state of affairs. One can only wonder which meaning is hidden behind more general formulations, but a neat distribution of the specified meanings suggests that battle cries of "Long live socialism!" might have been intended differently by the authors embedded in different semantic cultures of the respective parties. SDKPiL—more integrated with international socialist culture, the German SPD and the Russian SD—may have introduced the change in response to pan-European patterns. The more indigenous Polish tradition was still maintained among PPS writers. The difference is also present in party programs from that period. This bifurcation would one day have severe repercussions. Already in the political languages of socialism deployed from 1905 on, it is clearly visible that the PPS was not aiming at the "socialist" transformation of society but instead understood "socialism" as a movement allegedly leading to other goals: that is, a nation state.

The socialist leaflets were numerous and successful in achieving their goals. Alternative ideas were introduced only gradually. The resonance of the audience had to be taken into account, and accepted convictions could not be condemned straight away. The nationalists tested the limits of what they could say. At the beginning, they uttered shy suggestions that "we used to believe that socialism was a defense of workers" but "yesterday we saw that's a lie."[39] Later there was no need for such timidity, and growing antagonization ushered in open expressions of hostility and called for outright violence with instructions to "struggle against all bandits stalking our city: whether they are social scum, without party affiliation, anarchists, or bandits of socialism, we must crush them and eradicate them."[40] These slanders notwithstanding, for many, socialism was a core concept, which introduced a broader perception of the surrounding world.

New Social Space and New Subjects

Political discourses also aimed to deliver a general political orientation and ability to map causal and structural connections between various instances of everyday experience. Correspondingly, leaflets and proclamations explained the mechanisms of exploitation, the results of the partitions and Russian rule, and the reasons why the state army supported factory owners in their struggle with the workers. These steps were not ineffective, as some of the narrators quoted in the previous chapter testified—for instance, while recollecting the act of "becoming a mature man" and "comprehending life in a different way" after having read a leaflet.[41] The means used was to provide coherent explanations of ongoing processes and connect otherwise discrete events and actors in a broader picture of the social world. For example, let us consider the following statement from before the revolution, explaining the role of the tsarist administration in the economic crisis: "The Muscovite tsarat worries that the poor will revolt; as a result, it tracks them down diligently and with its brutal paw suppresses any striving of workers for a better living. Police, gendarmes, snoopers, and troops—here are the physicians that the tsarat gives us to heal the crisis!"[42] Similarly, the leaflets offered a coherent conceptual grid, enabling workers to project what they experienced—declining wages, violence, lack of recognition—onto a broader sociopolitical configuration known as "the Muscovite tsarat," "tsarist autocracy," or "capitalism."

Moreover, the overall economic situation was a subject of scrutiny in the leaflets, to counter claims that, for instance, the workers themselves caused the crisis by striking. Political writers focused on introducing and explaining various workers' institutions that were planned for the socialist future or already existed in the capitalist West. Some of them were presented as possible to introduce at that point in time to improve working conditions on the spot. In such cases, the leaflet showed what a given solution could do: for instance, politicized labor unions might intervene in the vicious cycle of capitalist exploitation. "The labor unions must participate in the political struggle; after all, it is their cause! The capitalist wants to lengthen the workday without restraint, wants to reduce workers' wages, does not want to spend money on protective measures that would limit factory accidents, [and] does not want to introduce healthy work conditions because all these things cost money. Where strong professional associations exist, they force capitalists to limit time at work, increase wages, and introduce protective measures and healthy work conditions."[43] Coming to understand an alternative mode of life was a powerful experience. It was usually connected with growing anxiety and a subsequent struggle to understand both the surrounding world and the socialist message itself. This message, however, was not intelligible all at once. One of the proletarian autodidacts recollected this experience as follows: "We faced unknown issues, begging for explanation, inducing anxiety and an exciting threat of danger. Not always were all the terms known, but the crucial content remained clear for proletarian children and left no doubt. It was understandable. The proclamations were a call for a struggle against harm and exploitation, poverty and degradation."[44] The ideological content of the proclamations was responsible for turning the workers into political subjects of a particular kind. The language of the leaflets constructed class and national identities as well as political affiliations. Finally, this political communication induced contentious stances—positions that disrupted the existing distribution of appearances.

The leaflets questioned the principle of integration of the body politic and urged a reordering of society across divisions. They stimulated the multidimensional process one may call—after Jacques Rancière—subjectification.[45] For this process, the exclamatory and direct language used in the leaflets mattered on a very immediate level. Pamphlets addressed the readers in particular ways, which were not always obvious. Acclamations of human dignity infused the content and style of the proclamations: for instance, grammatical structures implying the unity of the writer and the reader through a collective "we" were an important pillar of workers' self-recognition. A previously quoted SDKPiL supporter described his first contact with a proclamation addressing the readers as "comrades"; according to him, it was an experience of a "huge, if not decisive, significance to become humans." Bakery workers finally "were not working cattle, not two-legged animals but comrades."[46] Similarly, almost all leaflets, which retained a trace of oral speech transposed in time through writing, began by addressing the audience. These opening expressions were crucial in terms of calling the newly interpellated subject to action and rendering him or her in a particular mode of being and relationship to a broader social whole. While reading these variegated and not accidental phrases—Comrades! [also in the female form], Proletarians! Workers and working women! Colleagues! Brothers, Poles!—the recipient, without being aware of it, entered into a class of persons addressed in a particular way and identified with that group.

Such direct expressions of address directed toward workers/recipients had a large impact. Because such an expression is seemingly inclusive—regardless of whether it was issued by a political ally, polemicist, or enemy—it is not easy to avoid being self-classified as an addressee. To some extent the reader becomes a comrade, a worker, a brother, or a Pole, even if that was not his or her primary identification before. The interpellating phrase is constructed in a way that prevents rejection—assigning oneself to the group that is not included would mean self-exclusion from a general community, almost a human co-being. On the one hand, similar expressions were responsible for inducing a certain construction of the self, integrated in broader discourses, ideological dispositives, institutions, and, above all, regimes of power. On the other hand, though, they stimulated language-induced empowerment, leading recipients to acquire their own subjectivity *qua* dignity and an elementary self-conscious attitude to the self and the outer world.

The opening interpellating formulas were diversified and clearly indicative of the mode of subjectivity to be induced by a partisan discourse. SDKPiL called out to the addressees as "comrades," "workers," or "proletarians," stressing a class identity and bridging the gap between a writing and reading subject (we all are comrades, *and* workers as well). Similarly, the PPS preferred "comrades" (also in the feminine)[47] stressing the socialist tradition and solidarity, albeit not of a class-exclusionary kind (less often they called out to workers as an explicitly defined group). In contrast, the NZR used the form "compatriots" (Rodacy!) or "brothers and countrymen" (Bracia Rodacy), inducing national identification, already carried within it an ethnic component (the word *rodacy* in Polish is derived from *ród*, which relates to family affiliation or parentage), which was not without significance in a multiethnic setting with growing intergroup tensions. In turn, the equally often utilized expression "Brother workers" stressed this national unity but simultaneously separated within it a certain subgroup, implicitly suggesting its vocation in an organic division of roles in the national body. This corresponded with the hierarchical vision of the nation that was typical of the Polish National Democracy party.[48]

This effect of the concepts was multiplied by the grammatical structure of the leaflets, using different means to convey the activity of recipients and their corresponding place in the social whole. The mode of speech and syntax of sentences referring to action delimited the borders of the speakable and the doable, as Willibald Steinmetz notes in respect to English parliamentary discourse.[49] For instance, PPS leaflets often focused on tsarist oppression experienced by the workers. They stressed the violence of the oppressor as a hostile foreign force ("the government of conquest is harassing us"). This corresponds with the rejection of the "foreign yoke" and alleged necessity of overthrowing it to regain freedom. Simultaneously, it builds a transclass community of suffering, strengthening the national project of the party. PPS publications also contained many utterances asserting or stimulating the activity of workers. "There, where hitherto a despondency and slavish obedience ruled," one of the leaflets announced, "a sense of honor and personal dignity was awakened." "And we," the leaflet continued, "want to live a free life of our own, we must become free and independent people."[50] While the asserted state of affairs was conflated with calls to action, assertion of a *desired* state of affairs acted also performatively: "From miserable, gray slaves, despised by everybody, who were dragged through the mud by every chump, we became people, the great freedom fighters."[51] PPS writers used words that appealed to workers' dignity and courage, supplemented by political agency, which profoundly reorganized the former distribution of places, the ascribed right of speech, and the regime of political visibility.

PPS leaflets, in most cases, deploy the "we" form to build a sense of community between workers and the authors of the text, the party and the entire society. This reconstructed the assumed imaginary institution of society and separation of places within it, and thus new places of contentious utterance were created.[52] The newly acquired status of the workers was broadly announced and carried a powerful message. The workers became a collective political subject, self-conscious of its place and recognized by others as a legitimate claimant or at least the force of fear: "We gained very much, because we became a social class, which society and government started to consider seriously. All the bourgeois parties want to please the workers with their friendship, all the journals write about workers and for workers, all attempt to win the workers. This is a great victory!"[53] Correspondingly, the grammatical structure of PPS leaflets (later the PPS-Left) indicates active, conscious action on the side of workers. They also contain many calls to action directed at workers. The subject of such action is a collective of workers that decides the course of events: "Comrades! Of the proletariat's own will, under the command of the proletariat the normal course of events in our cities was stopped for a few days! With a strong hand, armed with solidarity, the working class of Lodz, in solidarity with the proletariat of all Poland, derailed the bourgeois life, and the government and the bourgeoisie were initially helpless in the face of the workers' dictates."[54]

Slightly different rhetorical strategies for constructing political subjects may be detected in SDKPiL publications. Here the dominant form is direct expressions addressed to the workers and calling for action. The postulated activities are justified with some form of normative necessity imbued in the sentence structure. These modal normative utterances ("The proletariat must," "One has to fight," "We, the workers, must be ready for the task awaiting us") usually refer to a more general order of justification (the historical dynamics of the revolution, historical laws). The party is in charge of detecting those laws and is a depositary of the historical course of events. Party functionaries may detect the resulting necessary actions of the revolutionary workers. This reference to the objective historical process is complicit with the intellectual horizon of the Second International, of which SDKPiL was a faithful adherent.[55] Within the middle echelons of socialist parties, the laws recognized by scientific socialism and predicted course of events described by Marxism often legitimized current decisions. Bearing a seal of highly revered science, it was a quite effective strategy of building a convincing program and mobilizing for action among the European socialist Left in those days.

This way of thinking may seem too complicit with stiff theorems and the arbitrary will of party functionaries imposed on workers' constituencies. This rigidity notwithstanding, one has to remember that it was SDKPiL that attempted most vehemently to build a horizontal bond with the workers through the mode of communication the party employed and its inner-party "workerist" ethos. For instance, party writers unanimously and unambiguously recognized the agency of workers and constructed a sense of unity above inner-party occupational divisions. The corresponding language of the leaflets often used forms suggesting the identity of the writer and the reader, and the (working-class) addressee was not distinguished from the (intelligentsia) writer or the party leadership. In these leaflets the "we" form encompassing all these groups is the most common. Opening phrases are directed to the workers, but the body text constructs the common, working-class-based task of the revolutionary struggle, of which the writers are part and parcel. This structure is epitomized in passages like the following, from a May 1 proclamation: "Against these hostile efforts, against the tight-knit phalanx of the counterrevolutionary elements, which aim at reversing this great movement of the people, to the old flume, which wants to solidify for the ages bondage and exploitation, we the workers, we revolutionaries, swordsmen of light and freedom, on the first day of May we utter our proud slogans."[56] In critical moments, the leadership of the socialist parties did not abstain from using the imperative or even issuing direct orders. There were two sorts of circumstances when such things happened. Leaflets opposing the draft used strong imperatives, thus mimicking and counterbalancing the military style of government announcements. The same occurred when the socialists were trying to stop anti-Jewish pogroms. This indicates the parties' determination to prevent anti-Jewish atrocities but simultaneously signifies that some of the recipients may have indeed required such a strong slap on the wrist.[57]

Contrary to its exceptional status in socialist printings, the poetics of command and creation of hierarchical distance are common in nationalist publications. On the grammatical level it is clearly visible that for NZR writers (mostly non-working-class members of the National Democracy party), the workers had a neatly delimited, prescribed place in their imagined social structure. Correspondingly, the authors of NZR publications aimed at re-creating this structure among their readers. To achieve this effect, the language of the leaflets utilizes imperatives and orders and creates a didactic relationship to the workers, who are methodically separated from the writing subject. The pragmatics of language create distance through deployment of the second-person plural and imperative clauses. An exemplary statement might be as follows: "Brothers! Do not let the foreign soldiers harass you."[58] Simultaneously, a sense of belonging to the higher-order community is suggested. This community, however, is hierarchically differentiated. This approach separated groups of different status, power, and political visibility, and the workers remained on its lower levels. The social distance grew when the leaflet directly instructed workers from the position of knowledge and power: "We warn you that nowadays, when industry and commerce are in disarray, we cannot gain any concessions from the capitalists. We warn you that strikes won't get you anything except ultimate poverty and despair. We warn you that today there is poverty and misery all over the country because of the work of the socialists."[59]

In similar instructions, the political imagination of the National Democracy party is revealed. Even if the social distance between the intelligentsia writers and the working-class readers was similar in all political parties, the national democratic discourse created the steepest hierarchy. It presupposed a hierarchical social order, establishing vertical relationships between groups composing the unity of an organic but functionally specialized nation. Thus the integration of community through expressions such as "brothers" is immediately supplemented by classification into groups hierarchized according to their access to power, knowledge, and political position, where the workers are subsumed under the control of the intelligentsia. These hierarchical orders of speech and corresponding discipline over working-class recipients were soon to gain prominence as the National Democracy party and the NZR established a growing presence in working-class politics.

Considering the grammatical means of conveying action and agency, there is also a noticeable temporal change. The revolution encompassed periods of upsurge and decline, times of active repression and relative respite. The presence of different modes of speech in the leaflets varied accordingly; the pragmatics of language registered the ups and downs of the revolutionary process. In the initial phase, the socialist parties did not control the course of events. However much they wanted to take charge, they were relatively impotent in the face of the power of the revolutionary streets. Just one day after Bloody Sunday in St. Petersburg, the SDKPiL leaflet asserted that "now over those crowds to a growing extent hovers a leading spirit of Social Democracy."[60] The statement was manifestly untrue. However, if such a declaration were to resonate with popular sentiment, it could substantially increase the party's influence. Working-class protest might be inscribed into the social democratic program, thus presenting the party as the main proxy of the workers' struggle. This stimulated shop-floor identification with the organization.

Subsequent leaflets of all socialist parties acted as important vehicles of subjectification by openly proclaiming working-class agency and confirming it through grammar and language. During the biggest wave of strikes (January and October 1905) there were numerous examples of praising the possibility of action and the power of organized workers. Almost every sentence of the leaflets of those days assigns an active role and revolutionary dignity to the workers. This must have had a strong appeal to those lacking recognition. In those texts, workers were no longer a passive mass either condemned because of moral deficiencies or at best deserving pity, as the prerevolutionary bourgeois press presented them. In the leaflets workers became an active part of society, changing the course of history. One proclamation announced: "The working people of all Russia and Poland rose to fight for freedom and rights! . . . We took the first revolutionary step already; we won the first huge victory over the tsarat! We have awoken the entire Polish proletariat to action in solidarity. The general strike, this massive demonstration of our powers, shook the tsarat. To overthrow and crush it entirely, a huge amount of work and enormous sacrifice is needed."[61] The leaflets explicitly acknowledged the performative dimension of struggle—the fact that it is in action that political subjects capable of further steps are forged. Political freedom must be secured through revolutionary practice and not donated from above; the latter only confirms the passivity of its recipients. "Popular Freedom cannot be and won't be introduced by the tsar himself or a government pack of thieves. True Freedom can be introduced only by the people."[62] This writer, perhaps Rosa Luxemburg herself, is here applying the conceptualization of political freedom, which was acquired through struggle, to agitational material.[63] For sure, the leaflet corresponded with the theoretical premises of SDKPiL. Therefore, not only explicit slogans but also a deeper conceptual structure of political agitation paralleled the broader theoretical thinking of a given party.

The mode of action ascribed to various groups fluctuated with changes in revolutionary dynamics. In moments of upsurge, calls for action were intensified; in phases of relative calm, when certain concessions had already been gained, such urging was replaced by performative statements that acknowledged the state of affairs they were intended to produce.[64] At such times, it was the tsarat that was rendered passive in the leaflets, or if it did act, its actions were portrayed as the swan song of a dying monster desperately trying to fight back. Some of the leaflets announcing the new might of workers were not entirely wrong. There was a change going on, and such sentences started for a while to not merely call for change but also describe the actual situation: "There is nothing of the past humility, pusillanimity. The awareness of past harms is awoken, the need for hard struggle with capital grows, the idea of solidarity encompasses broader circles in the name of the workers' cause."[65]

This surge in working-class self-assertion, however, was constantly undermined by conflicting party programs. Initially, the platforms merely induced ambiguity, but an unintended consequence was to enhance the communicative competence of workers. Interparty disputes ushered in a high level of intraclass warfare between adherents of conflicting political identities and between different ethnicities populating the cities.

The Route of Political Differentiation

After the first phase of general resistance against further participation in a system of oppression, the hardships of working-class life provided opportunities for political mobilization initially championed by the PPS.[66] The impetus for a proletarian riot crystallized in the form of opposition toward all-encompassing systemic oppression, at first linked to the tsarist regime. A proclamation made by another major combatant for workers' political commitments, SDKPiL, might be deemed typical of this early phase: "Our biggest enemy, and the protector of all our enemies, is the tsarist regime. We shall direct our struggle against it!"[67] In the beginning, almost every political program was at least partially based on rising hostility to the tsarist regime.[68] Indeed, such a negative frame of reference was an important factor contributing to the movement's coherence and intensity in the first phase, although it is not clear to what extent a conscious anti-tsarist political agenda was at play among workers. Suffice it to say that initially, among socialists, as well as among the industrial bourgeois, the strike was interpreted as a political expression of resistance against the autocracy.

The very articulation of a voice of refusal and the partial recognition of this act as legitimate in a broader social context certainly was a milestone. After this first achievement, economic demands gained more significance, aiming at a more concrete utilization of mass political action. These struggles also won partial success, but this success severely affected the character of subsequent strike waves—support, or just acceptance, by nonproletarian social strata diminished or entirely disappeared. The negative unity against the occupier receded and was replaced by antagonism defined in economic terms as successful economic claims induced further ones and thanks to the ideological work of socialist parties of all denominations. The bourgeoisie shifted its political position and became a group that was hostile to proletarian demands; a division not of "the people vs. the foreign invader" but of "the people vs. the regime of exploitation" (the tsar along with capitalism) began to organize the political field at the midpoint of 1905.

The social composition of the local bourgeoisie played an important role in this transformation. Although it was a very heterogeneous group, during this reconfiguration it was clearly defined in economic and not ethnic or

Fig. 3.2. The cover of the satirical magazine *Mucha* from December 1905 depicting the "ex-king, capital," illustrating the turn of the revolutionary surge against economic exploitation. Polish National Library Digital Collection.

national terms by its opponents. It was certainly important that German or Jewish entrepreneurs did not necessarily share the anti-Russian attitudes held by the Polish elite. As a result, Germans and Jews found it easier to cooperate with the tsarist administration in antilabor policies, including the use of military squads in factories. It was, therefore, easier to reclassify these national groups as part of the regime of exploitation alongside the Russian state.[69] In this way, the ethnic component had a negative impact (by not providing national or ethnic solidarity in practice and perceptions), but it did not prove significant as a possibly antisemitic undertone of class-based discourses.

Meanwhile, the programs of socialist parties (SDKPiL, the PPS, the Bund) required steps aimed at sufficiently differentiating the political identities involved, especially in the context of rhetorical presentations to agitated workers. During mass meetings in factories, speakers competed with each other, fighting with arguments and tugging on the emotions of the listening crowd. Usually, speakers concentrated on basic, easily perceptible differences in political programs or referred to various types of affiliations precious to workers.

SDKPiL unanimously called for class unity, convincing the audience that victory could be attained only by "ties between workers of all nationalities."[70] In comparison, the PPS promoted the postulate of rebuilding a Polish nation state while acknowledging the principle of class struggle, the struggle of the proletariat against the bourgeoisie.[71] Among PPS members, there was no agreement about the means of making socialist independence a reality or about possible alliances between different nations and classes. Although the use of dual categories potentially excluded some groups, such a proposition still appealed to many, confirming their hybrid identity as Poles and proletarians. However, the PPS also worked among Jews and moved over time from a tactical rivalry with the Bund and a rejection of Jewish socialists' national aspirations to realistic cooperation with their Jewish comrades even outside the party.[72] At the same time, the Luxemburg-led part of SDKPiL drifted from tacit support for Jewish organizations to outright hostility toward any form of national separatism.[73] Meanwhile, the parties working with the Jewish proletariat, also numerous, attempted to find a place for a distinct religious, national, or linguistic identity.[74]

As a result, most of the controversies concerned the national question, the relationship between the nation state and socialism, principal goals such as autonomy or independence, and appropriate means—including whether to cooperate with Russian socialists or engage in a separate struggle (ideas supported by SDKPiL and the PPS, respectively). Opinions on current tactics also diverged, with the PPS being much more inclined toward military-style action against tsarist officials performed by dedicated squads, and SDKPiL strongly opposing it in favor of the mass mobilization of factory workers in a party-led movement. Sometimes dates of forthcoming strike were announced deliberately to differentiate one socialist party from another, and not as an outcome of a broader political strategy. Of course, that led to some confusion and weakened the party's influence among workers as well as attenuating the overall political struggle.[75] Tensions emerging from the necessity of demarcating identity also grew inside parties; in SDKPiL it was mainly polemics about Rosa Luxemburg's theory of "organic incorporation," and in the PPS disputes concerned the increasing tendency toward a military struggle for national independence and differences in attitudes toward class struggle. This conflict eventually led to a split in the PPS in 1906: the PPS-Lewica (the Left) and the PPS-Frakcja Rewolucyjna (Revolutionary Faction) emerged as a result.[76] Thus the fragmentation of the socialist movement increased.

The formal characteristics of the parties' political discourse evolved accordingly. Already before the revolution the socialist parties published polemics in their more theoretically oriented journals. Even when they used the same concepts and basic premises, the assumed forms of community or meaning given to the events differed. For instance, when SDKPiL materials present the June barricade fights in Lodz, they describe them as part and parcel of the broader, historical process of the revolutionary struggle of the international proletariat. The PPS, in contrast, narrativized the events as an outburst of unrest in response to tyrannical tsarist oppression. In the first case, the presentation was in line with the socialist orthodoxy of the Second International. In the second, it was framed according to the insurrectionist tradition of the PPS, eager to stress the oppressive and foreign character of the tsarat, against which the socialist Poles should direct their blows. Another example is the bifurcation in meaning assigned to the concept of socialism examined above.

Such fragmentation also triggered a necessarily self-reflexive attitude to one's own discourse. The differences in defining terms and framing reality around them were obvious to the writers and at least some of the readers.[77] As a result, texts had to incorporate these variations in their own argumentative structures, utilizing much more advanced forms of interdiscourse than any simple presentation of the party program on a particular issue. Consequently, leaflets, and above all, the party press used self-reflexive explanations of differences between programs and concepts as their building blocks. They were supplemented with ironic reappropriations and mockery of the opponent's position or advanced forms of sarcasm. At least to some extent the reading competence of the audience had to keep pace; otherwise such articles would become completely impenetrable and useless for agitation.

To complicate the situation even further, the positions of the parties switched. For instance, at first socialist parties unanimously boycotted the Duma elections, but SDKPiL later decided to take part in the next round (after the tsar dissolved the first Duma) for agitational purposes. Adding insult to injury, at the beginning the party leadership was hesitant even to make a final decision. Correspondingly, the coverage of Duma elections had to explain the entire process, give arguments for changing the decision, and maintain credibility among the workers. All decisions were extensively justified, and leaflets contained abundant explanations about rejected political institutions and their more desirable alternatives.[78] Tactical moves did not always correspond to strategic goals. Nonetheless, both types of action might have unintended consequences stimulated by these self-reflexive explanations. They significantly contributed to the advancement in communicative competence imbued in printed communications.

In a mirror process, nationalist publications were initially explicated from a minority position. They had to constantly present the position they supported in reference to others. Only slowly did it become possible to move from gentle suggestions that the socialists were mistaken or manipulated to outright attack. Nevertheless, the arguments being presented always had to critically resonate with the grievances and basic demands of working-class life. For instance, there were arguments against strikes; some posited that better wages might be acquired through cooperation with Polish factory owners. So long as nationalists remained timid contenders, intraclass animosities were not yet a big deal, and despite the huge ethnic, religious, and national differentiation of the urban population, intergroup conflict was not yet a factor.

In those days, socialist parties unanimously called for joint action by Polish and Jewish workers, with the PPS recognizing the rights of both groups, and SDKPiL suggesting their common class identity.[79] With the Jewish population so numerous, and Jews present among every social strata except peasants, it was necessary to build broader class alliances and impossible to exclude one-third of the working class from contentious politics (and equally impossible to claim that *the* Jews were the exploiters). A clear class antagonism as a basis for political identity thwarted attempts to find another enemy.[80]

In this vein, leaflets stressed the class connections between Jewish and Polish workers that should overcome ethnic or religious divisions. It was suggested that pogroms victimize working-class people, not the elite, whom workers may see as hostile: "Comrade workers! Pogroms threaten not Jewish rich men and capitalists—the endangered are always the Jewish proletariat. Yet we all know that in the struggle for freedom, in the revolutionary struggle, the Jewish proletariat is on our side. It would be a dishonor if we did not stand as every mother's son in a defense of those under threat."[81]

Here the class structure of the local Jewish population was deliberately invoked to disrupt the association between Jews and exploiters. In this way, the class distribution among Jews acted to contest the ethnic division, both at the level of argument and in the everyday shop-floor experience of the readers addressed.

As a result, such battle cries of proletarian unity were largely successful, and workers of all origins marched together and acted in solidarity, celebrating the fallen victims from both groups.[82] After all, the most intense confrontation with tsarist troops on the streets of Lodz in June 1905 was triggered by a rumor about the secret burial of fallen comrades in an attempt to prevent further unrest. These fallen comrades were Jewish workers killed a few days earlier. Only sporadically did the socialists warn the workers in leaflets that the proletarian unity and solidarity with Jewish comrades should be sustained, in case tsarist emissaries attempted to induce anti-Jewish unrest.[83] The tsarist government was explicitly credited with fanning antisemitism.[84] Fears of such a threat seemed to dominate, and similar calls intensified after attempts to initiate pogroms unanimously associated with tsarist provocation.[85] Apparently, even though Russian officers already associated socialism with the Jews, they failed to convince the socialists themselves and their proletarian disciples. Moreover, their attempts were met with indifference by the workers and with ironic reappropriation by socialist writers. For instance, one PPS leaflet explicitly acclaims Jews for accounting for the lion's share in sacrificing their lives for the workers' cause: "The government is angry with the Jews . . . because the Jews take an active share in all revolutionary movements and do not spare their blood. . . . This Jewish blood, which blended with Polish and German [blood] flowing into the street sewers of Lodz, this blood demands only one hatred—against the tsarat."[86]

One thing here is beyond a doubt: it was not a libel to be associated with Jews and to claim officially that Jews are an important pillar of the socialist movement was not political suicide. The situation was about to change rapidly, however, with the growing presence of the NZR, tightly connected with the National Democracy party, on the political scene. The NZR, which was created in June 1905, was able to establish itself simply by being around at a time of general growth in political activism.[87] After the October Manifesto, in which the tsar granted some political freedoms to his subjects, political identities began to be displayed on the streets even more explicitly. Such displays exacerbated hostility against political and ethnic otherness, now visibly claiming the right to public expression.

The timing here is not coincidental: the beginning of national democratic agitation among workers coincided with the rise of political antisemitism. However, I neither claim that it was the proletarian branch of the National Democracy party that was the sole harbinger of political antisemitism, nor do I look for the answer as to whether "the elite" or "the masses" are to blame.[88] There are no simple causal connections that go directly in this or that direction. One should not replicate the elite-masses dichotomy—which although undoubtedly present in the thinking patterns of the time is not sufficient as an explanatory matrix today. At issue here is a general reconfiguration of the political field and the discursive constraints that made the rendition of National Democrats' preferred political identity impossible without reference to the strong constitutive outside.[89] The construction of national unity and a corresponding nationalist proletarian identity was not an easy task. The crucial step was managing fear of the Other, threatening the community but simultaneously securing its unity. Using this negatively evaluated Other confirmed, validated, and enforced the existing predilections of national democratic political leaders.

Making national unity meaningful to workers, although not an effort created de novo, had to take place against the everyday experience of shop-floor exploitation and the socialist mapping of the social world that had already become a common language to explain the world to workers.[90] Even if oppression could often be coded nationally (Polish worker vs. German foreman in the factory or the exploitation of German/Jewish entrepreneurs), providing meaningful evidence of cross-class national unity was a challenge.

For sure, the national identity of workers was not an invention of the NZR and existed before the revolution. Laura Crago has convincingly documented its social and economic background in the preceding years. German cultural hegemony and organizational domination encouraged workers to construct themselves as working-class Poles, striving for recognition of their cultural specificity (language, professional habits) and improving their job opportunities—mostly against Germans rather than Jews.[91] Nevertheless, as a political program and coherent identity explicitly antagonistic to socialist coworkers, nationalism was an offspring of the revolution and the emergence of the NZR. Considering the range of support for the NZR among workers and the intensity of their engagement, it cannot be written off as the "bourgeois manipulation of uneducated masses" of unconscious workers.[92] What, then, did such a reconstruction of the political field and the political identities of workers look like in detail?

The Triumph of Nationalism

The growth of working-class nationalism was a profound political transformation made through the medium of speech. These were "fighting words" that changed the political field.[93] The rapidity of the process and the step by step reconstitution of meaning given to the surrounding world testifies to the powerful role of language in politics. "We, the workers—Poles," announced the proclamation of the NZR, "consider national solidarity as a primary unity consolidating us; our holiest obligation is to respect this solidarity."[94] That meant abstaining from strikes in the name of national prosperity. "We call You, then, brother-workers to interrupt occupations in factories, to firmly resist pressure from agitators, to hold back on any demonstrations, processions, and, last but not least, military actions, bearing in mind the calamities they would bring."[95] Initially, the National Democracy party and the NZR had to fight an uphill battle. To ground such a position and make forging a coherent national identity among workers more feasible, references to an outside enemy were of great assistance.

At first sight, a convenient enemy was at hand: Poland had been partitioned by three imperial powers, and young nationalists above all directed their political energies against them to struggle for independence in the long run. Nevertheless, a problem appeared at the very heart of nationalist attempts at political practice and mobilization. The long-present threat of foreign rule, which had taken away Polish independence, was the center of

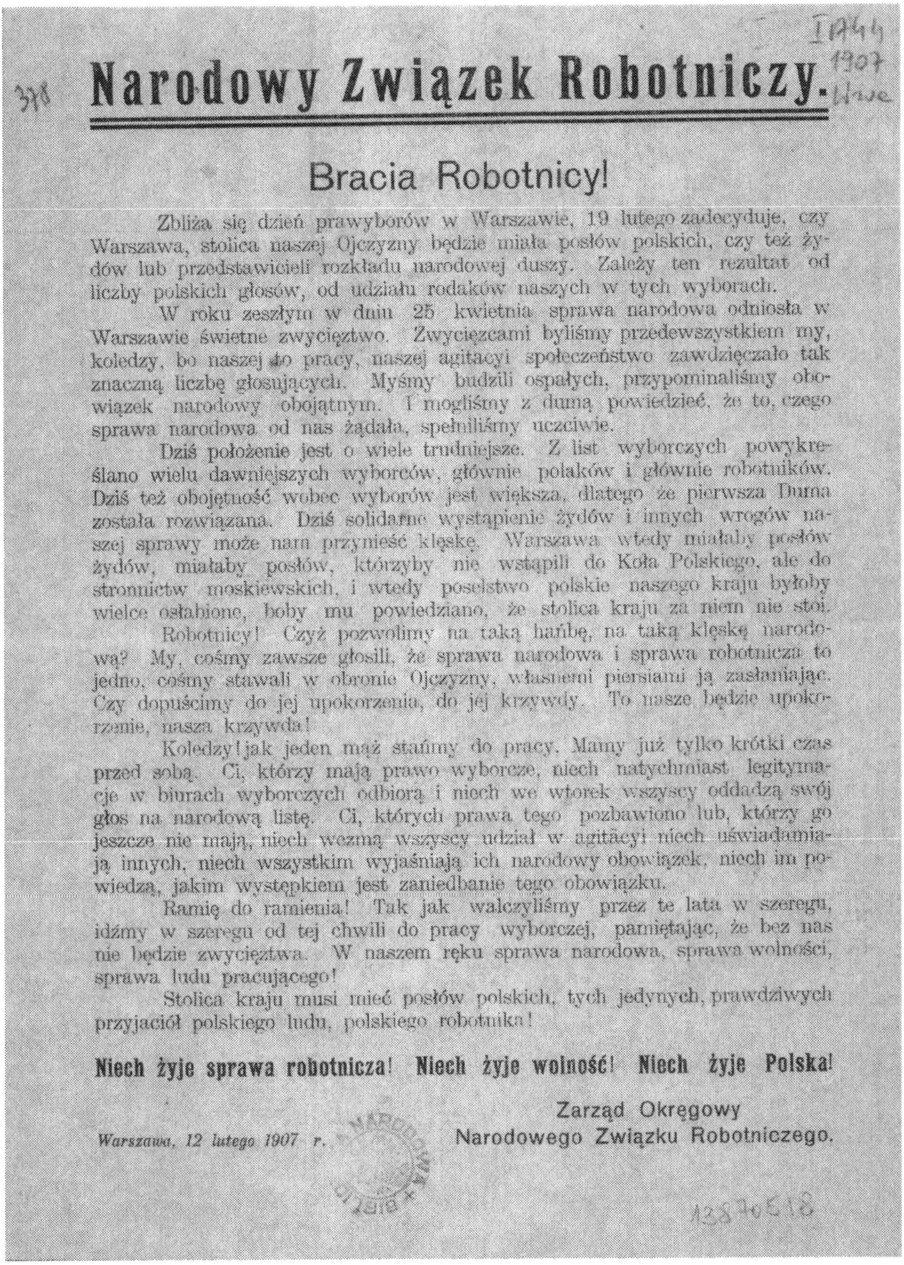

Narodowy Związek Robotniczy.

Bracia Robotnicy!

Zbliża się dzień prawyborów w Warszawie, 19 lutego zadecyduje, czy Warszawa, stolica naszej Ojczyzny będzie miała posłów polskich, czy też żydów lub przedstawicieli rozkładu narodowej duszy. Zależy ten rezultat od liczby polskich głosów, od udziału rodaków naszych w tych wyborach.

W roku zeszłym w dniu 25 kwietnia sprawa narodowa odniosła w Warszawie świetne zwycięstwo. Zwycięzcami byliśmy przedewszystkiem my, koledzy, bo naszej do pracy, naszej agitacyi społeczeństwo zawdzięczało tak znaczną liczbę głosujących. Myśmy budzili ospałych, przypominaliśmy obowiązek narodowy obojętnym. I mogliśmy z dumą powiedzieć, że to, czego sprawa narodowa od nas żądała, spełniliśmy uczciwie.

Dziś położenie jest o wiele trudniejsze. Z list wyborczych powykreślano wielu dawniejszych wyborców, głównie polaków i głównie robotników. Dziś też obojętność wobec wyborów jest większa, dlatego że pierwsza Duma została rozwiązana. Dziś solidarne wystąpienie żydów i innych wrogów naszej sprawy może nam przynieść klęskę. Warszawa wtedy miałaby posłów żydów, miałaby posłów, którzyby nie wstąpili do Koła Polskiego, ale do stronnictw moskiewskich, i wtedy poselstwo polskie naszego kraju byłoby wielce osłabione, boby mu powiedziano, że stolica kraju za niem nie stoi.

Robotnicy! Czyż pozwolimy na taką hańbę, na taką klęskę narodową? My, cośmy zawsze głosili, że sprawa narodowa i sprawa robotnicza to jedno, cośmy stawali w obronie Ojczyzny, własnemi piersiami ją zasłaniając. Czy dopuścimy do jej upokorzenia, do jej krzywdy. To nasze będzie upokorzenie, nasza krzywda!

Koledzy! jak jeden mąż stańmy do pracy. Mamy już tylko krótki czas przed sobą. Ci, którzy mają prawo wyborcze, niech natychmiast legitymacje w biurach wyborczych odbiorą i niech we wtorek wszyscy oddadzą swój głos na narodową listę. Ci, których prawa tego pozbawiono lub, którzy go jeszcze nie mają, niech wezmą wszyscy udział w agitacyi niech uświadamiają innych, niech wszystkim wyjaśniają ich narodowy obowiązek, niech im powiedzą, jakim występkiem jest zaniedbanie tego obowiązku.

Ramię do ramienia! Tak jak walczyliśmy przez te lata w szeregu, idźmy w szeregu od tej chwili do pracy wyborczej, pamiętając, że bez nas nie będzie zwycięstwa. W naszem ręku sprawa narodowa, sprawa wolności, sprawa ludu pracującego!

Stolica kraju musi mieć posłów polskich, tych jedynych, prawdziwych przyjaciół polskiego ludu, polskiego robotnika!

Niech żyje sprawa robotnicza! Niech żyje wolność! Niech żyje Polska!

Warszawa, 12 lutego 1907 r.

Zarząd Okręgowy
Narodowego Związku Robotniczego.

Fig. 3.3. An electoral leaflet of the NZR calling the workers to participate in the Duma elections. Polish National Library Digital Collection.

the Polish romantic imagination and later was inherited by the positivists.[96] The National Democrats were the offspring of this intellectual lineage.[97] However, this justification for national unity could not be adapted to the new revolutionary circumstances. The foreign oppressor during the revolutionary unrest was already a target of political contention organized by the socialists.

No wonder then that the tsarist regime, although explicitly challenged by the National Democrats, was not the best candidate to secure the unity of the nation. Even though the tsarat had been a traditional enemy of the Polish national struggle from the very beginning, it was no longer an appropriate focal point of negative unity for the workers' newly constructed national identity. First, since the socialists were already attacking this form of systemic oppression, joining the attack would not allow the National Democrats to differentiate themselves enough. Second, and most important, the National Democracy party gradually distanced itself from any revolutionary fervor, becoming openly hostile to it at the end of 1905. Fighting revolutionary "anarchy," managing fears of a destabilized society, and profiting heavily from the general fatigue with revolutionary unrest, the National Democrats felt uneasy about defining the tsarist regime as the main enemy.[98] Indeed, this would have been difficult to do while simultaneously condemning the skirmishes with tsarist troops with such intensity. Proclaiming themselves to be the main defenders of "order" and championing modern anxieties intensified by revolutionary dislocation, the political practice of the National Democrats to some extent converged with efforts made by the tsarist state, equally aiming at effectively governing this unrest and maintaining the existing order.[99]

For instance, the National Democrats referred to armed resistance or open street rallies as "anarchy demoralizing to the spirit and sapping national powers or pointless riots [*ruchawka*]" and to participating workers as an "unconscious mob, incapable of self-control."[100] Applying all the elements normally associated with political enemies to this anarchic, chaotic, and uncivilized pole of cultural signification was a logical next step. Taking that step also allowed the party to effectively "suture" the dissatisfactions of modernity to Jewishness and to socialism and revolutionary anarchy. Unleashed market forces might have been added to the list of enemies equally well. Interestingly, however, capitalism largely disappeared from nationalist discourse during the revolution. The reason was a serious ideological transformation of the National Democracy party.

Table 3.1. A cross-table with ideological elements on the verge of political modernity in Poland.

	LEFT	RIGHT
MODERN	socialism	nationalism
CONSERVATIVE	liberalism	Catholicism, monarchism

Party thinkers traveled a long way from popular radicalism to a conservative right wing representing middle and affluent social strata, profiting heavily from capitalist relations already common in the Russian Empire, especially its western fringes. National democratic ideology had once had a strong populist content, and for a long time the nation was virtually identical with the people (*lud*).[101] The turn of the nineteenth and twentieth centuries, however, brought a pivotal transformation of the National Democracy party from a progressive national-populist party to the modern Polish Right, replacing the old aristocratic formation on this side of the political spectrum.[102]

This transformation on the right can best be explained without citing the dualistic left-right model, which does not fit the reality of modern reshuffling of political identities. Even if the National Democracy party vehemently opposed the revolutionary upheavals and sided with certain conservative forces while looking for stability, it did not mean that the formation opted for old-line conservatism. Dmowski and his colleagues continued to insist that their movement was "democratic" and "modern," and undoubtedly it was. The Polish Right had its own version of modernity and revolution, though. The political field may be better characterized by a cross-table assigning to the modernizing and the conservative poles their distinctive left and right incarnations.

Alternatively, political positions may be located on the ideological triangle proposed by Brian Porter-Szűcs.[103] In this case the national democratic movement was moving up the scale along the right side of the triangle from populist democratic radicalism to a nationalism that mobilized the masses but sought to ground itself in tradition and looked for support among more conservatively oriented social strata.

In these circumstances, some reference to long-deployed patterns of Polishness based on a noble ethos was necessary to avoid having to build a national identity from scratch. Thus an initial and severe critique of the malfunctions of the Polish nobility gave way to general pride in past Polish

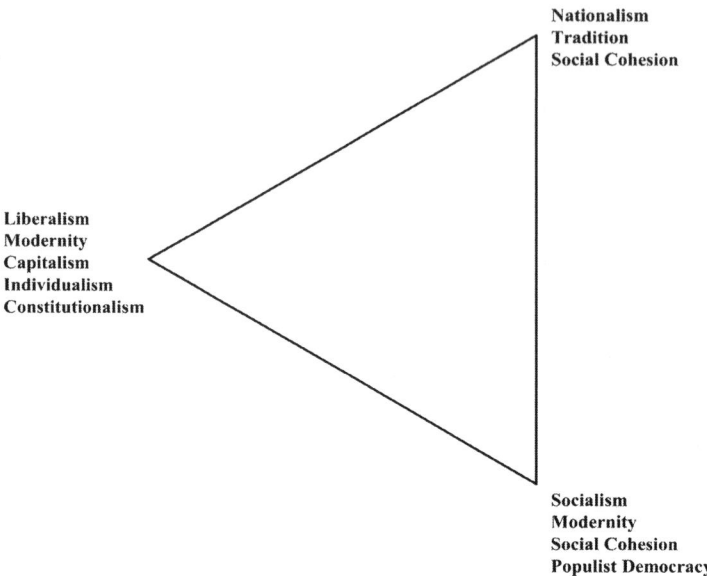

Fig. 3.4. Possible ideological positioning on a tridimensional political field.

(noble) glory. Consequently, the new nationalist program had to sublate class differences and antagonisms for the sake of a new national unity, which was by no means obvious in those days. However, nationalist programs and their relevant political mobilizations tend to be most effective when successfully integrated with social claims.[104] Only if a nationally defined group is relatively homogenous in class terms and deprived of significant privileges or possibilities in the ruling state can powerful social energies be created in the name of national revival. This was conspicuously not the case here.

An additional factor ensuring the coherence of national mobilization was needed, and references to the external enemy of Polishness and the Poles proved useful. The national democratic conception of "political realism" left much space to move within the "national cause," which might have been supported in many other ways besides simple insurrection. Moreover, in order to simultaneously retain its credentials as a nationalist movement while securing the preservation of existing social order whose chief guarantor was the tsarist state, the National Democracy party had to find "anti-Polish" forces other than the Russian tsar.

Undoubtedly, National Democrats could not and did not want to resign from the opposition against tsarist autocracy altogether. However, the tsarist empire could not easily serve as the primary enemy for National Democratic rhetoric in 1905: the movement's leaders did not see the regime as the primary threat facing the Polish nation. More immediately and more viscerally, nationalist Poles needed to establish their dominion within their own space. In that mission, the first task was to establish discipline and unity among the Poles, then to absorb the groups they saw as deviations from Polishness (Ukrainians, Belarusians) and, above all, defeat the Jews.[105]

To establish this problematic national unity, the National Democracy party did not hesitate to clearly exclude Jews, who in their discourse had already been assigned the role of the Other.[106] Earlier intellectual predilections of National Democrats were combined with a conjunctural situation and the residue of premodern popular anti-Judaism to create a powerful interpretation of current predicaments and antagonisms. Ceaseless attempts were undertaken to persuade Polish workers that indeed the Jewish proletariat initiated disturbances, which negatively influenced the condition of the Polish economy and Polish workers. Moreover, the National Democracy party and the NZR discouraged Polish workers from acting in solidarity with Jewish workers or just incited hostility against Jewish colleagues.

During the revolution the nationalists were increasingly critical of the revolutionary surge, and the general revolutionary disorder went farther. "The Jews" were successfully branded as a foreign element inducing disorder in the name of their own profits and gains. Revolution was allegedly made in the name of Jews: "A reason [for a strike] could always be found: . . . unfulfilled Jewish demands or the like," unambiguously suggested one leaflet.[107] This kind of Jewish interest was a hidden agenda of socialism, as the NZR leaflets and articles insinuated, thus constituting a bedrock for a "racialization" of political difference, later utilized in countless occasions: "It is high time every worker understood that listening to any orders, without even asking in whose name and in what aim are they given, is an affront for him. Who is ordering us? Who is pretending to be our rulers? Hobbledehoys and noisy Jewish snotnoses [*chłystki i żydziaki krzykliwe*]."[108] Not only can "the Jews" harvest the gains of the revolution, but they also allegedly profit from its failure. That is why they mislead Christian workers in false unity: "Revolution . . . would be profitable for the Jews, who after our weakness and harassment could spread all over the country even more," clarified one leaflet.[109]

This line of argument was complicated by the fact that it was actually the Poles who gained some freedoms (including in the realms of language and schooling, realms very precious to the National Democrats). In addition, the National Democracy party simultaneously looked for a language to describe the discontents of modernity, which were intensified by the revolution. It was not possible for the progressive, explicitly modern National Democrats, fighting for the cultural autonomy of the nation, to unambiguously condemn either modernity or the cultural gains of the revolution. (Un)luckily "the Jews" fit perfectly as a referent that could be invested with all the amorphous negativity. They were accused of introducing the discontents of modernity, capitalist speculation, and socialist destabilization alike. Simultaneously associating the Jews with socialism delegitimized a competitive language making sense of the modern world. Finally, "the Jews" were condemned for bringing revolutionary disorder, a move that merged the dangers of a victorious socialism and a defeat of the Poles. As a result, "the Jews" could be held responsible for any disadvantage to the Poles, seen both as an imagined nation dreamed of by the nationalists and a common people in the here and now whom National Democrats tried to convince to identify with this nation. This complex position combined contradictory elements with no obvious connection. Nevertheless, it appeared to be a powerful political machine.

I do not imply that National Democrats deliberately and cynically deployed antisemitism as a mere strategy. In their worldview, the Jewish danger was rational, real, and true. The nationalists' deeply ingrained antisemitism notwithstanding, these elements had not been broadly exploited in the political struggle before and did not penetrate the mainstream of political discourse. The movement's rapid rise and success require another explanation than national democratic antisemitism writ large during the revolutionary and counterrevolutionary mobilization. The success of antisemitism and the corresponding construction of viable identities may be explained through examination of the specific route of political differentiation.

Fig. 3.5 (*opposite page*). The cover of the satirical magazine *Kolce*. This issue was published in 1911, when antisemitic panic was already running at full throttle. It well illustrates the change—what had started in 1906 became a dominating motive in the entire political debate few years later. Note that this is the same journal that praised the working-class hero slashing bureaucracy in 1905. University of Warsaw Library, courtesy of Grzegorz Krzywiec.

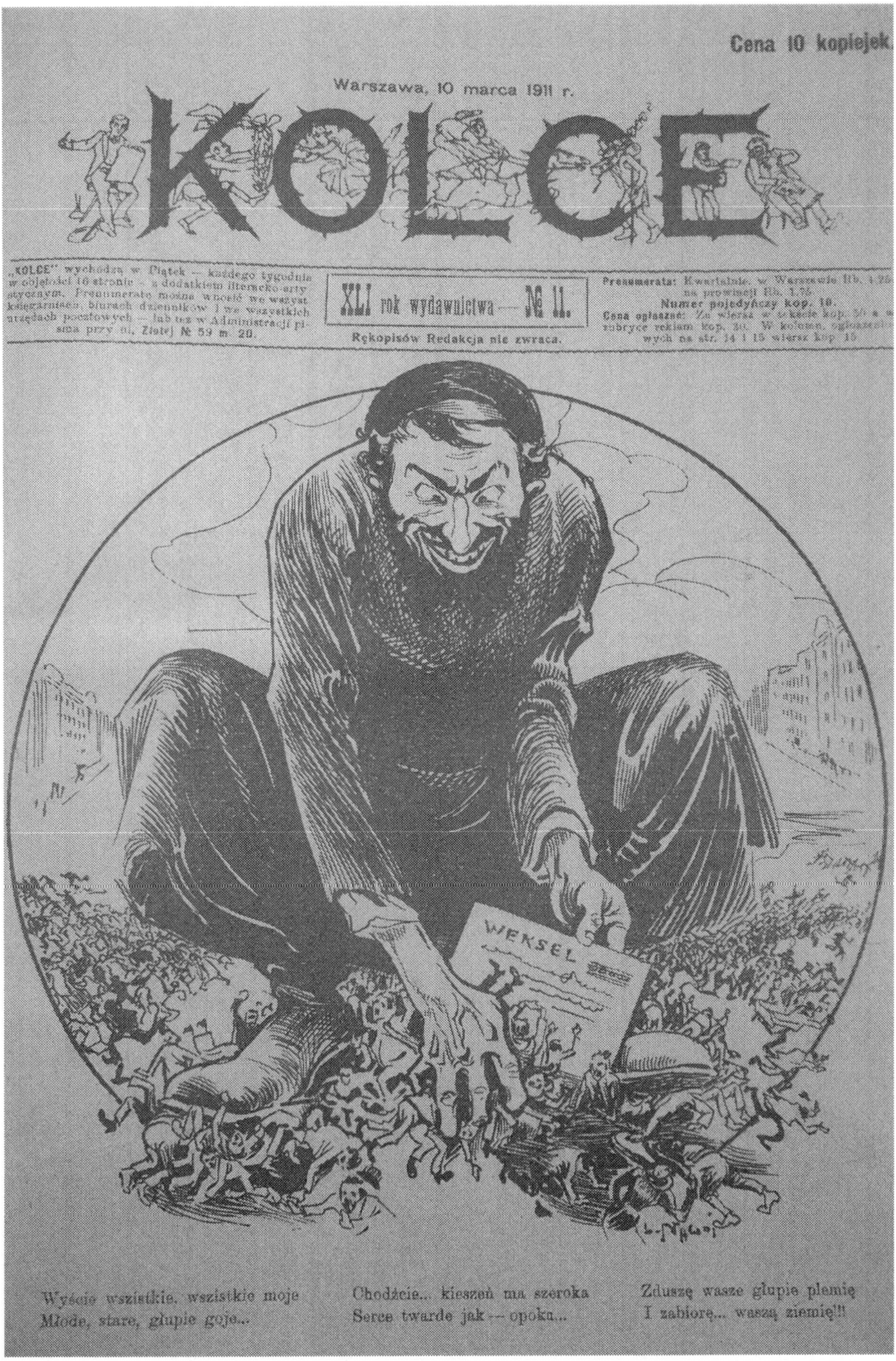

Cena 10 kopiejek.

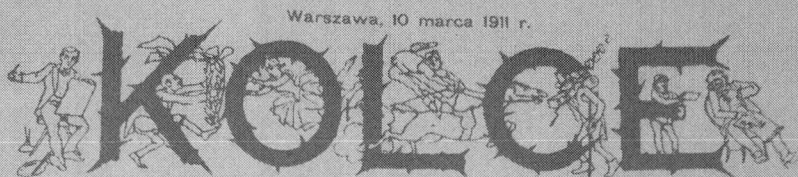

Warszawa, 10 marca 1911 r.

KOLCE

„KOLCE" wychodzą w Piątek — każdego tygodnia w objętości 16 stronic — z dodatkiem literacko-artystycznym. Prenumeratę można wnosić we wszystkich księgarniach, biurach dzienników i we wszystkich urzędach pocztowych — lub też w Administracji pisma przy ul. Złotej № 59 m. 20.

XLI rok wydawnictwa — № 11.

Rękopisów Redakcja nie zwraca.

Prenumerata: Kwartalnie: w Warszawie Rb. 1.25 na prowincji Rb. 1.75.
Numer pojedyńczy kop. 10.
Cena ogłoszeń: Za wiersz w ... kop. ... w rubryce reklam kop. 30. W kolumn. ogłoszeniowych na str. 14 i 15 wiersz kop. 15.

Wyście wszistkie, wszistkie moje
Młode, stare, głupie goje...

Chodźcie... kieszeń ma szeroka
Serce twarde jak — opoka...

Zduszę wasze głupie plemię
I zabiorę... waszą ziemię!!

Certain identities and political agendas were reinforced through dynamic interaction and a feedback loop between political discourse and popular response, while other messages could not be spread so widely. Seeing the problem in this way helps explain the rapid rise of political antisemitism without referring to simple political propaganda or inherent capacities of the (Polish?) masses in revolt. Simultaneously, this approach indicates why it was the nationalist Right that was able to capitalize on the drop in revolutionary enthusiasm. Not only were the nationalists able to give meaning to the perceived anarchy and collapse among the higher echelons of society, but they could also address the grievances of at least a segment of the dissatisfied and disappointed workers. For the elite antisemitism offered a handy explanation of the new activity of popular contenders without assigning agency to them; for at least some of the workers it was a powerful mobilizing language explaining their situation.

Moreover, national democratic politics of the ballot offered some perceived significance to working-class voters. Their labor unions offered perspectives for legal action, which was desired among people who may have been excited by underground militancy at one time but were unwilling to maintain such a risky life forever—especially in the face of harsh tsarist repression. Regardless, the initial puzzle of forging a viable identity and redefining the friend-foe distinction was positively resolved by the intensifying leaning toward antisemitism. That trend culminated in outright and vitriolic antisemitic campaigns during elections to the Third and Fourth Dumas, crowned by the boycott of Jewish enterprises in 1912.[110] This was not the only paramount change within the national democratic discourse, however.

The underlying story was also a complex change in respect to the relationship between the workers and political elements in nationalist thought. In the 1880s, when the National Democracy party was in its infancy, it was a populist radical party not only aiming for national revival but also postulating paramount social transformation in favor of the lower classes and their much more prominent place in politics. the National Democracy party was not capable of integrating the growing democratic tendency into its discourse and relevant practice. The result of this shortfall was a turn toward discipline and an organic political imaginary, and subsequently to a xenophobic, authoritarian, and socially conservative nationalistic project. Even if early proponents of the movement urged "the people" to become

Fig. 3.6. Nationalist rally in Warsaw, November 5, 1905. Polish National Library Digital Collection, BN F.434651.

involved in politics and nation building, as soon as the masses actually went out to the streets it appeared that they would not follow the directives of their self-proclaimed nationalist leaders.[111] This reversed the attitudes of these leaders and funneled their evolution into almost antipodean positions in comparison to their previous ideals.

The National Democrats did not try to pull workers back from public engagement, but at the same time they started to fear the masses, who were not behaving according to previous expectations. They absolutely wanted mass political engagement, which Dmowski and his colleagues considered essential to victory in "modern politics." But they wanted that engagement to be controlled from above. As Dmowski put it, "a disorganized, loose crowd has to transform itself into a highly organized, disciplined army."[112] This army was supposed to be engaged and committed, fervent in its identification with the nation and ready to struggle for survival, which is nonetheless a form of engagement, an illiberal democratization of sorts.

As the national democratic ideology transformed itself from a popular, democratic radicalism into an overtly elitist, exclusionary integral nationalism, it easily became the leading force setting the tone for the reaction

Speech and Action • 113

condemning the revolution and suppressing popular participation in politics. The nationalists limited the populace to circumscribed activity under the party leaders and relegated everything else to a murky realm of irrational outbursts of mob rule or animal instincts. This switch had long-lasting consequences and defined the overall nationalist project. The National Democracy party underwent an authoritarian turn, simultaneously "closing" and essentializing the concept of the nation in Polish political thinking for years, and largely reversing the shift toward the subjectification of workers within the political realm. This move resonated with fears of nonproletarian social strata. It simultaneously boosted support for the nationalists among those strata and blocked further development of proletarian constituencies.[113] The accompanying change in the bourgeois vision of politics and working-class participation, which became a backdrop for this convergence and resonance, is investigated in the next chapter.

Discourse in Action

In this chapter I investigate the evolving presence of speech, which constituted an important change in the public sphere. In particular, I scrutinize political leaflets as the material infrastructure of this transformation. Political publications were the main carriers of ideas and often the artifacts around which political communication revolved, since they were read aloud, debated, and contested. Their functions and the agency of language were multiple, and I have reconstructed several of them. As the first embodiments of political ideologies approached by many, they played an important role in disseminating new ideas. They intervened in the legitimization of the existing order by destroying the respect felt toward the ruling power—above all, the tsar. Simultaneously, they introduced new concepts that assisted people in expressing grievances and gave meaning to the performed practices. This contributed to the new cognitive mapping of the social space—the language of the leaflets allowed for the connection of personal experiences with the broader analysis of the social and political situation, thus rearticulating this experience as well.

The leaflets and proclamations consistently constructed the community of concepts and shared reference points. Repeatedly deployed and explained concepts and phrases saturated workers' vocabulary and thinking, building the (fractured) language of modern mass politics. This included concepts related to proletarian selves (comrades—also in the female—proletariat and proletarians, brothers in one nation), a diagnosis of the situation (capitalism, exploitation, revolutionary anarchy), political tools of change (strike, revolution), practices of public participation (debate, agitation, speech, rally, voting), political institutions (protests, manifestations, strikes, elections, parliament), and an envisioned final goal (national independence, freedom of the people, rule of the people, democracy, socialism, democratic republic). The same applies to means of identification—envisioned communities and the imaginary institution of society (nation, the people [*lud*], society, class, proletariat). The impact of the leaflets was not limited to such knowledge dissemination, however.

The language of the leaflets had an important pragmatic dimension. As performative statements, political texts were crucial in delimiting the domain of the speakable and the doable. In the descriptions of events and calls to action, various modes of agency were encrypted. While the issuance of a leaflet with a given political content (locutionary act in writing) had certain goals such as mobilizing for action or constructing a given political identity (intended illocutionary impact), the profound change it brought about happened on the side. It concerned what really happened with the recipient, and it might affect the sender or their mutual relationship as well (perlocutionary effect). Such utterances, according to the philosopher of language John L. Austin, "produce certain consequential effects upon the feelings, thoughts, or actions of the audience, or of the speaker, or of other persons," and reshape a relational configuration of places, actions and appearances.[114] Occasionally the perlocutionary dimension slips into illocutionary, as in explicit formulas indicating the empowerment of workers.[115] However, usually the performative device cannot be expressed (as would be the case in a hypothetical slogan "I hereby make you a political subject who is no longer the same as before" or something similar and equally absurd). This dimension is neither explicitly intended by the senders nor immediately realized by the recipients. Nevertheless, it constitutes change. Workers entered into politics through discourse, and discourse modified its new users in a variety of ways, depending on political and social imagination perpetuating respective writers and the development of the revolutionary process. I have analyzed modes of agency prescribed for the recipients in the leaflets of different parties, showing how tacit assumptions of the place of workers in society shaped political languages, becoming stable reservoirs for uttering political speech.

These political languages disseminated among proletarian readers helped construct a community of participants taking part in revolutionary events. This common conceptual horizon enabled hitherto passive workers to feel incorporated into a broader whole of politically active individuals whom they obviously could not know in person. Thus, to borrow Benedict Anderson's term, the language of the leaflets and political culture accompanying them were the means of building the new "imagined community" at both the general level—unified individuals participating in politics—and as fractured members of (differently envisioned) classes or nations.[116] The proclamations had the lion's share in the intellectual and cultural transformation of workers and the creation of a new political culture among a revolutionary public.

However, the level of conflict among parties, ideologies, and ethnicities grew, with flames of hostility fanned by new contenders eager to forcefully rebuild the emerging identities. That is why in the final section I present extensive analysis of the transformation of the political field. This field was marked with a growing presence of nationalist countermobilization, and national democratic antisemitism was neither an automatic activation of already present and popular anti-Jewish sentiments due to the rise of mass politics nor the sole creation of nationalist ideologues. It was the broader context of political struggle that ushered in a need for a negatively evaluated outsider. The Jews fit this role due to a particular social and demographic situation and older Judeophobic tendencies. Above all, this trend demonstrates the new power of language within the political field.

The aforementioned aspects of language action within the political arena could also be sequenced as dominating tendencies in subsequent phases of the revolution. Such a view allows for comprehension of the revolutionary process in an alternative way—as a transformation of language use within the political sphere. Although none of the distinctions or described "stages" can be circumscribed neatly, they nevertheless demonstrate the changing role of language. Initially, political speech carried forms of "epiphany" and cognitive "enlightenment"; later, it brought subjectification and created new places of political utterance for workers.[117] In parallel, the growing antagonism ushered in polemical interdiscourse and fostered additional abilities, described in the previous chapters as the democratic surplus.

The rapid change of conflicted identities and a profound reconfiguration of the political field testify to the power of language in politics. The scrutiny of the functions of language sheds light on these multilevel changes. It is a useful perspective to assist our understanding of modern politics and allow us to gauge our analysis so as to detect empirical traces of the transforming political scene. Viewed in this way, the revolutionary dynamic may also be informative in respect to the generic characteristics of the political process, as an unfolding mobilization and conflict performed in, and through, language. This language was later a means to narrativize and express the reconstructed self for working-class writers recollecting their political activity. Workers' own memory of their public involvement and its impact on the self may be revealed in biographical testimonies. Those inscriptions of politics in transformation are examined in the next chapter.

4

Life and Politics

> This year [1905] was a groundbreaking one for me. My concepts were entirely crystallized.

The revolutionary experience of protest, public self-assertion, and intellectual stimulation through reading and listening made an imprint on already committed circle participants but also led out to the streets people never mobilized before. In any case the 1905 Revolution was often considered by workers writing memoirs as the most important event in their lives. In autobiographies of politicized workers, as in the epigraph to this chapter, it is the 1905 Revolution that is the singular event structuring the memory. To understand the more subjective side of revolutionary politics and investigate the nexus between working-class life and politics, in this chapter I analyze written, autobiographical testimonies of the revolution.

In the life stories presented here biography as life (for the writers) and biography as narration (for us) meet politics. Political activity is viewed an important vehicle of biographical transformation and acts as the main means of storytelling regarding the remembered life. It must have been an important dimension of narrators' lives, allowing them to embark on a path they would not have realized otherwise. Reading biographical materials about revolutionary involvement, however diverse they may be, exposes the role of politics in working-class lives as reconstructed in biographical writing—a carrier and a result of those political experiences.

Biography and Its Politicization

The revolution did not come out of the blue, even if almost all participants and observers were astonished, if not shocked, by its appearance. Neither did it imprint on a blank canvas of the working-class self. The revolutionary events intervened in developing biographies by either providing the ultimate mobilization already dreamed about by political militants or by ushering novices into the realm of mass politics. In both cases it was an event reconfiguring selves, as reconstructed in biographical memory. Just as biographical memory is always entangled in institutionalized collective remembering, the actual effect of the revolution in real time cannot be neatly dissected from this memory.[1] Nevertheless, its overarching presence in the biographical reconstruction testifies to its significance, however entangled social mediation and memory culture may have been.

The political militants were not necessarily socialists, and sometimes just the opposite. So unlike previous scholars, I investigate all the narratives—socialist, patriotic socialist, and nationalist alike—on the same generic level.[2] This plurality of commitments and diverse motives present within a single tradition, or even autobiography, bears witness to the heterogeneity of revolutionary experience, which cannot be reduced to any linear emancipation. Not only the socialist promise of emancipation but also nationalist unity often brought pivotal changes of militants' selves, assertions, and feelings. Workers were mobilized in multiple and conflicting ways, and most of the identities thus forged had afterlives in parallel memory cultures. These cultures were, in turn, punctuated by important shifts in the general political landscape: the break with tsarism, the Polish interwar state under different political jurisdictions, and the socialist state after 1945—not to mention two world wars. This multiplicity of entanglements supports a more complex analysis of biographical encounters with politics.

In these circumstances, I see the discourse of the political self presented in autobiographies as a product of the layering of time.[3] All that defines the political self of the writing subject is a historical lamination created by the process they describe. Facts, experiences, and contexts presented in the biography are also elements of the self responsible for producing each biography in real time. The opposite is also true: what the manufactured biography is and what it presents as its transformative events may help us infer something about subject formation in history. It is the memory of past events, whatever they were, with all the orchestrated collective elements and conventionalized strategies of emplotment, that gives the actual self its place and meaning.

Along these lines, a socialist autobiography, for instance, conveys experiences typical of a working-class subject of a particular place and time, already reworked according to the available discursive and interpretative resources (as a socialist perception of the world). Later, it is rearticulated as the accumulated experience of the narrator, writing to reconstitute him- or herself as a veteran socialist militant (or some other relatively coherent identification, a context examined in the appendix). Meanwhile, the resources already available are supplemented by new impulses connected to the present situation, politics, and rhetoric of socialist writing.

The narrators wrote their testimonies in a given social and political context, and they must be seen as performative acts. They had definite purposes and actual effects (not always identical) on the authors, their readers, and their relationship. The narrators used their writing to convince the assumed reader of their own depiction of the past. Hence experience is (according to its double meaning in many languages) both the raw material reworked by the socially and discursively embedded self, living and developing in time, and the stock reservoir of reworked lore that the narrators actively reuse for the purpose of their writing.[4] Both dimensions are often unconsciously yet "purposefully" conflated in writing, which produces a certain poetics of authenticity. Working-class, revolutionary lives were experienced, memorized, and reintegrated in the meaningful construction of selves undertaken by political militants of different kinds and denominations and can be understood only as such in scholarship today. I try to follow this poetics and for a while place my faith to the narrators' storytelling while uncovering various tropes recurring in many stories. These tropes are nevertheless ushered in with the help of single protagonists, which allows me to introduce more contextual information regarding particular people. While maintaining critical awareness of the mediality of the source, I would like to understand the subjective impact of the revolution. Thus I occasionally block the operation of too many critical mirrors for the sake of hearing the stories.

A Sense of Misery and Increasing Self-assertion

The political transformation embodied in biography was embedded in a sense of self and an idea of the world that for some reason was considered unsatisfying. Władysław Kossek was the son of a skilled worker. However, at the age of twelve he lost his father, who died of a "typical workers' disease, tuberculosis."[5] Władysław had to give up a modest unauthorized education to help his semi-invalid father in the factory and took over the household after his death. Such a path represents a common arrangement: unavoidable and hardly reversible poverty resulting from the death of a male breadwinner. The story of a youth cut short, with limited opportunities for self-development, abruptly ended by a sudden death or deteriorating health is a repetitive pattern in working-class biographies in the prewelfare period in Europe; in Russian Poland this pattern continued for several decades.[6] In such a difficult situation, young Władysław, already on the verge of destitution, could not help wondering about his fate. His harsh circumstances gave rise to conscious critical reflection and were recalled as justifying action. To underline his sense of misery, he compared his living conditions with those of other people in a multiethnic and highly differentiated (in terms of class and status) urban environment. Indeed, various class milieus often existed cheek by jowl because of the relative proximity of factories, workers' districts or tenements, and entrepreneurs' villas and palaces (especially in Lodz and the Dąbrowa Basin).[7] "I wondered if all people lived and worked in the same way. Why—I used to think—when I was coming back from church [thus on Sunday, a festive day when traditionally a richer meal was eaten] and I would like to eat something better, I could not afford it. . . . Why are rich people everywhere liked, enshrined, and do not have to work as hard as me and my mother? Why do even the priests in the church like them more than us?"[8]

These doubts did not yet push Kossek to rethink his own position, and an external political intervention was needed. Kossek admitted in the same paragraph that in his "own opinion in those days, the most righteous was the Father God, giving health and power to work, and after him came the factory owner, Buhle, who after Father's death had given my mother a job and made it possible for us to exist."[9] Apparently, it would still take a lot of political work to forge militant workers out of passive laborers who took a capitalist moral economy for granted and saw the owners as merciful for giving them a job.

Agitation often built on existential grievances but also made them more conscious and acute. Even if cataloging misfortunes was a cold-blooded reconstruction of facts rather than a prolonged mourning, it drew on an emotional background of familial tragedy. A child who could not survive because of sanitary deficiencies or sheer hunger was a mundane experience, but the fate woven out of such sad events was an unbearable and inescapable burden: "The life of our family was very harsh; thirteen times a child was born, and eight times a funeral was arranged. For most workers, when one misfortune was gone, another one approached."[10] Against such a backdrop Kossek reconstructs his political affiliation. It was his brother who gave meaning to these perceived sufferings and offered a way out of a seemingly hopeless situation. "[My] brother Julian . . . used to say: 'Nobody is going to help us workers. We have to fight for better living conditions on our own.' Soon Julian started to broaden my consciousness and encouraged me to work for the party. He was bringing proclamations home, and once he said that he had been a member of the Polish Socialist Party for a long time and his pseudonym was Kostek. Since by then I was an adult man, I saw life differently and I ardently observed all that was happening around me."[11]

This political revelation resonated with Kossek's previous experience. Once the mystery was revealed, it was an important threshold in the formation of the revolutionary self, or just a "mature" consciousness, comprehended by writers as essentially coherent with the future state of mind in the moment of producing biographical narration. It was the shortest path leading to political involvement. Kossek entered the PPS as one of many workers, mobilized in the first days of revolutionary upheaval, finally making use of their long-maturing commitments. It was also a fundamental element of increasing self-assertion, presented as an important dimension of a biographical trajectory. It was further confirmed by the tangible experience of potential change. The reappearance of this moment in memory may be expressed as a short "syllogism" combining the success of strikes with further political mobilization in favor of the socialists.[12] It was aptly expressed by Kossek: after a strike succeeded, "the factory was on the move again. It was a great victory of the socialists. Everybody knew that we owed it to the socialists. Long live the socialists!"[13] Such a conclusion was well received in the context in which the memoir was written.

Kossek's autobiographical statement is part and parcel of an orchestrated commemorative effort undertaken by the Polish socialist state. This important subgroup consists of larger, book-size autobiographies (sometimes utilizing earlier manuscripts); testimonies given on various occasions such as anniversaries, open competitions, or radio calls to gather such memories; extensive, open-ended questionnaires collected by historians orbiting around the ruling party; and "resumes" written to prove entitlement for benefits as veterans of the proletarian movement. Without a doubt, the larger framing is no accident; Kossek's testimony is included in a collected volume gathering the writings of Polish veterans of 1905 and 1917. They are deliberately lumped together to stress the continuity of the "revolutionary struggle" between events in "Poland" (1905) and those happening elsewhere, which were later perceived as neutral if not hostile (1917—largely dismissed because of the later Polish-Soviet war of 1919–1921). On the micro level, however, there were hardly any interventions; the standard story of a militant socialist worker, conventionalized as it already was, was usually enough to fulfill the official requirements.

The sense of misery and deprivation was not incongruous with the ideological requirements but also not particularly encouraged. However, biographical testimonies may tend to project a subsequently acquired awareness of the context or patterns of interpretation onto the past. It is argued, for instance, that even the feeling of basic deprivation and defining the self as entangled and victimized by industrial production was acquired relatively late. Stimulated by upper-strata discourses on the social question, it appeared only after the nearly universal spread of postenlightenment aspirations to welfare and well-being.[14] It seems, however, that this frame was already present in the real-time experience of workers before 1905. The diagnosis of pure living conditions as a background for political activity appears in testimonies stemming from all the political denominations analyzed here. It is also confirmed by the moral economy of early petitions sent by workers to factory owners or the tsarist administration. If before 1905 they did not display any critique of the existing order, they nevertheless used poverty and unbearable conditions as a main justification of submitted claims.[15] In later recollections this approach was generalized into a more all-encompassing compassion and solidarity with others in similar situations. "I was suffering hunger and humiliation for a few coins as a sweeper in Mister Geyer's weaving factory. I felt with the sensitive heart of a child that all the workers of this enormous factory were suffering along with me—equally my peers and the adults, who previously had seemed to me always satisfied and self-assured. I pitied most of these exhausted women and elders, from whom Geyer's factory had taken away their entire lives, not giving them anything in its place."[16]

In this vein, the prerevolutionary situation was widely reconstructed as a time of passivity and obedience. Narrators use advanced introspection to understand their own initial position. They also stylize it as raw material for political mobilization, later pointing at the political framework that allowed them to "wake up." Alternatively, they reconstruct the political framework as resonating with their primordial sentiments or inborn dignity.[17] While a sense of misery as a precursor of militancy is a widespread motive in European labor biography, in the Polish conjuncture the striving for national recognition was as important as the economic deprivation and the rejection of inequality. These motives are present in narratives from all over the political spectrum, regardless of any obvious political incentives to hone the story of the self along one of those lines. For instance, one of the Sosnowiec workers, working under a German foreman's supervision, described his germinating pride and rejection of docility in contrast to his passive colleagues (who may just have better than the narrator at hiding their resentment):

> Some of my cooperators ignored it, not paying any attention to it. I do not know if they were convinced that it had to be like this, that we were outlawed people, or their thought was so dumb, so lazy, that they did not understand the disrespect against us as Poles. I also do not know why I felt that somebody was beating me with a stick when hearing a similar word [some offensive nickname derogatory against the Poles] directed at me or at some of my cooperators. It was like somebody was kicking me with his legs, that somebody treated me like dirt till I could not stand it anymore. I felt some unbearable, undefined pain, and it seemed to me that somebody was tearing out my heart and tearing out my guts. I felt a pain that human language cannot describe.[18]

Such feelings often supply a context explaining the writer's political alignment after the first contact with some nationalist association or socialist party circle. Later they triggered retributive acts asserting dignity during the revolutionary days, when long-maturing grievances and hidden fantasies of revenge might be reenacted for real. But the growing subjective dissatisfaction with the surrounding world and one's own place in it was above all presented as a background for attempts to change the situation. The stories, however, do not unfold straightforwardly. As a kind of *Bildungsroman*, they depict the narrator as a figure overcoming various threats and obstacles. Political involvement, or even initial interest, had to first go through layers of distrust, internalized feelings of hierarchy, and sheer fear of persecution.

The Hard Road of Autodidacticism

It is probably difficult to overestimate the obstacles that an illiterate worker had to overcome before he or she got involved politically. Working-class militancy in 1905 should be regarded as far from obvious; in the case of more experienced activists, it required a long period of self-education beforehand. A peasant's son and future professional writer, Lucjan Rudnicki, while pasturing geese, stole remnants of illustrated newspapers from a pile of burning papers and furniture. The goods being burned had come from the parish house, where the local priest had died of cholera. Rudnicki was severely beaten by his father, who found out what happened and confiscated the precious booty, which the boy had already hidden somewhere in the barn. The punishment was executed, however, not because the papers were "stolen" from the (dead) priest, or even because the boy exposed himself and his family to the risk of cholera. The problem was that he had not taken care of the geese properly.[19] The hierarchy in a peasant household was rigid and did not leave much space for education. "Taking the hard road" was the fate of everybody wanting to reach beyond village life.

For Rudnicki, forced migration to a large industrial hub first offered an escape from the "benign state of natural, almost primitive culture."[20] In this new environment he was soon ready to take on new intellectual activities. Following the standard path of autodidactic readers, from popular pulp novels he jumped to the Polish classics. He used to read insatiably "after coming back from the factory and satisfying hunger, from 8 to 11 PM with the whole family by the kitchen lamp." That led to ardent discussions of the characters' fate until "the aunt's repetitive calls to go to bed gradually calmed down the literary disputes."[21] Further studies indispensable to professional and intellectual mobility demanded exceptional effort, a painful self-perfection, and the breaching of subsequent borders of language and cultural exclusion. Rudnicki felt "uneducated in the simplest knowledge, knowledge of the mother tongue, as it was visible that what we knew was more imperfect, lower."[22] He consciously tried to overcome this obstacle, which not surprisingly was very difficult without any external assistance or even a simple dictionary.

Finally, he found assistance for his efforts in socialist mobilization. The alignment between the cognitive pursuits of proletarian autodidacts and political languages to explain the world was an important factor in political mobilization. Political language explained the world, then offered a sort of cognitive epiphany. Social processes, structural constraints, and mechanics of the world were convincingly connected with the everyday experience of the factory worker. For some not entirely obvious reason, the most self-reflexive testimonies about this shift are written by people of the Far Left (SDKPiL or the PPS-Left; Rudnicki fits this pattern as well). One may guess that the trend has to do with a highly theoretical party culture fueling the reflective effort of crafting the political self. Another reason might be the greater inner-party upward mobility of working-class militants, which both resulted in them living political lives worthy of being recorded and gave them the resources to do it. Suffice it to say, memoirs that are highly original, have literary value, and are long enough to investigate broader biographical processes were written by committed militants who were politicized men of letters with a longer party career behind them. These authors were not mobilized during the revolution but usually earlier; in 1905 they were already trained agitators, as was Rudnicki.

However, more typical biographies of rank-and-file workers follow a similar path. A description of a turbulent childhood is an important part of many life histories. Here narrators who were able to attain some degree of upward social mobility describe hardships imprinted in their memories, defining their yearning for an education against this backdrop. The not always merry days of urban childhood nevertheless offered some space for personal development, fantasies, dreams, thoughts, and speech. A number of working-class children did have time for play and a moderate education. This relatively "open" time was abruptly brought to an end by economic hardship—the necessity of wage labor. Artisanal cultures with a relatively high level of literacy, which still existed in places, offered alternative means of education at home.[23] The unskilled workers hired by large factories, however, no longer had access to such time reserves and intellectual resources. This confrontation with an unpleasant reality and the inability to fulfill dreams and aspirations is a common memory in written workers' biographies.[24] As one man put it: "Because I had not known life yet, with its economic relationships, I started to dream about a career as a doctor, a lawyer, or in another, similar profession. However, after leaving the old yeshiva I soon got disappointed. I noticed the class division of society: rich and poor. I realized that entry through the gates of European culture is not as easy as I imagined. Abilities alone do not suffice; above all one needs money, and this is the most important [thing]."[25]

Working-class adults were acutely aware that those early educational opportunities, which later often defined the course of their lives, were mostly a matter of luck or incredible stubbornness.[26] We can see evidence of this realization in the story of Franciszek Kujawa, a boy taught by an old political militant of Social Democracy, luckily living nearby:

> He stroked my head and began to ask if I attended school—I replied that for such poor children as I there was no place in school, because whenever my mother had taken me to the school there had been no place. The teacher for sure wanted to get a bribe, and in our family there was no money for bread. [He asked:] And can you read and write—I can read because my mother has taught me, but she cannot write so she has not taught me. [He asked again:] And do you want to learn how to write—I replied, that very much because boys who were attending school did not want to play with me because I could not write. [He replied:] From tomorrow onward I will teach you how to write—you want it desperately. I was waiting eagerly for this tomorrow, the night seemed to last forever. I woke up very early, and like never before and after I waited eagerly for this moment when I would finally start to learn the art of writing.[27]

Not only are enchantment and longing described here, but there is also a complex dynamic of the pain of rejection, an awareness of exclusion, and as yet unformed self-assertion. It is supplemented by a cognitive passion often present among future autodidacts—later party leaders, political militants, or class-milieu writers of the interwar years. The teaching they anticipated receiving was not a regular transfer of knowledge conceded from the enlightened elite to the people but instead a horizontal bricolage. Knowledge was reappropriated to be passed along in an alternative, class-based educational milieu. There it might be rearticulated and reused for these milieu-specific purposes. The roughly educated children often recirculated their skills, either teaching other children or reading newspapers or books aloud to their illiterate or barely literate parents and relatives.[28] Moreover, the childish universe hitherto directed to the everyday concreteness of working-class family life came face to face with an alternative order based on the abstract, seemingly useless practice of writing; the experience of reading triggered in the narrators an urge to rebuild their embodied knowledge, also their class habitus, and to use their minds and muscles differently than before. "At the beginning," recalled Kujawa, "the art of writing was very difficult for me. Drawing lines and circles on one side of the notebook was more tiresome for me than digging potatoes for the entire day or chopping wood out of an entire trunk."[29] This difficulty itself created a spirit of reverence and exaggerated attention in respect to the rebuilding of the self.

The writers willingly create the impression that homebred talents among the populace demanded extreme durability and persistence, if not wit or even cunning. There is an element of "poaching" in the attempts to gain access to knowledge and development in the stories told by past autodidacts. These "hidden transcripts" are forms of resistance directed not only against the access restrictions imposed by the "ruling classes," embodied in various forms of financial obstacles or lack of proper institutions. The opposition is not only various members of the elite who bar the gates against possibly dangerous knowledge.[30] The writers knew that they also had to question and outwit the tacit rules of their respective communities and their own habits and convictions.[31] Some of them become subcultural interclass subjects, intelligentsia workers, but they also had to stand guard against the constraints of their advancing life course.

The narratives I analyzed confirm the patterns recognized by historians to study the working-class life cycle. The free-spirited pursuit of knowledge was more typical of young workers.[32] Once the time of apprenticeship ended, there was a regular factory job available; young single males were better off, sometimes able to spend surplus cash on a newspaper, a shared book, maybe some type of popular entertainment or just fuel for a lamp to read after dusk. In those vivid years there were opportunities for small triumphs, used by narrators to stress their engagement and interest in spheres other than work: "We sometimes spent evenings more seriously . . . , on conversations about inventions, about science, and about superstitions. We used to buy popular and educational brochures from Arct [a Warsaw bookshop], and we learned on our own, however one could. Sometimes one of us brought an illegal printing. The rest ate it up like delicious prey. For instance, I was once able to get hold of a collection of revolutionary songs. . . . From those songs we learned to express our grievances."[33]

This is also evidence of the connection between materials read in the past and ways of writing in the (narrators') present. Some writers were perfectly aware of this relationship, openly thematizing the resources they used for understanding and later describing the world around them. The resulting self-assertion is brought forward as evidence of biographical change. Working-class writers display their courage to openly resist and question authority figures.

A socialist veteran, the tanner Michał Ostrowski, tells how he was taken to a hospital, still under religious jurisdiction, and was to undergo a compulsory confession. He vehemently resisted, responding to the medical staff: "My faith is grounded in my will and reason; these are my convictions, which I consider my personal issue, and that is why I won't allow religious practices to be forced upon me. I am a philosopher, and I believe in what science has investigated."[34] Such a statement was an expression of the writer's accomplished, resistant self. Even if it is a pure literary creation or a highly stylized memory—a description of words and deeds as imagined rather than done and spoken—the narrator's very mode of presentation to his readers speaks for itself.

The biographical dynamic is narrativized in a form resembling the bourgeois *Bildungsroman,* rearticulated in the mode of socialist transformation from a passive victim to an active and resistant challenger against oppressive circumstances.[35] Like every autobiographical writer, a working-class one is a bricoleur, recycling stock patterns to express his life story, which was also lived in real time within external benchmarks. In the case of politicized working-class autobiography, the meaningful world of work had to be replaced by other forms of emplotment acquired from socialist literature (where often a collective subject underwent maturation and awakening in history) or novels, saturating working-class writers with bourgeois personality models based on individual pursuits and heroism.[36]

The pattern of struggle against all odds for self-formation also comes back when writers describe later attempts to stay on the track of self-development. Some attempted to "cheat" their life course, corrupting it through a combination of the approaching stage of life with goals acquired before. Ostrowski writes:

> I had an enormous will to be educated, and just after leaving the orphanage I tried to read a lot. I was most interested in ancient history and natural sciences. Unfortunately, there was nobody around who would have given me any advice,

so I read everything randomly. . . . I always admired people who had at least some schooling, and I felt my nothingness, because I did not have this key to knowledge. I understood that school gives a foundation, and I had no such foundation. I always felt sad, and I dreamed that I would get a wife—a friend, who having any education could help me in further educating myself.[37]

This time the attempt failed miserably: "my 'Florka' [the wife's name] did not like my comrades, because they only used to tell fantastic fables about stupidities but did not dance."[38]

Political Initiation

If a stubborn autodidactic effort failed, and biographical assistance from elders or educated wives was not at hand, opportunity came from the worker's political involvement. Not only did parties spread literacy and new languages to describe the world, but they also organized more general education, such as open lectures or meetings. It was a collective form of a broader education, but above all it was political action where individual intellectual pursuits could also come to fruition.

In earlier times, the everyday life of workers in Russian Poland was seldom interrupted by a spark of political zeal. Considering the short life expectancy, an entire generation grew up between the scattered protests. The Lodz riot from 1892 was by early 1900 a vivid part of communicative memory; it was not a direct point of reference, however, but a distant story retold by the older generation of workers, not those most active in the heyday of 1905.[39] As a result, the stories of political beginning are told against the backdrop of mundane activity, endless toil, and hopelessness—narrativized as a fresh awakening; a slow move toward light, life, and hope. They are not presented as a taking of the baton of revolutionary struggle from older veterans. The veterans, however, sometimes played important biographical roles as crucial external actors spreading the news; they sometimes acted as biographical caretakers and educators infecting the narrators with germs of disruptive thinking and the initial imagining of a world different from the actual present.

Curiosity might also initiate a chain of events that pushed the young adept into deeper involvement. It could happen because of some form of positive outside pressure or in response to external persecution. Sometimes, improper behavior was reflexively changed into a positive identity as a part of biography management in the time of writing (and probably at the time of action as well). Józef Skowroński, a young worker from Zgierz, attended an ill-defined circle of "moderate protestants of Polish-socialist provenance."[40] There he became interested in the critique of religion, which removed the veil of mystery from religious ritual, thus resonating with his natural curiosity. Putting the acquired ideas into practice, he decided to investigate the Host, to check if it really contained "the blood of Lord Jesus." This scientific enterprise did not gain the endorsement of his mother, who after beating him severely gave him up to the priest. This threat immediately resulted in his forced escape to Lodz, a bigger city without the direct control of the clergy characteristic of his semiurban local community. As a result, he "joined the PPS and became an active member."[41] This is how the "moral career" of a revolutionary could be reconstructed.[42] In this case, the grip of standardized narrative is loosened, and a certain contingency of the biographical process is revealed.

In other cases, however, the ideological and experiential genesis of political commitment is covered with a thick crust of obviousness; the party road and political activism seem almost as natural as subsequent stages of the life course. As one of the narrators put it: "The labor movement started. Workers began strikes in factories, and I as a boy was needed in the party to distribute the leaflets."[43] Just like that. Such a presentation confirms the ideological choice as the right one, reassuring the coherence of the biography as a correct, unidirectional way of the revolutionary subject called upon to fulfill its historical task.

Such laconic expositions notwithstanding, political initiation was not always easy. It was a long and demanding intellectual journey, and access to the long-desired fresh ideas was fairly limited. Often a significant other, a kind of biographical patron, is introduced as a crucial protagonist of the biography. Such a patron either intervened at a crucial moment of the biographical path—for instance, by awaking educational aspirations—or acted as a political gatekeeper. A friend, family member, or just a more sympathetic party agitator provided the narrator with contact to the party structure and played an important role in politicization. This might be an extended process: "Zygmunt . . . talked a lot about a revolution, that every worker should be a socialist—and socialism leads to liberation and freedom—by then in the house various people gathered, and one avoided us [the younger freshmen]. I was desperate to hear something, but I only learned something from Zygmunt later."[44]

Already committed workers occasionally found it difficult to contact other militants plugged into the party structure. In conditions of illegality they were reluctant to reveal who they were or even respond to outsiders asking them about their party allegiance. Oftentimes the first point of contact was leaflets distributed broadly and "randomly."[45] Those luckier or more stubborn were able to get a political journal in their hands; however, it was expected they would pass it on. Such obstacles were common in memories of socialist adherents and nationalist freshmen alike. I now zoom in on the nationalists, whom we have not yet discussed.

Biographies of NZR members are authorized recollections of the movement, and they are clearly uttered as a reclaiming of polemics against the dominant memory. The problem was not that Polish nationalism was weak (quite the contrary) but that the NZR was separated from its main current.[46] When the NZR fostered the gathering and publishing of memoirs in the 1930s, it was already long detached from the National Democracy party, drifting to the almost fascist right in interwar Poland. The national democratic political syndicate, however, mobilized workers along nationalist, anti-minority and anti-Jewish lines and did not support a separate workers' movement. Thus the NZR memory was orphaned, and the association attempted to claim legitimacy among the insurrectionist tradition of Polish workers. It therefore rivaled the then dominant memory of the militarist right-wing faction of the PPS, by then enshrined as a prehistory of Józef Piłsudski's camp.

During the revolution, however, the National Democrats abandoned the insurrectionist tradition and were partially coopted by the Russian state, which saw them as a guarantor of order against revolutionary anarchy. Then the nationalists enjoyed slightly broader margins of legality, later trampled by the tsarist reaction. Initially, however, this milieu shared the experience of conspiracy with the socialists.

In such underground conditions, the future nationalist militant Michał Kosiorek "dreamed about joining the secret patriotic organization because illegal work for Poland excited [him]." Only after a long period of asking around and later occasional cooperation in the distribution of printouts was he admitted "to the first secret meeting," where he "was informed about the aims and tasks of the NZR."[47] Another national activist, Jan Posiak, picked up some "patriotic literature" in a physician's waiting room. Later he "read not only alone but accompanied by a couple of colleagues. In this way an informal, loose circle of workers was formed, collectively using the doctor's library."⁴⁸ A huge wave of new members entered the movement during the revolution. The NZR was officially founded in 1905, allowing for mass mobilization. As a result, Michalina Klimkiewiczówna, a female nationalist activist, "joined the organization in 1905, when people massively flocked to political parties—everybody was taken by a psychosis of struggle for a better tomorrow and freedom for the country."⁴⁹ Even if the political agenda of the NZR was openly hostile to the revolutionary turmoil, general invigoration and the rise in political interests perpetuated its growth.

Many nationalists, in their recollections of political beginnings, tend to focus on the interplay of the new political agenda with older commitments passed on to them by parents or more incidental teachers. The national tradition or spirit was carried forward or revived by the narrator's participation.⁵⁰ This evokes a certain primordiality of national feeling, thus allowing the narration to converge with the basic tenets of the narrator's nationalist commitments. One of the narrators recalled that "when the nationalist proclamations [odezwy narodowe] reached our factory, we became interested in their content, and I must admit that they appealed to my feeling stronger, with a certain sentiment, and they moved my heart; none of the socialist leaflets could do that. All the socialist leaflets were based on calculation and materialism, whereas from the nationalist leaflets faith was flowing, passion, a burning zeal which took the heart."⁵¹

If socialist materials indeed presented seemingly rational, economic arguments—say, in favor of an economic strike—the nationalist ones, often calling for calm, had to mobilize different feelings and attachments for the sake of counteragitation. For such purposes summoning tradition, ethnic bonds, or lore of the forefathers may have been helpful. Clearly, adherence to the nationalist camp was constructed by the narrators as much more emotional than among socialist writers. Such a construction was also strengthened by the dynamic of the overall political mobilization. For a long time nationalist workers were a minority, so they tended to stress this primary, "deep" conviction as the reason for their adherence—a reason good enough to win over a previous, allegedly only incidental fascination with socialism. Maksymilian Brzeziński admitted that initially it was the socialists who were better prepared for political agitation. However, "it was the cause itself, which helped us [nationalists], as it reached the hearth of the Polish worker."⁵² This clearly indicates a more polemical setting where equals could adhere to competing political programs and identities.

These primordial commitments mobilized to back up political identity forged in a polemical setting also bore traces of mobilization against the Other. Polish nationalists tended to suggest that the socialists were affiliated with the Jews, which helped them to discredit political opponents in the eyes of some workers. Antisemitic undercurrents present in nationalist materials were successful tools of political mobilization. This further encouraged the use of political antisemitism to secure the problematic unity of the Poles. For instance, Józef Drzewiecki (Dejot), a railway worker from the Dąbrowa Basin, explained this growing hostility, at the same time presenting the main antisemitic building blocks of the nationalist discourse of those days. They continued to be fanned and reached their pinnacle in the 1930s, when this narrative was written:

> Naturally, one resisted the socialists [*socjałom*—in Polish a more derogatory expression] at every step by debunking their specious program. The PPS members in deranged fury attacked our rallies, and at mass meetings and demonstrations they tore up and desecrated the banners with the white eagle [Polish national emblem], shouting "Down with the white goose." . . . Moreover, the ringleted comrades [*pejsaci towarzysze*—euphemism for the Jewish socialists] were numerous and controlled the socialist activists; they contributed significantly to the abomination of Marxist slogans and the Jewing of the PPS ranks with individuals who endlessly, in line with the received Talmud, called [*podjudzali*] for a struggle against the gentiles.[53]

Antisemitism was not the only emotion behind nationalist mobilization. A framing more convergent with the general will to improve, successfully perpetuated by the socialists, also found a place within nationalist writings: "Among workers hopes of a better future had awoken; . . . the workers were only preparing to struggle for their future rights."[54]

In the political cauldron at the turn of the century, which heated up in 1905, identities were still quite labile. Thus reverence for an organization was enhanced by various procedures confirming the status of belonging. Such rituals were much more present among the nationalists. Moreover, in nationalist milieus the structure of belonging was more explicitly hierarchical. Nevertheless, acceptance into the secret and hierarchical order was a source of significant pride. Years later, Stanisław Parkot-Wójt still underlined the emotional impact of the initiation ceremony: "A celebration of acceptance into the organization and the oath made a huge impression on me. I grew in my own eyes; I felt like a human bearing on his shoulders new obligations about which I had not thought before."[55]

The staged dignity of such procedures might also backfire. One of the socialist "converts" recollected the rapid switching of sides. After a secret oath of fidelity to the cross (*wierność na krzyż*) the leader tried to convince the novices of the revival of aristocratic Poland (at least it was perceived and remembered this way). When the listeners objected to this, they were slandered as "foreign socialists." The rebellious workers left the meeting to look for an appropriate organization that would combine their patriotic allegiance and reservations against the old class and state privileges (that is, the PPS).[56]

Often the story of political alignment is presented as turbulent and far from obvious, which renders the final choice a well-grounded one. Indeed, the political sphere was highly fractured, which affected the actual paths of narrators, but also the experience of plurality urged them even more to present assumed affiliations as conscious choices. In this vein, the story of initiation often assumes the form of a drama. However, the mantle of a party militant, once assumed—with accompanying sociality of the circle, the union, or the party—offered much more than the initial excitement. In the life course of a political activist, a crucial role was usually assigned to the practices of political life, with its mastery, alternative hierarchy, and solidarity in battle. They constituted a sense of belonging abundantly described by narrators.

Belonging and Recognition

Socialist or nationalist mobilization intervened in repetitive working-class life. Part and parcel of its appeal was the opportunity to enter a new social context with its own hierarchies, time management, and dignified self-assertion. The study of biographical materials leaves no doubt; few narrators mentioned the struggle for material improvements as an important incentive for joining the party. The same point applies to testimonies written under state socialism, when the default narrative suggested combining past efforts with resulting present welfare provisions. Some committed supporters of the Polish People's Republic constructed this bridge in their writing here and there, but it always remained rhetorical embroidery rather than the master frame of writing.

The sense of belonging and recognition acquired within the movement is most clearly present in narratives of older workers entering the revolution as experienced militants. For them, because any language of contention had had at best a weak presence in previous years, the first contact with the movement was the most significant. Arguably, for many people it was the very first moment when the desire for personal improvement appeared. The Catholic Church had taught for some time that the desire for improvement in one's lot in life was a sin, and an impossible goal in any case. Such an attitude must have remained influential among populations faithful to the Church's teachings.[57] This desire for self-creation was clearly something new, probably more important than in other contexts marked by existing artisanal networks, which had been able to deliver these components to their aspiring members (as in the case of French or German working-class biographies).[58]

An apt example is Marian Płochocki (pseudonym Olbrzymek), a baker with a turbulent biography, later a Bolshevik and a veteran in the All-Union Association of Old Bolsheviks, executed in the great purge of 1937. His biographical writing epitomizes a separate subset, close to the well-researched "Bolshevik autobiographies."[59] It consists of texts written by former SDKPiL and PPS-Left members who embraced the Polish Communist Party and in various circumstances immigrated to the Soviet Union. There they produced militant memoirs, fulfilling the requirements of the official memory of the Bolshevik revolution, which were also published in dedicated journals.[60] In this case, however, because of a certain distance from the epicenter of the debate on the memory of the October Revolution, the "Polish" part of the memoir was relatively free from the direct constraints put on writing.

The son of a poor rural agricultural official, Płochocki left for vocational training in Warsaw. Because his father was unable to pay anything for his placement, he was hired as a "boy" assistant in a bakery. There long, unpaid labor and harsh conditions compensated for the lack of an entry fee. In his later writing he presents a story of his slow "awakening" (a trope typical of Bolshevik biographies and most prominent among SDKPiL narratives) from the "presence tightly filled with heavy, monotonous, and murderous work" where "a day was so similar to any other day as brothers, and there were 361 of them per year" (bakers had no free Sundays, only the major holidays).[61] In this predicament it was his inborn curiosity, and love of nature and culture, that helped him and offered the way out of an unbearable life (again, a typical element in an autodidactic autobiography—narrators unable to resist listening to birds singing or a bourgeois girl playing the violin nearby, just as Płochocki used to do). Among other bakers, as he suggested, a seed of change, a shift in attitude toward themselves, had still to be sown. "The comparison of life and existence of then living as a baker [i.e., employee of a bakery, apprentice, or low-ranking unskilled boy assistant] to the existence of a prostitute or a thief was right, not only in a metaphorical sense. The baker in the bakery was only a drudge, powerless and dumb, just like the tools he worked with; beyond the bakery he was only a drunken and rugged two-legged animal, who was disrespected by everybody, and he hated everybody for that. Because he was not able to respect himself."[62]

To this problem party culture was an appropriate response. Political involvement and interparty communication offered ways "to respect oneself." Initially, revolutionary circles were, for the narrator, covered by a mist of mystery, often stimulating curiosity and interest rather than addressing specific grievances. The future revolutionary felt that in the beginning the older fellow workers in a bakery were unapproachable: "We were not aware at all in what name they were fighting and what they were dying for, but we felt that it was about a better life in a world for such beaten and kicked poor as we were, and we praised them as saints."[63] It is no wonder that, when recognized as equal comrades in common struggle, political novices felt dignified, just like Płochocki: "Only when Masłowski [another comrade with whom Płochocki was printing a leaflet] informed [Comrade Rosół] who I was, he shook my hand with his hand, hardened from work. It was factual, but not ceremonial, admittance to his circle."[64]

In such a situation an important gesture of acceptance was also the form of address. Relatively democratic party culture was a significant respite from the workshop reality where foremen and principals were not excessively polite and commonly called workers using an informal form of address implying a lack of respect. A change in this practice was later a common demand within the revolutionary struggle for recognition. Also, the opening words of address calling the receivers "comrades" in print appealed to workers thirsty for fundamental recognition. Płochocki describes the importance of his first contact with such a proclamation for his construction of selfhood:

> The proclamation, copied on huge sheets of paper, started with the words: "Comrades, bakers." I have seen old bakers wiping tears away from their drunken faces while reading this. So we were not working cattle, not two-legged animals, but "comrades," we—comrades . . . This feeling could be understood and shared only by these comrades-workers, who were themselves severely

beaten up and kicked, and for whom the word "comrade" and "strike" were not everyday or technical terms but an acclamation of their belonging to the grand Workers Family. . . . I am firmly convinced, and I claim that this moment has had a huge, if not decisive, significance for us, bakers, becoming people.[65]

Such imagined inclusion in the group was later secured by the practical sociality of the party circle, supportive comrades, cooperation between workers and intelligentsia agitators, and effective networks of solidarity. When, for instance, an older worker already versed in socialism (or national literature) approached a young recruit, that was already a distinction. If, on top of that, a youngster was addressed as a comrade, this was an honorable award. The fact that such a form of address was common and universally accepted among the socialists did not change the situation—quite the contrary. For the newcomers it was not a widely recognized fact, and later they enjoyed being accepted as members of such a horizontal yet dignified community. A future SDKPiL militant was invited by such a biographical counselor: "'Sit, my comrade!' I was astonished. . . . I was called with this most dignified title for a human. . . . With this word, comrade, he adopted me, considered me equal with himself, beckoned me with his hand."[66] To be successful, revolutionary movements, apart from sudden appeals triggered by the seizure of the moment, must be responsive to vital needs of their adherents. The form of belonging they deliver is one of the most important forms of such responsiveness. Research on social movements documents the emotional safety net that such adherence may deliver.[67] Revolutionary politics in the tsarist empire was also an important factor in reshaping forms of belonging. For many uprooted communities no longer able to maintain old communal networks, revolutionary activity seemed a paradoxical safe haven. This mattered especially to populations lacking paths of social integration under the conditions of tsarist discriminatory politics, such as the lower-ranking Polish intelligentsia or the Jewish urban poor from the Pale of Settlement.[68] Tsarist national policies, even if oppressive in terms of language and cultural issues, did not put so many limitations on Polish workers' migration and occupations.[69] Poles did not suffer from direct threats of violence and discriminatory policies of the tsarist administration to the same extent as their Jewish colleagues from the Pale. Nevertheless, they also felt uprooted and longed for a new community of belonging.

In this context, self-assertion and recognition also occupied a prominent place among the narrators' reconstructed motives for their actions. The situation of a factory worker under a hierarchical work culture and with class differences strengthened by national and ethnic tensions was not easy. These workers had little hope of improving their personal situation; channels of professional upward mobility were narrow. Alternative forms of community capable of funneling such needs were highly desired. Consequently, socialist circles or nationalist associations responded to those grievances and were able to integrate newcomers into the relatively horizontal structures of recognition and communal prestige.[70]

In addition, a committed militant might educate himself (more rarely herself), be heard, and then be acknowledged as versed in socialism or a "national issue." By personal sacrifice, he or she might strive for broader recognition as an agitator expert in political rhetoric and oral performance or as a skillful organizer of "party technique" (i.e., printing and distributing leaflets or newspapers). Assessing these skills when mentioning other people is a common trait in written biographies, testifying to the importance of those criteria to networks of cooperation and friendship.

The magic of the seemingly horizontal structure and democratic culture of communication concerned not only personal relationships. For instance, in the words of one narrator, "an older worker" offered a chance to participate in a party meeting, where one "could find out why the state power sees socialists as a grave danger," thus stimulating "first curiosity, then conviction" to "enter the path of revolution."[71] Narrators stress how their lives were henceforth constructed differently, no longer revolving around mundane toil but interrupted by the reference to outside goals worth striving for. The sense of belonging and sharing in organizations as equals provided important elements of recognition and self-assertion so different from the scorn they remember having encountered on the shop floor. After entering the organization, they expected exciting things to come, and they were not wrong. Apart from thriving public activities, a crucial experience presented by narrators as a threshold in the development of their political consciousness was the strike.

The Experience of the Strike

Much of the research in labor history has emphasized the maturation of the labor movement through subsequent waves of struggles, strikes, and protests. The standard narrative of the field acknowledges the significance of singular acts of resistance and accumulated experiences for future class formation on the subjective level: for example, the emergence of a militant worker.⁷² Yet one wonders why relatively little has been written about the grassroots experience of strike as a shop-floor event reconfiguring the selves of its participants. Only the mandarins of the labor movement participating in the revolutionary process on the spot produced analyses of the strike movement. For most theoretically if not philosophically oriented writers, the strike is almost a mythical act of resistance—as, for instance, in the work of George Sorel.⁷³ More down-to-earth interventions interwove theoretical analysis with current agitation to push the movement forward, as in Rosa Luxemburg's writing on the strike waves I investigate here. Earlier I discussed how strikes worked in practice, but here I seek to excavate the phenomenology of strikes for those who took part in them and for shop-floor agitators, who often engaged in vernacular theorizing on the strike's dynamic and significance.

One such agitator-theoretician was Wincenty Jastrzębski. His remarks on strikes are exceptionally revealing because they stick out from the overall memory culture of his party and forms of struggle exposed in parallel memoirs.⁷⁴ While strikes and mass mobilization were important to the left faction of the PPS and the class struggle launched by the SDKPiL, within Jastrzębski's PPS-Revolutionary Faction (PPS-RF) milieu a quasi-military heroism of street fights with tsarist troops was absolutely dominant.⁷⁵ Such an alignment corresponded with the nationalist goals of the party and was later solidified by the successful rebuilding of the party's self-defense into military structures crucial for the future struggle for Polish independence. Consequently, this aspect of memory was part and parcel of a successful story of the winners, codified by memory efforts in the Polish interwar state. These semiofficial party-centered memoirs from within the hegemonic memory mostly contained heroic memories of insurgents leading military resistance against the Russian autocracy.⁷⁶ They were published in dedicated journals, various anniversary publications, or separate books, aligned with the parallel historiographical effort to document the "militaristic" struggle with "the foreign yoke."⁷⁷ Indeed, Jastrzębski himself recalled the reluctance of his comrades to recognize the validity of his theorizing on strikes and the relevance of this form of struggle for the party goals. When he shared his excited remarks on the power of striking, his older colleague immediately condemned him as loitering on a "roadless track of syndicalism."⁷⁸ He was immediately moved to be trained in the party "military school."

In general, however, Jastrzębski's story bears many typical traces of the political militant biography. His relatively affluent background, with a father who worked as a miller and shared substantial meals with a local priest ("baked hooded crows"), gave him the initial impulses for development. However, the father wasted his property on drink, which, along with a later illness and the death of both parents, made a poor orphan out of the young Wincenty. In his writing, the elements of the tragic literary form allow for the narrator's exposition of his struggle with obstacles, which he successfully overcame due to his intellectual zeal and political activity. During the 1905 strike wave he was already an experienced agitator, sent by the party to mobilize agricultural workers. This experience allowed him to engage in a broad reflection on the nature of manorial work and, above all, to develop insights into the significance of strikes in the working-class struggle.

He considered the strike a factor that demonstrated the importance of workers and their labor in maintaining general social existence, let alone productivity. Abstaining from work was direct evidence of who was the real mover of society—when workers dropped out, cities as they knew them ceased to exist. This worked also on a smaller scale; for instance, the manorial economy collapsed if farm laborers refused to work. This gave Jastrzębski insights into the personal phenomenology of strike: "The strike uncovers the natural class consciousness of wage earners, deeply hidden in their souls. Its righteousness and infallibility are confirmed self-evidently by the tangible reality of the strike, and it is reducible to a basic, almost natural truth: without the labor of farm hands the manorial estate has no value. This truth . . . affects his [the agricultural laborer's] physical condition, his attitude, self-confidence, dignity, and conviction about the righteousness of his cause."[79]

There is no doubt that all the parties involved in a conflict were usually perfectly aware what was really at stake, and they expressed it explicitly in the press, leaflets, and reports. Even when staging a strike as a minor misunderstanding, the goal was to lessen the domination of the owner, and this confrontation of wills made an impression on Jastrzębski: "Everybody already knew what it was all about. So the faces of all those gathered acquired noble shapes; it looked like somebody washed out of them all the everyday sorrows and in their place put one great grievance; under the pressure facial lines hardened."[80] In many cases factory or manorial relationships were never again as before. All the people involved were able to "see, understand, and draw conclusions, bordering on a riot." Also, for Jastrzębski himself, "two weeks of striking . . . produced more class consciousness than the entire *Communist Manifesto.*"[81] No wonder that from the beginning every strike, even one of seemingly minor importance, was comprehended as an act of direct participation in a broader struggle and was explained that way by socialist agitators. This rhetorical framing allowed the narrators to inscribe individual effort and sacrifice for the broader struggle of the whole social group. On the flip side, a successful strike led to the rare outcome in which the power of collective action directly changed an individual's position. The strike interwove a particular experience with a universal cause.

The influence of strikes on workers, and the accompanying reconfiguration of places workers might inhabit in the broader social communicative space, is a prolific topic in written works. More experienced narrators like Franciszek Łęczycki especially engaged in a practical analysis of strike experience, using all the conceptual apparatus the party had given them. Not only did they stress enhanced networks of solidarity but also the meaning newly assigned to individual life and actions.[82] This acquired dignity was also present on a direct, mundane level of shop-floor reality, because the strike was also a renegotiation of factory relations of power. After all, the workers had a say during those days. "The strike ended after two weeks with a partial success; factory owners were forced to give up. A hundred times more important was the moral victory and awareness that it was only a first step in the forthcoming struggle. . . . The proletariat understood that it could fight and win only if the movement were a common thing, gathering the masses. . . . [I]t awoke the feeling of class solidarity, and the so-called patriarchal relationship between employer and employee was forever gone."[83]

This reconfiguration of the political space affected more than the general relationship hidden behind the labor contract or moral economy of employment. Strikes were one of the main pillars of revolutionary public activity. In participants' memoirs, they are a paramount setting for retracing the fragile limits of the possible. For instance, in seemingly unimportant descriptions of events, a profound questioning of the balance of power is detectable. Writers are most excited about the gradual pushing of hitherto powerful forces from their lives. They gain the upper hand over hated forms of power, if for only a moment. Let us look at the narrative microstructure of one testimony, seemingly written to record basic facts, as part and parcel of the orchestrated effort to gather the prehistory of the "Polish proletariat" in the socialist state:

> The police commander arrived in a coach assisted by Cossacks . . . and *asked to be allowed* to speak to those gathered. When he was *allowed to speak*, he *started to ask* those gathered to disperse because otherwise bloodshed might happen. In response, shouts were heard of "Down with him," and he *was not allowed to speak any more*. . . . Finally, *the troops left*, tables were *carried in*—and the speeches *commenced*—it was the first day. On the second day our Citizen's Militia *appeared, the tsarist police were not visible, they were hiding* or walked around dressed casually.[84]

The entire sequence attests to an active pushing away of the structure of domination and a reversal of previous hierarchies. In the place of the old domination, alternative activities emerged. New constituencies immediately entered the evacuated space of power. The implicit feeling of triumph over forces previously accepted without question is a repetitive theme in the narratives of less involved militants, often those who joined the movement only in 1905. The sense of victory might come in reference to the tsarist police or troops but also to a foreman (carried out on a wheelbarrow as described before) or a factory owner forced to negotiate. Every strike, no matter how economic the demands might have been, was also a purely political gesture. The goal of the strike was to gain political empowerment and a right to make public claims. One cannot overestimate the significance of such an experience for workers' definition of the self. It changed their place in the social imaginary—their own, as well as the one assigned to them by other social strata.

If power may be recognized by resistance, the symptom of its questioning is reaction. Here the response was a harsh class struggle from above and a massive mobilization of the factory owners. This pushback resulted in a nearly universal lockout of the great factories in Lodz launched in late 1906 and many smaller attempts in other cities to threaten employees with the closure of factories and rehiring of staff. They were targeted to at least superficially regain absolute control over the workplace. The great Lodz lockout encompassed all seven of the largest factories in the city and affected twenty-two thousand workers. Almost a hundred thousand people lost any hope of income in the winter months.[85] Lasting several months, it ended with a defeat of the workers' committees and triggered an intense debate all over the country, with many members of the intelligentsia involved in negotiations or organizing charity for starving factory crews.

The proclamations issued by the factory committees and declarations from factory owners left no doubt that all those involved were aware of the real stakes of the conflict. It was not because of a minor disturbance at Poznański's factory that the owners decided to cut short their own profits for a lengthy period. And it was not because of this single issue that workers struggled (and starved) for so long.[86] Above all, the goal of industrialists was to yet again seize absolute control over their factories, a power that had been severely undermined by strikes and the general self-assertion of the crews eager to take over their workplaces. Strikes were not, however, the only events where new identities might be forged.

Street Heroism and Masculine Ethos

The emerging ethos of the class struggle and shop-floor solidarity was inseparably mixed with working-class rearticulation of the insurrectionist tradition. Instead of a strike activist, a militant could become a member of a militarized defense squad, directly demonstrating heroism in the face of political enemies and a much-desired form of manliness.[87] This might lead to injury, imprisonment, or death but was certainly accompanied by a chance to become a hero, if not a martyr. The excitement of fighting in the streets competed with the gains of the economic struggle. Thus class-oriented parties trying to build mass organizations bent over backward to discourage such individualistic militarism.

Nonetheless, the early engagement described in autobiographies—even if later inscribed in a broader historical mission—was not free of boyish heroism and the distinctive romanticism of illegality. The distribution of leaflets and proclamations may be recalled as a mundane if dangerous activity, but political commitment could be combined with fantasy as well. In such passages a biography resembles a picaresque novel, a familiar genre for proletarian readers as such literature was available in popular libraries and eagerly read. Patriotic Polish publications also presented more light-hearted characters appealing to popular readers. As a result, some of the biographies are stylized as adventure stories.

Eugeniusz Pieńkowski, a self-proclaimed "child of the street," had been implanted with patriotic zeal by an underground teacher early on. As a truly urban kid, he immediately turned his knowledge of the urban space from below (holes in fences, various secret passages so precious to boyish runaways) into a resource in his struggle: for instance, to smuggle political materials. His childish conspiracy used to take on more explicit dimensions as well, such as using particular "weapons" against tsarist functionaries. Shooting at tsarist troops and, above all, horses—then running in panic—with a blow gun made of a small straw and beans was after all great fun.[88] Such an arsenal turned into a lethal weapon of the weak when the target was a tsarist soldier climbing to the top of a chimney to remove a red banner placed there by militant workers the previous night.

Playing revolution might deliver many emotions. It continued to do so, even after the stakes of the struggle were already much more profound. Another juvenile socialist remembered that "For a youngster as I was it was really exciting to sneak through the fields and bushes to an arranged meeting place. . . . I must confess that during the first weeks belonging to the military organization [a PPS department] was for me the greatest adventure of my life. Gaining awareness, understanding of the aims of our struggle came only later."[89] Once understood, however, political involvement and its accomplishments were of paramount significance. The simplest acts became part and parcel of an honorable struggle even if they were composed of normally mundane activities. "When we copied the first exemplar of a proclamation (and it was done clearly and perfectly) tenderness touched all of us: tears of joy, though strongly suppressed, filled our eyes and our voices were dull, everybody attempted to hide the emotion and remained silent so as not to be taken for a 'sissy.'"[90]

Apparently, in this autobiography the point of reference was a specific proletarian ethos of action, which organized emotions accordingly. The self-assertion was attained by a masterful action, street heroism, public performance as a speaker or agitator, and the autodidactic effort, combined in various proportions according to individual opportunities and skills. This ethos was highly masculine, as the above quoted fragment unambiguously demonstrates, and it supported a politicized form of manhood.[91] In its extreme form it was epitomized by a militarized ethos of "combat squads." While virtually every party maintained such groups, the use of them became most prominent in official enunciations of the right-wing faction of the PPS, which later split off into the PPS-Revolutionary Faction. As the party increasingly called for military resistance against tsarist police and troops, shooting, throwing bombs, and other militarized forms of action came to the fore of its activities. Its officially maintained image and internally propelled militant ethos evolved accordingly. Its later memory culture also revolved around street heroism, combat sacrifice, and a dubious mixture of excitement, violence, and romantic insurrectionism.

Speaking from a sober distance, one of the narrators told how he was fascinated by street violence: "I became an ardent supporter of terror; I simply hallucinated about various images of terrorist acts. A bomb became a daily dream for me, and a revolver, even a good one, did not have the same charm as a bomb. My imagination worked intensively; throwing bombs at governors was simply a deep spiritual experience. It seemed that such a vivid struggle soon would bring complete freedom, because tsarist servants would flee from Poland to Russia."[92] The spiritual dimension of "bomb throwing" had a firm foundation in the emotional background shared by those who engaged in it. Such a militant, if not *military* ethos and the charms of street heroism allowing for individual triumph over hated state power and everyday life were attractive to young workers. The multilayered, long-bred feeling of hopeless oppression could finally be revenged and overcome in a short yet priceless moment of triumph.

Confronted with such strong emotions, party leaders had a hard time persuading excited workers that military action on the streets was not always the best choice. One agitator regretted that even "the conscious working-class youth was eager to start a fight and dreamed about a gun as about a girl, with love."[93] Mundane work for the party such as printing and organizing factory committees or strikes was not that exciting. Moreover, these tasks were not directed against the tsarist police apparatus, hated more and more because of the growing repression. Sometimes violent acts were deemed to be the only way to press workers' demands, especially when parties called for moderation or wanted to stick to the accepted semilegal forms of organizing.[94] One of those who got frustrated with his work for the party and preferred to "beat the Muscovites" admitted: "I was not satisfied [with socialist party-centered activities], because all that had been done was not a job of a Polish soldier, and I and many others wanted to be one."[95] In addition, the heroic image and prospect of carrying a weapon excited people even more. This promised to cause trouble for recently formed party battle squads and was instantly recognized as such: "We had many volunteers for the combat squads, some drafted because they [liked the idea that they] would be nicely called 'fighters,' that they would have a shiny party Browning [the most popular pistol—WM]; after the rules were read aloud to them, many dropped out."[96]

Here too we should see a desperate attempt to acquire an alternative self of sorts, equipped with dignity and agency. The "fighter" might have left

Fig. 4.1. An illustration from the PPS-FR user's manual instructing militia members how to shoot with a Browning pistol, Wydawictwo Wydziału Bojowego PPS, Cracow, 1907. Polish National Library Digital Collection, 268.813 A Cim.

behind the passive "worker."[97] Such a masculine street hero ethos was further promoted by the peculiar martyr cult spread in the socialist and nationalist materials alike. Socialist leaflets eagerly commemorated past founding-father figures, including members of the early socialist Proletariat Party executed by the tsarist police apparatus in the mid-1880s.[98] Another generation of martyrs consisted of socialist militants shot dead in the streets in 1905 or captured and hanged thereafter. They were venerated either as persons (especially Marcin Kasprzak and Stefan Okrzeja) or as more anonymous paradigm worker-victims of the tsarist autocracy. In addition to being a form of collective remembering and an important cement securing the new collective identity of the militant working class, such "heroization" was also an important gesture of class-based self-assertion. The national hero, most often of noble origin and benign character, struggling with the foreign yoke and vices of the modern world, was an extremely important figure in the Polish collective imaginary of the late nineteenth century.[99] Reappropriating this elitist image by investing it in socialist militants as heroic figures of working-class origin was necessary to secure the new place of workers in their own social imaginary.

This democratization of the heroic pantheon notwithstanding, all those forms were largely organized around the nucleus of the male-dominated ethos. Less militarized forms of public participation were also largely male-oriented. Public gatherings and mastery in polemical speaking were accompanied by the highly masculinized sociability of the labor union and the tavern.[100] Exceptions had to be carefully negotiated. Unfortunately, the sources are also mostly male-dominated; not many working-class women decided to write. They might have been able to show how a manhood based on terror caused troubles as the revolutionary process unfolded.

The militarized ethos of street fighting contributed to the growing hostility between parties and greatly boosted the readiness to pull out weapons in skirmishes between different militias, thus fanning the flames of intra-class conflict. It was also difficult, if not impossible, for militia members to get back to everyday life. Not only were they confronted with police retaliations and court-martials, but it was difficult to give up an actionist spirit and violent street adventures. The experience of agency, temporary power over one's own life, and the possibility of revenge offered militants a powerful sense of dignity, hard to shelve overnight.[101] As parties such as PPS-RF turned to armed reappropriations (the most famous being the raids on

Fig. 4.2. A charity postcard with Marcin Kasprzak, a SDKPiL printer who was arrested and executed after an armed defense of the underground printing facility. He became a widely venerated socialist hero. Buying a postcard contributed to the political prisoners' relief fund, Związek Pomocy Wiezniom [sic!] politycznym, 1905. Polish National Library Digital Collection, DŻS XII 8b/p.28/155.

trains in Bezdany and Rogów), the border between revolutionary action and banditry, self-sacrifice and self-interest, blurred. Anarchist groups programmatically encroaching on state structures easily turned destruction and terror into robbery.[102] Some militants, seeking means of subsistence, crossed the border between party service and banditry. These developments contributed greatly to the general weariness with revolution and was grist to the mill of antirevolutionary discourses.

The Self and the Political

This chapter aims to reconstruct the layered selves of political militants. I analyze their narratives, detecting stable elements stemming from a conventionalized writing form but also a patterned working-class life course. Such conduct makes it possible to investigate the careers of political militants, who in their own eyes were shaping their selves in the moment of writing. Their self-reflexive vernacular sociology of education, mobilization, and action sheds light on the entangled relationship between biography and politics. The abundant resources of reflexive practical reasoning are mobilized precisely where intense, deeper biographical work is needed to understand and incorporate the changes into a readymade subject, expressed in writing. To the extent that the writers are accomplished political subjects, they personify the transformation of the regime regulating workers' political participation. Their biographies are inscriptions of change, and the subjective, narrativized course of this change is real in respect to its biographical consequences.

Undoubtedly the memory culture and the regime delimiting the speakable and important from the irrelevant and impermanent facilitated the inclusion of political commitments in any written life story. As one scholar of working-class life comments: "political activity provided working people with a level of self-awareness and a sense of purpose that could both structure a life and motivate writing a life story."[103] It was through politics that working-class narrators gained conviction that the story of their lives was worth telling. "Political life," combined with narrative devices drawn from the respective political languages, is the main form of emplotment that gives the stories their narrative features. These devices enable writers to convey events from their lives in a meaningful way. This process of convincing the self about the value of writing *through* and *in* politics is also reflexivized in the writing itself: "I have no ability and physical possibility to put [my biography] on several sheets of paper. Even more I understand your wish [the agenda of the communist party in Soviet Union who commissioned the memoir] that these few sheets should include a serious chapter and not a short talk about my fiery youth and about the inevitable old age of a man-wanderer beyond the borders of his homeland. Thus in a most comprehensive and succinct way in a few images I tell that I was an active member of the revolutionary movement in Lodz since 1904."[104]

The narrative forms available to proletarian memoir writers in the interwar years led them to identify political themes as fundamental in reshaping their identities. Such fragments demonstrate how politics was considered an important factor molding the way those people understood themselves and their role in society; the very fact they had decided to write is mediated evidence of how they had changed. Such a strong commitment shaping the entire self-definition sometimes remained the main frame of reference for the narrators, who decades later still wrote as a part and parcel of the revolutionary effort: "I wish that an unknown, sensitive youngster, after having read this, could understood how much beauty, happiness, and joy could be gained in life from disinterested, humble work in the name of a great idea. . . . If I would like to live again, it is only to be able to die for the revolution, in this 'last struggle.' It is my only unfulfilled dream from the beginning of my conscious life."[105]

The strong presence of conventionalized strategies of emplotment and weaving the self into the historical process are evident.[106] After all, reading biographies that emerged in the past is to ramble in the mists of a threefold mediation: that of past subjective experience, that of memory, and that of the (equally past) politics of writing. The examined autobiographies are highly diversified regarding these dimensions but not necessarily along the lines of simple divisions between political parties.

What differentiates them most is the type of political involvement and the place of the revolution in the biographical sequence. The stories of a revolutionary upsurge in activities, more typical for a broader group of workers, were usually written by shop-floor militants and not future professional party functionaries. They are far less extensive and not so abundant in ethno-sociological theorizing or ethnographic detail. While being, to a lesser extent, a part of the full-fledged autobiographical genre, they mimic the alleged official story of their respective party. Thus the more typical, mass experience of political mobilization and intervention of the revolutionary event into the biographical process may be reconstructed from pieces of narratives, rather than followed in larger biographies. The longer autobiographical texts, in turn, describe the paths of party functionaries with a working-class background. It is there, among more prolific biographical writers, where literary patterns are recycled in a creative bricolage to craft the autobiography. This patterned distribution is also an indirect piece of evidence of the impact politics made on the intellectual careers of the militants.

In both cases, the 1905 event intervenes in the processual unfolding of biography, albeit in different ways. While simpler stories stress the importance of the revolution, in the more developed ones it is an intensification of practices already performed. For the first group, the 1905 Revolution was a significant political initiation—oftentimes, however, without a direct effect on their professional career. They never ceased to be shop-floor workers. Nonetheless, the revolution triggered a cognitive switch: that is, it introduced additional layers of meaning that mobilized the worker to live his life and later to write down its course. For the second group, however, the 1905 threshold often sealed the career of a professional militant, either because of a personal conviction or police persecution. What is crucial in such biographies is the slow path of leaving behind the class-specific culture and habitus for the prize of estrangement, if not exclusion from class. For already liminal people on the edge of class, it was the feeling of "moral estrangement from both their own class and the larger society—their marginality—that attracted them to the idea of a class movement that promised to erase the boundaries of class," as one labor historian describes the motivation of the working class "moral vanguard" in the Russian context.[107] This dynamic parallels the entanglement of the proletarian public sphere, which harbored resistance and a way out of class-specific limits but simultaneously was forced to adapt to dominant patterns to be considered as legitimate public practice.

Otherwise, the retrospectively constructed life course in the testimonies from different political milieus and produced in different historical circumstances is strikingly similar. It is much more a class- and site-specific narrative of a militant life than a memory culture orchestrated by any particular political milieu. In the same way, the 1905 upheaval functions within narratives as a pivotal event reorganizing the self and giving sense to writing both for its ardent supporters (for whom it was a foundational myth for the collective memory of the revolutionaries) and opponents, who nevertheless recognized its significance. Autobiographies testify to the formation of the new type of self, embedded in the broader space of sense. What was done, read, and spoken was hence understood by narrators first and foremost as part of a broader collective biography of a class or nation striving for future improvement. The actions undertaken were inscribed in a form of narrative organizing the relationship between the self and the world, with certain formal features, unfolding from a beginning to an end, revolving around certain turning points and being populated by a stable set of protagonists.[108] This gave the respective actions a meaning when they were performed, and analogously this emplotment also allowed the writers to weave events into a meaningful story written as an autobiography later. Militants clearly remember their revolutionary practices as part and parcel of a broader effort, just as was suggested to them in the ideological language that they had just acquired: "The autodidactic effort was approached from the point of view of future work on revolutionary lines. One read intensively, one discussed days and nights, one repeated every school year since then. And all of this for Her—for the

Revolution."[109] Hence the new conceptual resources were largely successful. New activities offered alternative realms of mastery and self-improvement. Among peers, new forms of recognition and respect emerged because of acquired wisdom and the willingness to share with others: for instance, an expertise in public speaking. An important factor contributing to the popularity of the labor movement was precisely this will to improve and the actual promise of improvement. A harsh life could hardly be changed, but one could aspire to mastery in an alternative civil society, which mattered to many of the narrators discussed here. It might have been mastery in speaking or bravery in struggle; both offered the structure of meaning—of life, work, and sacrifice. Here lay the charm of socialist reading circles and successful economic strikes, but also street militias securing demonstrations with weapons or expropriating tsarist funds by robbing convoys of money for party purposes.

The resulting biography is a retrospective, layered construction of the self: a life story as memorized, recollected, narrated, and used in real time for self-maintenance. As such, the working-class narrative as a collective literary form with specific *loci communes* is an important element of working-class cohesion and capability for action. For this reason, it is also an important factor defining the political place of workers.[110] The accomplished selves manufactured in writing were also effective as social agents in history. In this context, the analysis performed on all the narratives, socialist and nationalist alike, demonstrates a predominantly shared repertoire of motives. On a formal level, an alternative education, political mobilization, and turbulent events of the revolution had a similar imprint on their writing and self-definition. Such a finding is contrary to the picture based on more event-based analysis, which shows growing hostility, or an investigation of political languages, which also display increasing divergence and antagonism.

Nonetheless, accumulated experiences were largely framed in interchangeable ways. Even if ideologically the national question was the main bone of contention, militants on all sides shared feelings of class oppression and national sentiments. They were not erased even in much later recollections, already written within defined memory cultures. This shared pool of experiences may help explain the fluidity of the political field and the successful coopting of most of the working-class population to the Polish nation state after 1918. This loyalty mattered especially during the Polish-Bolshevik war of 1919–1921 and was maintained even after the Polish state began to fulfill the Far Left's prophecies regarding class domination smokescreened by national unity.

In the working-class biography the 1905 Revolution was not an ordinary thing. It was an unexpected rupture, long memorialized and recollected as a pivotal event in the lives of narrators. Perhaps for themselves it was the only "historical" event in a life not always worthy of extensive reappearance in written form. The revolution was a rupture in the repetitive rhythm of days that allowed people to play a role in their own history. In the words of a female worker: "But in this ceaselessly continuous, dull everyday labor, in which one day resembled any other—there were such moments which I have remembered for my entire life. They have caused me to remember them as they were yesterday, even if today the years since have blurred the recollection and images in my memory. The fact that I have brought up my children as militants in our cause is a merit of those days from the 1905. It was hard, but I am proud of [those days and 1905 events] because I had a chance to participate in them."[111]

Biographies are told in a register based on political mobilization. As stories of conversion, they merge the processual time of an unfolding life and the "eventful" rupture of the revolution. The revolution intervenes as an event reconfiguring the self and its attitude to the world or solidifies an acquired militant identity. It is a pivotal event organizing other elements: (1) frames explaining the present situation and its potential for change; and (2) narratives about beginnings, perils, and goals and about protagonists of the drama, friends, and villains. They were later all means to make a story out of one's life, to be convinced that it was worth writing at all; that is, to bear witness to something beyond oneself, to have a meaning worth commemorating and sharing. Ultimately, isn't this entanglement the best evidence of the importance of the political commitments in reshaping the writer's self? These commitments and entrance to the public sphere did not remain unchallenged, however. The political conflict not only affected the workers' factions; it was even more acute between the workers and those opposed to their political subjectification. The fierce negotiation concerning this issue is the subject of the next chapter.

5

The Intelligentsia and Its Workers

> And after all, I say, the black, painful night full of longing will come to an end. It allegedly refuses to end, only it can't end, because in my jaw there is a sick, abscessed, and decaying tooth that must be removed.

In the early spring of 1905, the liberal daily *Goniec Łódzki* (The Lodz messenger) published a somewhat mysterious meditation on dreaming and awakening. The front-page article consisted of lengthy paragraphs regarding healthy dreaming, nightmares, sleepwalking, and the final return to consciousness, as quoted above. There were also short intermediary sections, pointing at the intended meaning of the entire article. These additions explained that such never-ending dreams, as when a troubled nightly sleep transforms itself into a hardly bearable dawn, "often happen in the life of entire generations, classes, states—nay, even nations." Without a doubt, it was Polish society that was in the painful process of awakening.

To make things easier, society could not rise out of its bedding of passivity by itself but had to be accompanied by a qualified dentist-physician, who "would strengthen the entire [patient's] constitution, and not some witch doctor." The linchpin of the argument was who this doctor was supposed to be. "There is no doubt that the physician is already on duty, has taken care of the patient, and—most important—a diagnosis has been made." This doctor-leader was to be the Polish intelligentsia, not the self-proclaimed

155

fugleman—allegedly the socialists. It is indeed a time-worn allegory of the rightful political leader embodied in a qualified physician replacing the impostor demagogues, known already from Plato's *Gorgias*. Its recirculation in the above-quoted article from *Goniec Łódzki* is one of many attempts to make sense of the new situation, which had challenged all expectations about politics among the Polish intelligentsia. How the working-class population should be admitted into the public sphere to raise its claims was a hotly debated topic, even if that debate took place behind esoteric code words to avoid censorship.

Here I investigate various topoi used to comprehend issues concerning workers in the officially recognized, "bourgeois" press written and addressed to nonproletarian social groups, which together make workers an object of discourse.[1] The rapid entrance of workers into the public sphere through protest made old recipes obsolete and forced all voices to adapt. The revolution posed a challenge to the hitherto established ways of comprehending workers, work, and their relationship to society and the political sphere. This comprehension had never been delimited by a rigid set of ideas. It was rather a panoply of positions in motion, mutually contested ideological worldviews. All of them circumscribed workers' participation in the public sphere and the right to make demands regarding their situation. For every contender in the political field, this space for workers may have been different; nevertheless, the discussion set the limits of what could be legitimately said and done. This equilibrium changed because of the revolution. This chapter examines how the old attitudes confronted the new situation, and how the place of workers within the political sphere was negotiated in the local press of the biggest industrial center in the country.

Lodz was undoubtedly the center of the debate on working-class citizenship and workers' right to claim a political role, even though Warsaw was the main hub of intellectual debates, political activity, writing, and publishing. Because the social structure in Lodz had sharper contours, the debate on the social question assumed the clearest form in the press of the textile hub. Moreover, the provincial press was an important vehicle for the local intelligentsia's self-assertion. Their drive to define themselves and their role concerned their local standing vis-à-vis commercial elites but also the position of the city and its intellectual elites—widely considered foreign, weak, or nonexistent—within the country as a whole.[2] This effort spurred writers to take stances on raging social problems and assume the mantle of local public opinion. Finally, the revolution had the most dramatic course there, and the workers were its greatest driving force. All these factors make Lodz a suitable context to investigate the changing relationship between the workers and the political scene.

For years, the city's rapid growth of the city made it difficult for the commercial press to keep up. Initially, the German-speaking population was more outspoken in forming local opinion, and the first newspapers were printed in German.[3] The first Polish newspaper, *Dziennik Łódzki* (The Lodz daily), was abandoned in 1892, after only six years of turbulent existence.[4] For a while, the city had no Polish dailies. Around 1898 two competitors suddenly appeared, at first similar in their intellectual profile. Both titles catered to the local educated public and Polish businesses. *Rozwój* (Development) was slightly more bourgeois (both in adhering to burgher values and in supporting the interests of industrial moguls) and oriented toward the nationalist agenda. *Goniec Łódzki*, which appeared soon after *Rozwój*, was more liberal and characterized by a stronger intelligentsia ethos. There is little point in analyzing here the complicated histories of both, including the subsequent renaming of the latter to *Kurier Łódzki*, then *Nowy Kurier Łódzki* (The Lodz courier and The new Lodz courier).[5] Instead I focus on the role that the language used within this plural press system played in the reconstruction of the political scene.

The role of newspapers is not limited to creating imagined communities of intended readers. There is a widely shared consensus among scholars of the social role of the press that "newspapers have always created readers, not news, as their primary function."[6] As seen in the pioneering contribution by Benedict Anderson, in the realities of Russian Poland the nation remained an important category of polity being forged in the press. Newspapers constituted a part and parcel of the local "print capitalism," and they delivered a crucial pillar of the nation-building project, even more profound within the stateless imperial context. Whereas this social embedding remains important, what is even more significant is the reproduction of an entire social imaginary, or an overall vision of a polity and the groups constituting it.[7] Newspaper language can be seen very much as a "social semiotic," which in its generic range draws particular social groups into particular styles of presentation.[8] Such coagulated forms of discourse have the capacity to reproduce social relationships with considerable power. In this sense, the imagination of a polity created and maintained by the language of the press is not only about

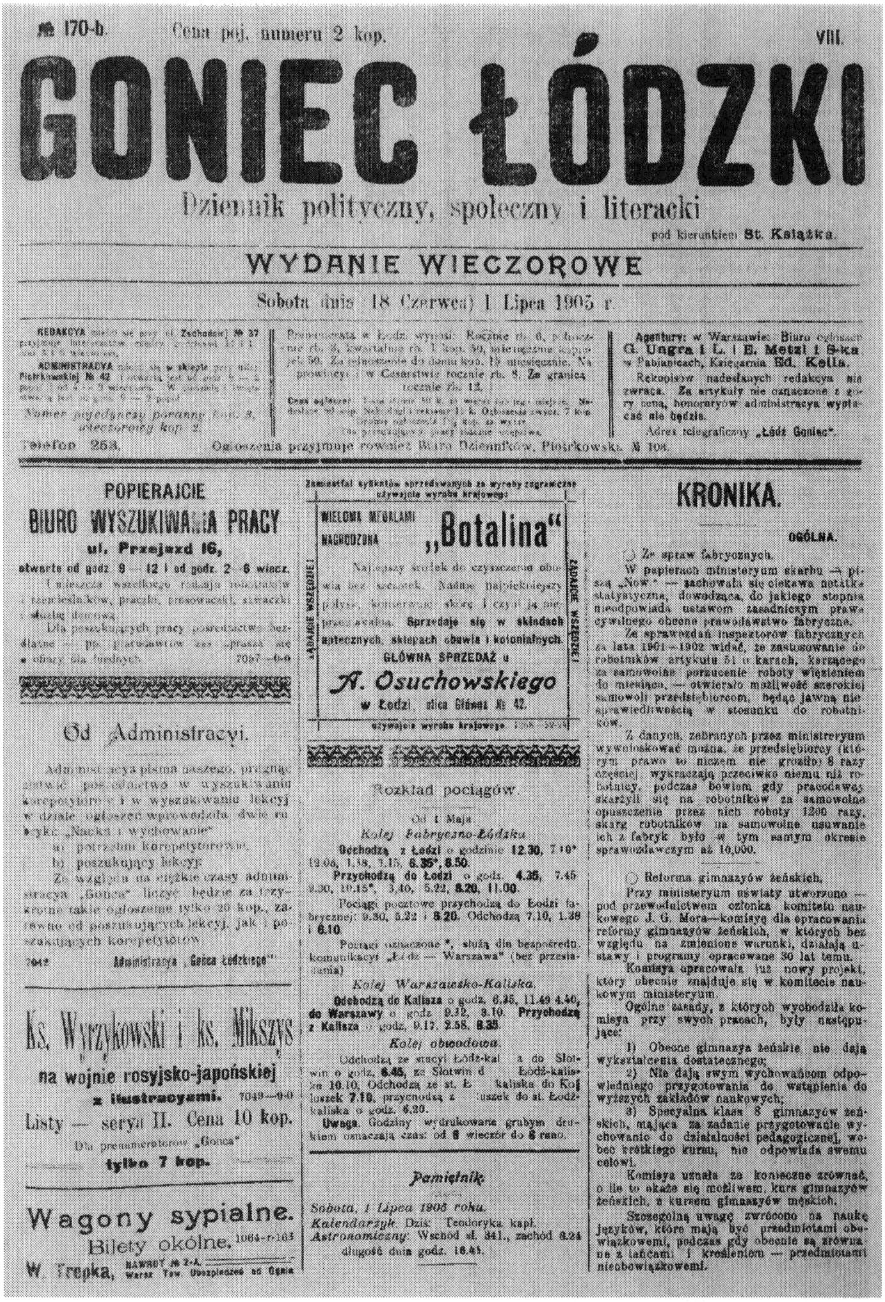

№ 170-b. Cena poj. numeru 2 kop. VIII.

GONIEC ŁÓDZKI

Dziennik polityczny, społeczny i literacki

pod kierunkiem **St. Książka.**

WYDANIE WIECZOROWE

Sobota dnia (18 Czerwca) 1 Lipca 1905 r.

Numer pojedynczy poranny kop. 3, wieczorowy kop. 2.

Prenumerata w Łodzi wynosi: Rocznie rb. 6, ... rocznie rb. 8. Za granicą rocznie rb. 12.

Agentury: w Warszawie: Biuro ogłoszeń **G. Ungra i L. i E. Metzl i S-ka** w Pabianicach, Księgarnia **Ed. Kolla.**

Rękopisów nadesłanych redakcya nie zwraca. **Za artykuły nie oznaczone z góry ceną, honoraryów administracya wypłacać nie będzie.**

Adres telegraficzny **„Łódź Goniec".**

Telefon 258. Ogłoszenia przyjmuje również Biuro Dzienników, Piotrkowska № 108.

POPIERAJCIE

BIURO WYSZUKIWANIA PRACY

ul. Przejazd 16,

otwarte od godz. 9 — 12 i od godz. 2 — 6 wiecz.

Dla poszukujących pracy pośrednictwo bezpłatne ... 7087—0-0

Od Administracyi.

Administracya pisma naszego, pragnąc ułatwić pośrednictwo w wyszukiwaniu korepetytorów i w wyszukiwaniu lekcyj w dziale ogłoszeń wprowadziła dwie rubryki: „Nauka i wychowanie"

a) potrzebni korepetytorowie,

b) poszukujący lekcyi.

Ze względu na ciężkie czasy administracya „Gońca" liczyć będzie za trzykrotne takie ogłoszenie tylko 20 kop., zarówno od poszukujących lekcyj, jak i poszukujących korepetytorów.

7042 Administracya „Gońca Łódzkiego"

Ks. Wyrzykowski i ks. Mikszys

na wojnie rosyjsko-japońskiej

z ilustracyami. 7049—0-0

Listy — serya II. Cena 10 kop.

Dla prenumeratorów „Gońca"

tylko 7 kop.

Wagony sypialne.

Bilety okólne. 1064-r-163

W. Trepka, NAWROT № 2-A.

Zamiast fal tysiąców sprzedawanych za wyroby zagraniczne używajcie wyrobu krajowego

WIELOMA MEDALAMI NAGRODZONA

„Botalina"

ŻĄDAJCIE WSZĘDZIE!

Najlepszy środek do czyszczenia obuwia bez szczotek. Nadaje najpiękniejszy połysk, konserwuje skórę i czyni ją nieprzemakalną. **Sprzedaje się w składach aptecznych, sklepach obuwia i kolonialnych.**

GŁÓWNA SPRZEDAŻ u

A. Osuchowskiego

w Łodzi, ulica Główna № 42.

używajcie wyrobu krajowego

Rozkład pociągów.

Od 1 Maja.

Kolej Fabryczno-Łódzka.

Odchodzą z Łodzi o godzinie **12.30**, 7.10* 12.06, 1.38, 3.15, **6.35***, **8.50**.

Przychodzą do Łodzi o godz. **4.35**, 7.45 9.30, 10.15*, 3.40, 5.22, **8.20**, **11.00**.

Pociągi pocztowe przychodzą do Łodzi fabrycznej: 9.30, 5.22 i **8.20**. Odchodzą 7.10, 1.38 i **6.10**.

Pociągi oznaczone *, służą dla bezpośredniej komunikacyi „Łódź — Warszawa" (bez przesiadania).

Kolej Warszawsko-Kaliska.

Odchodzą do Kalisza o godz. 6.35, 11.49 4.40, **do Warszawy** o godz. 9.12, 3.10. **Przychodzą z Kalisza** o godz. 9.17, 2.58, **8.35**.

Kolej obwodowa.

Odchodzą ze stacyi Łódź-kaliska do Słotwin o godz. **6.45**, ze Słotwin do Łódź-kaliskiej 10.10. Odchodzą ze st. Łódź-kaliska do Kojluszek **7.10**, przychodzą z Koluszek do st. Łódź-kaliska o godz. 6.20.

Uwaga. Godziny wydrukowane grubym drukiem oznaczają czas: **od 6 wieczór do 6 rano.**

Pamiętnik.

Sobota, 1 Lipca 1905 roku.

Kalendarzyk. Dziś: Teodoryka kapł.

Astronomiczny: Wschód sł. 341., zachód 8.24 długość dnia godz. 16.41.

KRONIKA.

OGÓLNA.

○ Ze spraw fabrycznych.

W papierach ministeryum skarbu — piszą „Now." — zachowała się ciekawa notatka statystyczna, dowodząca, do jakiego stopnia nieodpowiada ustawom zasadniczym prawa cywilnego obecne prawodawstwo fabryczne.

Ze sprawozdań inspektorów fabrycznych za lata 1901—1902 widać, że zastosowanie do robotników artykułu 51 o karach, karzącego za samowolne porzucenie roboty więzieniem do miesiąca, — otwierało możliwość szerokiej samowoli przedsiębiorcom, będąc jawną niesprawiedliwością w stosunku do robotników.

Z danych, zebranych przez ministeryum wywnioskować można, że przedsiębiorcy (którym prawo to niczem nie groziło) 8 razy częściej wykraczają przeciwko niemu niż robotnicy, podczas bowiem gdy pracodawcy skarżyli się na robotników za samowolne opuszczenie przez nich roboty 1200 razy, skarg robotników na samowolne usuwanie ich z fabryk było w tym samym okresie sprawozdawczym aż 10,000.

○ Reforma gimnazyów żeńskich.

Przy ministeryum oświaty utworzono — pod przewodnictwem członka komitetu naukowego J. G. Mora—komisyę dla opracowania reformy gimnazyów żeńskich, w których bez względu na zmienione warunki, działają ustawy i programy opracowane 30 lat temu.

Komisya opracowała już nowy projekt, który obecnie znajduje się w komitecie naukowym ministeryum.

Ogólne zasady, z których wychodziła komisya przy swych pracach, były następujące:

1) Obecne gimnazya żeńskie nie dają wykształcenia dostatecznego;

2) Nie dają swym wychowańcom odpowiedniego przygotowania do wstąpienia do wyższych zakładów naukowych;

3) Specyalna klasa 8 gimnazyów żeńskich, mająca za zadanie przygotowanie wychowanic do działalności pedagogicznej, wobec krótkiego kursu, nie odpowiada swemu celowi.

Komisya uznała za konieczne zrównać, o ile to okaże się możliwem, kurs gimnazyów żeńskich, z kursem gimnazyów męskich.

Szczególną uwagę zwrócono na naukę języków, które mają być przedmiotami obowiązkowemi, podczas gdy obecnie są zrównane z tańcami i kreśleniem — przedmiotami nieobowiązkowemi.

Fig. 5.1. The front page of *Goniec Łódzki* from 1905. Lodz University Library.

the community of readers but also about divisions separating the readers from other social groups and the tracing of the boundaries of presence (or imagining the place) for those groups.

Object of Welfare

Nineteenth-century European societies were battlegrounds of large urban populations striving for a better life. The growth of cities, worsening social problems, and political militancy created conditions different from those of the premodern period. The conundrum of poverty in the heart of industrial production was soon dubbed "the social question."[9] Increasing class struggle threatened to cause severe social turmoil, if not the overthrow of the capitalist mode of production. In addition, the recognition of work as a source of wealth and the emerging assumption of the basic equality of all people helped justify action.[10] In this situation, various solutions for reconstruction of the social bond were debated.

All those debates had counterparts in Polish intellectual life and journalistic accounts. In the beginning, they were rather abstract because the vagaries of industrialization were brought into debates between conservatives and proponents of potential modernization as distant examples from abroad, usually England.[11] Conservatives fiercely opposed industrialization because they were frightened by the dismantling of the traditional social bond. They dreamed about the development of an agrarian economy instead. The debate gained momentum with the arrival of the first serious industrial establishments. More tangible references were available on the spot, and the industrial hotbeds seemed to be harbingers of the capitalist future to come. Grounded in the agrarian heritage and the nobility's rural ethos, critiques of industrialization and urbanism mushroomed. Issues of industrial capitalism were a bone of contention between conservatives and positivists for years in the Polish debate.[12] Gradually the social question diffused and found its rearticulation in local circumstances.

However, it could not evolve for long because censors blocked explicit coverage of political topics. The higher echelons of Polish society hoped that the problems associated with the urban working class would miraculously bypass Polish lands.[13] Nevertheless, the awareness that the new social class was growing in numbers slowly came to the fore. As one commentator noted, it was high time to pay attention to those people, "whom we take into consideration so little, but they are decent, thrifty, full of solidarity, and working so hard that they deserve more general attention. This is unrecognized material full of new energies, which as soon as possible should be brought to light and simultaneously enlightened."[14]

As urban centers grew, they appeared to be quite different from the imagined benign rural industries run by modernized landed aristocrats. In sharp contrast to their predecessors, urban environments grew due to the influx of foreign capital, not the ingenuity of local agricultural business tycoons. The foreign origin of urban development was an object of public scorn, but at least the problem rose to prominence. It was clear that what was at stake—as one fearful writer warned—was "securing future generations against the worker question, which in Western Europe has swelled to the size of a social ulcer that makes abominable jokes."[15] Thus at first people tried to avoid the issue instead of addressing it. No wonder workers were seen as not holding any sway.

Simultaneously, much effort went into discrediting any attempt to organize workers politically. Not only were the tsarist authorities ruthless in suppressing early socialism, but the public elite bent over backward to show it in an unfavorable light.[16] Social conflict was perceived as an aberration that had to be policed and avoided at any cost. If only the dark forces of agitation had not incited narrow-minded workers, then a natural social harmony and cooperation between workers and their "bread givers" would have been possible. A particular form of liberalism, Polish positivism, arose to fill the ideological void after the collapse of the insurrectionist tradition. Polish liberals understood society as an organic whole, which enabled them to easily justify the existing social stratification and economic and legal differences between the higher and lower classes.[17] In an organic social body there was no place for conflict between the organs.

These exercises in political imagination initially had a spectral character. As was typical for a peripheral region with European ambitions, modernity was often disputed before any serious modernization began.[18] Correspondingly, the individual and collective rights of workers were debated too early because of the limited presence of the working class and too late in reference to "Western" developments.[19] Addressing this asynchronicity, more militant modern ideologies replaced the positivist-liberal consensus, also sidelining the old aristocratic conservatism. While explicitly conservative newspapers and magazines had low circulations, the ideas defended in those outlets were still distributed via the church pulpit to vast numbers of people. This is, however, a parallel story that rarely resurfaced in the urban press debate. There a plethora of new issues rose to prominence. The soaring yet still insular industrialization led the urban, social, and worker "questions" to be intensely debated.[20] There were already places in Russian Poland where capitalist modernization and the working-class presence could not be questioned. One of those was Lodz, where the social question was already a hotly, if timidly, disputed topic.

The issue of working-class life in Lodz was addressed as part of a broader discourse on the unequal development of the city and raging social and infrastructural problems. Before 1905 the "worker question" in a narrow sense was only occasionally present in the local press. Under censorship it would have been difficult to cover such a topic more extensively. It was also impossible, though, to ignore the vast domain of urban life in the industrial city. Although workers' living conditions were occasionally mentioned in *Dziennik Łódzki*, *Rozwój* and *Goniec Łódzki* gave workers full consideration.[21] In its first year, 1898, *Goniec Łódzki* noted that "the inhabitants of Lodz from other spheres paid little attention to this class and viewed people of workers' status as equivalent to machines."[22] In 1907 *Rozwój* reflected self-critically on its earlier negligence: "The workers' issue had already come to the fore because of the character of the city. Our paper, however, may not have treated it appropriately because of the exceptionally harsh censorship on that issue."[23] Meanwhile, working-class existence was part and parcel of the debate about urban life among outside observers astonished or shocked by Lodz reality, where people "live like scum and dregs of society."[24] The country-wide and local press criticized unfair social relationships, without questioning the basic tenets regulating them. Journalists were eager to expose the general ignorance, greed, and lack of civility in the wild, "Germanized" tumor on the Polish land, the vices that allegedly marked the urban polity and individual capitalists alike.[25] Occasionally, working-class life was a matter of scrutiny and moderate solutions proposed.

In the meantime, at the turn of the nineteenth and twentieth centuries, Lodz was no longer a city of workers and industrialists only. It started to attract a professional intelligentsia, and local multiethnic and multilanguage intellectual elites were slowly forged.[26] All these people considered Lodz to be somehow their "own" city; the Polish part ardently strove to make it acceptable to a harsh tribunal of Polish nationalism and general humanitarian sentiments.[27] A number of individuals overcame many hurdles to social activism. They—as one journalist expressed it—"wished to believe that regarding aspirations, one can find a lot of them," which could make up for "cultural traditions desperately lacking due to the city's short existence as an urban center."[28] They aimed at the improvement of workers' living conditions and "fulfillment of the basic requirements for a decent, healthy, and harmonious personal and public life."[29] While the mainstream press still harbored the positivist paradigm, it irreversibly declined in intellectual disputes heralding the changing direction of the 1890s.[30] Positivism's fratricidal offspring, new modern social and political movements spearheaded by socialism and nationalism, tended to perceive this "alien" and "bad" city as rather a challenge. This reaction stimulated new insight and invigorated the local debate as well. Lodz's public intellectuals ardently participated in the debate on welfare by rearticulating previously known diagnoses of the crisis. The local debate epitomized the general modern conundrum of how to organize societies facing industrial capitalism and defined the future trajectories of the local social welfare regimes.[31]

As has been widely documented by historians of the welfare state, a profound change in the assumed social order was indispensable for the introduction of general social provisions.[32] As Peter Wagner comments, "the introduction of early social policies obviously entailed to an intellectual transformation, in this case to a rethinking of the social bond, or of 'society.'"[33] Hence how society was conceptualized and imagined as a whole—and what kind of relationships between its groups, between individuals and impersonal mechanisms, such as the market were envisioned and reproduced in practice—all underwent powerful transformations.[34]

First of all, the lamented vagaries of capitalism had earlier been seen as transitory, and in the Polish case also as stemming from the distorted, foreign nature of capitalism. Consequently, people argued that the problems would go away, because the early stage had been passed and the proper, virtuous people had taken the reins of the market and production.[35] However, the much lamented problems refused to go away. Commentators realized that they were intransigent, entrenched products of industrial capitalism as such. As a result, they were ready to debate the possibilities of reform and intervention. Second, the growing awareness of these predicaments led to a certain generalization of responsibility. Individual misfortunes due to capitalist production and damage resulting from the new lifestyle were to be reframed as general consequences of a process one cannot individually control.

The belief grew that individuals should not be held entirely responsible for possible failures and harm that they experienced: for instance, in workplace accidents. It became possible to argue that industrialization had transformed the workplace reality into an essentially collective one in which industrial life itself, not the action(s) of any one individual, created new risks.[36] The urban poor's dwellings in shanty towns were no longer just temporary offshoots of urbanization or misfortunes haunting intellectually deficient and morally corrupt masses, deserving only of pity and some charity. They were seen as a problem that had to be somehow systemically overcome.[37] The situation was now perceived as structurally embedded in the existing conditions of urban capitalism.

In a similar vein, the discontents of early industrial capitalism stimulated local journalists in Lodz to expose the traps caused by private owners' limited liability. The sum of individual, profit-driven pursuits did not add up to a properly managed city. Although in early Russian Poland the state backed the development of capitalism, by the late nineteenth century the tsarist authorities exhibited a peculiar form of laissez-faire. As a result, capitalism in Russian Poland developed features much different from those of capitalism germinating in states with strong traditions of absolutist welfare. There flamboyant municipal buildings functioned in service to imperial states, and state-controlled policies took care of the biological stability of the urban population. In Russian Poland, however, the functions and real power of local government were mostly limited to military-style policing. The authorities were neither willing nor able to supplement urban social life with serious municipal management and protective institutions. And unsurprisingly, capitalist owners did not rush to build common infrastructure such as a sewer system, roads, and schools on their own.

In response, the local elites were called upon to take a more active stance in the "city with tens of thousands of Polish workers, and alongside them an entirely dispersed and idle intelligentsia, feeling completely alien in Lodz."[38] Articles in the local press engaged in an implicit critique of unregulated private property. The owners' selfishness was an equally common topic. The proponents of ideal hygiene singled out filthy, densely and carelessly built houses, which posed an epidemiological threat. "There is the power of millions, but there are no hospitals; there are many proudly protruding palaces but no hygienic flats for the hard-working masses; there are trimmed gardens but no public parks," reported one alarmed writer.[39] As the journalists looked for the reasons for such misery, they soon realized that these buildings were constructed in this way for a reason: a speculative rent extraction focused on short-term profits drawn from the poor and downtrodden inhabitants. Some tried to renegotiate the meaning of private property—arguing, for instance, that "a building in a large city is not only a property of this or that citizen, often a parvenu, who aims to draw the highest profits possible, but it is also to some extent common property."[40] It started to be a problem that "in Lodz, there are businesses worth millions gaining good profit but no schools."[41] Journalists were also acutely aware of the undesired consequences of the city's spatial layout. The aggregate of private plots and buildings did not help solve the problems of communal life, and all public spaces or facilities, from street lanterns and pavement to nonexistent urban greenery and a sewerage system, were neglected.[42] Thus the papers issued calls to take seriously one "of the long list of responsibilities of the city management" and regulate the spatial growth of the city, to "allow the growing population to settle properly."[43] In the ongoing attempts to find agencies capable of solving the problem, the reporters reevaluated private investment and attempted to appeal to certain moral commitments of the capitalists.[44] If the industrialists had become more integrated with local society, the common argument went, they would have undoubtedly been more eager to finance various benevolent establishments.

Philanthropic efforts were praised in those days of desperate need, when no other solution seemed viable to improve the pitiful conditions in the city. Various forms of "private biopolitics" were seen in a favorable light, as a benign effort to somehow improve the living conditions of the working class.[45] For example, in 1898, *Goniec Łódzki* reported on a factory district built by the textile tycoon Karol Scheibler for the upper echelons of his factory crew: "This is a district that in itself creates a small town. This is also the healthiest district, with many green areas, within easy reach of facilities and the rest of the city. Houses for workers in Księży Młyn, as well as the factory buildings, are decorated perfectly, both in terms of hygiene and practical use."[46]

Apt as it was, this description exemplifies the endorsement of any positive change without a broader critique targeting the existing institutional order. Some liberal writers considered similar projects as a viable alternative to the most rapacious type of capitalism yet did not question fundamental power and property relations or even invoke the idea of paternalistic care. The projects were clearly more than just philanthropy, and the owners of the associated factories made healthy profits from their investment in a less

Fig. 5.2. Karol Scheibler's factory in Lodz (Księży Młyn), the fire station, and workers' housing. Postcard. Courtesy of Łukasz Biskupski.

immiserated workforce. Later, although more systematic infrastructural projects, such as hospitals or the aforementioned district, still generated good publicity, the revolutionary turmoil led intellectuals to question the effectiveness of such efforts.

The scale of tension in 1905 made it clear that the meek steps undertaken by local civil society did not do enough to address the social question. The workers' outspoken political protest and explicit claims regarding their living and working conditions transformed the way the social question was conceptualized. The revolution encouraged new modes of critique to be expressed and bolder solutions to be debated. For instance, people said openly that voluntary measures did more for the reputation of local elites than the resolution of real social problems. They became increasingly regarded as for "capricious philanthropy," an almost useless hobby for factory owners' wives "who play in their own clique," which was nothing more than the publicly promoted "mountain that brought forth a mouse."[47] At first, the critics expected to see such efforts intensify, even if they continued to be based on principles of mercy, if not alms. After a while, however, the idea developed that philanthropy was more a symptom of pathological social relationships than a solution to local predicaments, as in an article from 1905: "Philanthropy has become such a fancy thing that [it seems that] philanthropists dress themselves and eat only to give people the possibility to earn money. But philanthropy exists only there, where poverty exists. A rich and well-organized country does not need philanthropy."[48] Similar diagnoses led commentators to postulate the creation of stable, impersonal institutions for taking care of the public good. Such a proposal encompassed the reconstruction of the alleged social bond. Not only were the poor not to blame for their hardships, but they deserved gestures of solidarity because the broader economic system had driven them into their present situation. Regrettably, as one contributor noted in 1907, society "was not able to create appropriate institutions." As a result, the most "vital needs of the population are entirely neglected or are taken care of by private institutions."[49] Even if such a plea was not considered a demand for universal public welfare, some assistance was deemed necessary for the greater good.

After all, some perils bred in urban slums would also harm affluent social strata. A contagious disease could easily spread throughout the city, germinating in dilapidated workers' housing, where "sewage-filled gutters flow across backyards with long ditches filled with swill and other filthy wastes."[50] Such a hygienist line of argument about the necessity to care for the public good was metonymically transferred to the economic-political nexus that was staked out during the revolution. Analogously, a miserable working-class district might be a source of uncontrollable social protest. Radiating out, it would infect other social strata until it endangered even the most detached urban elites. In press coverage during the revolution, pitiful living conditions were directly connected with moral degeneration and, later, political danger. The filthiness of a gutter was associated with moral decay, and contagious epidemics combined with moral illnesses: "starvation and plague will spread, poverty will grow, common despondency will increase, and against the backdrop of hunger and despair—immorality and felony will blossom with the most exuberant flowers again."[51] If seen in this light, both types of social problems demanded coordinated efforts toward their solution. For the first time a systemic proposal for reform emerged; one grounded in state-backed social institutions. The solution for the "stupidity and greed of the powerful, the only medicine," was a tax imposed by a more democratic state structure.[52]

The revolution made it clear that the worsening problems would not go away. A growing number of commentators noticed that the previous measures were not enough. Ideas for institutional reform mushroomed, and the social bond was consciously reconstructed. The social question was not an individual tragedy writ large and had to be addressed accordingly—but certainly not by waiting for aggregated individual efforts by the rich, made out of mercy or personal interest. The revolution spurred on the conceptualization of the social question as a political problem.

An Object of Pedagogy

Once workers descended from the heights of the abstract "social question" and "industrial squalor" to become a more tangible topic of reflection, they also became objects of moral supervision. Their general mores, drunkenness, and immodest living were scrutinized in the broader framework of moral indignation that targeted the vices of industrial cities. Such a city fostered a materialist attitude, which among workers "eliminates personal and national dignity, deforms characters, and develops brutish instincts."[53] Above all, however, the sexual misconduct of working women demanded regulation. Young working-class women were allegedly "spending their time on love affairs and mindless loitering," which made them susceptible to immoral living.[54] Such women were in the urban environment, and above all in the workplace, "exposed to temptations" in "the morally unhealthy atmosphere"; especially when "left without custody, they often massively derail" their lives.[55] Such presentations reinforced the widely held conviction that the urban employment of women led to prostitution.[56] Admittedly, in cases of obvious abuse, the foremen were openly accused as those who "throw handfuls of seeds of debauchery among the female workers, whispering ambiguous yet obscene words, cynical jokes or allowing themselves dirty jokes, which make their [the females'] faces flush."[57] Indeed, sexual harassment, such as coerced sexual services in exchange for factory employment, was a common practice and a hotly debated topic in public discourse.[58] While interventions were often targeted at individual villains such as seditious foremen, the main culprit of social critique generally remained the working class with its declining moral standards.

Before the revolution, a way out of moral degeneration was sought in a male breadwinner model and a tidy working-class household with a wife taking care of the children. This was usually a desired, yet by no means attainable, ideal. Hardly any working-class family could aspire to such comfort.[59] Thus additional assistance from those with more significant property was encouraged. Correspondingly, the new social contract, which might have stabilized the situation, was often modeled on restoring elements of the precapitalist moral economy. Oddly enough, it was often proselytized by local liberals. In the Polish context, they were more hesitant to endorse the marketization of the social bond than elsewhere. By this gesture they resisted foreign social models undermining Polish traditions, as in this statement from 1899:

> In the society of today it could not be any other way, for everything must have a value calculated with clanging coins. . . . Such an arrangement is very comfortable for one of the sides [of the labor contract] but does not go well with the obligations that every employer must take into consideration as a member of society. An employee [that is, worker in this context] is paid scandalously little. Apart from fulfillment of his material needs, the employee should feel that his work gains recognition, he should have signals that what he is doing brings some benefit, he desires to be a part of the enterprise not only materially but also integrated with ties of human feelings.[60]

This paternalist vision of the moral economy was supplemented with ideas of social amelioration. For a long time "alleviating the lot of the poor" was mostly conceptualized as a philanthropic activity, supporting those unable to keep up with modern life. Providing appropriate housing or pedagogical assistance was seen as a preventive measure against moral degeneration. The dreadful threat of riots, bred in those locales, rose to prominence when the situation became serious because of the massive political upheaval on the streets of Lodz in 1905. Then paternalistic projects were revived in the name of political control of the recalcitrant population.

In the opening months of the revolution, the press was very moderate in reporting the events and investigating their broader social contexts because of the still-present preventive censorship. Journalists, however, attempted various esoteric strategies to work in references to the ongoing events; it was essential for maintaining any credibility of their publications at a time of emerging mass protest, which was shaking the foundations of the existing order. References to the working-class protests were made by the extensive coverage of parallel events abroad, such as during the January general strike.[61] A few days later an extensive analysis of the state-backed insurance system for workers was presented, covering government statements but also clearly analyzing broader social implications of the new policies, which would stimulate "cultural and ethical development and enhance consciousness among workers."[62] Moreover, writers were occasionally quite explicit in explaining what could and what could not be said. It was, for instance, openly explained that only direct quotations from the Russian press, already approved by the censor, were an available source of information, before such a "readers' digest" could be presented.[63]

Apparently, the intellectual elites were already perfectly aware of the acuteness of the situation and sought desperately to comprehend the new reality in their thoughts and writings. Timidly, they started to problematize their own attitudes toward workers, becoming aware how much they neglected the social strata allegedly requiring moral leadership. The now successful socialist mobilization funneled emotions in a radical direction, not favorable to the intelligentsia. Facing such a situation, the liberal and nationalist intelligentsia was frightened by the independent activity of the people.

This independence was probably the biggest scandal. Whenever workers got the upper hand in their revolutionary activity, outside commentators immediately bent over backward to demonstrate some form of external leadership imposed on them. Clearly, the assumed hidden command and painstakingly revealed secret forms of control were a safe haven for the intelligentsia's mindset. While saving their general mode of social analysis, this thought pattern compromised any accurate insight into the situation. In a striking contrast to these allegations, in fact socialist parties tried hard, but they were not able to control the movement to a sufficient degree. Writers from the intelligentsia simply fantasized about a leadership that barely existed. Any action not compliant with the intelligentsia's imaginations was immediately associated with the intellectual, cultural, and above all political immaturity of a working class susceptible to foreign tutelage. The immediate answer, as in the story about the dream quoted above, was to call upon the right leader, personified by the intelligentsia itself. In the middle of 1905 one journalist stipulated:

> There could be only one answer—to get closer to the people and knock out of the hands of different social ferments the rudder over those unenlightened, hence little resistant, minds. Just as ears of grain are easily bent to the ground by a blow of wind, the poor masses [*rzesze*] follow the whispers of people foreign to the national good [*dobru krajowemu*], harming themselves and their [relatives]

and their country, harming the country that they undoubtedly warmly love. . . . The situation is serious. One must save the country against the approaching dangers. We must, as the country's intelligentsia, get close to the people, who today do not trust us; one must try to take the leadership to those broad strata.[64]

It seems that "foreign" tutelage of the Polish people—that is, the workers driven by Jewish or foreign socialist agitators—was easier to admit than a redistribution of social leadership. It became a stock explanation, trotted out to explain the new, "unbelievable" political agency. It blazed the path for various Jewish conspiracy theories that gradually came to the fore. The theories addressed the same need to explain the inexplicable (from an elitist point of view), rendering the masses as unavoidably passive and reactive.[65] Those who produced these theories built on the same scaffolding that was used by the more benign ethos of the social mission and tutelage. No doubt, however, there was an internal differentiation within this broader discourse.

The intelligentsia's paternalism had many faces. It was more oriented toward direct control, although sometimes it was less condescending in *Rozwój*. This journal was not willing to undermine the solid base of property ownership. Instead, it favored a rock-solid nation as a foothold for solidarity and cohesion. This view funneled its move in the direction of "sober" work with workers while keeping them in their inferior positions. Gestures intended to recognize workers' dignity at the same time verified their submission, solidifying their place in the social and national hierarchy. For instance, while calling for dignified workers' dress as a symbol of sober decency, the journal retained the image of the workers' submissive role as the gray mass of producers, with dignity assuming just the right social mantle.[66] Moreover, *Rozwój* was not reluctant to claim that the basic predicament was that "the worker walked alone and uncared for [*samopas*]," just like a child.[67] Journalists were at least aware how far their fantasies could be from the real social problems they attempted to address. To challenge this isolation, *Rozwój* launched a campaign aimed at revealing the "real being of the worker"—for instance, announcing a contest for a letter describing a worker's life and grievances.[68] This desire for knowledge, however, did not seem to lessen the yearning for power over the workers.

For its part, the more liberal *Goniec Łódzki* and its subsequent replacements were slightly more supportive of workers' claims. This enthusiasm notwithstanding, contempt for the uneducated masses was present as an undercurrent.

The more open the vision of society was, and the more prominent the place the popular classes occupied, the more liberal public opinion failed to conceal its disappointment with workers' actual political performance. The "leading broad popular masses" from 1905 were easily transformed into the "abysmally dark broader masses" of 1907, within the same generally liberal discourse on educating the people.[69] The masses in the streets made it clear that if the urban bourgeoisie and the Polish intelligentsia did not manage the social issue better, the revolution would pose a danger to their decent lives. Various political milieus called for action to either discipline, or at least educate, "the masses."

Even illiteracy was coded as a factor directly posing a threat of anarchy and disintegration. In a manifesto of sorts, directed at local intellectuals, *Goniec* announced: "Renewed social life—after overcoming the plague of anarchy—will pour into new forms and be organized anew."[70] This striking passage is calling for universal mobilization to fight illiteracy. The manifesto was to become one of the founding texts for the renewed ethos of social mission among the Polish provincial intelligentsia. The numerous members of the local elite who signed it, however, did not want to wait for it to happen—they "consider(ed) as [their] holy obligation now to declare war against illiteracy." The main point of reference was anarchy and disorder. Social life had to be rethought because "new foundations for social and state life were emerging." When the "wheel of history rotated exceptionally fast," there were "the broad, people's masses" who were to "retake the scepter of social leadership"—at least the intelligentsia thought so, not without fear for the future, when "the frightening power of illiterates" may take this scepter. Therefore, now for "everybody who was able to read and write," a "magnificent and holy obligation" was to "become a teacher of the people." Disorder had to be averted.[71] This caused a highly intensified feeling of obligation to line up and face the approaching challenge.

In the eyes of local journalists facing this crisis, moral and cultural rules were melting into thin air. The solution could be found only in the renewed sense of good and evil clearly provided by universal humanitarian values. They could be reestablished only—in the still positivist spirit shared among most of the local journalists from both dailies—through education: "This difficult and arduous task can be achieved by constant, well-organized, and intentionally peaceful work aimed at raising the level of ethical culture in our city, at making customs gentler [and] citizens more civilized, getting rid of illiteracy, making notions and terms rational, building wealth, developing a school system—in a word, propagating the ideals of work, justice, and a love of higher virtues."[72]

Rhetoric like the above came back with renewed intensity in the later phases of the revolution. The intelligentsia's belief in social vocation shaped its attitude toward the popular classes. Its educational mission helped maintain its conviction about immature, passive workers as an object of pedagogy and not an active counterpart in politics. This view in turn supported the perception of workers as always being either guided or manipulated, dependent on the intelligentsia's leadership but never genuinely active themselves. If the leadership was conspicuously nonexistent, it was invented by critics as a secret steering wheel behind the scenes. This idea filled in certain blanks in the existing grid of the intelligentsia's social imagination. Although the will to educate was maintained, its object evolved. It was no longer the unenlightened yet benign Polish people being shown the light but the dark masses that had to be forcefully returned from the road to crime. All in all, the treatment imagined by the intelligentsia was rejected by its resistant patients. Nonetheless, there were also other voices paying lip service to the "workers' cause."

Political Agents and Claimants

The revolution made the workers political actors who had to be taken into account even by the social strata that were most hostile to their political agency. Public opinion was divided in how it evaluated the performance of these new claimants. Many greeted with hope the new political regime characterized by mass participation. Even people who were not happy with workers asserting their power still believed that the working-class protest might push the tsar to introduce political reforms or expand the kingdom's autonomy. Others soon became frightened by the unleashed dynamics of mass politics, which clearly—in a vicious, inductive loop with tsarist repression—destabilized the country, threatening decent burghers and their property. The Lodz press tried to mediate between these positions, acknowledging some form of political citizenship for workers while carefully circumscribing its limits. At first the journalists could not express themselves openly, but from month to month, especially after the change in the censorship law in the fall of 1905, the potential for a vivid debate increased.

For instance, *Goniec Łódzki*'s coverage of the Lodz uprising and barricade fights in June 1905 was still scarce and rough; the paper reported only the censorship-approved facts without much commentary. Even within these narrow margins of freedom, one contributor managed to unambiguously suggest that the Jews were mostly involved. While giving an account of the transreligious solidarity among working-class contenders, he again denied the possibility of genuine working-class political action, pointing to forceful agitators, whom he held responsible for the unrest (and hence its victims).[73] It is noticeable that even under censorship a careful selection of words or connections between objects and actors might be indicative for readers. Moreover, the limits of the speakable were slowly broadened.

At roughly the same time in the same paper, there was already space to acknowledge the legitimacy of strike demands—above all, for an eight-hour workday, basic social insurance, and the right to strike as a guarantee for the legal negotiation of labor contracts.[74] An important step toward recognizing a strike as legitimate was to question the usual conviction about strikes ruining "the country," its factories, and the workers themselves. That was the chief argument of factory owners and many conservatives against protest activities. By referring to this debate and using economic reports and statistical data, the reporter argued that "it is not that bad" after all. Allegedly the factory owners were quoting data selectively to create the impression of misery. "Not only did the Lodz industry not collapse, . . . but it intensified," announced the paper, clearly siding with the workers, who were often accused of causing universal misery and ruination.[75] This approach paved the way for the recognition of working-class protest as legitimate.

With the journalists' hands still tied by censors, this legitimacy was carefully negotiated: for instance, by reprinting articles published elsewhere in Russia where censorship was less sensitive to the worker question.[76] Sometimes the bourgeoisie were held accountable for making a progressive proposal, framed as protecting the public peace and Russian statehood. It was the workers, however, who were to gain broader agency: "The industrialists do not believe in the efficacy of police assurances that they may calm minds. In their view, the only response that can stop the workers' movement throughout the state and urge workers to their proper work is legal equality between workers and other populations, giving them an opportunity to have their own representatives in the parliament. . . . This change may calm the workers and counteract the revolutionary agitation."[77] Liberals and nationalists alike understood that their political competitors succeeded for a reason. Socialists actually addressed serious social grievances. The old explanation about lacking social bonds lost any credibility, and journalists were ready to admit that some legal regulations in favor of workers' demands would be needed. "These were the employers who sinned; with a few exceptions, they treated their workers only as a labor force, did not penetrate their mental needs, did not attempt to get closer to them, and did not recognize an individual with equal social rights. . . . One may rein in socialist agitation in only one way: by taking into consideration the righteous demands of workers."[78] It was no longer a vague obligation to grant concessions out of humanitarian sensitivity. Now the demands that workers were making mattered. Such a shift opened a space for the explicit endorsement of certain economic demands made by protesters. For instance, striking female textile workers received explicit support when—as one journalist commented—"they understood the reason for their existential failures and unstable legal position and wished to improve their situation by stopping the exploitation." Their demands were explicitly considered as "moderate and righteous," and therefore it was deemed "surprising why they had not yet been fulfilled."[79] One reason was an increased awareness of the general working-class contribution to social life; the experience of strikes changed workers' sense of who they were, and outside observers realized that workers' contribution to the general social edifice had to be recognized. This led authors to draw effective conclusions from the initially liberal idea of social productivity based on labor.[80] While discussing the poor conditions of working-class housing, *Goniec* stated without hesitation: "Lodz owes its present growth, all its significance and might exclusively to the working mass, directly or indirectly."[81] This recognition of productive powers was accompanied by a more favorable attitude to workers' political practices. The space of the doable clearly expanded as well.

There were even authors ready to acknowledge the political competence of strikers and protesters. This argument was made not just in favor of the workers but also against those critics who dragged socialists through the mud as irresponsible rabble-rousers. Additionally, it also contrasted "Polish workers" with the alleged "Russian disorder," thus criticizing the Russian autocracy while assuming the mantle of the real supporters of order. "Thanks to the consciousness of our people, thanks to their political competence, anarchy is not ruling us. In moments of the greatest weakness of the old government, there was an exemplary order here. We have seen demonstrations of thousands kept in order not with a bayonet and a whip but by signs orchestrated by parties organizing the rallies."[82] Speaking about the political competence of the marching workers was a pivotal reversal of the previous paternalism. Some members of the intelligentsia decided to side with the rising working-class political constituencies. Amid the usual condescending pedagogy, examples of assigning to workers a sense of political responsibility expressed in their actions were significant. Similarly, during the Duma elections, people commented that "the workers gave yet more evidence of their political maturity and had convinced their elder brothers that they were not afraid of scarecrows at all" by not following the "reactionary" agitation.[83] All in all, the strike activity and political action around the ballot allowed working-class protesters to gain some recognition among the general public. While striking, their actual role in general social productivity was tangibly demonstrated by downing their tools. This helped them to be considered important—not only capitalists moved the wheels of progress. Many times, strikers were able to build new constituencies and show evidence of a systematic pursuit of social and political goals. As a result, workers were admitted to the category of active citizens by more progressive commentators.

Participants in Struggle

Although they admitted the workers into the political realm, the journalists did not easily abandon the vision of gradual social transformation. While not endorsing the revolution straight away, they did reverse the usual course of argumentation. Promises of modernity were, in their view, put into practice by none other than the workers. This time the capitalists were held responsible for preventing the organic social transformation from coming to fruition. The notion of the "righteous" and stable political regime was maintained, but in its new articulation it was the workers who facilitated its rise:

> A new political regime is only righteous and long-lasting if it rises by natural means—that is, the general work of creation. Thus the elements that in this mixture do not interact—that is, classes that during chaos and turmoil are not influencing each other—are simply to be considered superfluous. And among such redundant elements there is our capitalist class. Today, when turmoil and chaos have taken over classic relationships, the capitalist class has not taken any steps to create new, more appropriate modes of life and normalize the relationships between classes according to the requirements of life.[84]

This dubious social imaginary, not so deftly combining evolutionism and chemistry, was accompanied with quite open criticism of the existing state of affairs: "this blood-sucking hydra, this constrictor of any uninhibited life and development of the population, this executioner of the working class . . . [is] the old and rotten regime, whose one head is bureaucracy and the other—capitalism."[85]

Goniec was from 1906 on usually ready to admit divergent interests of conflicted social groups. Because of the revolution, which clearly pitted social groups against each other, it for the most part abandoned the imperative of social harmony and accepted the class-based description of society instead. Some journalists suggested the class nature of conflict straight away and did not hesitate to use language that was borderline Marxist. According to one journalist, "every sociopolitical revolution, and without a doubt the current revolution is like this, is a time of an intensified class struggle. The greater the struggle of the destitute class, the bigger are this class's gains after the revolution."[86] This wording hardly concealed an antagonistic vision of society and admitted the agency held by the "destitute class." It was already a critique explicitly addressing the features of the entire social and political system; from here it was only a small step to accepting the Marxist interpretation of social and economic reality. The *Goniec* publicists did not, however, adopt the Marxist concept of exploitation, as Kamil Śmiechowski has demonstrated.[87] Whenever the notion of exploitation appeared on their pages, it was in a commonsense meaning of abuse. Exploitation was an unfair relationship that put one side under economic pressure, and the mode of critique remained rather personal.

Nevertheless, in the press coverage it became a truism that the main parties in conflict were workers and factory owners. In the first months of the revolution broad social strata were supportive of (or at least not hostile to) the workers' struggle. Liberal writers hoped for a loosening of the grip of the tsarist autocracy and generally sympathized with the workers' demands for a more dignified existence. This support, however, did not change the condescending pedagogical attitude toward "the masses." The journalists hoped for the development of working-class politics directed against autocracy, under the leadership of the intelligentsia but with the tacit support of the capitalists. They were expected to make some minor concessions, just to keep class conflict at bay. These hopes appeared to be in vain, however, and the industrialists were soon blamed for the disorder: "Today, when disorder and chaos have entered into classical relationships, the capitalist class has not taken any steps to create new, more appropriate modes of life and form relationships between classes adequately."[88]

Instead of the "new modes of life" replacing "disorder and chaos," the tension grew after months of strikes. The owners decided to wage a deliberate and organized class struggle from above. Postponing the competition between factories, they cooperated to suppress workers' unrest. The goal was to leave no doubt as to who ruled the factories. Using some minor pretext, in late 1906 they instigated a lockout at the major Lodz factories.[89] Mutual assistance—earlier a pillar of prolonged protest—was no longer possible, as everybody was unemployed. The owners stated rather explicitly that their aim was to restore the relationships between employers and employees from before the revolution. The bone of contention was no longer the length of the workday or the daily wage. Trampling on the heads of workers, who dared to claim any agency while collectively bargaining about working conditions, was the agenda of the day. A harsh conflict began, ultimately won by the entrepreneurs.

During the great lockout, press opinion bifurcated. Initially, *Rozwój* clearly called for an agreement. In response to the capitalists' firmness, however, *Rozwój* called on workers to give up and accept the offered conditions.[90] Doing so would in many cases mean the return of prerevolutionary shop-floor reality. Not only would longer hours be back, but the hard-won right to take part in decisions about factory life would be lost. Some liberal commentators, however, clearly sided with the workers. This triggered a heated debate in the papers about industrial relations, human dignity, and justice. In the beginning, the line of contention concerned responsibility for the misery raging in the city. Later, however, more systematic approaches to the conflict were also proposed.

Just after the factories were closed, *Kurier* indirectly placed responsibility for the dramatic situation on party factionalism and revolutionary action sliding into quarrels, internal fights, and banditry.

> And—in the name of victory of narrow-minded party programs—we are ready to wreck the humanity, fatherland, and freedom in us. Woe to the vanquished! So here the nationalist parties blame the progressive ones and spit on them, the latter in turn give as good as they get, baptize the former as local hooligans [*chuliganeria rodzima*] . . . And against the backdrop of this party struggle a most

frightening abscess grows, signifying moral depravity and social anarchy—the banditry. . . . No, it's not a struggle, it's lethal insanity, sick madness, rising in revolutionary times among degenerated individuals, desiring and willing blood and murder, regardless why and to whom.[91]

Despite these initial accusations, the journalists were also critical of the owners. The attack on the industrialists was an implicit interdiscourse, targeting the national democratic offensive that had blamed socialist activists for all the misfortunes. Progressive liberals asserted that it was not workers' political activity but capitalist practices that were the true anarchy. One commentator stated: "I am one of the most ardent enemies of social anarchy, I am a supporter of a possibly high level of social order, and therefore I will always demonstrate that present social relations are grounded precisely on a deep anarchy—even worse, because in the present situation, a tiny minority is able to enact brutal physical violence over the overwhelming majority."[92] Such an analysis of the situation had an immediate effect. The journalists were now able to recognize the structural constraints that limited opportunities. Simultaneously, writers recognized in the conflict a final clash between two antagonistic forces. One of them, although stronger, could not deprive the other of its acquired agency:

> The brutal resistance, iron durability, and ruthless consistency of the stronger and mightier are not able to disarm the no less stubborn workers; on the contrary, [the opposition] stimulates them to struggle, to contest, to try out their powers. Workers believe today unbreakably in the power of Work to be bigger than the power of Capital; they believe today in the might of their righteousness and justice—and this faith is their undeniable feature, which nobody can take from them. This feature and other healthy convictions, the feeling of solidarity above all, will substitute entirely for the lack of strong and unified organization.[93]

What is clearly visible in this argument is a new mode of social analysis. It was no longer a critique targeting individual vices and the cultural mismatch of foreign capitalists not maintaining proper ties with the country hosting them. Instead, the left-liberal press clearly started to envision the social dynamic as a clash of antagonistic forces: classes with clear yet contradictory interests. The solution proposed could no longer be grounded in a reestablished social harmony. Now it was rather a matter of institutional transformation; the introduction of the state as a mediating agent was indispensable for working out any modus vivendi. Personal traits of "capitalists" were somehow related to their place in the organization of production, and their property created an insolvable disparity of power. This disparity effectively closed off any possibility for renegotiation or collective bargaining. A third party had to be brought in: "And here lies not only the source of dissatisfaction. The source of real poverty of the proletariat. Without state intervention, the proletariat is helpless against the conduct of factory owners. In the interest of factory owners always lies the subtlest utilization of everything that enables exploitation. Here too humanity is exploited. The high 'justice' and 'humanitarian values' of capitalists are well known to everybody who takes a closer look at the life of the proletariat or attempts to know the actual position of the proletariat in the world and the history of its movements."[94]

The critique went as far as to unambiguously equate capitalism with anarchy, which was previously expressed in this way only by the Social Democrats. An additional dimension was introducing the state into the analysis. More democratic relationships—as the assumption went—would allow for a more civilized articulation of interests and conflict resolution. Simultaneously, they would prevent the equally harmful disorders of class-state and popular rebellion. "Capitalist states only protected the justice of the owning classes and there was a disorder there; had they begun to democratize and slowly acknowledged the justice of workers, an order would have started to stabilize. . . . The removal of anarchy 'from above' is a condition for the removal of anarchy 'from below.'"[95] It is important to note that the social imaginary did evolve, and workers gained a certain right to act publicly and make demands. Some changes could not have been reversed. Even conservative spheres acknowledged that collective mediation was needed to solve the problem. One of the industrial moguls leading the lockout, Maurycy Poznański, admitted in an interview that collective negotiations were indispensable because the tsarist police apparatus was no longer able to secure any level of order. He also indirectly confirmed that it was the workers' protest that caused "the authority of a whip to be irreversibly gone" and remarked that it had "to be replaced with the self-consciousness of the workers."[96] In the nationalist bourgeois press tending toward the National Democracy party, such as Lodz's *Rozwój*, workers were also often presented as victims. Maybe they had violated the assumed codes of conduct, but only because of a lack of education and proper institutions.[97] The danger was seen as a general predicament demanding social reconstruction and not as an outcome of the admittance of improper actors to politics.

All in all, the dynamics of conflict reshuffled the social imaginary perpetuating press coverage. For many it was now clear that there was an unbridgeable antagonism between work and capital, represented by particular actors on the local scene. It was acknowledged as nonsense that industrialists would have acted benevolently toward their employees had they only recognized the principles of social harmony. As a result, the working-class protest gained the right of existence. In progressive titles, a more class-conscious discourse emerged. The situation was analyzed in terms of conflict between class-based interests, which, due to the inequality of power, turned into exploitation. Admittedly, the writers did not go so far as to adopt the Marxist analysis of social conflict. Some of them, however, clearly recognized the working-class protest as a legitimate, and in fact hardly avoidable, means of negotiation between the irredeemably conflicted parties. Once social antagonism was brought to the fore, proposals for its mediation by some neutral, higher-level institutions were forged. Thus the role of collective bargaining was for the first time seriously considered and the role of the state, even if in a hypothetical mode, was debated.

The Fear Factor

The public presence of new social groups was not, however, accepted with ease. Alternative public spheres and explicit claims undermining the existing order were perceived ambivalently. The proliferation of street violence did not help the cause. Mass politics on the streets was orchestrated by a new type of organization—mass, often illegal parties—if it was organized at all.[98] The politics of the ballot during subsequent Duma elections was not part and parcel of any full-fledged parliamentarian democracy; it nevertheless ushered in new phenomena and political tactics. The forceful electoral campaigning and bitter conflict about participation versus boycott of the election led to unrest and brawls, revealing the less pleasant face of mass democracy. All in all, as a revolution deserving its name, the events of 1905–1907 were far from the pastoral idealization of the people in politics. The ongoing events did not meet the expectations of the intelligentsia, even its radical segment. Progressive members of the elite were ready to accept a moderate redefinition of political visibility but rejected a deeper renegotiation of social roles and distribution of wealth. Frightened burghers and directly threatened factory owners were even more anxious and later hostile.[99] They were susceptible to the politics of fear.

Liberals also remained helpless. The revolution was simultaneously their biggest success and their greatest failure. They gained real opportunities when politics moved out of the underground, which had been their dream since the 1870s. During the 1905–1907 period former positivists and younger liberals, now called progressives, were able to organize active political organizations and corollary associations like the Polish Culture Association (Towarzystwo Kultury Polskiej). However, after this political coming out, the serious political weakness of the liberal intelligentsia and its alienation from the masses became apparent.[100] As Maciej Janowski notes, liberals "gained an opportunity to take political action exactly at the same time as they lost real political influence through a sudden radicalization of society."[101] The rise of "politics in a new key" heralded the twilight of the old-style liberalism proselytizing an elite ideal of decent and detached reasoning and debate.[102] In the reality of the revolution, neither activism nor retained social esteem were sufficient for an effective political bid.

The failure to grasp new circumstances characterized even noted intellectuals like Aleksander Świętochowski, the main figure of Polish liberalism.[103] It also haunted local leaders. The change in perceptions of the revolution can be traced through the memoirs of Aleksander Mogilnicki, a prominent liberal lawyer from Lodz. He initially collected contributions to the strike fund among local elites; later, however, he bitterly noted:

> It is easier to initiate a storm than to control it. Every revolution evolves differently than its initiators planned. Initial ideological reasons often perish when the masses reveal their worst instincts.... During the fight for freedom (which means just holding power) the biggest failure for socialist leaders is a wealthy worker. If workers were satisfied with their living conditions, socialist parties would become to a large extent obsolete and their leaders would have to undertake productive labor. Thus many socialist leaders had an interest in maintaining discontent among workers. As a result, the strikes, which were initially politically focused and directed against tsarist absolutism, which was so beneficial for the whole society, lost their political and national character. Political parties took control over them, and the workers, who were for ideological reasons not working for a long time, became happy with this idleness and began to organize militias murdering each other in madness.[104]

Such analysis underpinned presumptions about "the people" widespread in liberal circles. Not only did it express disappointment with the economic claims behind strikes, but it also offered a practical sociology of leadership explaining the activity of "the masses" without questioning the assumption about their apolitical passivity. The liberal diagnosis was clear: the workers were immature and too irresponsible for active participation in politics. The intelligentsia began to believe that the revolution was not a serious social movement, just a blind act of violence inspired by "aliens," including Jews and various socialist instigators who were either pursuing their own private interests or the wicked and bloody visions of political ideologues.

It would be an exaggeration to claim that the revolution triggered a direct oligarchic, counterdemocratic reaction among the Polish elite.[105] The growing civic activity of the Polish popular classes was undoubtedly crushed by the tsarist repression. However, the revolution among the Polish intelligentsia was both broadly greeted with awe and severely criticized as the uncontrolled outburst of the untamed masses, similar to the well-known late nineteenth-century pattern of conservative critique.[106] In the Polish context the anxiety about tsarist reprisal may have also played a role, especially among older generations still harboring the shock of repressions after the 1863 uprising and intellectually brought up in an atmosphere of positivist rejection of any confrontational measures. Regardless of the reasons, the reaction of the Polish intelligentsia to the masses protesting in the streets and reading and debating in factories was ambivalent at best and openly hostile at worst.[107] The intelligentsia's faith in a benign Polish people withered away, introducing an unbridgeable gap in the imagined body politic of the Polish nation.

Adding insult to injury, this tendency deepened the bifurcation of the public sphere into enlightened critique and popular protest, assuming a mantle even less acceptable to the nonproletarian social strata.[108] A powerful, conservative, discursive offensive was launched to condemn the "sewage masses" and "furious mobs" called to battle by "foreign socialists" and other "degenerated individuals," all in all "masons, Jews, and socialists, a perfectly matched trio heading toward the overthrow of Christian societies."[109] Some not so marginal commentators were ready to issue opinions usually seen rather as a satirical creation designed to mock dubious conspiracy theories: "the mob is today overtaken by socialists, who lead on a leash the factory folks and blindly obey the commands of foreign masonic and Jewish conspiracies."[110] This discursive configuration fostered the long-lived trope of

Judeocommunism nurturing Polish antisemitic discourses still used today, and in a less explicit way also penetrating more moderate forms of thought.[111] During the revolution it also spread widely, not limiting itself to antisemitic sectarianism, and often supported "racialized" hatred toward the masses.[112] Antisemitism was part and parcel of the antirevolutionary reaction and actually helped explain the new political reality with stock patterns of thought.

It was the nationalists who successfully addressed the growing unease and profited heavily from the general weariness with revolutionary unrest. Their political imagination and party structure took a turn toward discipline and autocratic order, which spurred on the fight against revolutionary "anarchy."[113] This offensive delivered the rhetorical ammunition for the successful management of the fears of a destabilized society. Anti-Jewish discourse introduced by the National Democrats helped find a culprit to blame for the disorder. Antisemitism also accompanied the politics of the ballot, spreading widely over many political discourses during the elections to the Third, and especially the Fourth, Dumas in 1907 and 1912, respectively.[114] Indeed, it proved powerful enough to make the National Democracy party a hegemonic power in the Polish public sphere for a number of years (even in the absence of formal power), thus infecting the political discourse and Polish national identity with the vicious germ of antisemitism.

Even Henryk Sienkiewicz, a leading Polish writer who had recently ascended the heights of fame, influence, and authority by receiving a Nobel Prize in 1905, chose to side with the National Democrats. He harshly criticized the revolution in his novel *Whirlpools* (*Wiry*). In one of the few fragments in which the writer/narrator, not one of the protagonists, directly states his opinion, he describes revolutionary events as "abominable screams, exciting the mob [*czerń*] more and more," among which a "human animal" is unleashed to get in on an "orgy of destruction"—that is, to plunder the property of decent citizens. The revolutionaries are described as "disheveled women, filthy juveniles with marks of crime on their degenerated facial lines and all sorts of ragamuffins with drunken faces."[115] Such physiognomic depictions mobilized anthropological categories known from the positivist criminology of Cesare Lombroso and supported the "racialization" of political difference.[116]

Only against the backdrop of this reaction raging among Polish public opinion can the specificity of the provincial press be grasped. It reflected these general tendencies but also tried to nuance voices and accommodate available conceptual grids to the actual situation in the working-class city. Undoubtedly, the power of the mass, anonymous crowd flocking to the streets and capable of pushing tsarist troops out of the way was an exciting yet frightening avatar of modern politics. Writers dreaming for decades about building the Polish political nation could not help but realize that the only chance to do it was slipping out of their hands. They proved completely incapable of tuning in to the moods of street politics. While remaining excited by politicized crowds, they were nonetheless fearful of their ultimate political choices. Against the backdrop of these fears, the interplay between the crowd and its leaders attracted special attention. It was believed to be key to understanding the new realities.

One such encounter was described in the following words: "A thin man, with pale, sunken cheeks, surrounded by a sparse, reddish growth of hair. Eyes small, running, shiny. On his face a smile scorning, scoffing. Hands in pockets of a worn-out overcoat. It seems that they [the people around] are moving, as if looking for something. . . . Looks like a shiver shook people gathered around. The adored lyrics of the 'Red Banner' moved like the wind over an ear of grain, and in his eyes bad reflexes appeared. He straightened, raised his hand, and his voice was almost a scream."[117]

The fragment is stylized as a documentary sketch rather than a standard newspaper article. Even if it admits the power of words, it nevertheless unambiguously suggests the hidden agenda of this interaction. The anthropological and behavioral details reveal the nature of the agitator between the lines. A handful of gentle measures suggests the foreign and inauthentic origins of the successful agitator. He may be triumphant in leading the crowd, but by no means was he a natural leader. His position is undeserved and usurping.[118] The mass under his tutelage is not realizing its potential and "natural" destinies.

There was a feedback loop between the agitator and his followers, which constituted the local variant of politics in the new key. It clearly ruined the political ambitions of the more moderate and patronizing intelligentsia. Members of the local intellectual elite had been dreaming for years about broadening the limits for civic activity in the state of the tsars and realizing the people's potential. The radical faction of the intelligentsia had often been involved in alternative education, whereas the more liberally inclined segment embarked on promoting philanthropy, municipal institutions, and popular education. Now both groups were terrified by the recursive interaction between people on the streets and their new leaders. Even if the

Fig. 5.3. Trojanowski's Coffee House on Miodowa St. in Warsaw after a bomb explosion, 1905. Photography by Stanisław Pęcherski, Koncern Ilustrowany Kurier Codzienny. National Digital Archives of Poland (NAC), 1-H-3.

possibilities of political action were fairly limited, for a while socialist leaders became the heroes of the day.

However, when the revolution revealed its darker face and the bloodily persecuted workers adopted terrorist tactics, the liberal press, seemingly with satisfaction, identified a mistake of those leaders:

> In the last week we had a very significant fact: one of the extreme parties repented and shouted loudly—we got lost! Indeed, the PPS-Revolutionary Faction [the more militarized, right-wing, nationalist splinter group] has made a huge mistake by giving out weapons to the mob and simultaneously giving it an impulse for expropriation and reappropriation. And in a relatively short time [the party] realized that it was not possible to differentiate between a bandit and a nonbandit. It is one more piece of evidence, of course an irrefutable one, of how abysmally dark are our broader masses. It may seem that at least individuals with any aspirations in their souls are somehow socialized, but it appeared that they willingly put dishonor on themselves and with this stigma they daringly stared into the eyes of honest people.[119]

It seems that—perhaps in contrast to the National Democrats—who condemned the anarchic, savage masses out of hand—the liberals constantly maintained their belief in an unenlightened people who just needed proper guidance. At the same time, however, they desperately attempted to deny the agency of those masses. Even if shooting and robbing in the streets were obviously individualized activities, it was still the party leaders who were allegedly in charge.

The intelligentsia employed a similar mechanism of attribution in response to the most widely commented on, singular act of economic terror. After several hours of fruitless negotiations with workers, Mieczysław Silberstein, a factory owner resistant to any concessions, took out a weapon and threatened the crowd. The gun was pulled out of his hand, and after another harsh exchange, at some point one worker shot dead the stubborn industrialist. The press unanimously pointed to the collective deficiencies of the factory workers and the abusive nature of political agitation: "Yesterday's crime demonstrated the frightening degeneration of the workers in their entirety, caused by a lack of culture and education, and recently use of the worker [allegedly by the parties] as a blind tool."[120] In similar circumstances *Rozwój* was eager to point out not only the harmful influence of agitation but also its foreign origin, usually allegedly Jewish but also Russian or "international." One writer suggested that "alien, hostile forces made people into murderers."[121] This killed two birds with one stone: it offered a scapegoat and saved the day for old convictions about benign, unenlightened people merely waiting to be awoken. All sides involved attempted to explain the turbulent situation. Narrative patterns helping to deal with the soaring crisis were varied. Those close to the political thinking of the National Democrats held sway.

> In the beginning of the so-called "freedom movement" two currents emerged, national and social. The latter had a hotbed in a neglected industrial city. It is redundant to repeat facts from that era: we remember vividly general strikes [*bezrobocia*], bloody June days, fratricidal struggles, terror, lockout. Perhaps it is too early to give a definite diagnosis of this time, especially since so many currents clashed: freedom struggle, economic struggle, struggle of the healthy part of the workers with the traces of the international. It could be stressed that national elements, acting in awful conditions, took the upper hand. The froth has fallen down and there is still some boiling, but in the cauldron a firm whole coagulates, a germ of a better national future.[122]

This mildly nationalist view of the events was still capable of recognizing the heterogeneous struggle and pluralism of the political world. It also revealed the dominant themes of the national democratic parlance. Foreign, anti-Polish socialism—which above all sowed seeds of anarchy, banditry and disorder—was fanned by vague interests acting against the Polish national cause and the "healthy" social body of the nation.[123] Workers should work harmoniously and docilely for the common national good. To attain this goal, a leading force capable of bringing discipline, getting rid of "social scum," and showing foreigners their place was needed. The National Democrats willingly offered their services in this matter, and they did as they said they would do: "took the upper hand." However, it was still important to present it as a somehow natural emanation of the national spirit, where people found the essence of their Polishness despite superficial yet multiple obstacles. In this vein, *Rozwój* announced that "the Polish nation has, especially in Lodz, many enemies, but it is irrepressible, so vital with its moral power that it will prevail over different mercenaries who would like to suppress the Polish spirit."[124] This claim reveals much about the future of Polish politics.

In sum, the commercial elite and large chunks of the Polish intelligentsia were frightened by the new modes of political action and above all by the agency of the new contenders. Consequently, they partially withdrew their approval of working-class politics. It was no longer possible to deny or simply ignore it. Instead, sometimes subtle, sometimes crude ways of pushing new groups out of the realm of legitimate political action appeared. Insinuations about foreign tutelage and the usurpatory character of leadership were multiplied to simultaneously delegitimize working-class politics and convince the frightened intelligentsia that its dated image of the situation was still valid. At the general level, however, the agency of workers was not turned into nothing. After all, pure fear is a form of recognition. The factor inducing fear must be at least considered as capable of action. It could be perceived, however, as a quasi-natural factor with little consciousness, a mere circumstance to be accounted for but not incorporated into the body politic. Against this backdrop, the rhetoric condemning the masses as a "natural," undifferentiated, savage, and dehumanized mob may be explained. Such a presentation allowed the elite to account for danger but simultaneously deny the agency of working-class contenders. Masses were not only actually existing groups but rather a product of a particular regime of political (mis)representation.

As a result, even if initially championed by the liberal intelligentsia, the press discourse often fostered the solutions proposed by the nationalists, with antisemitism, discipline of the nation, and rigid distribution of places within the body politic.

Aftereffects

In all the scrutinized dimensions, the 1905 Revolution was an important threshold in respect to the workers' presence in the press. The necessity to address the "worker question" was accepted. Old hopes for social harmony—dominant right after the infantile vagaries of peripheral capitalism went away—were shattered. After the revolution, the provincial intelligentsia retained the firm belief in education—propelled at the time, however, by horrific visions of the masses without proper resources to participate in public life: "The most necessary need of the masses is education: our masses should learn! For this goal there is never too much money or too many efforts!" *Kurier Łódzki* called just as the revolutionary wave calmed down.[125] Leaving vast swaths of society behind might have posed a threat to the most basic aspirations of other social spheres as well. There was no longer any doubt that more serious measures needed to be taken.

The left-leaning part of the local intelligentsia was unambiguous about the necessity of a more profound social transformation and systemic reform of the state and its welfare provisions.[126] As a partial solution, workers gained some recognition as legitimate members of the imagined social totality with their own place and set of separate interests, for which they were entitled to struggle.[127] The political imagination associated with this view registered the class division of society and acknowledged the possibility of conflict. The contributors to *Goniec Łódzki* and its heirs sometimes explicitly sided with the workers, envisioning a more equal distribution of social wealth as a desired goal. Strikes were considered a harmful but sometimes necessary means of negotiation. An established pattern of collective bargaining and legitimate representation of conflicted class interests was seen as a viable solution when thinking about state reform. The workers were recognized as political claimants.

At the same time, however, more conservative spheres still envisioned the working class as a passive object of intensified pedagogy and aimed to stop revolt and moral degeneration. While there was certainly an afterimage of a paternalistic bond haunting such statements, moderate conservative nationalists did rebuild their social imaginary as well. Their refurbished political imagination recognized a certain collective identity of "workers' status" but prescribed a particular place in the national body for laboring people "acting reasonably and not passionately." Within this corporatist idea proposed by *Rozwój*, "workers who strive for education and do useful work" might take "a prominent place in the newly organized social life."[128] However, such an independent place might be attained at the price of resignation from the organized struggle for a better life. Instead the workers were supposed to build national institutions. "Above all we have to make order in our own house; we have to be reborn morally and materially," *Rozwój* advised resolutely when outlining the project of the "house of the people," which was intended to be one of such institutions.[129] These institutions, one should add, would be carefully policed and kept under tight constraints by the more nationally educated spheres, securing the new national polity and its hierarchical order. More right-leaning nationalist writers also had to admit that social reality did not unfold toward organic harmony. Conflicting groups (albeit not explicitly called classes) could have irrevocably contradictory concerns.[130] Therefore, more active counteractions were to be taken, and socialists were widely accused of revolutionary anarchy and demoralization.

In this way, political antagonisms were spurred on by the revolution. Not only did it pit social contenders against each other, perpetuating class warfare and ideological polarization between parties, but it also catalyzed the differentiation of political programs supported by the provincial press. Before 1905 both *Rozwój* and *Goniec Łódzki* were "decently bourgeois," rather moderate and timid (also because of censorship), with slight shadings of nationalism and progressivism, respectively. During the heated days of the revolution, their profiles bifurcated. The former title sided with the National Democracy party and embraced integral nationalism, supporting on its pages "Polish national interests" and the vision of a disciplined national community. The latter (as *Kurier Łódzki*, then *Nowy Kurier Łódzki*) assumed the mantle of a progressive tribune of urban professionals, supporting a centrist political agenda and being more open to ethnic diversity and working-class claims that went beyond corporatist loyalty. Both titles were now orbiting closer to the party-led political camps and respective ideological languages, taking entrenched positions within the established political conflict. What accompanied this ideological polarization on both sides was fear of the masses, triggered by working-class protests on an unprecedented scale.

This ambivalence corresponded to the generally ambiguous role of the press in relation to the regime in power. The press played a major role in the reconstruction of political imaginations accompanying the revolution and the new political presence of workers. As it was revealed, however, this role was far from unidirectional. The situation in Russian Poland epitomizes the more general pitfalls inherent in the relationship between the press and the ruling order, be it the state or dominant social hierarchies of a less tangible kind. Newspapers were not actors pitted unanimously against autocratic rule that stimulated critical debate, which sooner or later would herald liberalization. To make such a claim would be to subscribe to the "Whig account of journalism,"[131] clearly stripped of its credibility even in the imperial borderlands, where the press was admittedly a national contender against the state autocracy. While the Polish press undoubtedly fostered the national project by the simple fact of supporting Polish language circulation and an Andersonian imagined community of addressees, it was also a factor policing the established boundaries of political participation.

In this vein, the Lodz press was a voice of the urban elites, more progressive or conservative but nevertheless understandably reluctant to acknowledge new political contenders without restrictions. The articles published in *Rozwój* or *Goniec Łódzki*, just like the leaflets analyzed in chapter 3, had to please their readers in order to stimulate a meaningful response and conversation. While the journalists may have been more open to new political constituencies, they nevertheless had to match their criticisms to the sensitivity of their readers. The readers often belonged to the propertied strata of the industrial city, so on a basic economic level they were more than interested in reviving the status quo ante regarding workers' rights to make claims on behalf of themselves.

Nevertheless, the revolution was a "juncture," which triggered "changes in what newspapers as an institution can say and what they are prevented from saying," as one scholar of the social role of the press put it.[132] The social reality and environment in which newspapers operated changed abruptly. The limits of the speakable expanded because of the abolition of preventive censorship and the powerful transformation of the political imagination. The press discourse, nevertheless, remained embedded in a dense net of readers' presumptions, editors' convictions, and the available stock language used to describe situations. This discourse underwent a significant change, sometimes assisting and sometimes resisting the general transformation of the political realm, which is the overarching topic of this study.

The limits of the doable established by discourse altered accordingly so as to accommodate the new political reality and comprehend the insurgent democratization of a social imaginary spearheaded by workers. The press delivered words, and hence mental images, explaining the new situation and allowing readers to make it intelligible in respect to the boundaries of the polity and the regime of action assigned to its parts. Chiara Bottici notes while investigating the entanglements of the political with the imaginal, as she termed it, that "what a given subject sees gathered together in the public sphere (the *agora*) is a set of bodies, not (yet) a *polis*. In order to perceive a *polis*, something that unifies all those scattered bodies, you need a pictorial (re)presentation that can include all of them. This can be given by the image of the *agora* itself or by the walls of the city, as was often the case in antiquity, or some other image of the common territory, but, in any case, it must be conveyed through a certain image that defines its boundaries."[133] While the *agora* is already a designated public space, the street becomes one only under special circumstances. In days of social crisis, the polity had to be reimagined anew, and images turning sets of bodies into *polis*, or conversely, denying this status to the scattered bodies, were eagerly sought. In the context of the 1905 Revolution, the borders and imaginings about the polity as applied to the populations flocking into the squares and streets were established and changed with significant input from the press discourse.[134] Analogously, the press accounts were also able to exclude people and delegitimize their claims, relegating them to a place beyond those boundaries.

Although opinions were more conflicted than before, the spectrum of the possible constituted by political imagination widened. Broader possibilities for action, however, did not mean broader acceptance of these actions, and the press also gave space to voices expressing the active pushback of the new contenders out of the public sphere through intensified policing of its limits.

Conclusion

The epigraphs that opened this study told the story of the revolution—an insurgent democratization and reconfiguration of the political arena—from contrasting angles. The imaginative vignettes of memory depicted, on the one hand, a heroic, bearded, aging figure building a barricade and performing his self-assertion on the revolutionary street, and on the other, working-class and Jewish impostors destroying the comfort zone of liberal politicians with their radical ideas and practices. On the level of cultural impact and political history, both depictions are true in their representation of increasingly antagonized sentiments. This bifurcation was present from the very beginning, in revolutionary politics that triggered many contrasting emotions. It grew alongside the antagonization of a politicized public and a crystallization of ideological identities. The confrontation of popular classes fighting for the right to *have* rights and a fearful elite reluctant to accept working-class rights or simply surprised by the scale of the unrest and the unavoidable disorders of a popular uprising interfered with the radicalized ideological programs of socialists and nationalists. These overlapping interests and emotions heightened interclass and intraclass struggle. The polyvalent conflict and the ambiguity of contested democracy has informed my thinking and writing throughout this study, aimed at an intelligible presentation of a powerful confrontation that lies at the foundation of the modern political sphere in Poland.

The 1905 Revolution in Russian Poland does not yield any simple narrative. Perhaps this is one reason for its relative historiographical invisibility, despite its profound impact on Polish social, political, and intellectual history. There are many reasons why it is difficult to square the revolution with any standardized story such as that of class struggle, national revival, or political modernization. What binds many previous studies is a binary political imagination of sorts. Even when specific works are far from Polish-centered martyrology pitting righteous challengers against the "foreign yoke," they nevertheless often maintain the fundamental opposition between autocracy and modern civic developments or the (Russian) state and (Polish) society. Reevaluation of such a framing does not necessarily lead to—as Abraham Ascher puts it, subscribing to this paradigm—"broadly liberal" revisionism reestablishing the prospects of an unrealized Russian path to liberal democracy or seeking pockets of civil society within and alongside the Russian state apparatus.[1] My aim was not to present a less repressive face of the tsarist state, even if I am far from accusing its functionaries of much excess beyond policing embedded in incentives of autocratic state self-preservation. Instead I focus on conflicting and conflicted tendencies and divisions fracturing the second part of the aforementioned binary historical imagination—Polish society.

While exploring the topic, I realized that more profound processes occurred between "the elite" and "the masses." Correspondingly, I examined class friction within a society in revolt. The backdrop for my source-based investigation is the broader historical narrative about waves of modern democratization and contraction. However, the case that I have examined from a refreshing, new perspective was a dense imperial situation with strong overdetermination by class, gender, ethnic, and national tensions. Initially, multiethnic groups and vast social strata rose up to contest an autocratic regime and a state widely perceived as a foreign occupier. All the involved parties entered a complex field of tensions, and the situation became very dynamic after this initial opposition started to dissolve. Whereas the elite could not smoothly side with the locus of state power, contenders from the populace were easily fractured along national lines and deemed a grave danger for national self-preservation. This multiplicity of conflicting identities notwithstanding, I decided to cast this study as an investigation of the workers contesting the intelligentsia's hegemony within the public sphere, as a crucial dimension rendering this configuration intelligible.

Circumscribing the Public Sphere

Approaching the problem from several complementary angles produces a satisfactory examination of the historically transforming political sphere in respect to the presence of the working class. Chapter 1 focuses on historical lineages of class formation and emerging working-class intellectual life. The examination of historical contexts demonstrates that the pattern of proletarianization in Russian Poland was a rapid but highly uneven one. Thus mostly the rural population entered the newly developed industrial hubs and only rarely approached established patterns of proletarian culture and networks capable of creating a launchpad for political militancy. It was political activity, initially induced by radicalized members of the intelligentsia vehemently organizing illegal political and intellectual activities, that provided the first point of entry into the world of letters and public participation for workers. During the revolution, however, the workers' "circle work" gave rise to various forms of more independent political practice on the streets and in the factories—the strike, the political rally, and the mass meeting or factory occupation, examined in chapter 2. The revolutionary dynamics spurred the development of a plebeian, working-class counterpublic as an alternative to the dominant means of circulation. It was also a field of experimentation and learning made possible in social situations where habits were broken, class boundaries were crossed in both directions, and questions were asked about fundamental issues.

Workers involved in that proletarian public sphere, from within which they contested the limitations imposed by the dominant public, successfully reconstructed the political community. They performed politics on their own, introducing new forms and subsequently forcing other social strata to consider the workers' social input and class-based arguments as important and legitimate. Workers nurtured plebeian, democratic politics while simultaneously struggling for individual and collective rights. Their voices and votes (words that in Polish have a common root) as individuals and as a class had to be partially recognized in the political realm. Their inclusion was not, however, greeted with enthusiasm by the propertied strata and a large proportion of the intelligentsia, which after its initial patriotic ardor withdrew its support and tended to see the revolution as an uncontrolled outburst of disorder. Various forms of fear of the masses perpetuated this discourse. Antisemitic undertones helped many members of the intelligentsia understand the new political situation by pointing at alleged foreign tutelage of the "mob," widely perceived as incapable of independent action and agency.

The overlapping political commitments expressed themselves in the prolific print production of the revolutionary public, situated between the radical intelligentsia and militant workers. Chapter 3 examines these printed materials—especially the leaflets—and their contribution to transforming political communication and its impact on readers and writers. What was speakable and what was doable expanded dramatically when politics came to include the lower classes, leaving behind old realities of bipolar competition between the aristocratic palace and the liberal salon. This "politics in a new key" was marked by a high level of antagonism and direct agency of political language. Political languages in conflict were powerful forces leading people into the streets and pitting them against each other in an unprecedented manner. Concepts used in leaflets or party journals were a means of ushering novices into the political realm. They led to a profound intervention in regimes of subjectification, not only delegitimizing the autocratic regime but also delivering active means of comprehension and self-placement of workers in the broader social order.

The "fighting words" uttered in the streets also had other effects. I scrutinize the role antisemitism played as a political device assisting in the construction of new political identities. When "nationalism began to hate," antisemitism appeared to be an extremely effective mobilizing device, and the Jews were cast as a negative, constitutive point of reference for the construction of national unity among the Poles. The new political reality modified the circuit between words and deeds, or language and action. The role of language changed when large constituencies were mobilized and pitted against each other and fighting words became a directly usable weapon.

In this antagonistic setting, working-class political militants themselves underwent a profound transformation. To explain the mechanics of this change, chapter 4 deals with the biographical implications of working-class involvement in politics. The revolution was often remembered as a pivotal event structuring a person's life story and restructuring the connections linking the self, politics, work, and life course of the writers. The entire emplotment of the militant biography revolves around the revolution. Political involvement not only gave meaning to each individual life, which was now perceived within a broader historical scheme of social and/or national liberation, but it also offered an alternative sociality and paths of upward mobility and recognition as speakers, organizers, or armed street militia members. Such a form of belonging was important for people deprived of it elsewhere and kept them involved despite the dangers that mode of life posed. Workers became conscious participants in a highly polemical culture of debate and challengers to a regime in retreat, capable of strategic action in favor of long-term goals. The revolution was an important trigger of change, simultaneously modifying the subjectively defined place of workers within society, the limits on what could be said and done, and the entanglement of the writers' lives with the public sphere.

These new modes of speech and thought left their imprint on working-class militants from different political milieus, including those opposed to the revolution. It had different impacts on already committed proletarian autodidacts and on freshly politicized workers who became involved only during the mass uprising. The former played an active role in the 1905 conflict and sealed their biographies as revolutionaries, whereas the latter often entered politics only in ephemeral ways and never ceased to be shop-floor workers. Nonetheless, for both groups the revolution was the main element structuring their written biographies. To a considerable extent, patterns of involvement were similar across political milieus, but the political self that revolution promoted may have been quite different.

Not only did workers perceive *themselves* differently because of the newly available language, but their political visibility to the outside world also changed. I examine the construction of "workers" in the press in chapter 5. The place of workers in journalistic discourse delimited their perceived and actual agency within the broader public sphere. Before the revolution, the rise of the "worker question" (and more broadly the "social question") in the press was slow, because of censorship and the long-maintained conviction that the predicaments of modernity would bypass Polish society. The revolution was a pivotal moment regarding the "social question," marking the modern renegotiation of the social system all over Europe. Censorship become milder, and revolutionized workers left little doubt about their presence and importance. As a result, the idea that it was necessary to address the "worker question" became ever more acceptable. Workers gained significant, albeit contested, recognition as legitimate members of an imagined social totality and as political claimants. The revolution catalyzed the reconceptualization of the social contract: more daring reform projects involved the state in the provision of welfare and expressed critique of capitalism and aggregate individual interests.

Nevertheless, the proliferating public presence of people previously forced to remain in the shadows triggered fear and hostility. The press debate reflected these reservations and problematized new modes of political action and leadership. Many elements of this debate are common tropes: criticism of illegitimate demagoguery, impostor leaders, or the immaturity of the new contenders. Various groups considered to be illegitimate were lumped together and became the object of elitist indignation fanned by nationalist sentiments. In this way, the elite's reaction worked in concert with nationalism among the populace to promote antisemitism as a means to exclude socialist workers on the grounds that they were manipulated by the Jews.

All in all, the distinctive type of human communicative activity conducive to establishing a specific sphere—the political sphere—underwent substantial transformation during the 1905 Revolution, leading to its modern form. This multidimensional transformation of the public sphere was facilitated by insurgent democratization, a bottom-up social struggle that included solid resistance. The rise of the proletarian public sphere, the public participation of workers claiming their rights, the people reshaping themselves through politics and performing political change, the new role of language within the masses' politics in a new key, and outsiders' changing perception of workers as political agents—all these dimensions constituted the contested change of the political sphere. The historical delimitation of this sphere and its enactment through discourse and practices touches on the principle of integration of the body politic. The "long 1905" had many consequences and can be regarded as a foundational moment for Polish modern politics and public sphere.

Revolutionary Aftermaths in Postimperial Comparison

Comparing tsarist borderlands at the fore of the revolutionary upheaval is especially revealing when considering the aftermath of the revolution in a broader perspective.[2] Intense political struggles after the First World War reshaped Eastern Europe. The idea of a social revolution created shock waves that interfered with the nationalist drive, aimed at creating nation states atop the debris of empire. Despite the high level of entanglement and influence of extramural forces, past legacies of political militancy, ideological landscape, and the balance of forces in respective areas had great significance. They often tipped the balance in favor of a particular option determining the existence and shape of emerging state polities. The power to control the situation or mobilize large groups of people for particular aims often resulted from the 1904–1907 clashes and their ambiguous aftermath.

In 1905 Latvian workers led some of the most powerful strikes, combining political and economic incentives, and local peasants rebelled against the Russian administration and the German landed gentry.[3] After failed attempts at Russification Finland secured a spectacular reform, not only restoring its traditional autonomy but also introducing universal suffrage for both men and women, all within the borders of the tsarist empire.[4] This victory enabled the Finnish Social Democrats to grow steadily and elect large numbers of delegates to the newly autonomous parliament. For Finland's socialists, the ballot box was not a coffin but a cradle. The workers in the Baku oilfields, despite initial ethnic clashes, also witnessed late but significant triumphs, including higher wages and a reasonable level of self-government for the multiethnic city.[5] In Georgia the regional revolution was championed by local Mensheviks, who retained a stable level of support in later years.[6]

A decade later, most of these regions were haunted by warfare and intense class conflict, albeit of diversified types. In Latvia support for social revolution was relatively high and was spearheaded by the famous Latvian Riflemen, leading to a bitter and complex conflict.[7] Finland experienced a civil war strictly divided along class lines; the Social Democrats defended previous electoral arrangements and were brutally defeated in the end.[8] The moderate Bolshevik Baku Commune was raided by Azeri nationalists, while Georgian Social Democrats were able to outmaneuver their opponents and create an independent, albeit short-lived state after 1918. All the nascent Transcaucasian states had to be reconquered by the Red Army. Former borderlands witnessed various patterns of revolutionary activity.

Poland, however, only a decade later remained relatively calm despite a devastating war ("the midwife of revolution") and the people's earlier impetus toward social revolution. The urban working class had a tradition of militancy and a vivid memory of the 1905 strikes and victories. Some workers were up for another radical upsurge, and so were some socialist parties that had time to develop much larger organizational capacities than twelve years before. Indeed, socialist milieus launched a vivid campaign pressuring the state-crafting elite. The initial proclamations of independence were made under socialist auspices, and significant social demands were addressed in their tentative programs (Ignacy Daszyński's Lublin government and later the Piłsudski-backed Moraczewski cabinet).[9] With significant concessions made to the populace, the revolutionary surge in Poland was weakened and the internationalist Left was unable to spark a larger movement. The pendulum had swung toward national unity and remained there even after the Polish state had already begun to fulfill the warnings of the Far Left that national unity would serve as a smoke screen for class domination. Polish workers refused to revolt against the Polish state when the Bolsheviks advanced and approached Warsaw to push the socialist revolution westward. The revolution had been aborted in Poland; in other regions, however, the situation evolved differently.

The tentative explanation of this conundrum is that the events of 1904–1907 pushed these regions along distinct trajectories. The 1905 upheavals were characterized by a high level of militancy in most of the nationally diversified borderlands. They constituted an important threshold in forging modern political spheres in every case. While the Revolution of 1905 was in all cases a tipping point, the resulting reconfigurations played out differently. Although this pivotal event may be legitimately narrated as an important stepping-stone for the later overthrow of the unreformable tsarist autocracy in mainland Russia, its results in the borderland regions bifurcated. To explain the postrevolutionary dynamic and its significance for the general layering of the public sphere in Poland, I need to return to the Polish context and, again tentatively, read it through the lens of broader sociological terms, to come to grips with larger forces and tendencies.

Outcomes of the Failed Revolution

The events of 1904–1907, however dramatic, did not bring about direct changes in the political system or class structure. The revolution failed and was bloodily suppressed, leading to profound social disintegration and political repression. The political compromises offered by the tsarist state, such as the October Manifesto—which included moderate political liberties, a loosening of censorship, and several rounds of Duma elections—were simply ignored or bypassed in practice by the still-autocratic state. The "national question," an additional dimension of struggle in Poland, also remained unresolved, and the striving for autonomy was in vain. Emerging civic institutions, such as various associations or labor unions, were brutally suppressed during the Stolypin reaction, with extensive repression and martial law sustained until 1913 or thereabouts in the most heated regions.[10]

Nevertheless, the revolution mobilized new groups of society, in particular urban workers, to actively participate in the public sphere. Languages and practices of the revolutions broadened the limits of the speakable and the doable. The events ushered the Polish Kingdom into modern politics. Mobilized workers who participated in the vivid civic culture or labor organizations, even if later deprived of similar opportunities, were no longer the same passive imperial subjects as before. They became subjects in a completely different sense—that is, bearers of at least the potential capacity for conscious political action and self-aware participants in the social world, hence the title of this study. In this sense, the revolution was undoubtedly an important threshold in the modern democratization of the social imaginary and general sense of citizenship. It convinced people that they might obtain the right to have rights—that is, in Hannah Arendt's wording, "to live in a framework where one is judged by one's actions and opinions," and not destitute of belonging to some form of polity.[11] Universal suffrage was introduced in the independent Polish state only in 1918, thanks to the powerful claim for citizenship uttered by the populace in 1905. The workers' successful political militancy might have fostered future radicalism and corresponding organizational capacities. The effect of the revolution could not be limited to political modernization, however.

In addition to this anticipatory democratization, the emerging modern political sphere was also preset ideologically. It was the point of ideological polarization and a tipping point for the creation of stable political encampments, mobilizing particular languages and emotions, which structured the political field for years. The opening circumstances of modern politics delimited future possibilities for action.[12] The revolution was a stage of the "operationalization" of political ideologies. What had earlier been only imagined in the writings of party thinkers was now turned into political practice. The assumed political community could no longer be postponed or deferred but had to be mobilized and disciplined in the here and now, without envisioning a future reconciliation of tensions within it.

Consequently, the democratizing aspect of the revolution was supplemented by the disciplinary practice of political organizations. The National

Democracy party took a turn toward discipline and autocratic order.[13] This tension was also revealed in the socialist milieu; some military squads of the PPS-Revolutionary Faction had to be disbanded because of the low level of central control and the specter of banditry. The top echelons of the party clearly opted for military discipline in the ranks, envisioning a regular army rather than a mass movement. Their later organizational practice outside the party fully confirmed this shift. The circles around Józef Piłsudski endorsed a project of creating Polish military forces in Austrian Galicia from 1908 onward. The ideological transformation of some party leaders drifting steadily in the national and socially conservative direction was also connected with their experience of a molten mass in the revolutionary street, as the memoirs of Michał Sokolnicki demonstrate.

The Far Left, SDKPiL, in turn, was to a growing extent marginalized as a proxy of cosmopolitan Jewry, blamed for the revolutionary turmoil, an accusation holding in its grip even former revolutionary activists, now bitter and disappointed.[14] The party itself got bogged down in sectarian quarrels, and its "workerist" organizational culture became obsolete because of its leaders' antidemocratic practices. It attempted to hold back the antisemitic wave, but it only worsened its own situation when the vitriolic tide was already too high.[15] Hoping in vain to stir a revolution during the Polish-Bolshevik war of 1919–1921, SDKPiL secured its place on the obscure, and later illegal, margins as the Polish Communist Party, a fate it shared with the PPS-Left after their merger.

After the revolutionary surge, progressive circles took a step backward, to an increasing degree hegemonized by the language of the political Right. The process went so far that instead of promoting a continuous, unambiguously liberal, secular, and progressive agenda resisting the wave, Polish liberals did not hesitate to launch a particular product of Polish politics, so-called progressive antisemitism.[16] This tendency aborted the development of the liberal "just milieu" as a significant political actor, even if some liberal ideas were recirculated elsewhere. When the liberals had the floor swept from under their feet, facing socialist contention and popular demands, the National Democrats (now transformed into modern nationalist conservatives) gained the upper hand.

As a result, to fully grasp the transformation during and after the 1905 Revolution in the Polish case, we must direct our attention to the right side of the political spectrum, rather than to the ups and downs of the fractured socialist Left. After initially fighting an uphill battle, the right-wing National Democracy party emerged to give meaning to the new situation and trace the symbolic contours of the nascent modern public sphere after 1905. The National Democrats successfully channeled the "fear of the masses" and the burnout of revolutionary zeal. They launched a powerful political discourse, which built their legitimacy on fighting "anarchy" and revolutionary disorder. Collective emotions were effectively redirected from recognition and economic demands into national unity, assisted by a growing hostility against various "others": above all, the Jewish population. The anti-Jewish scaremongering proved powerful enough to make the National Democracy party a powerful player in the Polish public sphere for a number of years (even if it never held formal power), thus infecting the political discourse and Polish national identity—forged those days in its modern form—with the vicious germ of antisemitism.

What followed was a long-lasting nationalist hegemony that blocked the articulation of social claims, setting the tone for mainstream political discourse. It was the National Democrats who orchestrated the public debate in subsequent rounds of Duma elections in 1907 and 1912. Not only did the party's influence significantly change the balance of forces, but it also reconfigured the lines of political division. Political differences were racialized along antisemitic lines; political opponents were often described as anti-Polish or accused of being Jewish proxies. This machinery was later powerfully used to agitate against any left-wing constituencies, from the Bolshevik menace to the democratically elected Polish president.[17] After the First World War, therefore, the National Democrats peeled away enough of the working class to prevent a groundswell of revolutionary support that could have undermined the national project.

Nonetheless, the nationally inclined socialists, the PPS, established a considerable degree of support after a sharp turn to the left after 1914. The PPS refused to enter a bloc with the National Democrats; instead, it successfully raised social demands and combined them with national goals in support of the Polish state project. Hence the state project gained enough legitimacy among popular classes and even urban workers—in other tsarist borderlands the most radical group tending to back local communists—maintained support for it. This made it possible to survive a bitter military conflict with Russian Bolsheviks and sideline the social tensions that never vanished and after 1917 grew once more as the window of historical possibility opened again. This sequence of the 1905 rebellion, reaction, and later aborted revolution for the sake of state crafting had important consequences for the structural composition of the Polish public sphere. Before I get back to that, though, let us reexamine the results of this study against the backdrop of European labor history and historical approaches to the developing public spheres, making these two bodies of literature speak to each other.

Labor and the Public Sphere

In the "long" nineteenth century, the working class made the most serious and contentious claims to enter the political sphere.[18] The multiple social struggles of the working population, not without turbulence, brought about the manifold democratization of the political and social orders, as well as patterns of redistribution.[19] Despite oligarchic reaction the encroaching democratization was ongoing, and this part of the story was the subject of my study. The electoral successes of social democracy and expansion of minimum liberal rights from the franchise to welfare provisions shifted trajectories of European politics on a continental scale.[20] Not only did working-class politics influence patterns of democratization, and thus recast the political arena, but political trajectories also shaped class formation.

The 1905 Revolution was a pivotal moment in determining the political choices and self-awareness of class among workers in Russian Poland. Workers performed acts of self-assertion; at the same time, for better or worse, their struggle was separated from a myriad of "progressive" or insurrectionary forces. This point in the history of Polish progressive radicalism was similar to 1848 in Western Europe in that it definitely separated the working-class "masses" from the bourgeois claims formerly invested in the "third estate."[21] Correspondingly, the memory of the revolution was long regarded as a founding myth of class militancy in the interwar period. It also integrated workers into the narrative of national revival as contributors to the history of national liberation who were no less important than the noble participants in earlier uprisings. The legacy of the revolution, however, also included a bifurcation of working-class identities.

Although socialism of many varieties gained massive support and inspired waves of strikes, urban workers in large numbers supported its more nationalist wing or the integral nationalist project. The former offered the enticements of street militarism and fights against the hated Russian oppressor, and the latter led the workers to the ballot box, offering an important sense of participation and a chance to express their preferences through voting. Therefore, a high level of antagonism marked shop-floor politics for years, and particular factories maintained cultures of protest and political identities often forged amid the revolutionary conflict and factory "cleansing" during fratricidal struggles. This high level of antagonism prevented future common mobilization in favor of simple economic demands, as calls for sociopolitical change were easily discounted as factional or socialist, if not as anti-Polish conspiracies. At the same time, however, people's experience of revolution might be similar despite the ideological differentiation. This shared pool of experiences may help explain the fluidity of the political field and the successful cooptation of the majority of the working-class population to the Polish nation state after 1918.

These seemingly contradictory processes may be explained as a form of ecological fallacy (or fallacy of division, more accurately speaking) in historical reasoning. The fact that nationalism gained adherents during the revolution does not necessarily mean that it attracted the same workers who had earlier supported socialism. Aggregated data on party membership cannot answer this question. This ambiguity is erased when one speaks just about the "working class" or "workers" (which in many cases is unavoidable without applying cumbersome labels). In a similar vein, the fact that part of the working class supported antisemitic politics did not in itself cancel out the democratic potential of the revolutionary public sphere. In both cases the historical analysis may concern completely different people. This clarification notwithstanding, workers' writings admitted confusion and volatility in their political identities, especially in prerevolutionary conditions. Considering that it was the more committed group that decided to write, and perhaps en masse confusion may have been a more widespread phenomenon, one should not reject personal political instability as an explanation out of hand.

The same misleading unitary effect haunts analytical concepts that are embedded in teleologies of modernity present in historical sociology. This study, dedicated to demonstrating ambivalence, raises such doubts in respect to democratization or civil society. The oppositions such as state vs. society or liberalization vs. autocracy do not necessarily have explanatory value. The conflicted Polish society produced many instances of civil society; not all of them, however, fostered democratization. Their creation, as an intermediary sphere between state and society, may have had unintended consequences, just as antagonistic pluralism supported some elements of a democratic worldview. But the liberalization of the state may have created space for reactionary organizations, and elections may have strengthened exclusionary identities.[22] Mass mobilization ushered in antisemitism and scaremongering about the effects of democracy. Such observations resonate with the conservative critique of political modernity and have been tentatively proposed by historiographical accounts seeking to explore ambiguous outcomes of major historical events.[23] What such arguments do not take into account, however—and what this book seeks to demonstrate—is that it is not mass politics but the oligarchic reaction to it that leads to an authoritarian turn in political practice.

The same conservative critique has often fueled multiple acts of exclusion by keeping workers, especially women, away from the public sphere. It is usually grounded in an imposed separation of private and public and the weeding out of many "persons and groups, particularly women and racialized groups culturally identified with the body, wildness and irrationality" as inappropriate, because they are considered too bound to particular situations and the domain of feelings.[24] Habermas's comments regarding the ideal of the bourgeois public sphere also apply to the materials analyzed here concerning the intelligentsia's reluctance to admit workers, women, and Jews to the public domain. Like the Western bourgeoisie and Habermas himself, the Polish intelligentsia featured in this book feared that the "laws which obviously have come about under the 'pressure of the street' can scarcely still be understood as arising from the consensus of private individuals engaged in public discussion. They correspond in a more or less unconcealed manner to the compromise of conflicting private interests."[25] Such a bourgeois (and intelligentsia) conception of the public sphere was premised on a clear separation of marketized society and state, thus neatly dissecting class-based claims from public reason, simultaneously founding its proclaimed universality on this very separation.[26]

Despite the different historical lineages in the Polish case, the political nation ruled by the early modern noble class was also premised on the commercial sphere. The separation of the manorial economy and the republic worked in parallel. These divisions were transferred to the antistate opposition after the partitions, when the intelligentsia conspired against the foreign state. These conditions eventually eroded as nonbourgeois strata gained access to the public sphere. When "the social question" came to the fore, "society was polarized by class struggle, and the public fragmented into a mass of competing interest groups," as Nancy Fraser comments on this far-reaching transformation in the Western configuration.[27] In this respect, the Polish story parallels the rise and fall of the bourgeois public sphere sketched by normatively oriented theorists generalizing the Western historical experience. However, its more modern development was—surprisingly—divergent, and not only because of the resilience of the older configuration. Thus the "modern transformation," despite the convergence of European political edifices during democratization, in the end took a distinct path.

Pathogenetic Conjuncture

The 1905 Revolution had many, not always explicit results on the development of the Polish public sphere. The story of this development—which affected structures of political action, the regime of class-based articulation, and modes of political thinking that the actors employed—may be dubbed a pathogenesis. Reinhart Koselleck originally applied the term to the patterns of thinking that emerged in opposition to the European absolutist state but appeared to be an indissoluble residue lasting long after its initial genesis.[28] Despite the different historical circumstances, I also trace the long-lasting effects on political thinking and practice back to the initial conjuncture of major elements in the public setting: namely, the tsarist state, the intelligentsia-led civil society, and the proletarian revolt and claims for public recognition. The emerging proletarian public was not one that had been imagined by the bourgeois elite. It came from different origins, engaged in different forms of participation, embraced alternative governing principles, and exemplified the divergence of class-based interests. It raised claims that ran counter to the social status quo, but that was only one side of the coin. The discounting of workers' claims also grew out of a particular regime of representation of private and collective demands that rendered the latter illegitimate.

The public sphere is not only a sphere "which mediates between society and state, in which the public organizes itself as the bearer of public opinion."[29] Historically, it has been a more "structured setting where cultural and ideological contest or negotiation among the variety of publics takes place."[30] In the Polish case, the forming of public opinion took place not between the society and the state but by the society *against* the state. That formation soon, however, gave rise to an additional, alternative form of public articulation that could not be integrated into the corrupted and judgmental mode of political reasoning forged in conditions of a nonexistent political sphere, properly speaking. According to Fraser, such an additional, subaltern public has a dual character; it functions as a "space of withdrawal and regroupment" and as a "base and training ground for agitational activities toward wider publics."[31] In this book I explore, among other things, the subaltern regroupment, which fostered alternative practices and training for effective articulation of interests in a broader public. Consequently, workers simultaneously confronted the state and the public sphere of the dominant groups, facing political violence and class-based exclusion.

Workers' public practices and modes of universalization of particular experiences and demands were difficult to integrate in a general public sphere that had been tainted by its (bourgeois, or in our case intelligentsia) context of emergence. Only the proverbial "street" offered a place where the proletarian public sphere could emerge and the populace's demands be debated. Only there could an impulse to integrate class-based demands into a legitimate pool of arguments arise.[32] Although there were moments when the interclass body politic with its high political potential emerged in the streets and squares and workers were given certain rights to the city, they only became urban dwellers and not fully recognized citizens.[33] If such an integration is inhibited and an oligarchic reaction is triggered, the class-specific public spheres develop separately, causing further divergence, as Craig Calhoun concludes from the story of English plebeian radicals and my investigation confirms.[34] Consequently, the popular demand, when not included in the public sphere, degenerates, and political liberalism cannot be practiced, maintained, or introduced without the basic needs of the claimants being met, as Hannah Arendt well understood.[35] Instead of coopting the popular revolt as a factor facilitating and later solidifying the political balance and civil institutions, the workers' claims were, as I argue, excluded from legitimate public activity and removed from the domain of rationality. This tendency led to suppression of the people's unrest and redirected it into social disintegration and unrestrained revolt.

Nevertheless, this conclusion does not fully explain why the previously progressive and prodemocratic intelligentsia also rejected general cooperation and identification with the proletarian surge. Following the rapid entrance of the populace into politics, the enlightened Polish elite remained almost helpless. "Fear of the masses" intensified in a way that prevented the liberal Polish intelligentsia from acknowledging and recognizing the proletarian public and its claims as a legitimate counterpart of the rising public sphere.[36] While the foreign tsarist regime inhibited any practical political action and modes of reasoning, the quasi-utopian way of thinking by the liberal salon detached it from political thinking proper, much more than when forged in opposition to the Western absolutist state or in the context of mainland Russia under the tsar.[37] The bourgeois press criticized the underdevelopment of public institutions and civic communities and envisioned their emergence as a way of securing the modernization of the Poles under imperial rule. Such a concept of public activity was apolitical, if not antipolitical, and opposed to the (hostile) state. The visions of the moral order of public activity harbored among the intelligentsia prevented them from including nonprescribed phenomena, both from above (state politics) and below (a popular contentious public and alternative public sphere). In these circumstances the liberal intelligentsia (if not, strictly speaking, the elite) aimed to spread knowledge among the people until they reached the "entry conditions" of rational public participation. Knowledge, however, is indivisible. Defining social status and political position by reference to knowledge, as Eastern European intelligentsias did, impedes possibilities for negotiating conflict with other social groups that are allegedly destitute of it.[38] In this realm, the prospective, utopian dimension of Polish liberalism unveils itself. This approach could simply not have worked during the rapid rise of mass politics.

In contrast, the long path followed by the lower classes in England or France was marked by gradual polemics, with proletarian contenders raising claims and renegotiating with a still not ossified capitalist order.[39] In such circumstances, it was possible for emerging elites to at least partially recognize their claim for political visibility. The oligarchic elite of the *ancien régime* and nouveau riche bourgeois alike were eagerly trying to define the situation in their own way; however, it was not possible to preclude and dismiss proletarian claims and the plebeian public as the mere inarticulate calls of an uneducated mob. In Russian Poland, it was much easier to make this distinction, as working-class radicalism was not based on an informed debate and did not meet the educated public on equal ground—as some earlier Western European plebeian radicals had done.[40] Polish progressive milieus, not to mention conservatives, were able to neglect the proletarian public with ease, excluding the democratic tendency brought about by popular struggle.[41] This exclusion happened even though the intelligentsia tradition had seemingly predisposed the public sphere to be much more receptive of emergent, contentious claimants. Its earlier endeavors to foster participation backfired;

once triggered, popular participation was still received with paternalism and condescension. The revolution erased much of the old composition of the intelligentsia ethos, sharply revealing its paradoxes, but nonetheless strengthened certain elements.

Above all, the revolution put an end to the ideal of national unity. Various elite Polish groups had long yearned for reconciliation between social groups and dreamed of a common struggle in the name of national goals—usually imagined as a fight for national liberation and independence. But if factory owners had no qualms about reaching out to tsarist troops to suppress labor unrest, workers did not hesitate to shoot dead their fellows from different parties, and priests called for an ultimate confrontation with the satanic socialists, sometimes leading to actual murders of rural agitators, then there was hardly any hope left for a reconciliation in the name of national revival. The very idea of this revival was contested, and its political nature conspicuously revealed. Within the homogeneous politics of nation, class-specific interests could hardly be expressed, but the rise of the labor movement and mass socialist parties temporarily brought them into the light. Such conflict, if mediated through mechanisms of political representation, is widely encountered in modern democracies. In this respect, therefore, revolution pushed the Polish public sphere into modernity. However, the lines of division, which here verged on antagonism, were not favorable for the long-term legitimacy of labor.

Although the class-oriented Left surfaced as a powerful movement, it was constrained by the conditions of a stateless nation under an imperial autocracy. The Left was fractured chiefly because of controversies over the "national question," a condition that appeared elsewhere in Europe only after the First World War. The PPS pioneered the combination of social struggle with national liberation, a pattern present in many anticolonial revolutions of the twentieth century.[42] But with the existing national elite entrenched in positions of status, there was little opportunity to express class-based claims as national-universal. Indeed, these claimants were easily delegitimized as fracturing the national unity, if not directly accused of acting against the national interest. Whether the interests in question were the well-being of "Polish industry" or the landholdings of the Polish gentry endangered by parcellation, the nationalist framework successfully prevented any debate about a more profound redistribution. The irredentist drive channeled social unrest into integral nationalism and effectively impeded any consensus in that regard. Adding insult to injury, the cultural heterogeneity of local populations impeded unidirectional political mobilization. As larger comparative research demonstrates, the basic level of an established (usually national) polity is an indispensable condition for the successful long-term mobilization of the Left, even in internationalist terms.[43] In the Polish case, however, emotions could either be funneled into interethnic conflict or invested in the interclass state-building project.

For that reason, major social demands (for instance, land reform) were also left practically unaddressed in the Polish Second Republic after the reconstruction of the Polish nation state. They were brought back to the table only after the catastrophe of the Second World War and later realized from above by the Stalinist state, which detached local populations from the empowering experience of successful social and political struggle. As a result, redistribution came to be seen as a foreign and hostile imposition. The resulting general contempt toward democratic demands and the impossibility of collective bargaining for the people's economic interests had an even longer afterlife. The intelligentsia mindset was preserved along with the social stratum itself, which appeared surprisingly resilient in terms of its cultural capital through subsequent historical turnovers.[44] After the fall of state socialism, it was again easier to delegitimize claims for redistribution; it resonated soundly with new neoliberal premises.[45] A bottom-up insurgent democratization—whether that of 1905 or the "first" working-class solidarity of the 1980s—was suppressed by the state structure. The delayed aftermath—1918 and 1989, respectively—were championed not by the initial authors of the upsurge but by their self-proclaimed leaders, the intelligentsia.[46] Going one step further, one may also float a hypothesis about the Polish intelligentsia's long-lasting moralized vision of politics and suppression of labor's class-based interests. [47] The events described here were a prelude to a complex conceptual-political lamination that lasted for years and haunts the Polish public sphere even today. Seen in this way, the 1905 Revolution, with its prelude and aftermath, proved to be a pivotal moment for placing workers within the political arena and forging the particular conceptual-political form of the Polish public sphere. Correspondingly, this case study informs the more general investigation of the lineages of public spheres and democratization.

Appendix

A Note on Methodology and Sources

This study tackles research problems associated with the historical sociology of the political arena. One may also call this research practice an enlarged intellectual history, systematically broadened to encompass also the lower classes—in this case, the workers. The general approach is a problem-driven one, designed to tackle the main questions with appropriate means and not with a stable methodological framework. As I zoom in, however, it is also a source-driven study. I apply research strategies to delimited sets of sources in a more selective way, and the archive delimits the realm of the possible in those chapters. Thus this study includes several prismatic insights of the core problem with different foci and substantially varying corpora of empirical material. It is designed to tackle the main issue from different yet supplementary angles.

The overarching "social ontology" is critically realistic and language-sensitive. I consider language as a crucial element constituting social reality but not coextensive with it. Moreover, language is an unavoidable mediator in research methods dealing with historical written sources. My approach to primary sources, necessarily textual in nature, is informed by post-linguistic-turn labor studies, on the one hand, and historically oriented discourse analysis and conceptual history, on the other. Research strategies regarding different groups of sources were varied, and I discuss necessary information in the text, including elements of source criticism appropriate for a given group of materials. Therefore, I offer only a brief overview of practical procedures here, focusing on the technical side and characteristics of the sources.

Biographical Testimonies

As a result of my archival research, I selected approximately 110 biographies as structurally developed enough to allow meaningful analysis. The collection consists of autobiographical testimonies of different sizes and characters, ranging from three-page resumes gathered from party or factory archives to thick-as-a-brick autobiographies.

As a result, besides anniversary collections and edited volumes,[1] many autobiographies were extensive enough to be published as separate books, contributing to the "autobiographical boom" of the postwar years.[2] They may be compared to the earlier memoirs published in the interwar years within partisan memory cultures in Poland and the Soviet Union. An important group consists of texts written by former SDKPiL and PPS-Left members who embraced the Polish Communist Party (KPP) and, in some cases, immigrated to the Soviet Union. There they produced militant memoirs, fulfilling the requirements of the official memory of the Bolshevik revolution, which were also published in dedicated journals.[3] In this case, however, because the writer could establish a certain distance from the epicenter of the debate over the memory of the October Revolution, the "Polish" part of the memoir was relatively free from the direct constraints put on writing. Meanwhile, veterans of the PPS were intensively writing in Poland. These semiofficial party-centered memoirs from within the hegemonic memory contained primarily heroic stories of insurgents leading military resistance against the Russian autocracy. They were published in dedicated journals, various anniversary publications, or separate books aligned with the parallel historiographical effort to document the "militaristic" struggle with "the foreign yoke."[4]

Moreover, I had access to about twenty testimonies written by NZR members or affiliates. They were published in dedicated journals and various anniversary publications in the interwar period as part and parcel of the semiofficial commemorative effort of the associated political milieu. The memory of NZR nationalist workers was pitted against socialism but also against the main current of Polish nationalism. The first collection was published in the anniversary issue of the journal *Kiliński* commemorating the foundation of NZR thirty years earlier, in 1905. Subsequent issues followed, filled with commemorative articles and autobiographical testimonies written by former members.

In addition, in all these contexts, unpublished memoirs emerged, later often gathered in "personal folders" in the PZPR archives. Many autobiographies were written in response to direct commissions from local party committees (cities and regions) for commemorative purposes. Bigger factories may have had an employee who collected memoirs of the "veterans of the proletarian movement." Later, such documents were preserved in the party archives too. Subsequent anniversaries (such as 1955 and 1975) produced additional impulses to actively seek autobiographical writers. Testimonies were written for various competitions, willingly organized by party historians or sociologists.[5] A separate category was personal surveys or file autobiographies, as Yury Zaretskiy called them.[6] They were filled in to confirm veteran status and may have resulted in various rewards, honorary titles, or increased pensions. One needs to keep in mind all these contexts and politics of writing while studying the biographical inscriptions of the revolution.

Precoded chunks of autobiographies relevant for this study were turned into computer-readable text and open coded using Weft-QDA software. Later, axial coding was used to build connections between literary forms and life cycle stages.[7] The material was later additionally selectively coded in order to structure the insights better and produce topic-oriented, sequenced pictures of the life course of political militants.

When quoted, notes contain full bibliographical reference. Additionally, journals (but not separate biographies published in them) and self-standing books are listed in the bibliography.

Political Leaflets

My investigation concerns a complete corpus of preserved political texts (ca. eight hundred items) published in Polish by party organizations in three major industrial centers of Russian Poland (Lodz, Warsaw, and the Dąbrowa Basin) and by the central committees of the parties. The analysis covered worker-directed political discourse in the leaflets issued by the major political parties, which included SDKPiL, the PPS, which later split into the PPS-Revolutionary Faction and the PPS-Left, and the National Democracy party with the National Workers Association—NZR. It is worth remembering that socialist parties also addressed German- and Jewish (Yiddish)-speaking workers, and Jewish socialist parties created another pillar of vivid political life during those days. Leaflets in Russian were directed chiefly at soldiers. However, non-Polish material was not systematically analyzed.

Digitalized leaflets were researched with computer-assisted qualitative analysis software (QDA Miner + WordStat) in order to shed light on discursive patterns emerging in the dense communicative setting of the revolution and the development of political languages in time. Every leaflet in the database was assigned variables such as party, place of publication, date, and topic. The material was open coded, and in certain aspects closed coding was later performed. The codes concerned themes, *topoi* used to express core issues, syntax applied to particular actors, passive and active structures, normative expectations toward readers, and assumed community coded via grammatical persons. Additionally, I performed basic lexicometrical analysis examining key concepts and collocations. The presence of all these features could be easily correlated with assigned variables; for instance, it was clearly visible how rhetorical strategies of a given party evolved over time. The data set, however, was manageable enough to read every text in a traditional way with full hermeneutic sensitivity. Data organization allowed me to easily return to the chosen themes and interpretatively reread relevant fragments or choose illustrative examples.

The insights presented here are informed by the analysis of the entire collection, but when exemplary items are quoted, then the bibliographical address is given (incipit and archival location). Leaflets were gathered from archives, libraries, and collections of primary sources with the help of a published bibliography.[8] Archival institutions storing the leaflets and published collections are listed separately in the bibliography.

The Press

The press was used as a source in two modes. The arguments presented in chapter 5 are grounded in a systematic analysis of Polish-speaking dailies in Lodz. The background was a complete query of all issues of two major dailies from 1899 to the outbreak of the First World War performed within a framework of another research project.[9] For the purposes of this study, I used the articles from the broader collection that concern social and political topics and, above all, workers. In addition, I reexamined all issues published during the revolution. Core articles were digitized and analyzed in QDA miner software (see above).

Republished collections of articles[10] were extremely useful. So too was preparatory research undertaken by the author of a monograph on one of the press titles (personal communication).[11] When quoting newspaper articles, I list the title of the article, year of publication, and the concurrent issue (roughly corresponding to the working days of the year), which allows for unambiguous identification, unlike the daily date given on a vignette according to two calendars.

In addition, I also made an extensive, albeit less systematic query of other titles, used throughout this study. This included Warsaw dailies, some influential weeklies dealing with political topics, and, above all, the illegal political press published by the parties. Titles are listed in the bibliography.

Other Materials

Apart from the abovementioned coherent corpora, I used a panoply of other, more scattered materials. The published collections of primary sources were of great assistance, and on occasion I drew directly from sources produced by the tsarist administration. As a contextual background I used larger socialist brochures, party programs (usually republished as collected volumes), some theoretical enunciations of party leaders, collections of letters, and political pamphlets.

Notes

Abbreviations Used in the Notes

Archival Sources

AAN	Archiwum Akt Nowych (Archive of Contemporary Files, Warsaw, Poland)
AGAD	Archiwum Główne Akt Dawnych (Main Archive of Old Files, Warsaw, Poland)
APŁ	Archiwum Państwowe w Łodzi (State Archive in Lodz, Poland)
AODRR	Akta Osobowe Działaczy Ruchu Robotniczego (Personal Files of the Activists of the Workers' Movement)
APPS	Archiwum Polskiej Partii Socjalistycznej (Archive of the Polish Socialist Party)
BN	Biblioteka Narodowa (National Library, Warsaw, Poland)
DŻS	Dokumenty Życia Społecznego (Documents of Social Life)
KGP	Kancelaria Gubernatora Piotrkowskiego (The Chancellery of the Piotrkow Governor-General)
KC PZPR	Komitet Centralny Polskiej Zjednoczonej Partii Robotniczej (Central Committee of the Polish United Worker's Party)
pdt.	podteczka (subfolder)
t.	teczka (folder)
t.os.	teczka osobowa (personal folder)
ZDiPU	Zbiór Druków i Pism Ulotnych (The Collection of Ephemeral Printings and Writings)
ZDU A. Br.	Zbiór Druków Ulotnych Anny Branickiej (The Collection of Ephemeral Printings of Anna Branicka)
ZŻGP	Zarząd Żandarmerii Guberni Piotrkowskiej (County Gubernial Head Office of the Gendarmerie)

Organizations and Party Bodies

CKR	Centralny Komitet Robotniczy (Central Workers' Committee)
KPP	Komunistyczna Partia Polski (Polish Communist Party)
KR	Komitet Robotniczy (Workers' Committee)
ŁKR	Łódzki Komitet Robotniczy (Lodz Workers' Committee)
ND	Narodowa Demokracja (National Democracy)
NZR	Narodowy Związek Robotniczy (National Workers' Association)

OKR	Okręgowy Komitet Robotniczy (Regional Workers' Commitee)
PD	Postępowa Demokracja (Progressive Democracy)
PPS	Polska Partia Socjalistyczna (Polish Socialist Party)
PPS-Left	Polska Partia Socjalistyczna Lewica (Polish Socialist Party-Left)
PPS-RF	Polska Partia Socjalistyczna Frakcja Rewolucyjna (Polish Socialist Party-Revolutionary Faction)
PZPR	Polska Zjednoczona Partia Robotnicza (Polish United Workers' Party)
SDKPiL	Socjaldemokracja Królestwa Polskiego i Litwy (Social Democracy of the Kingdom of Poland and Lithuania)
WKR	Warszawski Komitet Robotniczy (Warsaw Workers' Committee)
ZG	Zarząd Główny (Heading Committee)

Introduction

Epigraphs: Memory of the revolutionary events written down by one of the witnesses, Quoted in Karwacki, *Łódź w latach rewolucji 1905–1907*, 64; and Anna Skarbek Sokołowska, *Wspomnienia 1882–1914*, Ossolineum, rkps 14137II, k. 160–61, quoted in Stegner, "Rewolucja w opinii środowisk liberalnych Królestwa Polskiego 1905–1907," 33–34.

1. As in the case of the ethicized concept of nation, see Kizwalter, *O nowoczesności narodu*; and Porter, *When Nationalism Began to Hate*.

2. Próchnik, *Pierwsze piętnastolecie Polski niepodległej (1918–1933)*; Wapiński, *Pokolenia Drugiej Rzeczypospolitej*; Żarnowska and Wolsza, *Społeczeństwo i polityka*; Micińska, *Dzieje inteligencji polskiej do roku 1918*; Samuś, *Wasza kartka wyborcza*.

3. Kenney, *Rebuilding Poland*.

4. Zarycki, "Cultural Capital and the Political Role of the Intelligentsia in Poland"; Zarycki, "Class Analysis in Conditions of a Dual-Stratification Order."

5. Arndt, *Intellektuelle in der Opposition*; Laba, *Roots of Solidarity*; Cywiński, *Rodowody niepokornych*; Gawin, *Wielki zwrot*; Siermiński, *Dekada przełomu*.

6. Reasons for unrest and the unfolding of revolutionary events are presented in Blobaum, *Rewolucja*.

7. Blobaum, *Rewolucja*, 72–73.

8. Samuś, "Kobiety w ruchu socjalistycznym Królestwa Polskiego," 94; Blobaum, "'Woman Question' in Russian Poland, 1900–1914." See also Sikorska-Kowalska, "Polskie 'Marianny.'"

9. Lewis, "Revolution in the Countryside."

10. Quoted in Kalabiński and Tych, *Czwarte powstanie czy pierwsza rewolucja*, 116.

11. Porter-Szűcs, *Poland in the Modern World*, 44.

12. At the end of 1906, the three main socialist parties were as numerous as 55,000 (PPS), 35,000 (SDKPiL), Bund (30,000), accounting for 15 percent of workers in the Polish Kingdom, whereas directly before the revolution all three of them had no more than 1,500 members. The NZR had about 25,000 members. Christian labor organizations gathered another 20,000. For the data, see Monasterska, *Narodowy Związek Robotniczy, 1905–1920*, 34–40; Żarnowska, *Geneza rozłamu w Polskiej Partii Socjalistycznej*, 457–65;

Żarnowska, "Rewolucja 1905–1907 a aktywizacja polityczna klasy," 12–21; and Karwacki, *Łódź w latach rewolucji 1905–1907*, 10–32.

13. Samuś, *Wasza kartka wyborcza*, chap. 1; Blobaum, *Rewolucja*, 113.

14. Synthetic panoramas of competing ideologies were presented in Porter-Szűcs, *Poland in the Modern World*, chap. 2; and Blobaum, *Rewolucja*, 80–114.

15. Porter, "Democracy and Discipline in Late Nineteenth Century Poland."

16. Blobaum, *Rewolucja*, 189.

17. This idea was proposed by Brian Porter-Szűcs in in his comments on one of the drafts.

18. Kmiecik, *Prasa polska w rewolucji 1905–1907*; Myśliński, *Polska prasa socjalistyczna w okresie zaborów*; Śmiechowski, *Łódzka wizja postępu*.

19. Żarnowska and Wolsza, *Społeczeństwo i polityka*; Samuś, *Wasza kartka wyborcza*.

20. Blobaum, *Rewolucja*, 286–87.

21. Ury, *Barricades and Banners*, 216.

22. Marzec, "What Bears Witness of the Failed Revolution?"

23. Eley, "Nations, Publics, and Political Cultures."

24. See, respectively, Eley, *Forging Democracy*; Silver, *Forces of Labor*; Castel, *From Manual Workers to Wage Laborers*; Taylor, *Modern Social Imaginaries*.

25. Mulholland, *Bourgeois Liberty and the Politics of Fear*.

26. Katznelson and Zolberg, *Working-Class Formation*; Kocka, *Arbeiterleben und Arbeiterkultur*; Linden and Rojahn, *Formation of Labour Movements, 1870–1914*; Linden, "National Integration of the European Working Class."

27. McDaniel, *Autocracy, Capitalism, and Revolution in Russia*; Sewell, "Uneven Development, the Autonomy of Politics"; Kocka, *Arbeiterleben und Arbeiterkultur*.

28. Originally, this statement comes from the *Manifesto of the Communist Party*, in Marx and Engels, *Collected Works*.

29. Bendix, *Nation-Building and Citizenship*, 104. See also Moore, *Injustice*.

30. Mulholland, *Bourgeois Liberty and the Politics of Fear*; Losurdo, *Liberalism*. On the general matrix of separation of publics, see Calhoun, *Roots of Radicalism*. Comparative studies may be found in Kocka, "Die Trennung die burgerliche und proletarianische Demokratie"; Kocka and Muller-Luckner, *Arbeiter und Bürger im 19. Jahrhundert*; and Eisenberg, "Working Class and Middle Class Associations." It is also argued that the main line of division here is decisive. When working-class politics was directed against the state, a broad union-party front was formed (Germany). If the main addressees were factory owners and there were hopes for state cooperation, a nonpolitical labor movement triumphed (England). See Katznelson and Zolberg, *Working-Class Formation*, 28.

31. Bonnell, *Roots of Rebellion*, 448. For more on autocratic capitalism and its impact on state-labor relations, see McDaniel, *Autocracy, Capitalism, and Revolution in Russia*.

32. Rieber, "Sedimentary Society," 353.

33. Mulholland, *Bourgeois Liberty and the Politics of Fear*; Miliband, "Class Struggle from Above."

34. Surh, *1905 in St. Petersburg*.

35. Wood, *Becoming Metropolitan*; Zahra, *Great Departure*. On methodological nationalism, see Wimmer and Glick Schiller, "Methodological Nationalism and Beyond."

36. Jedlicki, *Błędne Koło 1832–1864*, 290. See also Siekierski, *Kultura szlachty polskiej*, 35–53.

37. Śmiechowski, "Searching for a Better City."

38. Żarnowski, *State, Society, and Intelligentsia*; Walicki, *Polish Conceptions of the Intelligentsia*; Micińska, *Dzieje inteligencji polskiej do roku 1918*.

39. I have developed this line of argumentation in Marzec and Śmiechowski, "Pathogenesis of the Polish Public Sphere."

40. As stressed in research on well-formed labor movements and accompanying institutions. See Kocka, *Arbeiterleben und Arbeiterkultur*, chap. 6; Welskopp, *Banner der Brüderlichkeit*; and Sewell, "Artisans, Factory Workers, and the Formation."

41. As happened in England, where radicals successfully petitioned Parliament and actively sought political alliances. See Breuilly, "Civil Society and the Labor Movement." On complex processes of polemical dialogue, renegotiation of the moral economy, and alliance building in England, see also Steinberg, *Fighting Words*.

42. On political thinking, see Freeden, *Political Theory of Political Thinking*. Earlier historical configurations are analyzed in Koselleck, *Critique and Crisis*. The situation in Russia has been studied in Bradley, "Subjects into Citizens," and some remarks on Poland may be found in Janowski, "Gab es im 19. Jahrhundert in Polen."

43. For comparison of the relative "weight" of working class protest in Poland and Russia, see Blobaum, *Rewolucja*; Harcave, *First Blood*; Shanin, *Roots of Otherness*; and Ascher, *Revolution of 1905* (2004).

44. Steenson, *After Marx, before Lenin*; Eley, *Forging Democracy*.

45. Kurzman, *Democracy Denied, 1905–1915*.

46. Blänkner, "Historizitat, Instituzionalitat, Symbolizitat." Core synthetic contributions in this broader debate are Habermas, *Structural Transformation of the Public Sphere*; Koselleck, *Critique and Crisis*; and Hoffmann, *Civil Society, 1750–1914*.

47. Steinmetz and Haupt, "Introduction," 20.

48. Habermas, "Public Sphere," 115.

49. Fraser, "Rethinking the Public Sphere"; see also Hauser, "Vernacular Dialogue."

50. This does mean, however, that it does not include elements referring to different national or ethnic groups. It is worth noting that language differentiation only partially overlapped with ethnic or national divisions, often blurred and hybrid. This decision is motivated by the economy of research and capacities to compare and trace the process of change, not any assumption about boundaries of identity. Thus, for instance, leaflets in Polish directed to Polish-speaking German or Jewish workers or their biographical testimonies were not excluded from the analysis.

51. Snyder, *Nationalism, Marxism, and Modern Central Europe*; Walicki, *Stanisław Brzozowski*; Marzec, "Reading Polish Peripheral Marxism Politically."

52. Bottici, *Imaginal Politics*, 81.

53. Porter, *When Nationalism Began to Hate*.

54. Jonsson, *Crowds and Democracy*, 26.

55. Habermas, *Structural Transformation of the Public Sphere*, 132. An essential critique regarding the core issues of this study is presented in Montag, "Pressure of the Street."

56. Jonsson, *Crowds and Democracy*, 27.
57. The expression comes from Hobsbawm, *Age of Extremes*. On the changing role of language, see Steinmetz, *Political Languages in the Age of Extremes*.
58. Müller, *Contesting Democracy*.

1. Workers and Their Intelligentsia

Epigraph: Edward Skórkiewicz, Pamiętnik rewolucji 1905 roku w Zagłębiu Dąbrowskim, APŁ, Komitet Łódzki PZPR, folder 11718, p. 4.

1. Influential works on the French Revolution include Hunt, *Politics, Culture, and Class*; Baker, *Inventing the French Revolution*; and Ozouf, *Festivals and the French Revolution*. On Russia in 1917, see Kolonitskii and Figes, *Interpreting the Russian Revolution*. On 1905, see Baberowski, *Imperiale Herrschaft in der Provinz*; and Huechtker, "'Politics and Poetics of Transgression.'"

2. Works that have particularly influenced my approach include Koselleck, *Critique and Crisis*; Koselleck, *Preußen zwischen Reform und Revolution*; Kocka and Muller-Luckner, *Arbeiter und Bürger im 19. Jahrhundert*; Kocka, *Arbeitsverhältnisse und Arbeiterexistenzen*; and Kocka, "Asymmetrical Historical Comparison."

3. For an overview, see Prazmowska, *History of Poland*; and Porter-Szűcs, *Poland in the Modern World*.

4. Kula, *Economic Theory of the Feudal System*; Małowist, *Western Europe, Eastern Europe and World Development*; Kochanowicz, *Backwardness and Modernization*. An interesting presentation of Lodz in the context of global economic entanglements is presented in Pobłocki, "Cunning of Class."

5. At that time Poland was in a constitutional personal union with the Russian Empire, created in 1815 by the Congress of Vienna. The tsars soon reduced Polish autonomy, and Russia eventually de facto annexed the country.

6. See Nietyksza, *Rozwój miast i aglomeracji*. At the beginning, however, the only industrial areas in the new country's frontiers were Staropolski Okręg Przemysłowy (the Old Polish Industrial Region) and Częstochowa; the rest of Congress Poland was rural. On early prepartition attempts to industrialize the country, see Assorodobraj-Kula, *Poczatki klasy robotniczej*.

7. Kołodziejczyk, "Pochodzenie i źródła rekrutacji klasy robotniczej"; Kula and Leskiewiczowa, *Przemiany społeczne w Królestwie Polskim*; Żarnowska, *Klasa robotnicza Królestwa Polskiego, 1870–1914*. For a comparative frame in England, France, and Germany, respectively, see Thompson, *Making of the English Working Class*; Sewell, *Work and Revolution in France*; and Kocka, *Arbeitsverhältnisse und Arbeiterexistenzen*. For an instructive comparative overview, see Katznelson and Zolberg, *Working-Class Formation*.

8. See "Wstęp," in Gąsiorowska-Grabowska and Kalabiński, *Źródła do dziejów klasy robotnicze*. Some of the paragraphs in this section first appeared in Marzec and Zysiak, "Days of Labour."

9. On the tsarist system and synthesis of autocracy with deficient governance, see Waldron, *Governing Tsarist Russia*. Political freedoms and actual cooperation between the state administration and social institutions were much more meager in Russian Poland

than in mainland Russia. After the January uprising of 1863, the autonomy of the region was practically abolished and meek attempts to liberalize the tsarist state (rural and urban self-governance, loosening of press censorship) did not affect the region later. See Jaśkiewicz, *Carat i sprawy polskie*; Weeks, "Nationality and Municipality"; Weeks, *Nation and State in Late Imperial Russia*; and Rolf, *Imperiale Herrschaft im Weichselland*.

10. Gatrell, *Tsarist Economy*.

11. The notion of proletarianization and its assumed indeterminate outcomes in respect to class-based culture and working-class politics draws on the perspective presented in Katznelson and Zolberg, *Working-Class Formation*. An earlier and equally useful model was proposed in Kocka, *Lohnarbeit und Klassenbildung*.

12. On Warsaw development and ethnic cauldron, see more in Corrsin, *Warsaw before the First World War*.

13. Żarnowska, *Robotnicy Warszawy na przełomie XIX i XX wieku*. On outcomes of this social composition for revolutionary protest, see Kiepurska, *Warszawa w rewolucji 1905–1907*.

14. Szajnowska-Wysocka, "Demographic Changes in an Industrial Centre," 193.

15. Walczak, *Dzieje robotnicze Śląska i Zagłębia Dąbrowskiego*. See also Kałuża, *Przeciw carowi!*

16. By the end of the century up to one-third of the workers were employed in factories hiring more than a thousand people (Pustoła, "Dynamika liczebności proletariatu przemysłowego").

17. Rosin and Bandurka, *Łódź 1423–1823–1973*, 18.

18. Puś and Pytlas, *Dzieje Łódzkich Zakładów*, 11.

19. Calculations in Podgórska, *Szkolnictwo elementarne w Łodzi*, 58. For more information on urban growth, see Fijałek et al., *Łódź*; and Janczak, "National Structure of the Population."

20. Missalowa, "Kształtowanie się klasy robotniczej," 23–24.

21. Żarnowska, *Klasa robotnicza Królestwa Polskiego, 1870–1914*, 132–36.

22. Żarnowska, "Rodowód i ruchliwość społeczna."

23. In bigger textile mills female workers could be a majority. See Puś and Pytlas, *Dzieje Łódzkich Zakładów*, 124.

24. Janczak, "National Structure of the Population," 25; Janczak, *Ludność Łodzi przemysłowej 1820–1914*, 11:109.

25. On local bourgeoisie and factory owners, see Pytlas, "National Composition of Łódź Industrialists"; Pytlas, *Łódzka burżuazja przemysłowa w latach 1864–1914*.

26. While older scholarship stresses the complete lack of educated groups, for a revision see Iwańska, "Garść refleksji i postulatów badawczych."

27. Janczak, *Ludność Łodzi przemysłowej 1820–1914*, 11:155. There are no precise data on national composition of classes. Censuses indicate the area of professional activity but not status, so they contain information about how many Jews were active in industry but do not indicate exactly how many of them were workers. Nevertheless, the general numbers and proportions of the population offer an estimate.

28. Nietyksza, *Ludność Warszawy na przełomie XIX i XX wieku*, 120.

29. According to the 1897 cenzus, 35 percent of male Jews in Warsaw were active in industry and craftsmanship, compared to 39 percent in commerce, finance, and insurance. See Nietyksza, *Ludność Warszawy na przełomie XIX i XX wieku*, 177; and Żarnowska, *Robotnicy Warszawy na przełomie XIX i XX wieku*.

30. Żarnowska, *Klasa robotnicza Królestwa Polskiego, 1870–1914*, 102–57; Żarnowska, "Rewolucja 1905–1907 a aktywizacja."

31. Kita, Królikowska, and Pawlak, *Bunt, masa, maszyna*.

32. On the burgeoning "national question" and tsarist responses, see Crago, "'Polishness' of Production"; and Kanfer, "Łódź."

33. On the repertoires of contention, see Tilly, *Popular Contention in Great Britain, 1758–1834*. For the somehow mysterious proceedings of this short-lived political constituency, see Próchnik, *Bunt łódzki w roku 1892*; Samuś, *"Bunt łódzki" 1892 roku*.

34. For more information on the level of education among workers, see Żarnowska, "Zasięg oświaty elementarnej wśród."

35. There were deliberate attempts to limit working-class children's access to any form of schooling apart from these three-year municipal schools. The Russian superintendent in charge of education, Alexander Apukhtin, issued a secret directive to the school directors to prevent them from accepting working-class children into gymnasiums. Special schools for this group were later created in urbanized areas. On general education, see Podgórska, *Szkolnictwo elementarne w Łódzi*; and Szymański, *Zarys polityki caratu wobec szkolnictwa*.

36. On various forms of informal and usually illegal private education, see Żarnowska, "Zasięg oświaty elementarnej wśród"; Żarnowska, *Robotnicy Warszawy na przełomie XIX i XX wieku*; and Światło, *Oświata a polski ruch robotniczy 1876–1939*.

37. On vocational training, see Miąso, *Szkolnictwo zawodowe*.

38. On one local debate about the catastrophic lack of professional schools, see Śmiechowski, *Łódzka wizja postępu*.

39. On synthetic presentation of the generic features of the informal and ongoing working-class education, see Johnson, "Really Useful Knowledge"; and Rose, *Intellectual Life of the British Working Classes*.

40. Miąso, *Uniwersytet dla Wszystkich*; Światło, *Oświata a polski ruch robotniczy 1876–1939*.

41. Szukiewicz, "Fragmenty mojej pracy partyjnej," 36.

42. On the intelligentsia's ethos and mission, see Walicki, *Polish Conceptions of the Intelligentsia*; Sdvizkov, *Zeitalter der Intelligenz*. "Organic work" was one of the core ideas developed by Polish positivism. Positivism as an intellectual movement in the Polish context used to have particular features. Although referring to the Comtean positive philosophy, it was more of a sociocultural program after the suppression of the 1863 January uprising. Instead of inducing insurrectionist tendencies, positivists called for "organic work," bringing mundane civilizational progress through progressive and liberal measures in culture and economy, as means of contesting partitions and lack of nation state. See "Positivism," in Miłosz, *History of Polish Literature*; Blejwas, *Realism in Polish Politics*; and Janowski, *Polish Liberal Thought before 1918*.

43. This particular form, allegedly strengthening some authoritarian disposition of

Eastern European intelligentsia is analyzed in Nicolaysen, "Looking Backward," 41–120; and Riga, "Identity and Empire," 136–49.

44. Polish circles were organized similarly to Russian ones, so the literature on the latter can be of some relevance here. See Pearl, *Creating a Culture of Revolution*, chap. 1; and Wildman, *Making of a Workers' Revolution*, chap. 4. On Russian Poland, see Miąso, *Uniwersytet dla Wszystkich*. On Polish alternative education seen through the lens of the history of the intelligentsia, see Mencwel, *Etos lewicy*.

45. Often the main aim of this general education was supplementing the very scarce body of skillful agitators, and for such work general knowledge was also useful. Such a situation is described for instance in Sternet, *Strejk styczniowo-lutowy r. 1905*, 241.

46. After the demise of positivism as a master framework of patriotic activity for the younger generation of intelligentsia now more prone to active radical politics, the generation of anti-system radicals emerged, subsequently splitting into socialist left and populist and national democratic right, see Cywiński, *Rodowody niepokornych*; Mencwel, *Etos lewicy*; Porter, *When Nationalism Began to Hate*.

47. Blobaum, *Feliks Dzierżyński and the SDKPiL*; Samuś, *Dzieje SDKPiL w Łodzi 1893–1918*; Radlak, *Socjaldemokracja Królestwa Polskiego i Litwy*.

48. Snyder, *Nationalism, Marxism, and Modern Central Europe*.

49. Żarnowska, *Geneza rozłamu w Polskiej Partii Socjalistycznej, 1904–1906*. On differences in theoretical sensitivity, see Possart, *Struktury myślenia teoretycznego*. There is no major work on the PPS in English. On negotiating the Jewish question, see Zimmerman, *Poles, Jews, and the Politics of Nationality*. The liberation struggle under the national banner as redeemable to socialism, and indeed more sensitive for intersection of identities and demands, is presented in Blanc, "National Liberation and Bolshevism Reexamined"; and Blanc, "Anti-Imperial Marxism."

50. Crago, "'Polishness' of Production"; Monasterska, *Narodowy Związek Robotniczy, 1905–1920*; Fountain, *Roman Dmowski*; Krzywiec, *Chauvinism, Polish Style*.

51. Tobias, *Jewish Bund in Russia*. On the immense influence of the Bund in local Jewish communities, see Shtakser, *Making of Jewish Revolutionaries*. Some other peculiarities of Jewish politics are scrutinized in Hoffman and Mendelsohn, *Revolution of 1905 and Russia's Jews*.

52. Zionism was apparently more attractive for people with middle class background and already gathered some support on the Pale, but not in Russian Poland, see Gitelman, "Century of Jewish Politics," 16.

53. Dąbrowski, *Czerwona Warszawa przed ćwierć wiekiem*, 111–12.

54. Żarnowska, "Rewolucja 1905–1907"; Żarnowska, "Klasa robotnicza Królestwa Polskiego w rewolucji 1905–1907."

55. Bradley, *State and Civil Society in Russia*; Bradley, "Subjects into Citizens"; Bradley, *Voluntary Associations in Tsarist Russia;* Janowski, "Gab es im 19. Jahrhundert"; Porter, "Emergence of Civil Society."

56. This surprise notwithstanding, some signs of tension were already visible before. Robert Blobaum is somewhat right in arguing that in the Polish Kingdom the relevant timing should incorporate the startup of 1904 events predating the 1905 clashes, already synchronous with the general upheaval in Russia (*Rewolucja*, 42–43). Scholars of the

Russian Revolution have also pointed to earlier tensions, effectively broadening the time scope of the revolution to 1904–1907 (e.g., Ascher, "Interpreting 1905").

57. Edward Skórkiewicz, Pamiętnik rewolucji 1905 roku w Zagłębiu Dąbrowskim, APŁ, Komitet Łódzki PZPR, folder 11718, p. 4.

58. Abundant documentation of the prerevolutionary language of claims may be found in petitions and protest letters sent to factory owners or different agencies of the tsarist administration. See the petitions in Korzec, *Źródła do dziejów rewolucji 1905–1907*, vol. 1, pt. 1; and Gąsiorowska-Grabowska and Kalabiński, *Źródła do dziejów klasy robotniczej*. More petitions may be found in tsarist files: for instance, APŁ KGP 546, 547.

59. Kalabiński and Tych, *Czwarte powstanie czy pierwsza rewolucja*, 116.

60. [Leon Wasilewski], *Strejk polityczny w Król. Polskiem, Nakładem Administracyi "Przedświtu" i "Naprzodu," Kraków 1905*, 22–23; see also Pestkowski, *Wspomnienia rewolucjonisty*, 32.

61. Brzozowski, *Kultura i życie*. Generally on Brzozowski, see Walicki, *Stanisław Brzozowski*; and Marzec, "Reading Polish Peripheral Marxism Politically."

62. Stanisław Brzozowski, *Literatura polska wobec rewolucji*, in Brzozowski, *Współczesna powieść i krytyka literacka*, 224.

63. "Wywiad u M. Poznańskiego," *Rozwój*, no. 6 (1907). One of the members of the liberal intelligentsia remembered: "So far [early 1905] everybody supported strikes. In the moment of outburst they were even supported by the factory owners against whom they were nominally directed," in Mogilnicki, *Wspomnienia*, 95. The Warsaw-based association of engineers also expressed its admiration of the calm and dignity of the striking workers (*Krwawe dnie w Warszawie*, 2). Many anecdotes from the early days use the description of a strike as a feast (święto).

64. Pestkowski, *Wspomnienia rewolucjonisty*, 32–33.

65. Party literature tried hard to build this sense of solidarity among factories, branches, and regions. Almost every socialist journal directed toward working-class readers contained a special section on "current news from factories and workshops," which was the most popular section among readers. For editorial commentary on this issue in SDKPiL's journal, see *Czerwony Sztandar*, no. 23 (1905): 9n.

66. For an overview, see Żarnowska, "Próba analizy ruchu strajkowego." On the dynamics in Lodz, see Karwacki, *Łódź w latach rewolucji 1905–1907*, 39–41. In Warsaw the rhythm of strikes was slightly different, with more involvement of non-working-class participants (Kiepurska, *Warszawa w rewolucji 1905–1907*, 79–97). On the Dąbrowa Basin, the best description may be found in Kałuża, *Przeciw carowi!*

67. For detailed information on concessions and the improvement of living conditions after the first strikes, see Kalabiński and Tych, *Czwarte powstanie czy pierwsza rewolucja*, 626–28; and Piskała, "1905—rok z dziejów polskiego Manchesteru," 221–22.

68. Even if Anderson (*Imagined Communities*) coined the term as referring to the perceived bond of national community, here it is rather class that became such a virtual yet no less effective frame of reference.

69. A detailed analysis of strike waves with participant number estimations, data on strike days, and change across time is presented for Lodz in Badziak and Samuś, *Strajki*

robotników łódzkich w 1905 roku. On Warsaw, see *Ruch strajkowy robotników przemysłowych Warszawy i guberni warszawskiej w okresie najwyższego jego natężenia*, pts. 1 and 2, in Kalabiński, *Polska klasa robotnicza*.

70. Tilly, *Popular Contention in Great Britain, 1758–1834*, 347–49.

71. A transformation masterfully described, concerning other factories on the industrial fringes of imperial Russia, in Zelnik, *Law and Disorder on the Narova River*.

72. Karwacki, "Walka o wprowadzenie"; Karwacki, *Związki zawodowe i stowarzyszenia pracodawców*, 45; Pestkowski, *Wspomnienia rewolucjonisty*, 35. For an analysis of party documents, see Strobel, *Partei Rosa Luxemburgs*, 227–31.

73. Some remarks on the dynamic relationship between parties and mass movements can be found in Kaczyńska, "Partie polityczne a masowy ruch robotniczy"; Żarnowska, "Rewolucja 1905–1907 a aktywizacja polityczna klasy"; and Żarnowska, "Spojrzenie na rewolucję 1905 r."

74. For narrators describing such events, either as their own experience or as a general practice of those days, see Relacja Feliksa Zimnocha, AAN, Zbiór relacji dotyczących ruchu robotniczego, R-141, p. 2; Władysław Nowicki ("Książę"), Wspomnienia z 1905–1906 roku, in Tych, *Archiwum ruchu robotniczego*, 95; Edward Skórkiewicz, Pamiętnik rewolucji 1905 roku w Zagłębiu Dąbrowskim, APŁ KŁ PZPR, t. 11718, p. 9; and Henryk Bitner, "Rok 1905 w Łodzi," *Z pola walki*, no. 11–22 (1931). On factory conflicts and complicated negotiations, see Karwacki, "Walka o wprowadzenie"; Karwacki, *Łódź w latach rewolucji 1905–1907*; and Lewis, "Labor-Management Conflict in Russian Poland."

75. It is widely documented by labor historians how important artisanal cultures were for early labor protests and the sprouting of socialism. They provided networks of communication and solidarity, delivered educated members to the movement, and fueled militant zeal with longing for a better future modeled on the imagined, long-gone past. In various ways and regarding different contexts, such argumentation is presented in Thompson, *Making of the English Working Class*; Shorter and Tilly, *Strikes in France, 1830–1968*; Sewell, *Work and Revolution in France*; Sewell, "Artisans, Factory Workers, and the Formation"; Calhoun, *Question of Class Struggle*; Bonnell, *Roots of Rebellion*; Welskopp, *Banner der Brüderlichkeit*; and Bauman, *Memories of Class*.

2. Workers and the Public Sphere

Epigraph: Szapiro, *Związki Zawodowe Robotnicze*, 5.

1. Eley, "Nations, Publics, and Political Cultures."

2. Negt and Kluge, *Public Sphere and Experience*.

3. Habermas, *Structural Transformation of the Public Sphere*.

4. Arditi, *Polemicization*.

5. For an alternative history of public practices as forms of popular contention, early strikes, and so on, see Negt and Kluge, *Public Sphere and Experience*, 42.

6. Lottes, *Politische Aufklärung und plebejisches Publikum*. On the plebeian political experience of English Jacobinism, see also Breaugh, *Plebeian Experience*. Thompson, *Making of the English Working Class*, gives a general context.

7. See also Tilly, *Popular Contention in Great Britain, 1758–1834*.

8. Lottes, *Politische Aufklärung und plebejisches Publikum*; Kocka and Muller-Luckner, *Arbeiter und Bürger im 19. Jahrhundert*; Eley, "Nations, Publics, and Political Cultures"; Calhoun, *Roots of Radicalism*.

9. Marzec and Śmiechowski, "Pathogenesis of the Polish Public Sphere."

10. Frykman and Löfgren, *Culture Builders*; Kocka and Mitchell, *Bourgeois Society in Nineteenth-Century Europe*. Therefore in Central and Eastern Europe the term "intelligentsia" is commonly understood slightly differently than in the Western world (and often in anglophone academia), where it is sometimes used interchangeably with the term "intellectuals." However, in local terms it is analytically more accurate to consider the Eastern European intelligentsia as a particular social strata, composed of the educated groups of society. In such depictions, intellectuals are just one part of the group; see Kurczewska, "Inteligencja." Other authors underline the psychological foundations of belonging to the intelligentsia. What allegedly characterized this group was its strong self-identity and certain exclusivity despite close links to other social strata (Micińska, *Dzieje inteligencji polskiej do roku 1918*, 111–13).

11. Chałasiński, *Społeczna genealogia inteligencji polskiej*; Kita, "Dwór po powstaniu."

12. Czepulis-Rastenis, *"Klasa umysłowa,"* 5.

13. Walicki, *Polish Conceptions of the Intelligentsia*.

14. Mencwel, *Etos lewicy*; Cywiński, *Rodowody niepokornych*.

15. Śmiechowski, Sikorska-Kowalska, and Fukumoto, *Robotnicy Łodzi drugiej połowy XIX wieku*.

16. "Echa bezrobocia," *Kurier Codzienny*, no. 56 (7 June 1905): 2, quoted in Kiepurska, *Warszawa w rewolucji 1905–1907*, 96.

17. On tsarist censorship in general, see Ruud, *Fighting Words*. On the situation in the Kingdom of Poland, see Szyndler, *Dzieje cenzury w Polsce do 1918 roku*. The local censors' offices were very sensitive for political and social issues, see Śmiechowski, "Strategie władz carskich wobec łódzkiej prasy."

18. "Echa bezrobocia," *Kurier Codzienny*, quoted in Kiepurska, *Warszawa w rewolucji 1905–1907*, 96.

19. Pestkowski, *Wspomnienia rewolucjonisty*, 35; Karwacki, *Związki zawodowe i stowarzyszenia*, 45–47; Blobaum, *Rewolucja*, 99.

20. Henryk Bitner, "Rok 1905 w Łodzi," *Z pola walki*, no. 11–12 (1931), quoted in Bąbol, *Łódzkie barykady*, 387.

21. Stefan Sobotka, "Wspomnienia Żyrardowiaka," *Niepodległość* 9 (1934): 377.

22. On public street performances, see Karwacki, *Łódź w latach rewolucji 1905–1907*.

23. Bodnar, "Reclaiming Public Space," 2091.

24. Samuś, *Wasza kartka wyborcza*, 210–13.

25. On attempts to call various political gatherings as reflected in tsarist reports, see Korzec, *Źródła do dziejów rewolucji 1905–1907*, vol. 1, pt. 2, 488–89. It is often hard to assess to what extent the speakers were workers or, rather, representatives talking on behalf of workers. However, workers speaking, for better or worse, definitely made their way into the memories of proletarian autobiographers and excited or frightened intelligentsia alike. Thus all the parties felt the difference in partitions of political visibility.

26. Józef Grabiec [Dąbrowski], "Pierwszy tydzień listopadowy Warszawy przed dwudziestu laty: Notatki," *Świat*, no. 47 (1925): 6, quoted in Samuś, *Wasza kartka wyborcza*, 213–14.

27. Grabiec [Dąbrowski], "Pierwszy tydzień listopadowy Warszawy," quoted in Samuś, *Wasza kartka wyborcza*, 213–14.

28. This is the main framing Scott Ury proposes to understand massive political participation of the Jews of Warsaw around 1905 (*Barricades and Banners*). For a poignant description of a transition from peasant child into conscious urban worker and immersion in the new world of a big city and modern factory, see Rudnicki, *Stare i nowe*.

29. As practiced among the people, according to some scholars of Marxism. For the best presentation of this line of argumentation, see Halfin, *From Darkness to Light*. My polemic with this position is presented in Marzec, "Vernacular Marxism."

30. For more historical detail on this complex relationship, see Chwalba, *Sacrum i rewolucja*.

31. Dąbrowski, *Czerwona Warszawa przed ćwierć wiekiem*, 113.

32. Ludwig Dziąg, "Ze wspomnien kilińczyka," *Kiliński*, no. 3 (1936): 123.

33. Płochocki, *Wspomnienia działacza SDKPIL*, 130.

34. An overview of singing culture and lyrics may be found in Ajnenkiel, *Czerwona lutnia*.

35. Karwacki, *Łódź w latach rewolucji 1905–1907*, 317–37. Alcohol and tobacco were banned to prevent demoralization and gather money for the strike fund as well. For a report of the tsarist police about this, see Korzec, *Źródła do dziejów rewolucji 1905–1907*, vol. 1, pt. 2, 9.

36. Karwacki, *Łódź w latach rewolucji 1905–1907*, 113–18.

37. Wacław Konderski, "Wspomnienia działacza związków zawodowych SDKPiL," *Z pola walki* no. 1 (1961): 74.

38. These were spaces typical of big factories hiring mostly Christian workers. Because of their size, private-public spaces could exist amid the production process and out of the sight of factory owners or military staff. In the case of smaller workshops with Jewish crews this function may have been played by the market (*birzha*), where Jewish employees met to exchange political ideas. They could also meet on the street because of a strong asset they had—an impenetrable language, which protected them from being easily overheard or infiltrated by policemen and spies. See Shtakser, *Making of Jewish Revolutionaries*.

39. Stanisław Nowosiński (Zawierucha), "Z czasów rewolucji 1905 roku i późniejszych walk o niepodległość Polski," *Niepodległość* 5 (1932): 385.

40. Władysław Nowicki ("Książe"), *Wspomnienia z 1905–1906 roku*, in Tych, *Archiwum ruchu robotniczego*, 91. This was a name day, politicized especially in respect to political militants who as this narrator had just been released from political imprisonment.

41. On this dimension in other factory contexts in the region, see Shtakser, *Making of Jewish Revolutionaries*; and Welskopp, *Banner der Brüderlichkeit*.

42. For regimes of speech and communication important for creating workers' institutions and "alternative cultures" in German contexts, see Lidtke, *Alternative Culture*; and Welskopp, *Banner der Brüderlichkeit*.

43. Stanisław Perkowski, *Życiorys*, AAN, AODRR, 4545, p. 12.

44. Minutes of party gatherings confirm that training working-class speakers was a serious issue and a deliberately pursued strategy. For instance, the leaders of the PPS before the revolution were already complaining about "lies" used by SDKPiL agitators but also admitted that their own speakers were just badly prepared to resist those "empty phrases" adequately and win the bids. See *Sprawozdanie z zebrania kierownictwa PPS w 1903 roku*, AAN, Mf 1256/10.

45. In this respect the change in the working class social world epitomized the modern experience as analyzed by classical sociology, see Simmel, *Conflict*.

46. On party polemics and prerevolutionary development of socialist programs, see Kancewicz, *Polska Partia Socjalistyczna w latach 1892–1896*; Radlak, *Socjaldemokracja Królestwa Polskiego i Litwy*; Żarnowska, *Geneza rozłamu w Polskiej Partii Socjalistycznej, 1904–1906*.

47. "Skałon sympatykiem socjalistów, Margrafskij narodowym demokratą," *Robotnik*, no. 161 (1906).

48. *Czerwony Sztandar* no. 375 (1906); "Dajcie sobie buzi," *Czerwony Sztandar*, no. 60 (1906).

49. Letter to Leon Jogiches-Tyszka, 26–27 October 1905, in Luksemburg, *Listy*.

50. Dobrowolski—kowal, "Kartka do historii SDKPiL," *Z pola walki*, no. 4 (1974): 194.

51. Piotr Szefer, "Ze wspomnień łódzkiego robotnika," *Z pola walki*, no. 3 (1927): 141.

52. It is worth adding that this is a memory of a Jewish militant affiliating himself with Polish culture. This testimony also demonstrates how open various identities still may have been in those days. The decision the narrator faced was between the (nationalist) Bund and international solidarity (this time between Poles and Jews) postulated by the PPS. See Mojżesz Kaufman (Mojsze Mezryczer), "Przyczynki do historji żydowskiej organizacji PPS," *Niepodległość* 12 (1935): 30.

53. Halfin, *Red Autobiographies*.

54. Radomski, "Wspomnienia technika partyjnego 1905–1907 rok," *Z pola walki*, no. 11–12 (1931), quoted in Kozłowski, *Z rewolucyjnych dni*, 234.

55. Pestkowski, *Wspomnienia rewolucjonisty*, 83.

56. There is no space here to explore this issue further. For a brief outline of the Duma elections and party strategies, see Blobaum, *Rewolucja*. Evolving strategies and Duma elections are also extensively examined in Samuś, *Wasza kartka wyborcza*. Leaflets, polemical strategies and political expertise surplus are examined in Marzec, *Rebelia i reakcja*.

57. On multiple labor unions, see Karwacki, *Związki zawodowe i stowarzyszenia pracodawców*. It seems that in this polemical culture the narcissism of small differences between parties and their supporters had much more importance than some researchers have suggested in respect to working-class militancy in tsarist Russia. It is argued (for instance in Pearl, *Creating a Culture of Revolution*) that all parties used the same literature and agitation techniques and that on the shop floor of late nineteenth-century Russian factories, most of the radical workers cooperated and considered themselves radical workers as such rather than adherents of a particular program. In the context researched here, however, some direct evidence of working-class discourse suggests the opposite. For instance, a

telling "kite" from the tsarist prison is a well-elaborated exchange of arguments on the national question, the main bone of contention between socialist parties. See AAN APPS 305/II/60.

58. The PPS leaflet explaining the rules of the game and calling for cultured discussion may be found in Korzec, *Źródła do dziejów rewolucji 1905–1907*, vol. 1, pt. 2, 661. Significantly, it proposes clear limits on "freedom of speech." Those calling for anti-Jewish violence should be treated as provocateurs and shot dead on the spot.

59. For more on "fratricidal" struggles, see Kalabiński and Tych, *Czwarte powstanie czy pierwsza rewolucja*, 279–81; and Karwacki, *Łódź w latach rewolucji 1905–1907*, 156–60.

60. Korzec, *Źródła do dziejów rewolucji 1905–1907*, vol. 1, pt. 2, 121; See also Karwacki, *Łódź w latach rewolucji 1905–1907*, 112.

61. Korzec, *Źródła do dziejów rewolucji 1905–1907*, vol. 1, pt. 2, 123.

62. This dimension as the most profound change brought about by 1905 is examined for Russian workers and, in more emotional detail, the Jewish poor in, respectively, Bonnell, *Roots of Rebellion*; and Shtakser, *Making of Jewish Revolutionaries*.

63. Antoni Kotyl, O dziłalnosci w SDKPiL, KPP oraz pracy w Polsce Ludowej, AAN, AODRR 3028, p. 5.

64. Korzec, *Źródła do dziejów rewolucji 1905–1907*, vol. 1, pt. 2, 568–69.

65. The staging of tsarist power, the loss of its appeal and legitimacy, and attempts to restore its public appearance are examined in Baberowski, *Imperiale Herrschaft in der Provinz*; and Rolf, "A Continuum of Crisis?"

66. "Wiece," *Kurier Warszawski*, no. 486 (3 November 1905): 1, quoted in Kiepurska, *Warszawa w rewolucji 1905–1907*, 204.

67. Karwacki, *Łódź w latach rewolucji 1905–1907*, 120.

68. Łęczycki, *Mojej ankiety personalnej punkt*, 35, 61.

69. Jaśkiewicz, *Absolutyzm rosyjski*, 80–145.

70. Wortman, *Scenarios of Power*.

71. For some reason, however, the impact of the vote is not a topic emphasized in memoirs. In the case of socialist militants, dismissal of the right to vote is in line with the rather marginal role of elections in socialist politics, which always claimed that they had been just a cheat (even the open bidding for votes was explicitly framed as a way to gain adherents, not seats in the Duma). In the case of nationalist workers, the situation is more mysterious. Perhaps the official trajectory of the NZR, from which the vast majority of narratives came, caused the narrators to diminish their involvement with the National Democracy party, as their association split with National Democrats in 1908 and later built a rather separate memory culture. It is a widely held and not untrue conviction that the main issue was the increasingly pro-Russian and reconciliatory position taken by the National Democracy party in subsequent Dumas (Monasterska, *Narodowy Związek Robotniczy, 1905–1920*, 67–80.) If so, this would confirm the ultimate success of nationalist mobilization among workers, which proved to be stronger than convictions of the (elite) National Democrats themselves. Although they initially stimulated that mobilization, they later engaged in political maneuvers unacceptable to their ardent supporters among workers. However, there is also another explanation: workers unwilling to accept greater

social conservatism and elitist hegemony. Indeed, factory nationalism was not an artificial project made up from scratch by the National Democracy party, and the intellectual milieu of the NZR workers and their aspirations were resistant to full submission to the national democratic leadership demanding transclass loyalty against class-based interests. Their imagined future nation, state, and professional life were still class-based, and their demands strictly referred to the class context of production (Crago, "'Polishness' of Production," 36–41).

72. See Krzywiec, "Z taką rewolucją musimy walczyć na noże"; Porter, *When Nationalism Began to Hate*.

73. The dark side of national democratic politics is analyzed in Ury, *Barricades and Banners*, chap. 6.

74. The transformation of "political culture" in reference to Polish politics is analyzed in Samuś, *Wasza kartka wyborcza*. For an interesting approach to implicit political change at the cultural and imaginary levels of citizenship in the early days of the Weimar democracy, similar to the transformation scrutinized here, see Canning, "Introduction."

75. Hillyar and McDermid, *Revolutionary Women in Russia, 1870–1917*.

76. Rosa Luxemburg (SDKPiL), Cezaryna Wojnarowska (SDKPiL), Estera Golde-Stóżecka (PPS-Left), and Maria Paszkowska (PPS), to name only a few.

77. Historians have attempted to fill this significant lacuna in knowledge of the period but have not had spectacular outcomes because of the lack of relevant sources. Many of the arguments presented are rather inferences from indirect clues, as in Sikorska-Kowalska, "Polskie 'Marianny.'"

78. Statistical data on Lodz are especially revealing; see Janczak, *Ludność Łodzi przemysłowej 1820–1914*, 11:96–99. A case study concerning the largest factory in the city confirms the high percentage of female workers (Puś and Pytlas, *Dzieje Łódzkich Zakładów*).

79. Samuś, "Kobiety w ruchu socjalistycznym Królestwa Polskiego," 94.

80. Samuś, "Kobiety w ruchu socjalistycznym Królestwa Polskiego," 91.

81. On the image and alleged role of women in different political milieus, trajectories of the women's movement and the changing role of female members of the nation see Blobaum, "'Woman Question' in Russian Poland, 1900–1914." On the particular, gendered image of women among the nationalists, see Pytka, "Policing the Binary."

82. Władysława Michałowska, "Wspomnienia robotnicy," *Niepodległość* 16 (1937): 380–81.

83. Maria Budkiewicz, AAN, AODRR, folder 12896, pp. 1–2.

84. Malinowski, *Materiały do historii PPS*, 1:158.

85. The reasons might be different. For one wife who preferred dance to socialism, see Michał Ostrowski, Wspomnienia, AAN, AODRR, folder 4386, t. 1, k. 2/2.

86. Zob. np. Elżbieta Żebrowska, Wspomnienia, APŁ, KW PZPR, 1605, 107.

87. Karwacki, *Łódź w latach rewolucji 1905–1907*, 123.

88. *Robotnik*, no. 54 (1904): 4.

89. *Robotnik*, no. 57 (1904): 4.

90. Snyder, *Nationalism, Marxism, and Modern Central Europe*; Zimmerman, *Poles, Jews, and the Politics of Nationality*; Blanc, "National Liberation and Bolshevism Reexamined."

91. Roman Dmowski, *Narodowcy i ugodowcy w czasie rewolucyjnym*, w: Dmowski, *Pisma*, 3:91. On nationalist institutions among workers, see Crago, "'Polishness' of Production"; and Kanfer, "Łódź."

92. An interesting study of the revolution perceived by the industrial bourgeoisie is Hofmann, "Biedermanns in the 1905 Revolution."

93. Michel Foucault, *Body/Power,* in: Foucault, *Power/Knowledge*.

94. Władysław Reymont, *Z konstytucyjnych dni: Notatki*, Wednesday, Nov. 1, in Klonowski, *1905 w literaturze polskiej*, 283. See also Zalewski, "Świat wyszedł z zawiasów."

95. Marzec, "Beyond Group Antagonism in Asymmetrical Counter-Concepts."

96. Examples could be found in pamphlets such as Ostoja, *Wobec zbrodni*; and Niedzielski, *Z burzliwych dni 1904–1905*.

97. The leader of the National Democracy party, Roman Dmowski, also expressed an ambivalent attitude to the initial revolutionary moment, which opened up new opportunities but also posed a danger to his political ideals. See *List Romana Dmowskiego do Zygmunta Miłkowskiego* (Cracow, 31 March 1905), in Kułakowski, *Roman Dmowski w świetle listów i wspomnień*, 312. On fighting anarchy, see leaflet of the Central Committee of the National Ligue, August 1, 1905, APŁ ZŻGP 12/1905/II, p. 918–919; leaflet of Lodz Department of the NZR, December 27, 1905, APŁ KGP 1553, p. 6; and National-Democratic Craftsmen and Workers Youth, APŁ ZŻGP 12/1905/I, p. 119.

98. Janowski, *Polish Liberal Thought before 1918*.

99. Aleksander Świętochowski, "Po roku," *Prawda*, no. 45 (1906), quoted in Stegner, "Rewolucja w opinii środowisk liberalnych," 33. For more on Świętochowski's changing position, see Petrozolin-Skowrońska, "'Liberum veto' A. Świętochowskiego," pts. 1–2.

100. Quoted from the memoir of Anna Skarbek Sokołowska, *Wspomnienia 1882–1914*, Ossolineum, rkps 14137II, k. 160–161, quoted in Stegner, "Rewolucja w opinii środowisk liberalnych," 33–34.

101. A collection of tsarist administrative reports giving a detailed overview of the contentious workers' politics without antisemitic additions and even confirming existing solidarity of workers with different ethnic and religious backgrounds can be found in Korzec, *Źródła do dziejów rewolucji 1905–1907*, vol. 1, pts. 1–2; and Kalabiński, *Carat i klasy posiadające*. There is no reason to suspect the tsarist administration of hiding antisemitic undertones, as it had an interest in inducing ethnic and religious antagonisms. The fact that administrators quite explicitly deny this, stating that Jewish and Polish workers took part together in demonstrations, backs up the statement. It is also worth mentioning that a direct impulse for the June uprising in Lodz in 1905 was the massacre that took place during a peaceful demonstration of workers. This gathering was organized because of gossip about two killed Jewish workers buried secretly to avoid a public (and possibly contentious) funeral (Kalabiński and Tych, *Czwarte powstanie czy pierwsza rewolucja*). Apparently, rumors about Jews could also play a role different from the one we are used to seeing in research on pogroms in the region.

102. Sokolnicki, *Czternaście lat*, quoted in Śliwa, "Rewolucja—przeszłość i kontynuacje," 38–39.

103. Kozicki, *Historia Ligi Narodowej*, 287.

104. I developed this argumentation in Marzec, "Modernizacja mas." See also Krzywiec, "Z taką rewolucją musimy walczyć na noże."

105. For a broader perspective on the Jewish revolutionary street in Warsaw, see Ury, *Barricades and Banners*.

106. Stanisław Kozicki, *Pamiętnik*, t. 1 k. 212–14, Biblioteka PAN w Krakowie, syg. 7849, quoted in Plennikowski, *Stanisław Kozicki*. Italics mine.

107. The battle for "national" Warsaw, fought on the street and around the ballot box during the Duma elections, and the raging antisemitism accompanying it has been examined in Corrsin, *Warsaw before the First World War*; Weeks, "Fanning the Flames"; Blobaum, "Politics of Antisemitism in Fin-de-Siècle Warsaw"; and Ury, *Barricades and Banners*.

108. This form of usurpatory nationalism reached its fullest form in the interwar period (Brykczynski, *Primed for Violence*).

109. In addition to the works on Warsaw listed above, see Blobaum, *Antisemitism and Its Opponents in Modern Poland*; Weeks, *From Assimilation to Antisemitism*; Krzywiec, "Eliminationist Anti-Semitism at Home and Abroad"; and Krzywiec, *Polska bez Żydów*.

110. The notion of intersectionality stems from feminist studies on multiple regimes of oppression, usually against black working-class females. See, esp., Crenshaw, *On Intersectionality*.

111. On the nationalist vision of gender and policing the gendered boundary within the movement see Pytka, "Policing the Binary."

112. Jaszczuk, *Spór pozytywistów z konserwatystami*.

113. Domagalska, *Zatrute ziarno*.

114. Jeleński, *Wrogom własnej ojczyzny*, 8. Other examples of antisemitic vitriol mixed with virulent antisocialism, a prototype of the trope of Judeo-communism still perpetuating Polish antisemitism today, may be found in Jeleński, *Bezrobocie rozumu*; Jeleński, *Siła przed prawem albo jak kto woli*; and Jeleński, *Robotniku polski!*.

115. Kościesza [Antoni Skrzynecki], *Wrogowie wiary i ojczyzny*, 10.

116. Friedrich, "Polish Literature's Portrayal of Jewish Involvement in 1905"; Garstka, "Revolution of 1905 in Polish Literature." See also Bohdan Urbankowski, *Rok 1905 przed sądem najwyższych autorytetów literackich*, in Maciejewska, *Rewolucja i niepodległość*; Magdalena Rumińska, *"Wiekuista maskarada" przed 1905 rokiem i krwawy karnawał po 1905 roku*, in Stepnik and Gabrys, *Rewolucja lat 1905–1907*; and Adam Tyszka, *Pozytywiści wobec rewolucji 1905–1907*, in Klonowski, *Pod czapką frygijską*.

117. Ury, *Barricades and Banners*, 216.

118. Wynn, *Workers, Strikes, and Pogroms*; Weinberg, *Revolution of 1905 in Odessa*.

119. Ruch robotniczy u nas przeżywa chwile przełomowe, Leaflet of the PPS-Lewica, 18 grudnia 1907, BN DŻS.

120. Wildman, *Making of a Workers' Revolution*, chap. 8; Schwarz, *Russian Revolution of 1905*. On the tensions in the practice of Polish parties, above all the nationalists, see Porter, "Democracy and Discipline."

121. Quoted in Krajewska, *Czytelnictwo wśród robotników*, 91.

3. Speech and Action

Epigraph: Łęczycki, *Mojej ankiety personalnej punkt 35*, 59–60.

1. Schorske, "Politics in a New Key."
2. Blobaum, *Rewolucja*.
3. Porter, "Democracy and Discipline."
4. Steinmetz, *Das Sagbare und das Machbare*.
5. Some of them were translated from socialist "classics," some written by Polish authors. Sometimes writing them led to an international career: for instance, in Russia. For more detailed analyses for Russia and Poland, respectively, see Pearl, *Creating a Culture of Revolution*, chap. 3; and Marzec, "Vernacular Marxism." The most important titles can be detected thanks to the detailed bibliography of Kormanowa, *Materiały do bibliografii druków socjalistycznych*. I list editions analyzed by myself elsewhere, sometimes republished later: Bracke, *Precz z socjalistami!*; Daszyński, *Pogadanka o socjalizmie*; Kautsky, *Zasady socjalizmu (Program Erfurcki)*; Kautsky, *Nauki ekonomiczne Karola Marksa*; Kelles-Krauz, *Czy teraz nie ma pańszczyzny?*; Kelles-Krauz, *Jak się narody rządzą?*; Kujawczyk, *Ojciec Szymon*; and Młot, *Kto z czego żyje?*
6. On the illegal socialist press, see Kmiecik, *Prasa polska w rewolucji 1905–1907*; and Myśliński, *Polska prasa socjalistyczna w okresie zaborów*. On the publishing activity of the National Democracy party, see Jakubowska, *Prasa Narodowej Demokracji w dobie zaborów*; and Dawidowicz and Maj, *Prasa Narodowej Demokracji, 1886–1939*.
7. On the role of the leaflets, see Karwacki, *Łódź w latach rewolucji 1905–1907*; Krajewska, *Czytelnictwo wśród robotników*; and Żarnowska, *Robotnicy Warszawy na przełomie XIX i XX wieku*. In other national contexts, the importance of leaflets and brochures for rank-and-file Marxism is demonstrated in Bonnell, "Did They Read Marx?" For useful terminology and classification of "ephemeral literature" such as leaflets, see Pimlott, "'Eternal Ephemera.'"
8. For instance, according to estimates by Władysław Karwacki, during 162 days of the year 1906, SDKPiL issued and distributed 992,000 copies of various publications in Lodz alone. The Lodz workers' committee of the PPS published thirty thousand copies in Polish of a leaflet commemorating the first anniversary of the outbreak of the revolution. In addition, ten thousand were published in German and several thousand in Yiddish were distributed, accompanied by another couple of thousand leaflets received from the central committee. At the same time, Social Democrats distributed 1,500,000. In conditions of conspiratory illegal work, it is hard to assume that the publishing quotas were overestimated. In addition, if a leaflet reached an interested worker, it used to be recirculated, read aloud, and discussed (Karwacki, *Łódź w latach rewolucji 1905–1907*, 170). For titles and topics, see the almost complete listing in Kiepurska, *Bibliografia pism*.
9. See, for example, Łęczycki, *Mojej ankiety personalnej punkt 35*, 59–60.
10. Szczepan Michalski, Wspomnienia, APŁ KŁ PZPR, t. 11541, k. 6; Feliks Piskorski, "Z nad dobrzanki," *Kiliński,* no. 3 (1936): 102–3.
11. See, respectively, Antoni Deka, Ankieta personalna z życiorysem, APŁ, KW PZPR, syg. 1958; Maksymilian Brzeziński, "Dzielnica 'Zielona' w Łodzi," *Kiliński*, no. 1 (1936): 24; Bronislaw Żukowski, "Pamiętniki bojowca," *Niepodległość* 1 (1929–1930):

115–16; Łęczycki, *Mojej ankiety personalnej punkt 35*, 66; Pestkowski, *Wspomnienia rewolucjonisty*, 55.

12. Karwacki, *Łódź w latach rewolucji 1905–1907*, 169–70; Negt and Kluge, *Public Sphere and Experience*.

13. Quentin Skinner demonstrated how political thought and concrete interventions in politicking could be read as Austinian performatives (*Visions of Politics,* 82). See also Palonen, *Quentin Skinner*.

14. Palat, "Regulating Conflict through the Petition"; Frank and Steinberg, *Cultures in Flux*.

15. Karwacki, *Łódź w latach rewolucji 1905–1907*, 176.

16. Marzec, "1905–1907 Revolution in the Kingdom of Poland."

17. Chwalba, "Rola socjalistycznych druków ulotnych," 163; Karwacki, *Łódź w latach rewolucji 1905–1907*, 175.

18. "Do społeczeństwa polskiego. Chwila obecna jest przełomową," CKR PPS, AAN APPS, 11/II-2, k. 41–42a.

19. "Towarzysze! Mury wszechrosyjskiej twierdzy," ŁKR PPS, January 14, 1905, AAN, APPS 305/III/35, pdt 6, k. 15.

20. Respectively: "Robotnicy! Od dwóch miesięcy blisko sercem Polski robotniczej," ZG SDKPiL July 1, 1905, AAN SDKPiL, 9/VII-t. 5, k. 32–32a; AAN SDKPiL, 9/II-t.23, k. 63–64; APŁ ZŻGP 12/1905/II k.738–739 and "Na 1 maja 1906. r. Międzynarodowe Święto robotnicze w roku rewolucji," ZG SDKPiL, April 1906, AAN SDKPiL, 9/VII-t. 6, k. 17–20a.

21. Koselleck, "Begriffsgeschichte and Social History." Newer works debate whether it is possible to write a history of concepts in the twentieth century with enlarged sensitivity to new users and modes of circulation and describe thresholds in the history of concepts after the primary modern change analyzed by Koselleck for the—roughly—eighteenth century. See Geulen, "Plädoyer für eine Geschichte"; and Hoffmann et al., "Geschichtliche Grundbegriffe Reloaded?"

22. Blit, *Origins of Polish Socialism*.

23. "Historical Criteria of the Modern Concept of Revolution," in Koselleck, "Historical-Political Semantics."

24. "Strajk powszechny i rewolucja w Petersburgu," ZG SDKPiL, January 23, 1905; Daniszewski, *SDKPiL w rewolucji 1905 roku*, 65–67.

25. About the heterogeneity of struggles, see Shanin, *Roots of Otherness*. Of course this process resembles (and to some extend consciously repeats) that which occurred during and after the series of events we are used to describing as the French Revolution. Initially disarticulated and as a whole unprecedented events began to be presented, interpreted and remembered in relatively coherent categories—as a revolution, see Hunt, *Politics, Culture, and Class*; Baker, *Inventing the French Revolution*.

26. Kripke, *Naming and Necessity*. The act of naming executes its power also within academic discourse. After all, these events do not meet the criteria of revolution properly speaking formulated by political science or historical sociology to call something a revolution. See Brinton, *Anatomy of Revolution*; and Skocpol, *States and Social Revolutions*.

27. Possart, *Struktury myślenia teoretycznego*.

28. "Niech będzie pochwalony Jezus Chrystus! Bracia Rodacy! Słyszeliście chyba wszyscy," Komitet Zagłębia Dąbrowskiego NZR, March–April 1906 r., AAN NZR, 41-II, k. 34.

29. "Bracia robotnicy! Rzucono wam wielkie hasło rewolucyi. Hasło to rozpaliło wasze serca i umysły," Narodowo-demokratyczna Młodzież Rzemieślnicza i Robotnicza, APŁ ZŻGP 12/1905/I, k.119.

30. "Bracia robotnicy! Znowuż krążą po kraju naszym pogłoski, partie socjalistyczne," ZG NZR, June 1, 1905, APŁ ZŻGP, 390, k. 382–383.

31. "Rodacy! Parokrotnie od początku wojny obecnej wzywaliśmy Was do trzeźwości . . . , Komitet Centralny Ligi Narodowej," August 1, 1905, APŁ ZŻGP 12/1905/II k. 918–919; APŁ ZDiPU, 411, k. 28. For more on the trope of anarchy, important for almost all political languages in the game, but invested with different meanings, see Marzec, "Beyond Group Antagonism."

32. "Bracia Rodacy! Strejk powszechny, zapowiedziany przez socyalną demokracyę na poniedziałek nie udał się," ZG NZR, July 1, 1905, BN DŻS.

33. This was a time of certain flexibility in spelling patterns. The old-Polish long group *-ija, -yja* in words of foreign origin (Latin or French) had already vanished in most cases, but the choice between *-ya* and *-ja* particle was still hotly debated, often marking the "political" position of the contenders. Although the choice of spelling in printed materials of different political groups was probably not entirely conscious, it may indicate appropriation and domestication of the world *socjalizm* among its supporters. The unequal distribution of both variants in time and along party lines is clear in lexicometrical analysis of the leaflets. The spelling of *rewolucja* was already more stabilized. The final codification of the modern spelling came only with the state-supported standardization of the Polish language in 1918. See Jodłowski, *Losy polskiej ortografii*, 81–95; and Klemensiewicz, *Historia języka polskiego*, 605–7.

34. "Towarzysze! Towarzyszki! Od lat 17-tu proletarjat świętuje dzień 1-go maja, a świętowanie to jest dlań jutrznią nowego życia i jest zapowiedzią burzy, mającej zahuczeć wkrótce nad głowami jego ciemiężców," CKR PPS, April 30, 1906, AAN, APPS 305/III/34, pdt. 4, k. 26

35. "Towarzysze i Towarzyszki! Cały świat robotniczy święcił święto," Lodz Committee of the PPS, May 3, 1906.

36. A good example of this type is a text translated from German, Wilhelm Bracke's *Precz z Socjalistami!* [Down with the Socialists!]. Its argumentative structure resembles the common polemical situation, which socialist beginners may have encountered pretty often. The brochure is a stylized answer to the critiques and attacks on socialism executed by the doubtful. Apparently such a polemical handbook of arguments was attractive also to those readers who themselves were not so sure what socialism could mean and what goals its proponents pursued. The brochure clarifies that socialism in not the parceling out of land but common ownership, that it won't bring the abolition of property but its true realization is when everybody retains the right to retain what he or she has created and the like (Bracke, *Precz z socjalistami!* Originally published as *Nieder mit den*

Sozialdemokraten! [Braunschweig, 1876]). On other brochures, see Marzec, "Vernacular Marxism." On similar publications in Russian, see Pearl, *Creating a Culture of Revolution*.

37. "Rok Rewolucji. Dzień 22 stycznia zamyka pierwszy rok Rewolucji w caracie, która taki sam przełom stanowi w dziejach ludzkości, jak przed stu laty Wielka Rewolucja Francuska," ZG SDKPiL, January 1, 1906, AAN SDKPiL, 9/VII-t.33, k. 2–3a.

38. See, for instance, the so-called "Warsaw dictionary," the most prominent setter of language norms at that time. In "official" language this concept was not widely recognized—in the Warsaw dictionary socialism is mentioned only as an example of collectivism, and in other entries on betrayal and cheating, as an example of (rejected) ideological manipulation ("nie mnie brać na socjalizm"). The separate entry defines it as a social, political, and economic system aiming at the equality of rights and redistribution of property (Kryński and Niedźwiedzki, *Słownik języka polskiego*).

39. "Do Braci Robotników i całego społeczeństwa. Towarzysze! Rodacy!,'' National Democracy (signed as "a group of workers," as such significant in this context), Warsaw, November 4, 1905, BN DŻS IA 4h Cim.

40. "Rodacy! Dnia 3-go marca r. b. zamordowany został robotnik fabryczny," a leaflet of the Central Committee of the Association of National Defense (one of the impromptu national democratic political emanations), Warsaw, March 6, 1906, BN DŻS IA 4h Cim.

41. Władysław Kossek, "Kartki z życiorysu proletariusza," in Spieralski, *Wspomnienia weteranów rewolucji 1905 i 1917 roku*, 18. .

42. "Towarzysze! Nie widać końca kryzysu, który już tak dawno panuje," CKR PPS, November 13, 1901, in Korzec, *Źródła do dziejów rewolucji 1905–1907 w okręgu łódzkim*, vol. 1, pt. 1, 20.

43. "Obłuda pod maską bezpartyjności. Od kilkunastu lat walczy klasa robotnicza Polski i Rosji o prawo łączenia się w związki," Komisja Organizacyjna Związków Zawodowych SDKPiL, BN DŻS; APŁ KGP 1581, k. 4–11.

44. Łęczycki, *Mojej ankiety personalnej punkt 35*, 60.

45. Rancière, *On the Shores of Politics*; Deranty, *Jacques Rancière*.

46. Olbrzymek, "Wspomnienia starego robotnika 1893–1918," *Z pola walki*, no. 3 (1927): 57.

47. Explicitly including female members and readers, which was not that common at the time.

48. Porter, *When Nationalism Began to Hate*.

49. Steinmetz, *Das Sagbare und das Machbare*.

50. "Nasza deklaracya polityczna. Towarzysze i towarzyszki! Gnieciony i nękany przez," ŁKR PPS, February 5, 1905, AAN, APPS 305/III/35, pdt. 6, k. 18; APŁ KGP 1515 II, k. 518.

51. "Towarzysze Robotnicy! "Gorze Wam, bracia, iżeście słuchali socjalistów," krzyczy rozwydrzona reakcją rządu," Okręgowy Komitet Robotniczy Zagłębia Dąbrowskiego PPS; Okręgowy Komitet Robotniczy Zagłębia Dąbrowskiego PPS, BN DŻS IB Cim.

52. Rancière, *Disagreement*, 37.

53. "Towarzysze Robotnicy! 'Gorze Wam, bracia, iżeście słuchali socjalistów,' krzyczy rozwydrzona reakcją rządu," Okręgowy Komitet Robotniczy Zagłębia Dąbrowskiego

PPS; Okręgowy Komitet Robotniczy Zagłębia Dąbrowskiego PPS, BN DŻS IB Cim.

54. "Do łódzkich robotników. Towarzysze! Zwoli proletariatu," ŁKR PPS, February 8, 1905, APŁ ZŻGP, 390, k. 251–52.

55. Renton, *Classical Marxism*.

56. "Towarzysze! Robotnicy! Zbliża się dzień 1 maja, dzień święta robotniczego i demonstracji rewolucyjnej," ZG SDKPiL, April 1, 1907, in Daniszewski, *SDKPiL w rewolucji 1905 roku*, 545–47.

57. Marzec, "Under One Common Banner"; Śliwa, "Jewish Problem in Polish Socialist Thought."

58. "Bracia robotnicy! Trzy tygodnie minęło, jak zaprzestaliście pracować, Koło Okręgowe Stronnictwa Demokratyczno-Narodowego w Łodzi," in Korzec, *Źródła do dziejów rewolucji 1905–1907 w okręgu łódzkim*, vol. 1, pt. 2, 205–6.

59. "Baczność, Bracia Robotnicy, bo grozi nam nowe niebezpieczeństwo! Przez cały rok ubiegły 1905 obiecywali nam socyaliści we wszystkich swoich gazetach, odezwach i przemowach poprawę losu," Komitet Okręgowy Narodowego Związku Robotniczego na Zagłębie Dąbrowskie, February 1906, BN DŻS IB Cim.

60. "Strajk powszechny i rewolucja w Petersburgu, ZG SDKPiL," January 23, 1905, in Daniszewski, *SDKPiL w rewolucji 1905 roku*, 65–67.

61. "Towarzysze i Towarzyszki! Lud roboczy całej Polski za pomocą olbrzymiego strejku powszechnego," Warszawski Komitet Strejkowy PPS, February 12, 1905, BN DŻS, IB Cim.

62. "Towarzysze! Robotnicy! Lud roboczy całej Rosji i Polski powstał do walki," Łódzki Komitet SDKPiL, October 29, 1905, in Daniszewski, *SDKPiL w rewolucji 1905 roku*, 258–59.

63. This aspect figured prominently in Luxemburg's theoretization of the revolutionary movement made on the spot, especially in short but theoretically sound correspondences. See Luksemburg, *O rewolucji*. I have analyzed these writings in Marzec, "Róża Luksemburg i konstruowanie podmiotu politycznego."

64. "Na 1 maja 1906 Niech się nasze święto święci . . . Robotnicy! Lat temu 14 w dzień 1 maja," Komitet Łódzki SDKPiL, April 1906, in Korzec, *Źródła do dziejów rewolucji 1905–1907 w okręgu łódzkim*, 2:182–84.

65. "Do robotników fabryki Biedermanna. Towarzysze! Mało jest chyba fabryk, gdzie postawa zarządu," ŁKR PPS, 5 July 1906, in Korzec, *Źródła do dziejów rewolucji 1905–1907 w okręgu łódzkim*, 2:272–74.

66. It is worth mentioning that the left wing of the PPS had a particular influence on shop-floor activism, so the disseminated agenda was even more consciously socialist and economically focused than the general picture of the PPS in those days might suggest. On earlier, already indicative divisions concerning factory activism, see Kancewicz, *Polska Partia Socjalistyczna*; on growing differences and the ultimate split in the PPS, see Żarnowska, *Geneza rozłamu*. Because of this withdrawal of a significant part of the PPS from factory agitation, the general influence of the party on workers was initially severely limited (Crago, "'Polishness' of Production").

67. Korzec, *Źródła do dziejów rewolucji 1905–1907 w okręgu łódzkim*, vol. 1, pt. 1, 104.

68. Żarnowska and Wolsza, *Społeczeństwo i polityka*, 5–6.

69. For an intersection of class and national politics (which for a long time was more anti-German than anti-Jewish!) see Crago, "'Polishness' of Production."

70. Korzec, *Źródła do dziejów rewolucji 1905–1907 w okręgu łódzkim*, vol. 1, pt. 1, 239.

71. Tomicki, *Polska Partia Socjalistyczna, 1892–1948*, 77.

72. Wróbel, "From Conflict to Cooperation"; Piasecki, *Żydowska Organizacja PPS*; Zimmerman, *Poles, Jews, and the Politics of Nationality*.

73. While party writers such as Luxemburg or Julian Marchlewski offered sophisticated theoretical and historical refutations of antisemitism, they remained assimilationist hardliners and party polemical writings occasionally yielded to antisemitic language. See Jacobs, "Kautsky on the Jewish Question," 176–81; Ury, *Barricades and Banners*, 248–49; and Strobel, *Die Partei Rosa Luxemburgs, Lenin und die SPD*, 591–93; I developed this argumentation in Marzec, "Under One Common Banner."

74. Zimmerman, *Poles, Jews, and the Politics of Nationality*; Hoffman and Mendelsohn, *Revolution of 1905 and Russia's Jews*; Ury, *Barricades and Banners*.

75. Korzec, *Źródła do dziejów rewolucji 1905–1907 w okręgu łódzkim*, 2:42.

76. Żarnowska, *Geneza rozłamu*. A sophisticated analysis of the difference in political thinking that lay behind the split is presented in Possart, *Struktury myślenia teoretycznego*.

77. Łęczycki, *Mojej ankiety personalnej punkt 35*, 66; Rudnicki, *Stare i nowe*, 408.

78. The self-thematization as a feature of modern political languages is described in Steinmetz, *Political Languages in the Age of Extremes*, introduction.

79. Leaflet of ŁKR PPS, July 1905, in Korzec, *Źródła do dziejów rewolucji 1905–1907 w okręgu łódzkim*, vol. 1, pt. 2, 371–72.; leaflet of Head Committee of the SDKPiL, May 1905, in Daniszewski, *SDKPiL w rewolucji 1905 roku*, 165–66.

80. The most "antisemitic" option held officially by some people was universal assimilation. This certainly is a denial of full national and cultural rights but still far from antisemitism as such. Such a position was maintained by many Jewish militants in many varieties (internationalist assimilation of the SDKPiL, national assimilation of some PPS Jewish socialists). For a debate and internal polemics of the PPS (also members resisting unfair policies toward Jewish national aspirations in the days of initial heated political competition with the early Bund, see Piasecki, *Żydowska Organizacja PPS*, 35. For an overview of the PPS's relationship with other Jewish political parties, see Zimmerman, *Poles, Jews, and the Politics of Nationality*. For more about paradigmatic dilemmas of identity politics among Jewish members of SDKPiL, see Castle, "'You Alone Will Make Our Family's Name Famous.'"

81. Leaflet of the Warsaw Committee of the SDKPiL, June 16, 1906, in Daniszewski, *SDKPiL w rewolucji 1905 roku*, 401–2.

82. Report of the policmaster of Lodz, June 21 1905, in Korzec, *Źródła do dziejów rewolucji 1905–1907 w okręgu łódzkim*, vol. 1, pt. 2, 230–231.

83. Leaflet of the Central Committee of SDKPiL, November 14, 1905, in Daniszewski, *SDKPiL w rewolucji 1905 roku*, 263–65; leaflet of Lodz Committee of SDKPiL, November 9, 1905, in Daniszewski, *SDKPiL w rewolucji 1905 roku*, 271–72; leaflet of Workers Committee of the Dąbrowa Basin of the PPS, no date, APŁ, ZŻGP 12/1905/I, pp. 598–99.

84. Leaflet of the Peasant Department of the PPS, November 1, 1905, APŁ ZŻGP 12/1905/II, pp. 1204–5; ŁKR PPS, December 24, 1905, APŁ KGP, 1553, p. 3.

85. The role of the tsarist secret services or even the police and military in pogroms during the revolution was later confirmed, especially concerning the "closest" events in Białystok and Siedlce in 1906 (Korzec, "Pogrom białostocki i jego polityczne reperkusje"; Rudnicki, "Pogrom Siedlecki"; Kurkiewicz and Plutecka, "Rosyjskie pogromy"). For the broader context of this time and varied genesis of other pogroms, see Shlomo Lambroza, "The Pogroms of 1903–1906," in Klier and Lambroza, *Pogroms*.

86. Lodz Committee of the PPS, July 1905, in Korzec, *Źródła do dziejów rewolucji 1905–1907 w okręgu łódzkim*, vol. 1, pt. 2, 371–72.

87. Monasterska, *Narodowy Związek Robotniczy, 1905–1920*, 15–45.

88. As two paradigmatic answers to this question would suggest. See, respectively, Porter, *When Nationalism Began to Hate*, 158; and Ury, *Barricades and Banners*, 216.

89. On the origins of national democratic antisemitism, see Krzywiec, *Chauvinism, Polish Style*.

90. Marzec and Piskała, "Proletariaccy czytelnicy."

91. Crago, "'Polishness' of Production." The general discursive framing of Polishness for a long time (until about 1900) was rather anti-German—as can be seen in local newspapers, especially concerning the city of Lodz being under constant threat of being perceived as not Polish but foreign, German, even if Jews constituted up to one-third of its population (Śmiechowski, *Z perspektywy stolicy*).

92. As classical Stalinist historiography would have it (Kalabiński, *Antynarodowa polityka endecji*). In Lodz NZR once had extensive support. The local proletariat was composed of recent newcomers from poor village settlements with strong traditional values and religious beliefs. In the late nineteenth century, only 10–15 percent of inhabitants were born in Lodz (Żarnowska, *Klasa robotnicza Królestwa Polskiego, 1870–1914*; Monasterska, *Narodowy Związek Robotniczy, 1905–1920*, 27). However, national democratic thinking was heavily tainted by conscious obscurantism aimed at ruling over the masses, increasingly seen as a savage mob requiring taming (Marzec, "Modernizacja mas").

93. Mark W. Steinberg initially coined the term to describe a plural political field with utterances powerfully transforming patterns of political mobilization and the moral economy in early industrial England (*Fighting Words*).

94. Korzec, *Źródła do dziejów rewolucji 1905–1907 w okręgu łódzkim*, vol. 1, pt. 2, 174.

95. Korzec, *Źródła do dziejów rewolucji 1905–1907 w okręgu łódzkim*, vol. 1, pt. 2, 205–6, 656.

96. Walicki, *Philosophy and Romantic Nationalism*; Modzelewski, *Naród i postęp*.

97. Porter, "Social Nation and Its Futures"; Porter, *When Nationalism Began to Hate*.

98. This converged with a shift in Dmowski's position when he started to perceive the Russian Empire as a lesser danger and an actor with whom he could tactically cooperate.

99. Krzywiec, "Z taką rewolucją musimy walczyć na noże."

100. Leaflet of the Central Committee of the National League, August 1, 1905, APŁ ZŻGP 12/1905/II, pp. 918–19; leaflet of Lodz Department of the NZR, December 27, 1905, APŁ KGP 1553, p. 6; National-Democratic Craftsmen and Workers Youth APŁ ZŻGP 12/1905/I, p. 119.

101. Porter, "Who Is a Pole and Where Is Poland?"; Żurawicka, "Lud w ideologii"; Wolsza, *Narodowa Demokracja*; Kulak, *Jan Ludwik Popławski*; Puszkow-Bańka, *Polska i Polacy*.

102. The National Democrats took the baton from the old-line, elitist conservatives, who were declining in numbers and incapable of facing modern challenges and appealing to broader audiences (Grott, *Zygmunt Balicki*, 30; Jaszczuk, *Spór pozytywistów z konserwatystami*, 286). This shift had consequences. Social milieus previously hostile, or at least indifferent, to National Democracy party began to actively support and enter the party: during the revolution, the involvement of Polish landed gentry in its institutions grew (Wapiński, *Roman Dmowski*, 157). This also opened the door to an alliance with the Polish Catholic Church, which was equally interested in preserving the existing social order and not so opposed to antisemitism (Blobaum, "Revolution of 1905–1907"; Zaleska, *Kościół a Narodowa Demokracja*).

103. Porter-Szűcs, "Exclusionary Egalitarianism."

104. Hroch, *Social Preconditions of National Revival in Europe*; Gellner, *Nations and Nationalism*.

105. Wapiński, *Roman Dmowski*, chap. 4; Wapiński, *Pokolenia Drugiej Rzeczypospolitej*.

106. Wapiński, *Narodowa Demokracja 1893–1939*, 101; Krzywiec, *Szowinizm po polsku*. For an early socialist response to maturing radicals/future National Democratic antisemitic tendencies, see *Pobudka*, no. 5 (1889): 26; and Mishinsky, "Turning Point."

107. Korzec, *Źródła do dziejów rewolucji 1905–1907 w okręgu łódzkim*, vol. 1, pt. 2, 351.

108. Leaflet of the Central Committee of the NZR, June 1, 1905, APŁ KGP, 390, pp. 382–83.

109. Leaflet of the Central Committee of the NZR, June 1, 1905, APŁ KGP, 390, pp. 382–83.

110. On the rapid rise of political antisemitism, see Blobaum, "Politics of Antisemitism in Fin-de-Siècle Warsaw"; Weeks, *From Assimilation to Antisemitism*; and Ury, *Barricades and Banners*.

111. This transformation is analyzed in Porter, *When Nationalism Began to Hate*. More about the early populist writings of the National Democrats can be found in Kulak, *Jan Ludwik Popławski*; and Bończa-Tomaszewski, *Demokratyczna geneza nacjonalizmu*. A representative collection of press articles from the populist and progressive period may be found in Balicki, *Parlamentaryzm*; and Popławski, *Naród i polityka*. I investigated this transformation and confrontation with the revolution as a reason for the National Democracy party's increasingly authoritarian tendencies in Marzec, "Modernizacja mas."

112. Dmowski, *Pisma*, 3:342.

113. On the changing social base of the National Democracy party, see Kozicki, *Historia Ligi Narodowej*, 284–85; and Wapiński, *Roman Dmowski*, 157. Contemporary supporters also registered the change: for example, S. Skarzyński, *W obronie Narodowej Demokracji*, (Słowo, 1907), 291, quoted in Kidzińska, *Stronnictwo Polityki Realnej*, 118.

114. Austin, *How to Do Things with Words*, 101.

115. "Towarzysze Robotnicy! 'Gorze Wam, bracia, iżeście słuchali socjalistów,' krzyczy rozwydrzona reakcją rządu," OKR Zagłębia Dąbrowskiego PPS, BN DŚS IB Cim.

116. Anderson, *Imagined Communities*.

117. A process that one theorist calls polemicization (Arditi, *Polemicization*).

4. Life and Politics

Epigraph: Radomski, "Wspomnienia technika partyjnego 1905–1907 rok," *Z pola walki*, no. 11–12 (1931), quoted in Kozłowski, *Z rewolucyjnych dni*, 234.

1. The literature on biography, memory, life story, and narrative is obviously so vast that it cannot be presented here in detail. My approach is mostly inspired by the studies of biography with respect to political involvement. A heterogeneous catalog of works important here includes Kaźmierska, *Biography and Memory*; Steinmetz, "Reflections on the Role of Social Narratives"; Lyons, *Ordinary Writings, Personal Narratives*; Andrews, *Shaping History*; Passerini, *Fascism in Popular Memory*; Polletta, *It Was Like a Fever*; Brock, *Alltägliche Arbeiterexistenz*; and Scholz, *Arbeiterselbstbild und Arbeiterfremdbild*.

2. On the culture of revolution, see Kolonitskii and Figes, *Interpreting the Russian Revolution*. On orchestrating biographical memory and its role in "initiating the Bolshevik self" see Halfin, *Red Autobiographies*. The manufacturing of memory of the 1917 Revolution through its retelling is analyzed in Corney, *Telling October*.

3. This strategy is inspired by the approach to the history of concepts by the late Reinhart Koselleck with its focus on the layered sediments of historical meaning within a single concept, which is also a part of the present, synchronous semantic field. On the debate on layers of time in single concepts, see Koselleck, "Begriffsgeschichte and Social History"; Jordheim, "Does Conceptual History Really Need a Theory?"; Jordheim, "Against Periodization"; and Olsen, *History in the Plural*.

4. Scott, "Evidence of Experience"; in the context of autobiographical writing, see Smith and Watson, *Reading Autobiography*, 24.

5. Władysław Kossek, *Kartki z życiorysu proletariusza*, in Spieralski, *Wspomnienia weteranów rewolucji*, 15.

6. Vincent, *Bread, Knowledge, and Freedom*; Maynes, *Taking the Hard Road*.

7. Nietyksza, *Rozwój miast i aglomeracji*.

8. Kossek, *Kartki z życiorysu proletariusza*, 17–18.

9. Kossek, *Kartki z życiorysu proletariusza*, 17.

10. Kossek, *Kartki z życiorysu proletariusza*, 12.

11. Kossek, *Kartki z życiorysu proletariusza*, 18.

12. As the NZR in most cases opposed strike activity, this section is dedicated to the socialists. Nationalist memoirs are mostly silent on that matter.

13. Kossek, *Kartki z życiorysu proletariusza*, 25.

14. Brock, *Der schwierige Weg in die Moderne*.

15. Abundant documentation of the prerevolutionary language of claims may be found in petitions and protest letters issued to factory owners or different agencies of the tsarist administration. See petitions in Korzec, *Źródła do dziejów rewolucji 1905–1907 w okręgu łódzkim*, vol. 1, pt. 1; and Gąsiorowska-Grabowska and Kalabiński, *Źródła do dziejów klasy robotniczej*. More petitions may be found in tsarist files: for instance, APŁ KGP 546, 547.

16. Stanisław Michalski, *Na obu brzegach Atlantyku*, in Spieralski, *Wspomnienia weteranów rewolucji*, 113. See also Kossek, *Kartki z życiorysu proletariusza*, 12.

17. Thus constructing a vernacular frame analysis of a kind. On the academic concept of frame alignment, see Benford and Snow, "Framing Processes and Social Movements."

18. F. (full name unknown) Bereza, *Wspomnienia z dni rewolucyjnych czyli przebieg rewolucji z roku 1904 i dalej*, AAN, Instytut Badania najnowszej historii Polski, Wspomnienia nadesłane do redakcji pisma Niepodległość 1930–1937, syg 357/4, folder 3, p. 34.

19. Rudnicki, *Stare i nowe*, 21–22.

20. Rudnicki, *Stare i nowe*, 94.

21. Rudnicki, *Stare i nowe*, 104–5.

22. Rudnicki, *Stare i nowe*, 107.

23. Interesting examples from England may be found in Johnson, "Really Useful Knowledge."

24. It seems to be a pan-European pattern of worker autobiography. After all, the course of a working-class life was similar in many contexts, despite differences in proletarianization patterns and local industries. See, for instance, Vincent, *Bread, Knowledge, and Freedom*, chaps. 4–5.

25. Mojżesz Kaufman (Mojsze Mezryczer), "Przyczynki do historii żydowskiej organizacji PPS," *Niepodległość* 12 (1935): 26.

26. This also seems to be a broader pattern. Those who change their educational and social positions usually recollect some form of external biographical intervention (Maynes, *Taking the Hard Road*).

27. Franciszek Kujawa, *Wspomnienie z pobytu mego w byłej SDKPiL i KPP*, APŁ KW PZPR 1923, pp. 15–16.

28. Łęczycki, *Mojej ankiety personalnej punkt 35*, 40. For more on reading practices, see Krajewska, *Czytelnictwo wśród robotników*.

29. Franciszek Kujawa, *Wspomnienie z pobytu mego w byłej SDKPiL i KPP*, APŁ KW PZPR 1923, pp. 15–16.

30. The metaphors used to describe these autodidactic subversions are inspired by works on popular resistance and obstinacy such as de Certeau, *Practice of Everyday Life*; Scott, *Domination and the Arts of Resistance*; and Lüdtke, *Eigen-Sinn*.

31. Olbrzymek, "Wspomienia starego robotnika 1893–1918," *Z pola walki*, no. 4 (1927): 52–53; Łęczycki, *Mojej ankiety personalnej punkt 35*, 87. Some other ways of creative appropriation of the read content out of the box are documented in Vincent, *Literacy and Popular Culture*; and Lyons, "Reading Experience in Workers-Autobiographies."

32. Some remarks on general patterns of the working-class life cycle and its transformation, see Kohli, "World We Forgot." The life cycle as topic of autobiography is examined in Vincent, *Bread, Knowledge, and Freedom*, chap. 3; Bidinger, *Ethics of Working Class Autobiography*; and Simmons, *Factory Lives*.

33. Bronislaw Fijałek, Życiorys, personal folder, AAN AODRR, folder 1520, p. 1.

34. Michał Ostrowski, Wspomnienia, AAN AODRR, personal folder 4386, f. 2, p. 12.

35. Commentary on such narrative devices making it possible to integrate a biography may be found in Maynes, *Taking the Hard Road*, chap. 2; See also Steinmetz, "Reflections

on the Role of Social Narratives." For more about the particular socialist eschatology of light, activation, and emancipation, see Halfin, *From Darkness to Light*.

36. On the nonaccidental interdependent relationship between bourgeois and working-class narrative patterns and the role of politics as a vehicle for working-class writing, see Gagnier, "Social Atoms"; and Maynes, *Taking the Hard Road*, 322.

37. Ostrowski, Wspomnienia, f. 1, p. 2/1.

38. Ostrowski, Wspomnienia, f. 1, p. 2/2.

39. For the generational forgetting of experiences and lost conclusions from past political upheavals, see Suter, "Kulturgeschichte des Politischen."

40. In Skowroński's wording: *nieznaczne kółko protestantów polsko-socjalistycznego tołku* [sic!]. Most probably he meant just those who used to protest, affiliated with the PPS. Wypis z ankiety personalnej Józefa Skowrońskiego, in AAN, AODRR, Józef Skowroński, sygn. 11365.

41. Skowroński, Wypis z ankiety personalnej Józefa Skowrońskiego.

42. On the origins of the concept, see Goffman, "Moral Career of the Mental Patient."

43. Ignacy Kuświk, Moje wspomnienia, APŁ, KŁ PZPR, syg. 11442, p. 3. A similar "natural" way through friendship and personal bonds was described in Marceli Staszewski, Mój pamiętnik, APŁ, KW PZPR w Łodzi, syg. 1951. Strikingly, sometimes reasons or broader reflection on political choices made their way even to book-size memoirs of a (future) active politician, as in Kwapiński, *Moje Wspomnienia 1904–1939*.

44. Edward Skórkiewicz, Pamiętnik rewolucji 1905 roku w Zagłębiu Dąbrowskim, APŁ, KŁ PZPR, t. 11718, p. 4.

45. The party practice and the challenge of successful agitation are analyzed in the case of the SDKPiL in Radlak, *Socjaldemokracja Królestwa Polskiego i Litwy*; and Samuś, *Dzieje SDKPiL w Łodzi*.

46. On the NZR's split with the national democratic movement, see Monasterska, *Narodowy Związek Robotniczy*. Some analysis of its reasons is offered in Crago, "'Polishness' of Production."

47. Michal Kosiorek, "Skład bibuły w Warszawie," *Kiliński*, no. 1 (1936): 36.

48. Jan Posiak, "Dzielnica 'Górna' w Łodzi," *Kiliński*, no. 3 (1936): 108.

49. Michalina Klimkiewiczówna, "Praca organizacyjna w Żyrardowie," *Kiliński*, no. 3 (1936): 134.

50. For example, see Maksymilian Brzeziński, "Dzielnica 'Zielona' w Łodzi," *Kiliński*, no. 1 (1936): 17–18; Feliks Piskorski, "Z nad dobrzanki," *Kiliński*, no. 3 (1936): 102–3; Jan Posiak, "Dzielnica 'Górna' w Łodzi," *Kiliński*, no. 3 (1936): 108; and Bronisław Żukowski, "Pamiętniki bojowca," *Niepodległość* 1 (1929–1930): 115–16.

51. Czesław Łączny, "Początki buntu," *Kiliński*, no. 1 (1936): 24.

52. Maksymilian Brzeziński, "Dzielnica 'Zielona' w Łodzi," *Kiliński*, no. 1 (1936): 17–18.

53. "Jewing" (*zażydzenia*)—the act of making Jewish, contaminated with Jewishness—a derogatory expression with clearly antisemitic undertones. Józef Drzewiecki (Dejot), "Okręg w Zagłębiu Narodowego Kola Kolejarzy w 1905 roku," *Kiliński*, no. 3 (1936): 175.

54. Czeslaw Łączny, "Początki buntu," *Kiliński*, no. 1 (1936): 24.

55. Stanisław Parkot-Wojt, "W NZR, katordze i na sybirze," *Niepodległość* 12 (1935): 222.

56. Bolesław Mierzwiński, "Wspomnienia z czasów konspiracyjnej działalności w Łodzi i na wsi," *Kronika ruchu rewolucyjnego* 4, no. 3 (15) (1938): 168–69.

57. Porter, *Faith and Fatherland*, chap. 4.

58. For examples, see Vincent, *Bread, Knowledge, and Freedom*; Maynes, *Taking the Hard Road*. Scarce forms of artisanal solidarity are noted by those narrators who approached them; however, it is by any means common and is limited almost exclusively to Warsaw; see Jastrzębski, *Wspomnienia, 1885–1919*, 76.

59. Zelnik, "Russian Bebels," July 1976, October 1976; Halfin, *From Darkness to Light*; Halfin, *Red Autobiographies*.

60. It is worth mentioning that the very presence of journals publishing autobiographical materials actually contributed to the production of unpublished manuscripts because veterans had written them hoping for publication that did not necessarily happen. Such materials might have been published decades later or remained forever archival manuscripts. About efforts to gather such materials in the Soviet Union, see Corney, *Telling October*.

61. Płochocki, *Wspomnienia działacza SDKPIL*, 25. Fragments from the biography of Olbrzymek (his party pseudonym) are of the same writer and are only different in detail, however shorter. If possible, I quote from the earlier version, but in most cases the later book is its verbatim copy.

62. Olbrzymek, "Wspomnienia starego robotnika 1893–1918," *Z pola walki*, no. 4 (1927): 43.

63. Olbrzymek, "Wspomnienia starego robotnika 1893–1918," 45.

64. Comrade Rosół, called "the father," was a veteran socialist, working-class militant with much authority among SDKPiL workers (Płochocki, *Wspomnienia działacza SDK-PIL*, 57).

65. Olbrzymek, "Wspomnienia starego robotnika 1893–1918," *Z pola walki*, no. 3 (1927): 57.

66. Łęczycki, *Mojej ankiety personalnej punkt 35*, 61–62.

67. Ron Eyerman, "How Social Movements Move."

68. In particular, this new form of affiliation as an incentive for revolutionary mobilization is analyzed for Polish Jews and Jews from the Pale, respectively, in Ury, *Barricades and Banners*; and Shtakser, *Making of Jewish Revolutionaries*. The general situation of the Jewish population in Russian Poland is analyzed in Weeks, *From Assimilation to Antisemitism*. For Jews of the Pale see also Tobias, *Jewish Bund in Russia*; and Hoffman and Mendelsohn, *Revolution of 1905 and Russia's Jews*. On the specific position of radical Polish intelligentsia, see Mencwel, *Etos lewicy*. On the broader context of imperial minorities, see Riga, "Identity and Empire."

69. For the nationality policies of the late tsarist empire, see Weeks, *Nation and State in Late Imperial Russia*. The Polish context in the multiethnic city of Lodz and the changing situation of Polish workers are discussed in Crago, "Nationalism, Religion, Citizenship, and Work"; and Kanfer, "Łódź."

70. For similar mechanisms in early German social democracy, see Welskopp, *Banner der Brüderlichkeit*.

71. Tomasz Maciejowski, "Trzydzieści lat w walce", in Spieralski, *Wspomnienia weteranów*

rewolucji, 135. On the disappointment of an apprentice with no chance to make a professional career or even to learn anything, see Olbrzymek, "Wspomienia starego robotnika 1893–1918," *Z pola walki*, no 4 (1927); and Łęczycki, *Mojej ankiety personalnej punkt 35.*

72. See, for instance, Sewell, "Artisans, Factory Workers, and the Formation"; and Kimeldorf, *Reds or Rackets?*

73. Sorel, *Reflections on Violence*, 148; Bottici, *Philosophy of Political Myth.*

74. One has to remember, however, that he later changed his mind and embraced the Russian Revolution of 1917, later even coming back to Poland as an economic negotiator for the Soviet government. This partially explains his odd behavior toward his former party comrades.

75. On the ideological divergence of factions in this respect, see Kancewicz, *Polska Partia Socjalistyczna*. The growing discrepancy of the party tactics before the split during the revolution is analyzed in Żarnowska, *Geneza rozłamu.*

76. An exemplary narrative written in a "militaristic" and martyrological mode is Malinowski, *Z krwawych dni*. Other numerous examples may be found in the interwar journal *Niepodległość* (Independence).

77. For instance, journals prominent in maintaining this tradition in the interwar period are filled with similar memories of street fights with Cossacks, tales of bomb-throwing heroism, and recollections of Siberian martyrdom. See *Niepodległość* from 1930 onward, edited by Leon Wasilewski; *Kronika ruchu rewolucyjego w Polsce*; or *Organ Stowarzyszenia więźniów politycznych*, edited by Jan Krzeslawski and Adam Próchnik. There were also numerous book publications presenting such a military history of the nationalist socialist movement. One of the well-established authors championing the genre was Stanisław Martynowski. See Martynowski, *Łódzka dziesiątka bojowa*; Martynowski, *Łódź w ogniu*; and Martynowski, *Polska bojowa*. There were also attempts to canonize the street tactic as a cornerstone of military expertise in the later, independent Polish state, as done in Błotnicki, *Przez rewolucję 1905 r. do legionów 1914 r.*

78. Jastrzębski, *Wspomnienia, 1885–1919*, 146.

79. Jastrzębski, *Wspomnienia, 1885–1919*, 138.

80. Jastrzębski, *Wspomnienia, 1885–1919*, 140.

81. Jastrzębski, *Wspomnienia, 1885–1919*, 139.

82. This dimension is also clearly detectable in written material created on the spot, such as letters (Shtakser, *Making of Jewish Revolutionaries*). On the changing balance of power, see Karwacki, "Walka o wprowadzenie."

83. Łęczycki, *Mojej ankiety personalnej punkt 35*, 104.

84. Edward Skórkiewicz, Pamiętnik rewolucji 1905 roku w Zagłębiu Dąbrowskim, KŁ PZPR, t. 11718, p. 5. Italics mine.

85. On the great Lodz lockout, see Lewis, "Labor-Management Conflict in Russian Poland."

86. Abundant quotes from primary sources can be found in a documentary narrative of one PPS supporter (Aleksy Rżewski, "Lokaut łódzki," *Niepodległość* 5 [1931]).

87. Huechtker, "'Politics and Poetics of Transgression.'" On the socialist martyr cult, see Karwacki, *Łódź w latach rewolucji 1905–1907*, 56.

88. Eugeniusz Pieńkowski, "Wspomnienia 'dziecka ulicy' z lat 1905–1907," *Niepodległość* 6 (1932): 233–35.

89. Józef Szynkielewicz, "Młodość nie lęka się śmierci," in Spieralski, *Wspomnienia weteranów rewolucji*, 166.

90. Koral, *Przez partie, związki, więzienia i Sybir*, 33.

91. Manliness as an important element of the socialist ethos and public performance of workers is stressed by Welskopp, *Banner der Brüderlichkeit*.

92. Ludwik Śledziński, "Wspomnienia z Łodzi 1899–1901 (dokończenie)," *Kronika ruchu rewolucyjnego* 33, no 1 (9) (1937): 29.

93. Rudnicki, *Stare i nowe*, 372.

94. Surprisingly, even among nationalist workers associated with the NZR, the ideal of a street fighter took hold, regardless of the group's openly antirevolutionary rhetoric. This movement appealed to the calmness and reasoning of the Poles, not allowing themselves to get involved in the allegedly foreign affairs of Jews and socialists. The interwar protocols of the Medal Committee offer insight into the assumed personal characteristics of the movement's genuine hero. There biographical notes written to "nominate" fallen veterans for rewards are full of reverence for the "relentless struggle with the Muscovite invasion" (AAN NZR, Materiały Komisji Odznaczeniowej, AAN, syg. 41/IV, p. 1).

95. Kazimierz Pielat, "Z pamiętnika bojowca," *Niepodległość* 17 (1938): 83.

96. Bereza, *Wspomnienia z dni rewolucyjnych czyli*, 44.

97. For some remarks on performing masculinity during the street fight, see Huechtker, "'Politics and Poetics of Transgression,'" 96.

98. Blit, *Origins of Polish Socialism*; Naimark, *History of the "Proletariat."*

99. Micińska, *Między królem duchem a mieszczaninem*; Bończa-Tomaszewski, *Źródła narodowości*.

100. Welskopp, *Banner der Brüderlichkeit*.

101. A detailed analysis of this structure of feeling regarding the Jewish militants is available in Shtakser, *Making of Jewish Revolutionaries*.

102. On terror, expropriations, and banditry among PPS militias and anarchists, see Potkański, "Wokół koncepcji ideologicznej"; Potkański, "Eskalacja przemocy rewolucyjnej"; Potkański, *Terroryzm na usługach*; and Sekura, *Rewolucyjni Mściciele*.

103. Maynes, *Taking the Hard Road*, 39.

104. Józef Skowroński, biographical testimony, untitled, AAN, AODRR, sygn. 11365, p. 1.

105. Jozef Nowicki, "Wspomniena starego dzialacza," *Niepodległość* 13 (1936): 37.

106. For some remarks on political biography as a genre, applying mostly to elite professional politicians' biographies but to some extent also relevant to the present investigation, see Egerton, "Politics and Autobiography"; and Andrews, *Shaping History*.

107. Steinberg, "Vanguard Workers and the Morality of Class," 67; Rancière, *Nights of Labor*.

108. Steinmetz, "Reflections on the Role of Social Narratives."

109. Nowicki, "Wspomniena starego działacza," 39.

110. On the role of the working-class narrative, see Steinmetz, "Reflections on

the Role of Social Narratives." The model of class formation, where narratives are an important aspect of its subjective component, is discussed in Katznelson and Zolberg, *Working-Class Formation*.

111. "Wspomnienia weteranów rewolucji 1905 roku: Zwyciężyliśmy . . . mówi tow. Bronisława Łuczakowa—emerytka pracy," APŁ, KŁ PZPR, syg. 11484, p. 3.

5. The Intelligentsia and Its Workers

Epigraph: "Sen i przebudzenie," *Goniec Łódzki*, no. 67 (1905). All unmarked quotations below and the epigraph are from the same article. See also the analysis of this article in Śmiechowski, *Łódzka wizja postępu*, 124–25.

1. An attempt loosely inspired by the path taken in Palonen, *Struggle with Time*.

2. Kamil Śmiechowski, *Z perspektywy stolicy*; Marzec and Zysiak, "'Journalists Discovered Łódź Like Columbus.'"

3. Jaworska, "Prasa"; Kucner, "Prasa niemiecka w Łodzi 1863–1939."

4. Gostkowski, *Dziennik Łódzki w latach 1884–1892*.

5. See, respectively, Chańko, *Gazeta "Rozwój" (1897–1915)*; and Śmiechowski, *Łódzka wizja postępu*. For an overview, see Śmiechowski, "Początki prasy łódzkiej."

6. Conboy, *Language of Newspapers*, 8. On imagined communities, see Anderson, *Imagined Communities*.

7. See Taylor, *Modern Social Imaginaries*.

8. Halliday, *Language as a Social Semiotic*; Bell, *Language of News Media*.

9. Case, "'Social Question,' 1820–1920."

10. The core of this argument is presented in Moore, *Injustice*. On the early debate surrounding wealth and social questions and the reconfiguration of meaning of labor, see Stedman Jones, *End to Poverty?* The long-term debate on moral economy of labor is investigated by Biernacki, *Fabrication of Labor*. For the story told by changing concepts, see Conze, "Arbeit." Investigations on the beginnings of the welfare paradigm are presented in, among others, Castel, *From Manual Workers to Wage Laborers*; Hennock, *Origin of the Welfare State*; and Swaan, *In Care of the State*.

11. Kizwalter, "Nowatorstwo i rutyny," 27.

12. Kizwalter, "Nowatorstwo i rutyny," 28–29. On later debates, see Jaszczuk, *Spór pozytywistów z konserwatystami*. On antimodern and antiurban sentiments, see Jedlicki, *Suburb of Europe*; and Jedlicki, *Świat zwyrodniały*.

13. Krzywobłocka, "Stosunek burżuazji do klasy robotniczej."

14. *Opiekun domowy*, no. 46 (1872), quoted in Krzywobłocka, "Stosunek burżuazji do klasy robotniczej."

15. *Niwa* 12 (1877): 953, quoted in Krzywobłocka, "Stosunek burżuazji do klasy robotniczej,"147.

16. Golsztyńska, "Początki ruchu robotniczego i myśli socjalistycznej."

17. Although a long way from accepting the laissez-faire doctrine in toto, Polish positivism retained many convictions from various syntheses of liberalism and organicism. On the relationship between positivism and liberalism, see Janowski, *Polish Liberal*

Thought before 1918; and Porter, "Social Nation and Its Futures." On the discourse of nation suppressing that of class, see Modzelewski, *Naród i postęp*.

18. An interesting analysis of a similar cultural situation of an emerging national press in the borderlands of the Russian Empire—with a constant oscillation of European ambitions, peripheral realities, and ambiguous imperial presence—is presented in Manning, *Strangers in a Strange Land*.

19. See, for instance, *Kurier Warszawski*, no. 140 (1843): 670; *Kurier Warszawski*, no. 149 (1850): 800; *Korespondent Handlowy, Przemysłowy i Rolniczy*, no. 86, no 87, and no. 89 (1849), quoted in Kizwalter, "Nowatorstwo i rutyny," 30–31.

20. On the emerging rhetoric of "questions," see Case, "'Social Question,' 1820–1920."

21. Some earlier researchers argued that the "social question probably did not exist" for the founding editor of the paper (Gostkowski, *Dziennik Łódzki w latach 1884–1892*, 204). A contrary opinion backed up with abundant empirical evidence is presented in Śmiechowski, Sikorska-Kowalska, and Fukumoto, *Robotnicy Łodzi drugiej połowy XIX wieku*, 16.

22. "Robotnicy łódzcy," *Goniec Łódzki*, no. 40 (1898).

23. "Robotnicy," *Rozwój*, no. 245 (1907).

24. Starkman, *Łódź i łodzianie*, 40. A representative collection of contemporary articles is Boczkowski, *Łódź, która przeminela w publicystyce i prozie*. On the broader context, see Marzec and Zysiak, "'Journalists Discovered Łódź Like Columbus.'" On internal debates, see Śmiechowski, *Łódzka wizja postępu*; Śmiechowski, "Searching for a Better City; Zysiak, "Desire for Fullness"; and above all Zysiak et al., *From Cotton and Smoke*.

25. On the problem of the "Germandom" of Lodz in the Warsaw press, see Śmiechowski, *Z perspektywy stolicy*. On the particular image of local capitalists and petty business people based on their interethnic background, see Schuster, "Stadt der Vielen Kulturen'"; and Chu, "'Lodzermensch.'"

26. Hensel, *Polen, Deutsche und Juden in Lodz*.

27. The intelligentsia in Lodz was from the beginning much more socially active than Warsaw's, which aspired more to upper-class status (Iwańska, "Garść refleksji i postulatów badawczych").

28. "Z dnia na dzień," *Goniec Łódzki*, no. 78 (1900).

29. "Z dnia na dzień," *Goniec Łódzki*, no. 78 (1900). An example of such endeavors was the debate on housing and deteriorating living conditions, examined in Śmiechowski, "Warunki mieszkaniowe robotników."

30. Weiss, *Przełom antypozytywistyczny w Polsce*.

31. For a comparison, see the cases of Manchester or Bristol: Gorsky, *Patterns of Philanthropy*; and Shapely, *Charity and Power in Victorian Manchester*.

32. On the turbulent and variegated origins of welfare state paradigm, with the important role of a discursive framing of the problem, see, among others, Hennock, *Origin of the Welfare State*; Swaan, *In Care of the State*; and Stolleis, *Origins of the German Welfare State*.

33. Wagner, "As Intellectual History Meets Historical Sociology."

34. Reddy, *Money and Liberty in Modern Europe*.

35. On the Polish case and the debate on the capacity of benign nobles' national

capitalism to turn even Lodz into an island of moral order, see Zysiak, "Desire for Fullness."

36. Rabinbach, "Social Knowledge, Social Risk."

37. A similar transformation among local elites, press authors, and reformers is described in Steinmetz, *Regulating the Social*; and Lees, *Cities, Sin, and Social Reform*.

38. "Łódź przed dwudziestu laty," *Rozwój*, no. 11 (1905).

39. "W sprawie kąpieli," *Goniec Łódzki*, no. 90 (1898). For a comparative context and general remarks, see also Moreno Martínez, "Hygienist Movement," 794.

40. "Budownictwo łódzkie," *Rozwój*, no. 50 (1899).

41. "Szkoły fabryczne," *Rozwój*, no. 194 (1898).

42. "Zygzaki," *Rozwój*, no. 215 (1898); "Drzewostan w Łodzi," *Rozwój*, no. 41 (1900).

43. "W sprawie przyłączonych przedmieść," *Kurier Łódzki*, no. 535 (1908).

44. "W sprawie kąpieli," *Goniec Łódzki*, no. 90 (1898).

45. The term "private biopolitics" comes from Marzec and Zysiak, "Days of Labour."

46. "Kronika Łódzka. Księży Młyn," *Goniec Łódzki*, no. 114 (1898). It is worth noting that earlier the first Polish-language magazine *Dziennik Łódzki* (not of direct interest here), sponsored by Scheibler, the owner of this district, used these improved living conditions to discredit all other workers' demands as inappropriate: "when we see thousands of workers walking to work and getting back every day with a bright face, we cannot complain about their miserable fate" (Małagowski, Łódź–Księży Młyn, 26).

47. "Nasza filantropia," *Kurier Łódzki*, no. 6 (1906). See also "Echa tygodnia," *Kurier Łódzki*, no. 370 (1907); and "Filantropia a potrzeby ludności," *Kurier Łódzki*, no. 27 (1907).

48. "Zachloroformowani," *Goniec Łódzki*, no. 117 (1905).

49. "Filantropia a potrzeby ludności," *Kurier Łódzki*, no. 27 (1907).

50. "Budownictwo łódzkie," *Rozwój*, no. 50 (1899).

51. "Zarys sytuacji w Łodzi," *Kurier Łódzki*, no. 7 (1907).

52. "Filantropia a potrzeby ludności," *Kurier Łódzki*, no. 27 (1907).

53. "Potrzeby filantropijne Łodzi," *Rozwój*, no. 268 (1898).

54. "Robotnicy łódzcy," *Goniec Łódzki*, no. 40 (1898).

55. "Robotnicy łódzcy," *Goniec Łódzki*, no. 40 (1898).

56. Sierakowska, "Rodzina robotnicza w Królestwie Polskim," 327.

57. Untitled, *Rozwój*, no. 108 (1899).

58. On the debate about the conditions of women in the factories, see Sikorska-Kowalska, *Wizerunek kobiety łódzkiej*; and Żarnowska, *Workers, Women, and Social Change*. The importance of the problem is confirmed by petitions sent by indignant workers to factory inspectors, such as the documents presented in Korzec, *Źródła do dziejów rewolucji 1905–1907 w okręgu łódzkim*, vol. 1, pt. 1.

59. See, for instance, "Robotnice i gospodynie," *Goniec Łódzki*, no. 24 (1899); and "Jedna z wielu," *Goniec Łódzki*, no. 2 (1902).

60. "Chiński mur," *Goniec Łódzki*, no. 54 (1899).

61. "Bezrobocie," *Goniec Łódzki*, no. 25 (1905). The article covers strikes in the Rhineland and rebuts suggestions that Polish migrant workers destabilized wages there. The extensive presentation of the development of the strike, the reasons for it, and the

strategies of the parties involved, printed just two days after the general strike in Łódź had broken out (January 25), leaves little doubt that it was intended largely to improve understanding of local events.

62. "Państwowe ubezpieczenie robotników," *Goniec Łódzki*, no. 27 (1905).

63. "Prasa rosyjska o bezrobociu," *Goniec Łódzki*, no. 31 (1905). This time there is also an editorial commentary, arguing (contrary to the common mood and usual presentation) that the background of the strike is not anti-Russian but purely social. One may wonder to what extent it was a deliberate misconception intended to lower the level of state repression or an early expression of the writer's genuine confusion. Indeed both components were intermingled, and in those days it was far from clear who was fighting for what.

64. "Co czynić," *Goniec Łódzki*, no. 170a (1905).

65. How this trope, which appeared in a similar fashion in Russia, was exaggerated to the point of absurdity, and then brutally reversed, is documented in Halfin, "Rape of the Intelligentsia."

66. "Kronika tygodniowa," *Rozwój*, no. 195 (1907), in Sikorska-Kowalska, *"Wolność, czy zbrodnia?,* 284.

67. "Robotnicy," *Rozwój*, no. 245 (1907).

68. "Nasz Konkurs," *Rozwój*, no. 119 (1905), in Sikorska-Kowalska, *"Wolność, czy zbrodnia?,* 288. The paper also published letters from workers explaining their situation and desperate desire to receive an education. The letters' style and content, however, suggest extensive editing by the journal, if not outright falsification. See "Kronika tygodniowa," *Rozwój*, no. 94 (1905).

69. "Odezwa do inteligencji naszego miasta," *Goniec Łódzki*, no. 298a (1905); "Echa tygodniowe 2," *Kurier Łódzki*, no. 307 (1907).

70. "Odezwa do inteligencji naszego miasta," *Goniec Łódzki*, no. 298a (1905). All quotations in the paragraph are from the same source.

71. Marzec, "Beyond Group Antagonism."

72. "Dom ludowy," *Rozwój*, no. 221 (1907).

73. "Zaburzenia w Łodzi," *Goniec Łódzki*, no. 178 (1905).

74. "Sprawy fabryczne," *Goniec Łódzki*, no. 167a (1905).

75. "Nie jest tak źle!," *Goniec Łódzki*, no. 185. (1905).

76. In some provincial areas the censors just did not care, as the industrial issues were considered more exotic and not easily referable to the local situation. When such an article had already been accepted by a censors' office, it was possible to reprint it elsewhere. Even if the reprint was a verbatim copy, in a new setting it gained an entirely new, more contentious meaning.

77. "Uspokojenie robotników," reprinted from the journal *Ruś*, *Goniec Łódzki*, no. 254 (1905).

78. "Z minionych chwil," *Goniec Łódzki,* no. 260 (1905).

79. "Strajk szwaczek," *Kurier Łódzki*, no. 65a (1906), in Sikorska-Kowalska, *Czego chce współczesna kobieta?*, 102.

80. Stedman Jones, *End to Poverty?*

81. "Tanie mieszkania dla robotników," *Goniec Łódzki*, no. 269b (1905).
82. "Ratujmy przyszłość," *Goniec Łódzki*, no. 295 (1905).
83. "Listy z ulicy Św. Andrzeja," *Kurier Łódzki*, no. 33 (1906).
84. "Zachloformowani," *Goniec Łódzki*, no. 117 (1905).
85. "Kilka uwag refleksyjnych," *Goniec Łódzki*, no. 5 (1906), quoted in Śmiechowski, Łódzka wizja postępu, 125. See also "Fabrykanci a robotnicy, cz. II," *Kurier Łódzki*, no. 259a (1906).
86. "Walki bratobójcze," *Kurier Łódzki*, no. 63a (1906).
87. Śmiechowski, *Łódzka wizja postępu*, 120–28.
88. "Zachloroformowani," *Goniec Łódzki*, no. 117 (1905).
89. Lewis, "Labor-Management Conflict in Russian Poland."
90. A detailed reconstruction of the journal's position is presented in Chańko, "Gazeta 'Rozwój' wobec wielkiego lokautu łódzkiego."
91. "Echa tygodniowe," *Kurier Łódzki*, no. 9 (1907).
92. "Lokaut w świetle prądów demokratycznych," *Kurier Łódzki*, no. 13 (1907).
93. "Zwodniczy most," *Kurier Łódzki*, no. 27 (1907).
94. "Lokaut w świetle prądów demokratycznych," *Kurier Łódzki*, no. 13 (1907).
95. "Lokaut w świetle prądów demokratycznych," *Kurier Łódzki*, no. 13 (1907).
96. "Wywiad u M. Poznańskiego," *Rozwój*, no. 6 (1907), in Sikorska-Kowalska, *"Wolność, czy zbrodnia?*, 79.
97. This trend can be traced in articles about the revolution in *Rozwój* conveniently available collected and published in one volume: Sikorska-Kowalska, *"Wolność, czy zbrodnia?*
98. On the transformation of politics in Russian Poland, see Blobaum, *Rewolucja*, chap. 6; Ury, *Barricades and Banners*; and Kaczyńska, "Partie polityczne a masowy ruch robotniczy."
99. Several interesting works on Western Europe offer useful theoretical insights and comparative material. On the concept of "fear of the masses," see Balibar, Stolze, and Giancotti, "Spinoza, the Anti-Orwell"; Hill and Montag, *Masses, Classes and the Public Sphere*; and Mulholland, *Bourgeois Liberty and the Politics of Fear*.
100. Stegner, *Liberałowie Królestwa Polskiego 1904–1915*, 135–85; Janowski, *Polish Liberal Thought before 1918*, 219–44; Stegner, "Rewolucja w opinii środowisk liberalnych"; Jaszczuk, *Liberalna Atlantyda*; Śmiechowski, *Łódzka wizja postępu*, 245–50.
101. Janowski, *Polish Liberal Thought before 1918*, 220.
102. See Schorske, *Fin-de-Siecle Vienna Politics and Culture*. For a comparative context, see Freifeld, *Nationalism and the Crowd*.
103. On the evolution of his personal views on the revolutionary movement see Petrozolin-Skowrońska, "'Liberum veto' A. Świętochowskiego," pts. 1 and 2.
104. Mogilnicki, *Wspomnienia*, 96.
105. Rancière, *Hatred of Democracy*.
106. Jonsson, *Crowds and Democracy*.
107. Szwarc, "Rewolucja 1905 roku na ziemiach polskich"; Micińska, *Dzieje inteligencji polskiej do roku 1918*.

108. Similar bifurcations in different circumstances are described in Lottes, *Politische Aufklärung und plebejisches Publikum*; Eley, "Nations, Publics, and Political Cultures"; and Calhoun, *Roots of Radicalism*.

109. Kościesza [Antoni Skrzynecki], *Wrogowie wiary i ojczyzny*, 10. For other examples, see Jeleński, *Siła przed prawem albo jak kto woli*; and Jeleński, *Robotniku polski!*

110. Jerzy Moszyński, "List do redakcji," *Słowo*, no. 81 (1905), quoted in Micińska, "'Wieść z dna polskiego piekła.'"

111. Krzywiec, "Eliminationist Anti-Semitism."

112. Weeks, "Polish 'Progressive Antisemitism,' 1905–1914"; Micińska, "'Wieść z dna polskiego piekła'"; Krzywiec, "Polish Intelligentsia."

113. Porter, *When Nationalism Began to Hate*; Krzywiec, "Z taką rewolucją musimy walczyć na noże."

114. For an overview of these dynamics, see Weeks, *From Assimilation to Antisemitism*; Weeks, "Fanning the Flames"; Blobaum, "Politics of Antisemitism in Fin-de-Siècle Warsaw"; and Ury, *Barricades and Banners*.

115. Sienkiewicz, *Wiry*, 2, chap. 23. Some information on the novel and the plot may be found in Garstka, "Revolution of 1905 in Polish Literature."

116. Not incidentally, Lombroso's work was widely known and commented on in Poland thanks to a translation made by one of the leading National Democrats, Jan Ludwik Popławski (Lombroso, *Geniusz i obłąkanie w związku z medycyną sądową, krytyką i historyą*).

117. "Na tle rewolucji," *Goniec Łódzki*, no. 320 (1905).

118. For other discourses theorizing the feedback loop between docile masses and an impostor leader see Jonsson, *Brief History of the Masses*.

119. "Echa tygodniowe 2," *Kurier Łódzki*, no. 307 (1907).

120. "Zabójstwo Mieczysława Silbersteina," *Rozwój*, no. 206 (1907), in Sikorska-Kowalska, *"Wolność, czy zbrodnia?,* 154.

121. "Wolność czy zbrodnia," *Rozwój*, no. 249 (1906), in Sikorska-Kowalska, *"Wolność, czy zbrodnia?,* 117.

122. "Ruch polityczny w Łodzi," *Rozwój*, no. 245 (1907).

123. "Czerwona sotnia," *Rozwój*, no. 79 (1907), in Sikorska-Kowalska, *"Wolność, czy zbrodnia?,* 122.

124. Sikorska-Kowalska, *"Wolność, czy zbrodnia?,* 121.

125. "Echa tygodniowe 2," *Kurier Łódzki*, no. 307 (1907); for a later example, see "Za dużo oświaty," *Nowy Kurier Łódzki*, no. 208 (1912).

126. Some examples of arguments from the postrevolutionary period are in "Uspołecznienie robotników," *Nowy Kurier Łódzki*, no. 156 (1912).

127. This conviction was inspired by the inflow of socialist ideas. At the same time, however, it sealed the basic principle of a "market culture" grounded in self-interest. Along with the ideal of organic harmony, the nonmarket incentives driving working-class protests were sidelined. The prize for political legitimacy was the requirement to argue on the grounds of market rationality. See Reddy, *Rise of Market Culture*.

128. "Robotnicy," *Rozwój*, no. 245 (1907).

129. "Dom ludowy," *Rozwój*, no. 221 (1907).

130. [Untitled], *Rozwój*, no. 127 (1909).

131. Curran and Seaton, *Power without Responsibility*.

132. Conboy, *Language of Newspapers*, 12.

133. Bottici, *Imaginal Politics*, 90–91.

134. A similar approach to the press as a constitutive factor in reconstructing the social imaginary on the working class, although under different historical circumstances, is Zysiak, *Modernizacja, socjalizm, nauka*.

Conclusion

1. Ascher, *Revolution of 1905* (1988); Ascher, "Interpreting 1905"; Bradley, "Subjects into Citizens"; Bradley, *Voluntary Associations in Tsarist Russia*; Porter, "Emergence of Civil Society in Late Imperial Russia."

2. Rieber, *Struggle for the Eurasian Borderlands*.

3. White, "Revolution in the Baltic Provinces."

4. Polvinen, *Imperial Borderland*; Kujala, "Finland in 1905."

5. Suny, *Baku Commune, 1917–1918*; Swietochowski, *Russian Azerbaijan, 1905–1920*.

6. Suny, *Making of the Georgian Nation*; Jones, *Socialism in Georgian Colors*.

7. Rauch, *Baltic States*.

8. Upton, *Finnish Revolution, 1917–1918*; Alapuro, *State and Revolution in Finland*.

9. Porter-Szűcs, *Poland in the Modern World;* Wróbel, "Rise and Fall of Parliamentary Democracy."

10. Pyotr Stolypin was the Russian prime minister and home secretary between 1906 and 1911. He was the main tsarist politician responsible for suppression of the revolution and accompanying harsh repressions. On the Stolypin reaction in Russian Poland, see the last chapter of Blobaum, *Rewolucja*. For the context of conservative reform, see Ascher, *P. A. Stolypin*; and Waldron, *Between Two Revolutions*.

11. Arendt, *Origins of Totalitarianism*, 296–97. See also Somers, *Genealogies of Citizenship*.

12. At this point my argument gets closer to Pierre Bourdieu's analysis of the political field and of language as a carrier of power. On the whole, though, I did not use Bourdieu's terms, and the notion of the political field is taken rather as a descriptive and generic label and not a technical term. See Bourdieu, *Politische Feld;* Bourdieu, *Language and Symbolic Power*. On more general understanding of the field as a theoretical category, see Fligstein and McAdam, *Theory of Fields*.

13. Porter, "Democracy and Discipline." Indeed, a more authoritative tone saturated with patronizing power aimed at the reader is easily detectable in NZR materials directed at workers.

14. Apart from standard antisemitic and antisocialist literature, former socialists also accused Social Democracy of worse—the most spectacular examples being the writings of Julian Unszlicht, author of *Socjal-litwactwo w Polsce* and *O Pogromy ludu polskiego*. On the intellectual biography of this author, a self-hating Jew who became a fanatical Catholic priest, see Krzywiec, "Nadwiślański Weininger?"

15. On the later faith of the SDKPiL and its attempts to stop antisemitism, see Strobel, *Partei Rosa Luxemburgs, Lenin und die SPD*. The core statements of this debate were

published by Rosa Luxemburg in the journal *Młot* (Hammer). Some of them were translated and published in Fetscher, *Marxisten Gegen Antisemitismus*.

16. Weeks, "Polish 'Progressive Antisemitism,' 1905–1914"; Krzywiec, "Polish Intelligentsia"; Janowski, *Polish Liberal Thought before 1918*.

17. Brykczynski, *Primed for Violence*.

18. Leaving aside its specifics or coherence. For the debate on the nature of the working class, above all see Calhoun, *Question of Class Struggle*; and Calhoun, *Roots of Radicalism*.

19. Eley, *Forging Democracy*; Castel, *From Manual Workers to Wage Laborers*; Silver, *Forces of Labor*.

20. Eley, "Cultural Socialism, the Public Sphere, and the Mass Form."

21. Jonsson, *Brief History of the Masses*, 75. See also Mulholland, *Bourgeois Liberty and the Politics of Fear*.

22. On this contradiction and ambiguity of civil society in Russia, see Rogger, *Jewish Policies and Right-Wing Politics*; and Hohler, "Radical Right Civil Society."

23. The seminal example in political theory is Arendt, *Origins of Totalitarianism*. The example directly referring to the events covered in this study is Ury, *Barricades and Banners*. For an interesting criticism of this argument, see Jonsson, *Crowds and Democracy*. A balanced overview of European trajectories is presented in Müller, *Contesting Democracy*.

24. Young, "Impartiality and the Civic Public," 73.

25. Habermas, "Public Sphere," 118.

26. Montag, "Pressure of the Street."

27. Fraser, "Rethinking the Public Sphere."

28. Koselleck, *Critique and Crisis*.

29. Habermas, "Public Sphere," 115.

30. Eley, "Nations, Publics, and Political Cultures."

31. Fraser, "Rethinking the Public Sphere."

32. Montag, "Pressure of the Street."

33. Bodnar, "Reclaiming Public Space"; Lefebvre, "Right to the City"; On the local context of the right to the city, see Śmiechowski, "Hierarchia czy demokracja?"; and Śmiechowski, Sikorska-Kowalska, and Fukumoto, *Robotnicy Łodzi drugiej połowy XIX wieku*.

34. Calhoun, *Roots of Radicalism*.

35. Arendt, *On Revolution*.

36. For more on "fear of the masses," see Balibar, Stolze, and Giancotti, "Spinoza, the Anti-Orwell."

37. See respectively Freeden, *Political Theory of Political Thinking*; Koselleck, *Critique and Crisis*; and Bradley, "Subjects into Citizens."

38. In respect to Russia, a similar argument was made in McDaniel, *Autocracy, Capitalism, and Revolution in Russia*, chap. 9.

39. Thompson, *Making of the English Working Class*; Steinberg, *Fighting Words*; Lottes, *Politische Aufklärung und Plebejisches Publikum*; Aminzade, *Ballots and Barricades*; Sewell, *Work and Revolution in France*.

40. Lottes, *Politische Aufklärung und plebejisches Publikum*; Eley, "Nations, Publics, and Political Cultures"; Calhoun, *Roots of Radicalism*.

41. Eley, "Nations, Publics, and Political Cultures"; Montag, "Pressure of the Street."

42. Blanc, "National Liberation and Bolshevism Reexamined"; Blanc, "Anti-Imperial Marxism"; Kula, *Narodowe i rewolucyjne.*

43. Bartolini, *Political Mobilization of the European Left, 1860–1980*, chap. 4.

44. Zarycki, "Cultural Capital and the Political Role of the Intelligentsia in Poland"; Zarycki, "Class Analysis in Conditions of a Dual-Stratification Order."

45. On the working-class place within the social imaginary and political sphere, see Dunn, *Privatizing Poland*; and Ost, *Defeat of Solidarity*. These authors do not necessarily stress the long-term intransigencies of political thinking that might have supported the marginalization of workers.

46. From the abundant literature on the tormented interaction between workers and the intelligentsia in the first Solidarity movement and after, see Laba, *Roots of Solidarity*; Kennedy, *Professionals, Power, and Solidarity in Poland*; and Ost, *Solidarity and the Politics of Anti-Politics.*

47. On the later intellectual history of Polish dissidents, self-aware continuators of the intelligentsia's ethos, see Arndt, *Intellektuelle in der Opposition*; Gawin, *Wielki zwrot*; and Siermiński, *Dekada przełomu.*

Appendix

1. Spieralski, *Wspomnienia weteranów rewolucji*; Tych, *Archiwum ruchu robotniczego.*

2. Lisowski, *Etapy;* Łęczycki, *Mojej ankiety personalnej punkt 35*; Płochocki, *Wspomnienia działacza SDKPIL*. An overview of the autobiographical writing in the postwar period is presented in Zysiak, "Polish Method."

3. Above all, *Z pola walki* in the late 1920s and early 1930s. This group is the closest to the "Bolshevik autobiography" analyzed, among others, by Hernandez, "Confessions of Semen Kanatchikov"; and Halfin, *Red Autobiographies.*

4. For instance, journals prominent in maintaining this tradition in the interwar period are filled with similar memories of street fights with Cossacks, tales of bomb-throwing heroism, and recollections of Siberian martyrdom. See, for instance, *Niepodległość* from 1930 onward, edited by Leon Wasilewski; *Kronika ruchu rewolucyjego w Polsce*; or *Organ Stowarzyszenia wieźniów politycznych*, edited by Jan Krzeslawski and Adam Próchnik. There were also numerous book publications presenting such a military history of the nationalist socialist movement. One of the well-established authors championing the genre was Stanisław Martynowski. See Martynowski, *Łódzka dziesiątka bojowa*; Martynowski, *Łódź w ogniu*; and Martynowski, *Polska bojowa*. There were also attempts to canonize the street tactic as a cornerstone of military expertise in the later, independent Polish state, as done, for instance, in Błotnicki, *Przez rewolucję 1905 r. do legionów 1914 r.*

5. This was no accident, because for decades Polish social science specialized in collecting and researching ego documents. The prewar tradition was cultivated and developed within socialist memory culture.

6. Zaretskiy, "Confessing to Leviathan."

7. Gerhardt, "'Ideal Type' and the Construction of the Life Course"; Strauss and Corbin, *Basics of Qualitative Research.*

8. Kiepurska, *Bibliografia pism.*

9. "Four Discourses of Modernity. Modernism of the Periphery on the Example of Lodz," project hosted in the Department of Sociology of Culture at the University of Lodz, financed by the Polish National Science Center (contracted as UMO-2011/03/B/HS6/01874). The project findings are presented in Zysiak et al., *From Cotton and Smoke*.

10. Sikorska-Kowalska, *Wizerunek kobiety łódzkiej przełomu XIX i XX wieku*; Sikorska-Kowalska, "Wolność, czy zbrodnia?"

11. Śmiechowski, *Łódzka wizja postępu*.

Selected Bibliography

Primary Sources

Archives

Archiwum Akt Nowych w Warszawie
    Akta Osobowe Działaczy Ruchu Robotniczego
    Archiwum Polskiej Partii Socjalistycznej
    Instytut Badania Najnowszej Historii Polski, Wspomnienia nadesłane do redakcji pisma Niepodległość
    Narodowy Związek Robotniczy
    NZR, Materiały Komisji Odznaczeniowej
    Socjaldemokracja Królestwa Polskiego i Litwy

Archiwum Główne Akt Dawnych
    Zbiór Druków Ulotnych Anny Branickiej

Archiwum Państwowe w Łodzi
    Kancelaria Gubernatora Piotrkowskiego
    Komitet Łódzki PZPR
    Komitet Wojewódzki (dla woj. Łódzkiego) PZPR
    Piotrkowski Zarząd Żandarmerii Guberni Piotrkowskiej
    Zbiór Druków i Pism Ulotnych

Biblioteka Narodowa w Warszawie
    Dokumenty Życia Społecznego

Newspapers and Periodicals

Czerwony Sztandar (SDKPiL)
Dzwon Polski
Głos
Goniec Łódzki, 1898–1906; renamed *Kurier Łódzki*, 1906–1911; renamed *Nowy Kurier Łódzki*, 1911–1914
Kiliński, ed. Stanisław Nowicki, 1936–1937
Kronika Ruchu Rewolucyjnego w Polsce, ed. Adam Próchnik and Jan Krzesławski, 1935–1939
Liberum veto
Łodzianin (PPS)

Niepodległość, ed. Leon Wasilewski, 1929–1939
Pobudka
Pochodnia (NZR)
Prawda
Przegląd Wszechpolski (National Democracy, published openly in Austrian Galicia)
Przedświt (PPS)
Robotnik (PPS)
Rozwój, 1897–1914
Z pola walki (SDKPiL)
Z pola walki, Moscow, 1927–1931
Z pola walki, Warsaw, 1958–1989

Published Collections of Sources and Documents, Bibliographies, And Inventories

Daniszewski, Tadeusz, ed. *SDKPiL w rewolucji 1905 roku: Zbiór publikacji*. Warsaw: Książka i Wiedza, 1955.

Gąsiorowska-Grabowska, Natalia, and Stanisław Kalabiński, eds. *Źródła do dziejów klasy robotniczej na ziemiach polskich*. Vol. 1. Warsaw: Państwowe Wydawnictwo Naukowe, 1962.

Kalabiński, Stanisław, ed. *Carat i klasy posiadające w walce z rewolucją 1905–1907 w Królestwie Polskim: Materiały archiwalne*. Warsaw: Państwowe Wydawnictwo Naukowe, 1956.

Kiepurska, Halina. *Bibliografia pism ulotnych rewolucji 1905–7 w Królestwie Polskim*. Warsaw: Biblioteka narodowa, 1963.

Kormanowa, Żanna. *Materiały do bibliografii druków socjalistycznych na ziemiach polskich w latach 1866–1918*. Warsaw: Książka i Wiedza, 1949.

Korzec, Paweł, ed. *Źródła do dziejów rewolucji 1905–1907 w okręgu łódzkim*, tom 1, cz. 1. Warsaw: Książka i Wiedza, 1957.

Korzec, Paweł, ed. *Źródła do dziejów rewolucji 1905–1907 w okręgu łódzkim*, tom 1, cz. 2. Warsaw: Książka i Wiedza, 1958.

Korzec, Paweł, ed. *Źródła do dziejów rewolucji 1905–1907 w okręgu łódzkim*, tom 2. Warsaw: Książka i Wiedza, 1964.

Malinowski, Aleksander, ed. *Materiały do historii PPS i ruchu rewolucyjnego w zaborze rosyjskim 1893–1904*. Vol. 1: *1893–1897*. Warsaw: Wydawnictwo "Życie," 1907.

Missalowa, Gryzelda, and Natalia Gąsiorowska-Grabowska, eds. *Źródła do historii klasy robotniczej okręgu łódzkiego*. Warsaw: Książka i Wiedza, 1957.

Tych, Feliks, ed. *PPS-Lewica, 1906–1918: Materiały i dokumenty*. Warsaw: Książka i Wiedza, 1961.

Published Correspondence, Speeches, Political Pamphlets, Contemporary Writings, Literary Works, and Collected Journal Articles

Ajnenkiel, Eugeniusz. *Czerwona lutnia: Pieśni robotnicze*. Lodz: Wydawnictwo Łódzkie, 1964.

Balicki, Zygmunt. *Parlamentaryzm: Wybór pism*. Cracow: Ośrodek Myśli Politycznej, 2008.

Boczkowski, Piotr. *Łódź, która przeminęła w publicystyce i prozie (antologia)*. Lodz: eConn, 2008.

Brzozowski, Stanisław. *Kultura i życie: Zagadnienia szutuki i twórczości w walce o światopogląd*. Warsaw: Państwowy Institut Wydawniczy, 1973.

Brzozowski, Stanisław. *Współczesna powieść i krytyka literacka*. Warsaw: Państwowy Instytut Wydawniczy, 1971.

Daszyński, Ignacy. *Pogadanka o socyalizmie*. Lwów: Latarnia, 1900.

Dmowski, Roman. *Pisma: Dziesięć lat walki*. Vol. 3. Częstochowa, 1938.

Jeleński, Jan. *Bezrobocie rozumu*. Warsaw: Księgarnia "Roli," 1905.

Jeleński, Jan. *Robotniku polski! Ratuj siebie przed zgubą a kraj swój przed ruiną! (głos swojego do swoich)*. Warsaw: Księgarnia "Roli," 1907.

Jeleński, Jan. *Siła przed prawem albo jak kto woli: Wolność socjalistyczna*. Warsaw: Księgarnia "Roli," 1906.

Jeleński, Jan. *Wrogom własnej ojczyzny (jeszcze słów parę ku opamiętaniu)*. Warsaw: Księgarnia "Roli," 1906.

Kelles-Krauz, Kazimierz. *Czy teraz nie ma pańszczyzny?* London: Drukarnia Partyjna PPS, 1903.

Kelles-Krauz, Kazimierz. *Jak się narody rządzą?* Warsaw: Towarzystwo Wydawnictw Ludowych, 1906.

Klonowski, Stefan, ed. *1905 w literaturze polskiej*. Warsaw: Wydawnictwo Ministerstwa Obrony Narodowej, 1955.

Kościesza [Antoni Skrzynecki], Zbigniew. *Wrogowie wiary i ojczyzny: Kilka spostrzeżeń na czasie*. Warsaw: Wydawnictwo Kroniki Rodzinnej, 1905.

Kozicki, Stanisław. *Historia Ligi Narodowej (Okres 1887–1907)*. London: Myśl Polska, 1964.

Kozłowski, Aleksander. *Z rewolucyjnych dni (Wspomnienia z lat 1904–1907)*. Warsaw: Państwowe Zakłady Wydawnictw Szkolnych, 1963.

Krwawe dnie w warszawie. Warsaw, 1905.

Kujawczyk, Tomek. *Ojciec Szymon*. London: Wydawnictwo Polskiej Partyi Socyalistycznej, 1896.

Kułakowski, Mariusz. *Roman Dmowski w świetle listów i wspomnień*. London: Gryf Publications, 1968.

Lombroso, Cesare. *Geniusz i obłąkanie w związku z medycyną sądową, krytyką i historyą*. Translated by Jan Ludwik Popławski. Warsaw: Skład główny w Księgarni Gebethnera i Wolffa, 1887.

Luksemburg, Róża. *O rewolucji: Rosja 1905, 1917*. Warsaw: Książka i Prasa, 2008.

Luksemburg, Róża. *Listy do Leona Jogichesa-Tyszki, 1908–1914*. Warsaw: Książka i Wiedza, 1968.

Martynowski, Stanisław. *Łódź w ogniu*. Lodz: Drukarnia Udziałowa, 1931.

Martynowski, Stanisław. *Łódzka dziesiątka bojowa*. Lodz: Wydawnictwo Stowarzyszenia Byłych Więźniów Politycznych, 1928.

Martynowski, Stanisław. *Polska bojowa*. Lodz: Nakładem autora, 1937.

Młot, Jan. *Kto z czego żyje?* Warsaw: Książka i Wiedza, 1952.

Ostoja, Eustachy. *Wobec zbrodni*. Cracow: Nakładem autora, Skład główny księgarni Goebethnera i sp., 1906.

Popławski, Jan Ludwik. *Naród i polityka: Wybór pism*. Cracow: Ośrodek Myśli Politycznej, 2012.

Sienkiewicz, Henryk. *Wiry*. Vol. 2. Warsaw: Zakład Narodowy im. Ossolińskich, 1932.

Sikorska-Kowalska, Marta, ed. *Czego chce współczesna kobieta? Problematyka kobieca na łamach polskiej prasy w Łodzi przełomu XIX i XX wieku*. Lodz: Wydawnictwo Uniwersytetu Łódzkiego, 2013.

Sikorska-Kowalska, Marta. *"Wolność, czy zbrodnia?": Rewolucja 1905–1907 roku w Łodzi na łamach gazety "Rozwój."* Lodz: Wydawnictwo Uniwersytetu Łódzkiego, 2012.

Unszlicht, Julian. *O Pogromy ludu polskiego: Rola socyal-litwactwa w niedawnej rewolucyi*. Cracow: Nakładem autora, 1912.

Unszlicht, Julian (Sedecki). *Socjal-litwactwo w Polsce (z teorji i praktyki "Socjaldemokracji Królestwa Polskiego i Litwy")*. Cracow: Wydawnictwo Życie, 1911.

Memoirs and Autobiographies Published as Books or Collections

Bąbol, Feliks. *Łódzkie barykady: Wspomnienia uczestników rewolucji 1905–7 roku*. Lodz: Komitet PZPR i Woj. Rady Związków Zawodowych, 1955.

Błotnicki, Adam. *Przez rewolucję 1905 r. do legionow 1914 r.* Lwów: Nakładem "Panteonu Polskiego," 1929.

Bracke, Wilhelm. *Precz z socjalistami!* London: Drukarnia Partyjna PPS, 1904.

Dąbrowski, Józef. *Czerwona Warszawa przed ćwierć wiekiem: Moje wspomnienia*. Poznań: Karol Rzepecki, 1925.

Durko, Janusz, ed. *W pracy i w walce: Wspomnienia robotników warszawskich z przełomu XIX i XX wieku*. Warsaw: Państwowy Instytut Wydawniczy, 1970.

Humnicki, Antoni. *Wspomnienia z lat 1888–1892 (przyczynek do historyi naszego ruchu socyalistycznego)*. Warsaw: Wydawnictwo Życie, 1907.

Jastrzębski, Wincenty. *Wspomnienia, 1885–1919*. Warsaw: Państwowe Wydawnictwo Naukowe, 1966.

Koral, Wacław. *Przez partie, związki, więzienia i Sybir: Wspomnienia drukarza z działalności w ruchu socjalistycznym i zawodowym 1898–1928*. Warsaw: Związek Zawodowy Drukarzy i Pokrewnych Zawodów w Polsce, oddział Warszawa, 1933.

Kwapiński, Jan. *Moje Wspomnienia 1904–1939*. Paris: Księgarnia Polska w Paryżu, 1965.

Lisowski, Ignacy. *Etapy*. Warsaw: Ksiażka i Wiedza, 1975.

Malinowski, Marjan. *Z krwawych dni*. Lublin: Ludowa Spółdzielnia Wydawnicza, 1919.

Mogilnicki, Aleksander. *Wspomnienia: Spisane w Łodzi w latach 1949–1955*. Warsaw: Barbara Izdebska, 2008.

Niedzielski, Kazimierz. *Z burzliwych dni 1904–1905*. Warsaw: Księgarnia Ignacego Rzepeckiego, 1917.

O wolność i niepodległość: Wspomnienia robotników fabryki I. K. Poznańskiego w Łodzi w 20 rocznicę odzyskania niepodległości. Lodz: Komitet Fundacji Tablicy Pamiątkowej 20-lecia Niepodległości Polski, 1938.

Pestkowski, Stanisław. *Wspomnienia rewolucjonisty*. Lodz: Wydawnictwo Łódzkie, 1961.

Płochocki, Marian. *Wspomnienia działacza SDKPiL*. Warsaw: Iskry, 1956.
Rudnicki, Lucjan. *Stare i nowe*. Warsaw: Państwowy Instytut Wydawniczy, 1979.
Sokolnicki, Michał. *Czternaście lat*. Warsaw: Inst. Badania Najnowszej Historji Polski, 1936.
Spieralski, Zdzisław, ed. *Wspomnienia weteranów rewolucji 1905 i 1917 roku*. Lodz: Wydawnictwo Łódzkie, 1967.
Szapiro, Bernard. *Związki Zawodowe Robotnicze*. Warsaw: Towarzystwo Wydawnictw Ludowych, 1906.
Tych, Feliks, ed. *Archiwum ruchu robotniczego*. Vol. 3. Warsaw: Książka i Wiedza, 1976.

Secondary Literature

Alapuro, Risto. *State and Revolution in Finland*. Berkeley: University of California Press, 1988.
Aminzade, Ronald. *Ballots and Barricades: Class Formation and Republican Politics in France, 1830–1871*. Princeton, NJ: Princeton University Press, 1993.
Anderson, Benedict R. O'G. *Imagined Communities: Reflections on the Origin and Spread of Nationalism*. Rev. ed. New York: Verso, 2006.
Andrews, Molly. *Shaping History: Narratives of Political Change*. New York: Cambridge University Press, 2007.
Angenot, Marc. "Social Discourse Analysis: Outlines of a Research Project." *Yale Journal of Criticism* 17, no. 2 (2004): 199–215. doi:10.1353/yale.2004.0008.
Arditi, Benjamín. *Polemicization: The Contingency of the Commonplace*. Edinburgh: Edinburgh University Press, 1999.
Arendt, Hannah. *The Human Condition*. 2nd ed. Chicago: University of Chicago Press, 1998.
Arendt, Hannah. *On Revolution*. New York: Penguin Books, 2014.
Arendt, Hannah. *The Origins of Totalitarianism*. New York: Harcourt, Brace, and World, 1968.
Arndt, Agnes. *Intellektuelle in der Opposition: Diskurse zur Zivilgesellschaft in der Volksrepublik Polen*. Frankfurt am Main: Campus, 2007.
Ascher, Abraham. "Interpreting 1905." In *The Revolution of 1905 and Russia's Jews*, edited by Stefani Hoffman and Ezra Mendelsohn, 128–41. Philadelphia: University of Pennsylvania Press, 2008.
Ascher, Abraham. *P. A. Stolypin: The Search for Stability in Late Imperial Russia*. Stanford, CA: Stanford University Press, 2001.
Ascher, Abraham. *The Revolution of 1905*. Stanford, CA: Stanford University Press, 1988.
Ascher, Abraham. *The Revolution of 1905: A Short History*. Stanford, CA: Stanford University Press, 2004.
Assorodobraj-Kula, Nina. *Poczatki klasy robotniczej: Problem rak roboczych w przemysle polskim epoki Stanislawowskiej*. Warsaw: Państwowe Wydawnictwo Naukowe, 1966.
Austin, John L. *How to Do Things with Words*. Cambridge, MA: Harvard University Press, 1975.
Baberowski, Jörg, ed. *Imperiale Herrschaft in Der Provinz: Repräsentationen Politischer Macht Im Späten Zarenreich*. Frankfurt am Main: Campus, 2008.
Badziak, Kazimierz, and Paweł Samuś. *Strajki robotników łódzkich w 1905 roku*. Lodz: Wydawnictwo Łódzkie, 1985.

Baker, Keith Michael. *Inventing the French Revolution: Essays on French Political Culture in the Eighteenth Century*. New York: Cambridge University Press, 1990.

Balibar, Etienne, Ted Stolze, and Emilia Giancotti. "Spinoza, the Anti-Orwell: The Fear of the Masses." *Rethinking Marxism* 2, no. 3 (September 1989): 104–39. doi:10.1080/08935698908657878.

Bartolini, Stefano. *The Political Mobilization of the European Left, 1860–1980: The Class Cleavage*. New York: Cambridge University Press, 2000.

Bauerkämper, Arndt, ed. *Die Praxis der Zivilgesellschaft: Akteure, Handeln und Strukturen im internationalen Vergleich*. Frankfurt am Main: Campus, 2003.

Bauman, Zygmunt. *Memories of Class: The Pre-History and After-Life of Class*. London: Routledge, 2009.

Bell, Allan. *The Language of News Media*. Cambridge, MA: Blackwell, 1991.

Bendix, Reinhard. *Nation-Building and Citizenship: Studies of Our Changing Social Order*. Berkeley: University of California Press, 1977.

Benford, Robert, and David Snow. "Framing Processes and Social Movements: An Overview and Assessment." *Annual Review of Sociology* 26 (2000): 611–39.

Berlanstein, Lenard R., ed. *Rethinking Labor History: Essays on Discourse and Class Analysis*. Urbana: University of Illinois Press, 1993.

Bidinger, Elizabeth. *The Ethics of Working Class Autobiography: Representation of Family by Four American Authors*. Jefferson, NC: McFarland, 2006.

Biernacki, Richard. *The Fabrication of Labor: Germany and Britain, 1640–1914*. Berkeley: University of California Press, 1995.

Black, Antony. "The 'Axial Period': What Was It and What Does It Signify?" *Review of Politics* 70, no. 1 (2008). doi:10.1017/S0034670508000168.

Blanc, Eric. "Anti-Imperial Marxism Borderland Socialists and the Evolution of Bolshevism on National Liberation." *International Socialist Review*, no. 100 (2016).

Blanc, Eric. "National Liberation and Bolshevism Reexamined: A View from the Borderlands." *John Riddell Marxist Essays and Commentary*, May 20, 2014. http://johnriddell.wordpress.com/2014/05/20/national-liberation-and-bolshevism-reexamined-a-view-from-the-borderlands/.

Blänkner, Reinhard. "Historizitat, Institutionalitat, Symbolizitat: Grundbergiffliche Aspekte einer Kulturgeschichte des Politischen." In *Was heißt Kulturgeschichte des Politischen?*, edited by Barbara Stollberg-Rilinger. Berlin: Duncker & Humblot, 2005.

Blejwas, Stanislaus A. *Realism in Polish Politics: Warsaw Positivism and National Survival in Nineteenth Century Poland*. New Haven: Yale Concilium on International and Area Studies, 1984.

Blit, Lucjan. *The Origins of Polish Socialism: The History and Ideas of the First Polish Socialist Party, 1878–1886*. Cambridge: Cambridge University Press, 1971.

Blobaum, Robert, ed. *Antisemitism and Its Opponents in Modern Poland*. Ithaca, NY: Cornell University Press, 2005.

Blobaum, Robert. *Feliks Dzierżyński and the SDKPiL: A Study of the Origins of Polish Communism*. Boulder, CO: East European Monographs, 1984.

Blobaum, Robert. "The Politics of Antisemitism in Fin-de-Siècle Warsaw." *Journal of Modern History* 73, no. 2 (2001): 275–306.

Blobaum, Robert. "The Revolution of 1905–1907 and the Crisis of Polish Catholicism." *Slavic Review* 47, no. 4 (1988): 667–86.

Blobaum, Robert. *Rewolucja: Russian Poland, 1904–1907*. Ithaca, NY: Cornell University Press, 1995.

Blobaum, Robert. "The 'Woman Question' in Russian Poland, 1900–1914." *Journal of Social History* 35, no. 4 (2002): 799–824.

Bodnar, Judit. "Reclaiming Public Space." *Urban Studies* 52, no. 12 (2015): 2090–104. doi:10.1177/0042098015583626.

Bończa-Tomaszewski, Nikodem. *Demokratyczna geneza nacjonalizmu: Intelektualne korzenie ruchu narodowo-demokratycznego*. Warsaw: S. K. Fronda, 2001.

Bończa-Tomaszewski, Nikodem. *Źródła narodowości: Powstanie i rozwój polskiej świadomości w II połowie XIX i na początku XX wieku*. Wrocław: Wydawnictwo Uniwersytetu Wrocławskiego, 2006.

Bonnell, Andrew G. "Did They Read Marx? Marx Reception and Social Democratic Party Members in Imperial Germany, 1890–1914." *Australian Journal of Politics and History* 48, no. 1 (2002): 4–15. doi:10.1111/1467–8497.00248.

Bonnell, Victoria E. *Roots of Rebellion: Workers' Politics and Organizations in St. Petersburg and Moscow, 1900–1914*. Berkeley: University of California Press, 1983.

Bottici, Chiara. *Imaginal Politics: Images beyond Imagination and the Imaginary*. New York: Columbia University Press, 2014.

Bottici, Chiara. *A Philosophy of Political Myth*. Cambridge: Cambridge University Press, 2007.

Bourdieu, Pierre. *Language and Symbolic Power*. Translated by Gino Raymond. Cambridge, MA: Harvard University Press, 2003.

Bourdieu, Pierre. *Das politische Feld: Zur Kritik der politischen Vernunft*. Translated by Roswitha Schmid. Konstanz: UVK-Verl.-Gesellschaft, 2001.

Bradley, Joseph. *State and Civil Society in Russia: The Role of Nongovernmental Associations*. Washington, DC: National Council for Soviet and East European Research, 1997.

Bradley, Joseph. "Subjects into Citizens: Societies, Civil Society, and Autocracy in Tsarist Russia." *American Historical Review* 107, no. 4 (2002): 1094–123.

Bradley, Joseph. *Voluntary Associations in Tsarist Russia: Science, Patriotism, and Civil Society*. Cambridge, MA: Harvard University Press, 2009.

Breaugh, Martin. *The Plebeian Experience: A Discontinuous History of Political Freedom*. Translated by Lazer Lederhendler. New York: Columbia University Press, 2013.

Breuilly, John. "Civil Society and the Labor Movement, Class Relations and the Law: A Comparison between Germany and England." In *Arbeiter und Bürger im 19. Jahrhundert: Varianten ihres Verhältnisses im europäischen Vergleich*, edited by Jürgen Kocka and Elizabeth Muller-Luckner, 297–318. Munich: Oldenbourg, 1986.

Brinton, C. *The Anatomy of Revolution*. New York: Vintage Books, 1965.

Brock, Ditmar. *Alltägliche Arbeiterexistenz: Soziologische Rekonstruktionen des Zusammenhangs von Lohnarbeit und Biographie*. Frankfurt am Main: Campus, 1982.

Brock, Ditmar. *Der schwierige Weg in die Moderne: Umwälzungen in der Lebensführung der deutschen Arbeiter zwischen 1850 und 1980*. Frankfurt am Main: Campus, 1991.

Brykczynski, Paul. *Primed for Violence: Murder, Antisemitism, and Democratic Politics in Interwar Poland*. Madison: University of Wisconsin Press, 2016.

Brym, Robert J. *Jewish Intelligentsia and Russian Marxism: A Sociological Study of Intellectual Radicalism and Ideological Divergence*. Basingstoke: Palgrave Macmillan, 1978.

Burke, Martin J. *The Conundrum of Class: Public Discourse on the Social Order in America*. Chicago: University of Chicago Press, 1995.

Butler, Judith, Ernesto Laclau, and Slavoj Žižek. *Contingency, Hegemony, Universality: Contemporary Dialogues on the Left*. London: Verso, 2000.

Calhoun, Craig J. *The Question of Class Struggle: Social Foundations of Popular Radicalism during the Industrial Revolution*. Chicago: University of Chicago Press, 1982.

Calhoun, Craig J. *The Roots of Radicalism: Tradition, the Public Sphere, and Early Nineteenth-Century Social Movements*. Chicago: University of Chicago Press, 2012.

Canning, Kathleen. "Introduction." In *Weimar Publics/Weimar Subjects: Rethinking the Political Culture of Germany in the 1920s*. New York: Berghahn Books, 2010.

Case, Holly. "The 'Social Question,' 1820–1920." *Modern Intellectual History*, 2015, 1–29. doi:10.1017/S1479244315000037.

Castel, Robert. *From Manual Workers to Wage Laborers: Transformation of the Social Question*. New Brunswick, NJ: Transaction Publishers, 2003.

Castle, Rory. "'You Alone Will Make Our Family's Name Famous': Rosa Luxemburg, Her Family and the Origins of Her Polish-Jewish Identity." *Praktyka Teoretyczna*, no. 6 (2012): 93–125.

Certeau, M. de. *The Practice of Everyday Life*. Translated by Steven Rendall. Berkeley: University of California Press, 2011.

Chałasiński, Józef. *Społeczna genealogia inteligencji polskiej*. Cracow: Czytelnik, 1947.

Chańko, Jan. *Gazeta "Rozwój" (1897–1915): Studium źródłoznawcze*. Lodz: Uniwersytet Łódzki, 1982.

Chańko, Jan. "Gazeta 'Rozwój' wobec wielkiego lokautu łódzkiego." *Rocznik Łódzki* 20 (23) (1975): 143–71.

Chu, Winson. "The 'Lodzermensch': From Cultural Contamination to Marketable Multiculturalism." In *Germany, Poland, and Postmemorial Relations in Search of a Livable Past*, edited by Kristin Leigh Kopp and Joanna Niżyńska, 239–58. New York: Palgrave Macmillan, 2012.

Chwalba, Andrzej. *Historia Polski, 1795–1918*. Cracow: Wydawn. Literackie, 2000.

Chwalba, Andrzej. "Rola socjalistycznych druków ulotnych w kształtowaniu wiedzy i postaw politycznych robotników w dobie rewolucji 1905–1907." In *Społeczeństwo i polityka*, edited by Tadeusz Wolsza and Anna Żarnowska, 161–72. Warsaw: DiG, 1993.

Chwalba, Andrzej. *Sacrum i rewolucja: Socjaliści polscy wobec praktyk i symboli religijnych, 1870–1918*. Cracow: Universitas, 1992.

Conboy, Martin. *The Language of Newspapers: Socio-Historical Perspectives*. London: Continuum, 2010.

Conze, Werner. "Arbeit." In *Geschichtliche Grundbegriffe*, 1:49–109. Stuttgart: Klett-Cotta, 1972.

Corney, Frederick C. *Telling October: Memory and the Making of the Bolshevik Revolution.* Ithaca, NY: Cornell University Press, 2004.

Corrsin, Stephen D. *Warsaw before the First World War: Poles and Jews in the Third City of the Russian Empire, 1880–1914.* Boulder, CO: East European Monographs, 1989.

Crago, Laura. "Nationalism, Religion, Citizenship, and Work in the Development of the Polish Working Class and the Polish Trade Union Movement, 1815–1929: A Comparative Study of Russian Poland's Textile Workers and Upper Silesian Miners and Metalworkers." PhD diss., Yale University, 1993.

Crago, Laura. "The 'Polishness' of Production: Factory Politics and the Reinvention of Working-Class National and Political Identities in Russian Poland's Textile Industry, 1880–1910." *Slavic Review* 59, no. 1 (2000): 16–41.

Crenshaw, Kimberlé. *On Intersectionality: The Seminal Essays.* New York: New Press, 2012.

Curran, James, and Jean Seaton. *Power without Responsibility: The Press and Broadcasting in Britain.* New York: Routledge, 1997.

Cywiński, Bohdan. *Rodowody niepokornych.* Warsaw: Wydawnictwo Naukowe PWN, 2010.

Czepulis-Rastenis, Ryszarda. *"Klasa umysłowa": Inteligencja Królestwa Polskiego, 1832–1862.* Warsaw: Książka i Wiedza, 1973.

Czepulis-Rastenis, Ryszarda. *Z dziejów rewolucji 1905–1907 roku na ziemiach polskich: Szkic popularnonaukowy.* Warsaw: Państwowe Wydawnictwo Naukowe, 1955.

Dawidowicz, Aneta, and Ewa Maj, eds. *Prasa Narodowej Demokracji, 1886–1939.* Lublin: Wydawnictwo Uniwersytetu Marii Curie-Skłodowskiej, 2010.

Deranty, Jean-Philippe. *Jacques Rancière: Key Concepts.* Durham, UK: Acumen, 2010.

Dijk, Teun A. van. *Discourse and Power.* New York: Palgrave Macmillan, 2008.

Dijk, Teun A. van. *News as Discourse.* New York: Routledge, 2013.

Domagalska, Małgorzata. *Zatrute ziarno: Proza antysemicka na łamach "Roli" (1883–1912).* Warsaw: Wydawnictwo Neriton, 2015.

Dunn, Elizabeth C. *Privatizing Poland: Baby Food, Big Business, and the Remaking of Labor.* Ithaca, NY: Cornell University Press, 2004.

Egerton, George. "Politics and Autobiography: Political Memoir as Polygenre." *Biography* 15, no. 3 (1992): 221–42. doi:10.1353/bio.2010.0368.

Eisenberg, Christiane. "Working Class and Middle Class Associations: An Anglo-German Comparison 1820–1870." In *Bourgeois Society in Nineteenth-Century Europe*, edited by Jürgen Kocka and Allen Mitchell, 153–78. Oxford: Berg, 1993.

Eley, Geoff. "Cultural Socialism, the Public Sphere, and the Mass Form." In *Between Reform and Revolution: German Socialism and Communism from 1840 to 1990*, edited by David Barclay and Eric Weitz, 315–40. New York: Berghahn Books, 2009.

Eley, Geoff. *Forging Democracy: The History of the Left in Europe, 1850–2000.* New York: Oxford University Press, 2002.

Eley, Geoff. "Nations, Publics, and Political Cultures: Placing Habermas in the Nineteenth Century." In *Habermas and the Public Sphere*, edited by Craig J. Calhoun, 289–339. Cambridge, MA: MIT Press, 1992.

Elsaesser, Thomas. *Fassbinder's Germany: History, Identity, Subject.* Amsterdam: Amsterdam University Press, 1996.

Engelstein, Laura. *Moscow, 1905: Working-Class Organization and Political Conflict*. Stanford, CA: Stanford University Press, 1982.

Eyerman, Ron. "How Social Movements Move. Emotions and Social Movements." In *Emotions and Social Movements*, edited by Helena Flam and Debra King, 42–56. New York: Routledge, 2005.

Fetscher, Iring, ed. *Marxisten Gegen Antisemitismus*. Hamburg: Hoffman und Campe, 1974.

Figes, Orlando. *A People's Tragedy: The Russian Revolution, 1891–1924*. London: Jonathan Cape, 1996.

Fijałek, Jan, Kazimierz Badziak, Ryszard Rosin, and Bohdan Baranowski, eds. *Łódź: Dzieje miasta do 1918 r.* Warsaw: PWN, 1988.

Fischer von Weikersthal, Felicitas, ed. *The Russian Revolution of 1905 in Transcultural Perspective: Identities, Peripheries, and the Flow of Ideas*. Bloomington, IN: Slavica Publishers, 2013.

Flam, Helena, and Debra King. *Emotions and Social Movements*. New York: Routledge, 2005.

Fligstein, Neil, and Doug McAdam. *A Theory of Fields*. Oxford: Oxford University Press, 2015.

Flyvbjerg, Bent. *Making Social Science Matter: Why Social Inquiry Fails and How It Can Succeed Again*. New York: Cambridge University Press, 2001.

Foucault, Michel. *Power/Knowledge: Selected Interviews and Other Writings, 1972–1977*. Edited by Colin Gordon. New York: Pantheon Books, 1980.

Foucault, Michel. *Security, Territory, Population: Lectures at the Collège de France, 1977–1978*. Edited by Michel Senellart. Translated by François Ewald and Alessandro Fontana. New York: Picador, 2009.

Fountain, Alvin Marcus. *Roman Dmowski: Party, Tactics, Ideology, 1895–1907*. Boulder, CO: East European Monographs, 1980.

Frank, Stephen, and Mark D. Steinberg. *Cultures in Flux: Lower-Class Values, Practices, and Resistance in Late Imperial Russia*. Princeton, NJ: Princeton University Press, 2001.

Fraser, Nancy. "Rethinking the Public Sphere: A Contribution to the Critique of Actually Existing Democracy." *Social Text*, no. 25/26 (1990): 56. doi:10.2307/466240.

Freeden, Michael. *The Political Theory of Political Thinking: The Anatomy of a Practice*. Oxford: Oxford University Press, 2013.

Freifeld, Alice. *Nationalism and the Crowd in Liberal Hungary, 1848–1914*. Baltimore: Johns Hopkins University Press, 2000.

Friedrich, Agnieszka. "Polish Literature's Portrayal of Jewish Involvement in 1905." In *The Revolution of 1905 and Russia's Jews*, edited by Stefani Hoffman and Ezra Mendelsohn, 143–51. Philadelphia: University of Pennsylvania Press, 2008.

Frykman, Jonas, and Orvar Löfgren. *Culture Builders: A Historical Anthropology of Middle-Class Life*. Translated by Alan Crozier. New Brunswick: Rutgers University Press, 1987.

Gagnier, Regenia. "Social Atoms: Working-Class Autobiography, Subjectivity, and Gender." *Victorian Studies* 30, no. 3 (1987): 335–63.

Garfinkel, Harold. *Studies in Ethnomethodology*. Cambridge: Polity, 1984.

Garstka, Christoph. "The Revolution of 1905 in Polish Literature: Henryk Sienkiewicz's Wiry (Whirls) and Andrzej Strug's Dzieje Jednego Pocisku (The Story of One Bomb)." In *The Russian Revolution of 1905 in Transcultural Perspective: Identities, Peripheries, and the

Flow of Ideas, edited by Felicitas Fischer von Weikersthal, 245–55. Bloomington, IN: Slavica Publishers, 2013.

Gatrell, Peter. *The Tsarist Economy 1850–1917*. London: Batsford, 1986.

Gawin, Dariusz. *Wielki zwrot: Ewolucja lewicy i odrodzenie idei społeczeństwa obywatelskiego 1956–1976*. Cracow: Znak, 2013.

Geary, Dick. "Labour History, the 'Linguistic Turn' and Postmodernism." *Contemporary European History* 9, no. 3 (2000): 445–62.

Gellner, Ernest. *Nations and Nationalism*. Ithaca, NY: Cornell University Press, 2008.

Gerhardt, Uta. "'Ideal Type' and the Construction of the Life Course: A New Look at the Micro-Macro Link." In *Society and Biography: Interrelationships between Social Structure, Institutions and the Life Course*, edited by Ansgar Weymann, Walter R. Heinz, and Peter Alheit, 21–50. Weinheim: Studien, 1996.

Geulen, Christian. "Plädoyer für eine Geschichte der Grundbegriffe des 20. Jahrhunderts." *Zeithistorische Forschungen/Studies in Contemporary History*, no. 7 (2010): 79–97.

Glynos, Jason, and David Howarth. *Logics of Critical Explanation in Social and Political Theory*. New York: Routledge, 2007.

Goffman, Erving. "The Moral Career of the Mental Patient." *Psychiatry* 22, no. 2 (1959): 123–42. doi:10.1521/00332747.1959.11023166.

Golsztyńska, Alina. "Początki ruchu robotniczego i myśli socjalistycznej w publicystyce warszawskiej w latach 1876–1886." *Studia z dziejow myśli spolecznej i kwestii robotniczej w XIX wieku* 1 (1964): 159–88.

Gorsky, Martin. *Patterns of Philanthropy: Charity and Society in Nineteenth-Century Bristol*. Rochester, NY: Boydell and Brewer, 1999.

Gostkowski, Zygmunt. *Dziennik Łódzki w latach 1884–1892: Studium nad powstawaniem polskiej opinii publicznej w wielonarodowym mieście fabrycznym*. Lodz: Wydawnictwo Wyższej Szkoły Finansów i Informatyki, 2008.

Grott, Bogumił. *Zygmunt Balicki: Ideolog Narodowej Demokracji*. Cracow: Arcana, 1995.

Habermas, Jürgen. "The Public Sphere: An Encyclopedia Article." In *The Idea of the Public Sphere: A Reader*, edited by Jostein Gripsrud and Martin Eide, 114–20. Lanham, MD: Lexington Books, 2010.

Habermas, Jürgen. *The Structural Transformation of the Public Sphere: An Inquiry into a Category of Bourgeois Society*. Translated by Thomas Burger and Frederick G. Lawrence. Cambridge, MA: MIT Press, 1989.

Haimson, Leopold. "The Problem of Social Stability in Urban Russia, 1905–1917 (Part One)." *Slavic Review* 23, no. 4 (1964): 619–42. doi:10.2307/2492201.

Haimson, Leopold. "The Problem of Social Stability in Urban Russia, 1905–1917 (Part Two)." *Slavic Review* 24, no. 1 (1965): 1–22. doi:10.2307/2492986.

Haimson, Leopold. *Russia's Revolutionary Experience: 1905–1917: Two Essays*. New York: Columbia University Press, 2005.

Halfin, Igal. *From Darkness to Light: Class, Consciousness, and Salvation in Revolutionary Russia*. Pittsburgh: University of Pittsburgh Press, 2000.

Halfin, Igal. "The Rape of the Intelligentsia: A Proletarian Foundational Myth." *Russian Review* 56, no. 1 (1997): 90–109.

Halfin, Igal. *Red Autobiographies: Initiating the Bolshevik Self.* Seattle: University of Washington Press, 2011.

Halliday, Michael A. K. *Language as a Social Semiotic: The Social Interpretation of Language and Meaning.* Baltimore: University Park Press, 1977.

Harcave, Sydney. *First Blood: The Russian Revolution of 1905.* New York: Macmillan, 1964.

Hauser, Gerard A. "Vernacular Dialogue and the Rhetoricality of Public Opinion." *Communication Monographs* 65, no. 2 (1998): 83–107. doi:10.1080/03637759809376439.

Hennock, E. P. *The Origin of the Welfare State in England and Germany, 1850–1914: Social Policies Compared.* New York: Cambridge University Press, 2007.

Hensel, Jürgen, ed. *Polen, Deutsche und Juden in Lodz 1820–1939: Eine Schwierige Nachbarschaft.* Osnabrück: Fibre, 1999.

Hernandez, Richard. "The Confessions of Semen Kanatchikov: A Bolshevik Memoir as Spiritual Autobiography." *Russian Review* 60, no. 1 (2001): 13–35.

Hill, Mike, and Warren Montag, eds. *Masses, Classes, and the Public Sphere.* New York: Verso, 2000.

Hillyar, Anna, and Jane McDermid. *Revolutionary Women in Russia, 1870–1917: A Study in Collective Biography.* New York: Manchester University Press, 2000.

Hobsbawm, Eric J. *The Age of Extremes: The Short Twentieth Century, 1914–1991.* London: Abacus, 2011.

Hoffman, Stefani, and Ezra Mendelsohn, eds. *The Revolution of 1905 and Russia's Jews.* Philadelphia: University of Pennsylvania Press, 2008.

Hoffmann, Stefan-Ludwig. *Civil Society, 1750–1914.* New York: Palgrave Macmillan, 2006.

Hoffmann, Stefan-Ludwig, Kathrin Kollmeier, Willibald Steinmetz, Philipp Sarasin, Alf Lüdtke, and Christian Geulen. "Geschichtliche Grundbegriffe Reloaded? Writing the Conceptual History of the Twentieth Century." *Contributions to the History of Concepts* 7, no. 2 (2012): 78–128. doi:10.3167/choc.2012.070204.

Hofmann, Andreas R. "The Biedermanns in the 1905 Revolution: A Case Study in Entrepreneurs' Responses to Social Turmoil in Łódź." *Slavonic and East European Review* 82, no. 1 (2004): 27–49.

Hohler, Susanne. "Radical Right Civil Society." In *The Russian Revolution of 1905 in Transcultural Perspective: Identities, Peripheries, and the Flow of Ideas,* edited by Felicitas Fischer von Weikersthal, 93–104. Bloomington, IN: Slavica Publishers, 2013.

Hroch, Miroslav. *Social Preconditions of National Revival in Europe: A Comparative Analysis of the Social Composition of Patriotic Groups among the Smaller European Nations.* New York: Cambridge University Press, 1985.

Huechtker, Dietlind. "'The Politics and Poetics of Transgression': Die Revolution von 1905 im Koenigreich Polen." In *Revolution in Nordosteuropa,* edited by Detlef Henning, 81–104. Wiesbaden: Harrassowitz, 2011.

Hunt, Lynn. *Politics, Culture, and Class in the French Revolution.* Berkeley: University of California Press, 1984.

Iwańska, Marzena. "Garść refleksji i postulatów badawczych w związku ze stanem badań nad inteligencją łódzką w dobie zaborów." *Rocznik Łódzki* 53 (2006): 89–113.

Jacobs, Jack Lester. "Kautsky on the Jewish Question." PhD diss., Columbia University, 1983.

Jakubowska, Urszula. *Prasa Narodowej Demokracji w dobie zaborów*. Warsaw: Państwowe Wydawnictwo Naukowe, 1988.

Janczak, Julian. *Ludność Łodzi przemysłowej 1820–1914*. Vol. 11. Lodz: Wydawnictwo Uniwersytetu Łódzkiego, 1982.

Janczak, Julian. "The National Structure of the Population in Łódź in the Years 1820–1938." *Polin*, no. 6 (1991): 20–26.

Janion, Maria, ed. *Literatura polska wobec rewolucji*. Warsaw: Państwowy Instytut Wydawniczy, 1971.

Janowski, Maciej. "Gab es im 19. Jahrhundert in Polen eine Zivilgesellschaft? Erste Überlegungen." In *Die Praxis der Zivilgesellschaft: Akteure, Handeln und Strukturen im internationalen Vergleich*, edited by Arndt Bauerkämper, 293–318. Frankfurt [u.a.]: Campus-Verlag, 2003.

Janowski, Maciej. *Polish Liberal Thought before 1918*. New York: Central European University Press, 2004.

Jaśkiewicz, Leszek. *Absolutyzm rosyjski w dobie rewolucji 1905–1907: Reformy ustrojowe*. Warsaw: Państwowe Wydawnictwo Naukowe, 1982.

Jaśkiewicz, Leszek. *Carat i sprawy polskie na przełomie XIX i XX wieku*. Pułtusk: Wyższa Szkoła Humanistyczna w Pułtusku, 2001.

Jaszczuk, Andrzej. *Liberalna Atlantyda: Główne Nurty Liberalizmu Polskiego 1870–1939 r.* Warsaw: Nakładem autora, 1999.

Jaszczuk, Andrzej. *Spór pozytywistów z konserwatystami o przyszłość Polski 1870–1903*. Warsaw: Państwowe Wydawnictwo Naukowe, 1986.

Jaworska, Janina. "Prasa." In *Łódź: Dzieje miasta do 1918 r.*, edited by Jan Fijałek, Kazimierz Badziak, Ryszard Rosin, and Bohdan Baranowski. Warsaw: PWN, 1988.

Jedlicki, Jerzy. *Błędne Koło 1832–1864*. Warsaw: Wydawnictwo Neriton, 2008.

Jedlicki, Jerzy. *A Suburb of Europe: Nineteenth-Century Polish Approaches to Western Civilization*. New York: Central European University Press, 1999.

Jedlicki, Jerzy. *Świat zwyrodniały: Lęki i wyroki krytyków nowoczesności*. Warsaw: Wydawnictwo Sic!, 2000.

Jodłowski, Stanisław. *Losy polskiej ortografii*. Warsaw: Państwowe Wydawnictwo Naukowe, 1979.

Johnson, Richard. "Really Useful Knowledge: Radical Education and Working Class Culture." In *Working-Class Culture: Studies in History and Theory*. New York: Routledge, 2006.

Jones, Stephen F. *Socialism in Georgian Colors: The European Road to Social Democracy, 1883–1917*. Cambridge, MA: Harvard University Press, 2005.

Jonsson, Stefan. *A Brief History of the Masses (Three Revolutions)*. New York: Columbia University Press, 2008.

Jonsson, Stefan. *Crowds and Democracy: The Idea and Image of the Masses from Revolution to Fascism*. New York: Columbia University Press, 2013.

Jordheim, Helge. "Against Periodization: Koselleck's Theory of Multiple Temporalities." *History and Theory*, no. 51 (2012): 151–71.

Jordheim, Helge. "Does Conceptual History Really Need a Theory of Historical Times?" *Contributions to the History of Concepts* 6, no. 2 (2011): 21–41.

Joyce, Patrick. *Democratic Subjects: The Self and the Social in Nineteenth-Century England.* New York: Cambridge University Press, 1994.

Joyce, Patrick. *Visions of the People: Industrial England and the Question of Class, 1848–1914.* New York: Cambridge University Press, 1991.

Kaczyńska, Elżbieta. *Dzieje robotników przemysłowych w Polsce pod zaborami.* Warsaw: Państwowe Wydawnictwo Naukowe, 1970.

Kaczyńska, Elżbieta. "Partie polityczne a masowy ruch robotniczy." *Przegląd Historyczny*, no. 1–2 (1990): 125–38.

Kaczyńska, Elżbieta. "Tłum i margines społeczny w wydarzeniach rewolucyjnych (Królestwo Polskie 1904–1907)." *Dzieje Najnowsze* 15, no. 1–2 (1983): 221–30.

Kaczyńska, Elżbieta, and Zbigniew W. Rykowski. *Przemoc zbiorowa: Ruch masowy. Rewolucja.* Warsaw: Wydawnictwo Uniwersytetu Warszawskiego, 1990.

Kalabiński, Stanisław. *Antynarodowa polityka endecji w rewolucji 1905–1907.* Warsaw: Państwowe Wydawnictwo Naukowe, 1955.

Kalabiński, Stanisław, ed. *Polska klasa robotnicza: Studia historyczne.* Vol. 5. Warsaw: Państwowe Wydawnictwo Naukowe, 1973.

Kalabiński, Stanisław, and Feliks Tych. *Czwarte powstanie czy pierwsza rewolucja: Lata 1905–1907 na ziemiach polskich.* Warsaw: Wiedza Powszechna, 1976.

Kałuża, Adam. *Przeciw carowi! Rok 1905 w Zagłębiu Dąbrowskim.* Sosnowiec: Muzeum w Sosnowcu, 2005.

Kancewicz, Jan. *Polska Partia Socjalistyczna w latach 1892–1896.* Warsaw: Państwowe Wydawnictwo Naukowe, 1984.

Kanfer, Yedida S. "Łódź: Industry, Religion, and Nationalism in Russian Poland, 1880–1914." PhD diss., Yale University, 2011.

Karwacki, Władysław L. *Łódź w latach rewolucji 1905–1907.* Lodz: Wydawnictwo Łódzkie, 1975.

Karwacki, Władysław L. "Walka o wprowadzenie tzw. 'konstytucjonalizmu fabrycznego' w latach rewolucji 1905–1907 w Łodzi." *Rocznik Łódzki*, no. 15 (18) (1971): 153–64.

Karwacki, Władysław L. *Związki zawodowe i stowarzyszenia pracodawców w Łodzi (do roku 1914).* Lodz: Wydawnictwo Łódzkie, 1972.

Katznelson, Ira, and Aristide R. Zolberg, eds. *Working-Class Formation: Nineteenth-Century Patterns in Western Europe and the United States.* Princeton, NJ: Princeton University Press, 1986.

Kautsky, Karl. *Zasady socjalizmu (program Erfurcki).* Warsaw: Wydawnictwo "Życie," 1911.

Kautsky, Karol. *Nauki ekonomiczne Karola Marksa.* Warsaw: Książka i wiedza, 1950.

Kaźmierska, Kaja. *Biography and Memory: The Generational Experience of the Shoah Survivors.* Boston: Academic Studies Press, 2012.

Kennedy, Michael D. *Professionals, Power, and Solidarity in Poland: A Critical Sociology of Soviet-Type Society.* New York: Cambridge University Press, 1991.

Kenney, Padraic. *Rebuilding Poland: Workers and Communists, 1945–1950.* Ithaca, NY: Cornell University Press, 2012.

Kidzińska, Agnieszka. *Stronnictwo polityki realnej, 1905–1923.* Lublin: Wydawnictwo Uniwersytetu Marii Curie-Skłodowskiej, 2007.

Kiepurska, Halina. *Warszawa w rewolucji 1905–1907*. Warsaw: Wiedza Powszechna, 1974.

Kimeldorf, Howard. *Reds or Rackets? The Making of Radical and Conservative Unions on the Waterfront*. Berkeley: University of California Press, 1992.

Kita, Jarosław. "Dwór po powstaniu. Zmierzch dominacji ziemiaństwa." *Powstanie styczniowe 1863: Klęska i chwała, Pomocnik Historyczny. Dodatek do "Polityki"* (2013): 72–75.

Kita, Jarosław, Natalia Królikowska, and Cezary Pawlak. *Bunt, masa, maszyna: Protesty łódzkich tkaczy w kwietniu 1861 roku*. Lodz: Łódzkie Towarzystwo Naukowe, 2011.

Kizwalter, Tomasz. *"Nowatorstwo i rutyny": Społeczeństwo Królestwa Polskiego wobec procesów modernizacji, 1840–1863*. Warsaw: Państwowe Wydawnictwo Naukowe, 1991.

Kizwalter, Tomasz. *O nowoczesności narodu: Przypadek Polski*. Warsaw: Semper, 1999.

Klemensiewicz, Zenon. *Historia języka polskiego*. Vol. 9. Warsaw: Wydawnictwo Naukowe PWN, 2007.

Klier, John D., and Shlomo Lambroza, eds. *Pogroms: Anti-Jewish Violence in Modern Russian History*. Cambridge: Cambridge University Press, 2004.

Klonowski, Stefan. *Pod czapką frygijską*. Warsaw: Książka i Wiedza, 1975.

Kmiecik, Zenon. *Prasa polska w rewolucji 1905–1907*. Warsaw: Państwowe Wydawnictwo Nauk, 1980.

Kochanowicz, Jacek. *Backwardness and Modernization: Poland and Eastern Europe in the 16th–20th Centuries*. Aldershot: Ashgate Variorum, 2006.

Kocka, Jürgen. *Arbeiterleben und Arbeiterkultur: Die Entstehung einer sozialen Klasse*. Bonn: Dietz, 2015.

Kocka, Jürgen. *Arbeitsverhältnisse und Arbeiterexistenzen: Grundlagen der Klassenbildung im 19. Jahrhundert*. Bonn: Dietz, 1990.

Kocka, Jürgen. "Asymmetrical Historical Comparison: The Case of the German Sonderweg." *History and Theory* 38, no. 1 (1999): 40–50. doi:10.1111/0018-2656.751999075.

Kocka, Jürgen. *Lohnarbeit und Klassenbildung: Arbeiter und Arbeiterbewegung in Deutschland 1800–1875*. Berlin: Dietz, 1983.

Kocka, Jürgen. "Die Trennung von bürgerlicher und proletarischer Demokratie im europäischen Vergleich: Fragestellungen und Ergebnisse." In *Europäische Arbeiterbewegungen im 19. Jahrhundert: Deutschland, Österreich, England und Frankreich im Vergleich*, edited by Jürgen Kocka, 5–20. Göttingen: Vandenhoeck & Ruprecht, 1983.

Kocka, Jürgen, and Allen Mitchell, eds. *Bourgeois Society in Nineteenth-Century Europe*. Oxford: Berg, 1993.

Kocka, Jürgen, and Elizabeth Muller-Luckner, eds. *Arbeiter und Bürger im 19. Jahrhundert: Varianten ihres Verhältnisses im europäischen Vergleich*. Munich: Oldenbourg, 1986.

Kohli, Martin. "The World We Forgot: The Historical Review of the Life Course." In *The Life Course Reader: Individuals and Societies across Time*, edited by Walter R. Heinz, Johannes Huinink, and Ansgar Weymann, 64–90. Frankfurt am Main: Campus, 2009.

Kołodziejczyk, Robert. "Pochodzenie i źródła rekrutacji klasy robotniczej." In *Polska klasa robotnicza: Zarys dziejów*, vol. 1, part 1:85–116. Warsaw: Państwowe Wydawnictwo Naukowe, 1974.

Kolonitskii, Boris, and Orlando Figes. *Interpreting the Russian Revolution: The Language and Symbols of 1917*. New Haven: Yale University Press, 1999.

Korzec, Paweł. "Pogrom białostocki i jego polityczne reperkusje." *Rocznik Białostocki* 3 (1962): 149–82.

Koselleck, Reinhart. "Begriffsgeschichte and Social History." In *Futures Past: On the Semantics of Historical Time*, translated by Keith Tribe. New York: Columbia University Press, 2004.

Koselleck, Reinhart. *Critique and Crisis: Enlightenment and the Pathogenesis of Modern Society*. Cambridge, MA: MIT Press, 1988.

Koselleck, Reinhart. "Einleitung." In *Geschichtliche Grundbegriffe*, 1: xiii–xxvii. Stuttgart: Klett-Cotta, 1972.

Koselleck, Reinhart. "The Historical-Political Semantics of Asymmetric Counterconcepts." In *Futures Past: On the Semantics of Historical Time*, translated by Keith Tribe, 155–91. New York: Columbia University Press, 2004.

Koselleck, Reinhart. *Preußen zwischen Reform und Revolution: Allgemeines Landrecht, Verwaltung und soziale Bewegung von 1791 bis 1848*. Munich: Taschenbuch, 1989.

Krajewska, Jadwiga. *Czytelnictwo wśród robotników w Królestwie Polskim, 1870–1914*. Warsaw: Państwowe Wydawnictwo Naukowe, 1979.

Kripke, Saul A. *Naming and Necessity*. Cambridge, MA: Harvard University Press, 1980.

Kryński, Adam, and Władysław Niedźwiedzki. *Słownik języka polskiego*. Warsaw: nakładem prenumeratorów i Kasy im. Mianowskiego, 1901.

Krzywiec, Grzegorz. *Chauvinism, Polish Style: The Case of Roman Dmowski (Beginnings: 1886–1905)*. Frankfurt am Main: Peter Lang, 2016.

Krzywiec, Grzegorz. "Eliminationist Anti-Semitism at Home and Abroad: Polish Nationalism, the Jewish Question, and Eastern European Right-Wing Mass Politics." In *The New Nationalism and the First World War*, edited by Lawrence Rosenthal and Vesna Rodic, 65–91. New York: Palgrave Macmillan, 2014.

Krzywiec, Grzegorz. "Nadwiślański Weininger? Przypadki Juliana Unszlichta (1883–1953)." *Holocaust: Studies and Materials (Zagłada Żydów: Studia i materiały)*, no. 5 (2009): 243–57.

Krzywiec, Grzegorz. "The Polish Intelligentsia in the Face of the 'Jewish Question' (1905–1914)." *Acta Poloniae Historica*, no. 100 (2009): 133–69.

Krzywiec, Grzegorz. *Polska bez Żydów: Studia z dziejów idei, wyobrażeń i praktyk antysemickich na ziemiach polskich początku XX wieku (1905–1914)*. Warsaw: Instytut Historii PAN, 2017.

Krzywiec, Grzegorz. *Szowinizm po polsku: Przypadek Romana Dmowskiego (1886–1905)*. Warsaw: Wydawnictwo Neriton, 2009.

Krzywiec, Grzegorz. "Z taką rewolucją musimy walczyć na noże: Rewolucja 1905 roku z perspektywy polskiej prawicy." In *Rewolucja 1905: Przewodnik*, edited by Wiktor Marzec and Kamil Piskała, 326–50. Warsaw: Wydawnictwo Krytyki Politycznej, 2013.

Krzywobłocka, Bożena. "Stosunek burżuazji do klasy robotniczej w latach 1864–1879 w świetle prasy." *Studia z dziejów myśli społecznej i kwestii robotniczej w XIX wieku* 1 (1964): 132–58.

Kucner, Monika. "Prasa niemiecka w Łodzi 1863–1939." In *Niemcy w dziejach Łodzi do 1945 roku*, edited by Krzysztof Kuczyński and Barbara Ratecka, 259–79. Lodz: Wydawnictwo Uniwersytetu Łódzkiego, 2001.

Kujala, Atti. "Finland in 1905: The Political and Social History of the Revolution." In *The Russian Revolution of 1905: Centenary Perspectives*, edited by Jon Smele and Anthony Heywood, 79–93. New York: Routledge, 2005.

Kula, Marcin. *Narodowe i rewolucyjne*. Warsaw: Aneks, 1991.

Kula, Witold. *An Economic Theory of the Feudal System: Towards a Model of the Polish Economy, 1500–1800*. New York: Verso, 1987.

Kula, Witold, and Janina Leskiewiczowa. *Przemiany społeczne w Królestwie Polskim, 1815–1864*. Wrocław: Zakład Narodowy im. Ossolińskich, 1979.

Kulak, Teresa. *Jan Ludwik Popławski: Biografia polityczna*. Wrocław: Zakład Narodowy im. Ossolińskich, 1994.

Kurczewska, Joanna. "Inteligencja." *Encyklopedia socjologii*. Warsaw: Oficyna Naukowa, 1998.

Kurkiewicz, Michał, and Monika Plutecka. "Rosyjskie pogromy w Białymstoku i Siedlcach w 1906 roku." *Biuletyn Instytutu Pamięci Narodowej*, no. 11 (120) (2010): 20–24.

Kurzman, Charles. *Democracy Denied, 1905–1915: Intellectuals and the Fate of Democracy*. Cambridge, MA: Harvard University Press, 2008.

Laba, Roman A. *The Roots of Solidarity: A Political Sociology of Poland's Working Class Democratization*. Princeton, NJ: Princeton University Press, 1991.

Laclau, Ernesto. *New Reflections on the Revolution of Our Time*. New York: Verso, 1990.

Łęczycki, Franciszek. *Mojej ankiety personalnej punkt 35*. Warsaw: Czytelnik, 1969.

Lees, Andrew. *Cities, Sin, and Social Reform in Imperial Germany*. Ann Arbor: University of Michigan Press, 2002.

Lefebvre, Henri. "The Right to the City." In *Writings on Cities*, edited and translated by Eleonore Kofman and Elizabeth Lebas, 147–59. Cambridge, MA: Blackwell, 1996.

Lefort, Claude. *Democracy and Political Theory*. Cambridge: Polity, 1988.

Lewis, Richard D. "Labor-Management Conflict in Russian Poland: The Lodz Lockout of 1906–1907." *East European Quarterly* 7, no. 4 (1974): 413–34.

Lewis, Richard D. "Revolution in the Countryside: Russian Poland, 1905–1906." *Carl Beck Papers in Russian and East European Studies*, no. 506 (1986). doi:10.5195/CBP.1986.26.

Lidtke, Vernon L. *The Alternative Culture: Socialist Labor in Imperial Germany*. New York: Oxford University Press, 1985.

Lih, Lars T. "1905 and All That: The Revolution and Its Aftermath." *Kritika: Explorations in Russian and Eurasian History* 8, no. 4 (2007): 861–76. doi:10.1353/kri.2007.0055.

Linden, Marcel van der. "The National Integration of the European Working Class." In *Workers of the World: Essays toward a Global Labor History*. Boston: Brill, 2008.

Linden, Marcel van der, and Jürgen Rojahn, eds. *The Formation of Labour Movements, 1870–1914: An International Perspective*. New York: Brill, 1990.

Lipiński, Wacław. *Walka zbrojna o niepodległość Polski w latach 1905–1918*. Warsaw, 1931.

Losurdo, Domenico. *Liberalism: A Counter-History*. Translated by Gregory Elliott. New York: Verso, 2014.

Lottes, Günther. *Politische Aufklärung und plebejisches Publikum: Zur Theorie und Praxis des englishen Radikalismus im späten 18. Jahrhundert*. Munich: Oldenbourg, 1979.

Lüdtke, Alf. *Eigen-Sinn: Fabrikalltag, Arbeitererfahrungen und Politik vom Kaiserreich bis in den Faschismus*. Hamburg: Ergebnisse, 1993.

Lyons, Martyn, ed. *Ordinary Writings, Personal Narratives: Writing Practices in 19th and Early 20th-Century Europe*. New York: P. Lang, 2007.

Lyons, Martyn. "The Reading Experience of Worker-Autobiographers in 19th-Century Europe." In *Reading Culture and Writing Practices in Nineteenth-Century France*. Toronto: University of Toronto Press, 2008.

Maciejewska, Irena. *Rewolucja i niepodległość: Z dziejów literatury polskiej lat 1905–1920*. Kielce: Wydawnictwo Szumacher, 1991.

Małagowski, Andrzej. *Łódź–Księży Młyn: Historia ludzi, miejsca i kultury*. Lodz: Księży Młyn, 1998.

Małowist, Marian. *Western Europe, Eastern Europe and World Development, 13th–18th Centuries: Collection of Essays of Marian Małowist*. Edited by Jean Batou and Henryk Szlajfer. Boston: Brill, 2010.

Manning, Paul. *Strangers in a Strange Land: Occidentalist Publics and Orientalist Geographies in Nineteenth-Century Georgian Imaginaries*. Boston: Academic Studies Press, 2012.

Marchart, Oliver. *Post-Foundational Political Thought: Political Difference in Nancy, Lefort, Badiou and Laclau*. Edinburgh: Edinburgh University Press, 2007.

Marx, Karl, and Friedrich Engels. *Collected Works*. New York: International Publishers, 1975.

Marzec, Wiktor. "The 1905–1907 Revolution in the Kingdom of Poland—Articulation of Political Subjectivities among Workers." *Contention* 1, no. 1 (2013): 53–74.

Marzec, Wiktor. "Beyond Group Antagonism in Asymmetrical Counter-Concepts: Conceptual Pair Order and Chaos and Ideological Struggles in Late 19th–Early 20th Century Poland." In *"Hellenes" and "Barbarians": Asymmetrical Concepts in European Discourse*, edited by Kirill Postoutenko. New York: Berghahn Books, in press.

Marzec, Wiktor. "Modernizacja mas: Moment polityczny i dyskurs endecji w okresie rewolucji 1905–1907." *Praktyka Teoretyczna*, no. 3 (2014): 99–132. doi: 10.14746/pt.2014.3.5.

Marzec, Wiktor. "Reading Polish Peripheral Marxism Politically." *Thesis Eleven* 117, no. 1 (2013): 6–19. doi:10.1177/0725513613493992.

Marzec, Wiktor. *Rebelia i reakcja: Rewolucja 1905 roku i plebejskie doświadczenie polityczne*. Cracow: Universitas, 2016.

Marzec, Wiktor. "Róża Luksemburg i konstruowanie podmiotu politycznego." *Praktyka Teoretyczna*, no. 6 (2012): 155–81.

Marzec, Wiktor. "Under One Common Banner: Antisemitism and Socialist Strategy during the 1905–7 Revolution in the Kingdom of Poland." *Patterns of Prejudice* 51, no. 3–4 (2017): 269–91. doi: 10.1080/0031322X.2017.1353723.

Marzec, Wiktor. "Vernacular Marxism. Proletarian Readings in Russian Poland around the 1905 Revolution." *Historical Materialism* 25, no. 4 (2017): 65–104. doi: 10.1163/1569206X-12341543.

Marzec, Wiktor. "What Bears Witness of the Failed Revolution? The Rise of Political Antisemitism during the 1905–1907 Revolution in the Kingdom of Poland." *Eastern European Politics and Societies* 30, no. 1 (2016): 189–213. doi:10.1177/0888325415581896.

Marzec, Wiktor, and Kamil Piskała. "Proletariaccy czytelnicy—marksistowskie i socjalistyczne lektury we wczesnej proletariackiej sferze publicznej Królestwa Polskiego." *Sensus Historiae* 12, no. 3 (2013): 83–103.

Marzec, Wiktor, and Kamil Piskała, eds. *Rewolucja 1905: Przewodnik*. Warsaw: Wydawnictwo "Krytyki Politycznej," 2013.

Marzec, Wiktor, and Kamil Śmiechowski. "Pathogenesis of the Polish Public Sphere: Intelligentsia and Popular Unrest in the 1905 Revolution and After." *Polish Sociological Review*, no. 4 (2016): 437–57.

Marzec, Wiktor, and Agata Zysiak. "Days of Labour: Topographies of Power in Modern Peripheral Capitalism. The Case of the Industrial City of Łódź." *Journal of Historical Sociology* 29, no. 2 (2016): 129–59. doi:10.1111/johs.12080.

Marzec, Wiktor, and Agata Zysiak. "'Journalists Discovered Łódź like Columbus': Orientalizing Capitalism in the Late Nineteenth and Early Twentieth Century Polish Modernization Debates." *Canadian-American Slavic Studies* 50 (2016): 235–65. doi:10.1163/22102396-05002007.

Maynes, Mary Jo. *Taking the Hard Road: Life Course in French and German Workers' Autobiographies in the Era of Industrialization*. Chapel Hill: University of North Carolina Press, 1995.

McDaniel, Tim. *Autocracy, Capitalism, and Revolution in Russia*. Berkeley: University of California Press, 1988.

Melancon, Michael S., and Alice K. Pate, eds. *New Labor History: Worker Identity and Experience in Russia, 1840–1918*. Bloomington, IN: Slavica Publishers, 2002.

Mencwel, Andrzej. *Etos lewicy: Esej o narodzinach kulturalizmu polskiego*. 2nd ed. Warsaw: Wydawnictwo "Krytyki Politycznej," 2009.

Methods of Critical Discourse Analysis. Thousand Oaks, CA: SAGE, 2001.

Miąso, Józef. *Szkolnictwo zawodowe w Królestwie Polskim w latach 1815–1915*. Wroclaw: Zaklad Narodowy im. Ossolinskich, 1966.

Miąso, Józef. *Uniwersytet dla Wszystkich*. Warsaw: Państwowe Zakłady Wydawnictw Szkolnych, 1960.

Micińska, Magdalena, ed. *Dzieje inteligencji polskiej do roku 1918*. Warsaw: Wydawnictwo Neriton, 2008.

Micińska, Magdalena. *Między królem duchem a mieszczaninem: Obraz bohatera narodowego w piśmiennictwie polskim przełomu XIX i XX w., 1890–1914*. Wrocław: Wydawnictwo Leopoldinum Fundacji dla Uniwersytetu Wrocławskiego, 1995.

Micińska, Magdalena. "'Wieść z dna polskiego piekła': Problem oskarżeń o zdradę narodową w okresie rewolucji 1905–1907 roku." In *Rewolucja 1905–1907 w Królestwie Polskim i w Rosji*, edited by Marek Przeniosło, Stanisław Wiech, and Barbara Szabat, 59–82. Kielce: Wydawnictwo Akademii Świętokrzyskiej, 2005.

Miliband, Ralph. "Class Struggle from Above." In *Social Theory and Social Criticism: Essays for Tom Bottomore*, edited by Michael Mulkay and William Outhwaite. Oxford: Basil Blackwell, 1987.

Miłosz, Czesław. *The History of Polish Literature*. Berkeley: University of California Press, 1983.

Mishinsky, Moshe. "A Turning Point in the History of Polish Socialism and Its Attitude towards the Jewish Question." *Polin*, no. 1 (1986): 111–29.

Missalowa, Gryzelda. "Kształtowanie się klasy robotniczej przemysłu włókienniczego Łodzi w latach 1815–1870." In *Włókniarze łódzcy: Monografia*, edited by Józef Spychalski and Edward Rosset. Lodz: Wydawnictwo Łódzkie, 1966.

Modzelewski, Wojciech. *Naród i postęp: Problematyka narodowa w ideologii i myśli społecznej pozytywistów warszawskich*. Warsaw: Państwowe Wydawnictwo Naukowe, 1977.

Molenda, Jan. *Chłopi, naród, niepodległość: Kształtowanie się postaw narodowych i obywatelskich chłopów w Galicji i Królestwie Polskim w przededniu odrodzenia Polski*. Warsaw: Wydawnictwo Neriton, 1999.

Monasterska, Teresa. *Narodowy Związek Robotniczy, 1905–1920*. Warsaw: Państwowe Wydawnictwo Naukowe, 1973.

Montag, Warren. "The Pressure of the Street: Habermas's Fear of the Masses." In *Masses, Classes, and the Public Sphere*, edited by Mike Hill and Warren Montag, 132–45. New York: Verso, 2000.

Moore, Barrington. *Injustice: The Social Bases of Obedience and Revolt*. White Plains, NY: M. E. Sharpe, 1978.

Moreno Martínez, Pedro L. "The Hygienist Movement and the Modernization of Education in Spain." *Paedagogica Historica* 42, no. 6 (2006): 793–815. doi:10.1080/00309230600929542.

Mouffe, Chantal. *On the Political*. New York: Routledge, 2005.

Mulholland, Marc. *Bourgeois Liberty and the Politics of Fear: From Absolutism to Neo-Conservatism*. Oxford: Oxford University Press, 2012.

Müller, Jan-Werner. *Contesting Democracy: Political Ideas in Twentieth-Century Europe*. New Haven: Yale University Press, 2011.

Myśliński, Jerzy. *Polska prasa socjalistyczna w okresie zaborów*. Warsaw: Książka i Wiedza, 1982.

Naimark, Norman M. *The History of the "Proletariat": The Emergence of Marxism in the Kingdom of Poland, 1870–1887*. Boulder, CO: East European Quarterly, 1979.

Negt, Oskar, and Alexander Kluge. *Public Sphere and Experience: Toward an Analysis of the Bourgeois and Proletarian Public Sphere*. Translated by Peter Labanyi, Jamie Daniel, and Assenka Oksiloff. Minneapolis: University of Minnesota Press, 1993.

Nicolaysen, Helena. "Looking Backward: A Prosopography of the Russian Social Democratic Elite, 1883–1917." PhD diss., Stanford University, 1991.

Nietyksza, Maria. *Rozwój miast i aglomeracji miejsko-przemysłowych w Królestwie Polskim, 1865–1914*. Warsaw: Państwowe Wydawnictwo Naukowe, 1986.

Olsen, Niklas. *History in the Plural: An Introduction to the Work of Reinhart Koselleck*. New York: Berghahn Books, 2012.

Ost, David. *The Defeat of Solidarity: Anger and Politics in Postcommunist Europe*. Ithaca, NY: Cornell University Press, 2005.

Ost, David. *Solidarity and the Politics of Anti-Politics: Opposition and Reform in Poland since 1968*. Philadelphia: Temple University Press, 1990.

Ozouf, Mona. *Festivals and the French Revolution*. Translated by Alan Sheridan. Cambridge, MA: Harvard University Press, 1991.

Palat, Madhavan K. "Regulating Conflict through the Petition." In *Social Identities in Revolutionary Russia*, edited by Madhavan K. Palat, 86–112. New York: Palgrave, 2001.

Palonen, Kari. *Quentin Skinner: History, Politics, Rhetoric*. Cambridge: Polity, 2003.

Palonen, Kari. *The Struggle with Time: A Conceptual History of "Politics" as an Activity*. Hamburg: Lit, 2006.

Passerini, Luisa. *Fascism in Popular Memory: The Cultural Experience of the Turin Working Class*. New York: Cambridge University Press, 1987.

Passerini, Luisa. "Women's Personal Narratives: Myths, Experiences, and Emotions." In *Interpreting Women's Lives: Feminist Theory and Personal Narratives*, edited by Personal Narratives Group. Bloomington: Indiana University Press, 1989.

Pearl, Deborah Lee. *Creating a Culture of Revolution: Workers and the Revolutionary Movement in Late Imperial Russia*. Bloomington, IN: Slavica Publishers, 2015.

Petrozolin-Skowrońska, Barbara. "'Liberum veto' A. Świętochowskiego wobec rewolucji 1905–1907: Część I." *Rocznik Historii Czasopiśmiennictwa Polskiego* 9, no. 2 (1970): 183–96.

Petrozolin-Skowrońska, Barbara. "'Liberum veto' A. Świętochowskiego wobec rewolucji 1905–1907: Część II." *Rocznik Historii Czasopiśmiennictwa Polskiego* 9, no. 3 (1970): 339–60.

Piasecki, Henryk. *Żydowska Organizacja PPS: 1893–1907*. Warsaw: Wydawnictwo Polskiej Akademii Nauk, 1978.

Pimlott, Herbert. "'Eternal Ephemera' or the Durability of 'Disposable Literature': The Power and Persistence of Print in an Electronic World." *Media, Culture, and Society* 33, no. 4 (2011): 515–30. doi:10.1177/0163443711398690.

Pipes, Richard. *The Russian Revolution*. New York: Vintage, 1991.

Piskała, Kamil. "1905—rok z dziejów polskiego Manchesteru." In *Rewolucja 1905: Przewodnik*, edited by Wiktor Marzec and Kamil Piskała, 211–43. Warsaw: Wydawnictwo "Krytyki Politycznej," 2013.

Plennikowski, Waldemar. *Stanisław Kozicki: W kręgu propagandy idei i polityki Narodowej Demokracji*. Toruń: Grado, 2008.

Pobłocki, Kacper. "The Cunning of Class: Urbanization of Inequality in Post-War Poland." PhD diss., Central European University, 2010. http://etnologia.amu.edu.pl/go.live.php/PL-H648/dr-kacper-poblocki.html.

Pocock, J. G. A. *Political Thought and History: Essays on Theory and Method*. New York: Cambridge University Press, 2009.

Podgórska, Eugenia. *Szkolnictwo elementarne w Łódzi w latach 1808–1914*. Lodz: Łódzkie Towarzystwo Naukowe, 1966.

Polletta, Francesca. *It Was Like a Fever: Storytelling in Protest and Politics*. Chicago: University of Chicago Press, 2006.

Polvinen, Tuomo. *Imperial Borderland: Bobrikov and the Attempted Russification of Finland, 1898–1904*. Durham, NC: Duke University Press, 1995.

Portelli, Alessandro. *The Death of Luigi Trastulli, and Other Stories: Form and Meaning in Oral History*. Albany: State University of New York Press, 1991.

Porter, Thomas Earl. "The Emergence of Civil Society in Late Imperial Russia. The Impact of the Russo-Japanese and First World Wars on Russia." *War and Society*, no. 23 (2005): 41–60.

Porter[-Szűcs], Brian. "Democracy and Discipline in Late Nineteenth Century Poland." *Journal of Modern History* 71, no. 2 (1999): 346–93.

Porter-Szűcs, Brian. "Exclusionary Egalitarianism and the New Cold War." *Slavic Review* 76, no. S1 (2017): S81–97. https://doi.org/0.1017/slr.2017.160.

Porter-Szűcs, Brian. *Faith and Fatherland: Catholicism, Modernity, and Poland*. Oxford; New York: Oxford University Press, 2011.

Porter-Szűcs, Brian. *Poland in the Modern World: Beyond Martyrdom*. Chichester: Wiley-Blackwell, 2014.

Porter[-Szűcs], Brian. "The Social Nation and Its Futures: English Liberalism and Polish Nationalism in Late Nineteenth-Century Warsaw." *American Historical Review* 101, no. 5 (1996): 1470–92.

Porter[-Szűcs], Brian. *When Nationalism Began to Hate: Imagining Modern Politics in Nineteenth-Century Poland*. New York: Oxford University Press, 2000.

Porter[-Szűcs], Brian. "Who Is a Pole and Where Is Poland? Territory and Nation in the Rhetoric of Polish National Democracy before 1905." *Slavic Review* 51, no. 4 (1992): 639–53.

Possart, Jadwiga. *Struktury myślenia teoretycznego a kontrowersje ideologiczne: Polemiki w publicystyce PPS w okresie rozłamu 1906–1908*. Warsaw: Książka i Wiedza, 1963.

Potkański, Waldemar. "Eskalacja przemocy rewolucyjnej na przykładzie Łodzi w 1905 roku." *Przegląd Humanistyczny Pedagogika. Politologia. Filologia*, no. 5 (2011): 294–308.

Potkański, Waldemar. *Terroryzm na usługach ugrupowań lewicowych i anarchistycznych w Królestwie Polskim do 1914 roku*. Warsaw: Wydawnictwo DiG, 2014.

Potkański, Waldemar. "Wokół koncepcji ideologicznej oraz praktycznej terroru w ujęciu liderów i szeregowych członków PPS na przełomie XIX i XX w." In *Wybrane zagadnienia bezpieczeństwa dla edukacji*, edited by S. Bukowski and M. Cupryjak, 25–47. Szczecin: Szczecińska Szkoła Wyższa Collegium Balticum, 2009.

Prazmowska, Anita. *A History of Poland*. Houndmills: Palgrave Macmillan, 2004.

Próchnik, Adam. *Bunt łódzki w roku 1892: Studium historyczne*. Warsaw: Książka i Wiedza, 1950.

Próchnik, Adam. *Pierwsze piętnastolecie Polski niepodległej (1918–1933): Zarys dziejów politycznych*. Warsaw: Wydawnictwo Robotnik, 1933.

Próchnik, Adam. *Studia z dziejów polskiego ruchu robotniczego: Pisma*. Warsaw: Książka i Wiedza, 1958.

Przeniosło, Marek, and Stanisław Wiech, eds. *Rewolucja 1905–1907 w Królestwie Polskim i w Rosji*. Kielce: Wydawnictwo Akademii Świętokrzyskiej, 2005.

Puś, Wiesław, and Stefan Pytlas. *Dzieje Łódzkich Zakładów Przemysłu Bawełnianego im. Obrońców Pokoju "Uniontex" (d. Zjednoczonych Zakładów K. Scheiblera i L. Grohmana) w latach 1827–1977*. Warsaw: Państwowe Wydawnictwo Naukowe, 1979.

Pustuła, Zbigniew. "Dynamika liczebności proletariatu przemysłowego." In *Polska klasa robotnicza: Zarys dziejów*, vol. 1, part 2, 106–21. Warsaw: Państwowe Wydawnictwo Naukowe, 1978.

Puszkow-Bańka, Agnieszka. *Polska i Polacy w myśli narodowej demokracji na przełomie XIX i XX wieku (Jan Ludwik Popławski, Zygmunt Balicki, Roman Dmowski)*. Cracow: Wydawnictwo WAM, 2013.

Pytka, Meghann. "Policing the Binary—Patrolling the Nation: Race and Gender in Polish Integral Nationalism, from Partitions to Parliament (1883–1926)." PhD diss., Northwestern University, 2013.

Pytlas, Stefan. *Łódzka burżuazja przemysłowa w latach 1864–1914*. Lodz: Wydawnictwo Uniwersytetu Łódzkiego, 1994.

Pytlas, Stefan. "The National Composition of Łódź Industrialists before 1914." *Polin*, no. 6 (1991): 37–56.

Rabinbach, Anson. "Social Knowledge, Social Risk, and the Politics of Industrial Accidents in Germany and France." In *States, Social Knowledge, and the Origins of Modern Social Policies*, edited by Dietrich Rueschemeyer and Theda Skocpol, 48–89. Princeton, NJ: Princeton University Press, 1996.

Radlak, Bronisław. *Socjaldemokracja Królestwa Polskiego i Litwy w latach 1893–1904*. Warsaw: Państwowe Wydawnictwo Naukowe, 1979.

Rancière, Jacques. *Disagreement: Politics and Philosophy*. Translated by Julie Rose. Minneapolis: University of Minnesota Press, 1999.

Rancière, Jacques. *Hatred of Democracy*. Translated by Steve Corcoran. New York: Verso, 2014.

Rancière, Jacques. *The Nights of Labor: The Workers' Dream in Nineteenth-Century France*. Philadelphia: Temple University Press, 1989.

Rancière, Jacques. *On the Shores of Politics*. London: Verso, 2007.

Rauch, Georg von. *The Baltic States: The Years of Independence. Estonia, Latvia, Lithuania 1917–1940*. London: Hurst, 1995.

Rawson, Don C. *Russian Rightists and the Revolution of 1905*. New York: Cambridge University Press, 1995.

Reddy, William M. *Money and Liberty in Modern Europe: A Critique of Historical Understanding*. Cambridge: Cambridge University Press, 1987.

Reddy, William M. *The Rise of Market Culture: The Textile Trade and French Society, 1750–1900*. Cambridge: Cambridge University Press, 1987.

Renton, Dave. *Classical Marxism: Socialist Theory and the Second International*. Cheltenham: New Clarion, 2002.

Rieber, Alfred J. "The Sedimentary Society." *Russian History* 16, no. 2/4 (1989): 353–76.

Rieber, Alfred J. *The Struggle for the Eurasian Borderlands: From the Rise of Early Modern Empires to the End of the First World War*. New York: Cambridge University Press, 2014.

Riga, Liliana. *The Bolsheviks and the Russian Empire*. Cambridge: Cambridge University Press, 2012.

Riga, Liliana. "Identity and Empire: The Making of the Bolshevik Elite, 1880–1917." PhD diss., McGill University, 2000.

Rogger, Hans. *Jewish Policies and Right-Wing Politics in Imperial Russia.* Berkeley: University of California Press, 1986.

Rolf, Malte. "A Continuum of Crisis? The Kingdom of Poland in the Shadow of the Revolution (1905–1915)." In *The Russian Revolution of 1905 in Transcultural Perspective: Identities, Peripheries, and the Flow of Ideas,* edited by Felicitas Fischer von Weikersthal, 159–74. Bloomington, IN: Slavica Publishers, 2013.

Rolf, Malte. *Imperiale Herrschaft im Weichselland: Das Königreich Polen im russischen Imperium (1864–1915).* Berlin: De Gruyter Oldenbourg, 2015.

Rose, Jonathan. *The Intellectual Life of the British Working Classes.* 2nd ed. New Haven: Yale University Press, 2010.

Rosin, Ryszard, and Mieczysłąw Bandurka. *Łódź 1423—1823—1973: Zarys dziejów i wybór dokumentów.* Lodz: WKiSUM, 1974.

Rudnicki, Szymon. "Pogrom Siedlecki." *Kwartalnik Historii Żydów,* no. 1 (2010): 18–39.

Rumińska, Magdalena. "'Wiekuista maskarada' przed 1905 rokiem i krwawy karnawał po 1905 roku. Wybrane *Kroniki i Dzieci* Bolesława Prusa." In *Rewolucja lat 1905–1907: literatura—publicystyka—ikonografia,* edited by Krzysztof Stępnik and Monika Gabryś, 175–85. Lublin: Wydawnictwo Uniwersytetu Marii Curie-Skłodowskiej, 2005.

Ruud, Charles A. *Fighting Words: Imperial Censorship and the Russian Press, 1804–1906.* Toronto: University of Toronto Press, 2009.

Samuś, Paweł, ed. *"Bunt lódzki" 1892 roku.* Lodz: Wydawnictwo Uniwersytetu Łódzkiego, 1993.

Samuś, Paweł. *Dzieje SDKPiL w Łodzi 1893–1918.* Lodz: Wydawnictwo Łódzkie, 1984.

Samuś, Paweł. "Kobiety w ruchu socjalistycznym Królestwa Polskiego w latach rewolucji 1905–1907." *Rocznik Łódzki* 56 (2009): 85–115.

Samuś, Paweł. *Wasza kartka wyborcza jest silniejsza niż karabin, niż armata . . . : Z dziejów kultury politycznej na ziemiach polskich pod zaborami.* Lodz: Wydawnictwo Uniwersytetu Łódzkiego, 2013.

Sarasin, Philipp, ed. *Fremdkörper.* Innsbruck: Studien, 2005.

Scholz, Otfried. *Arbeiterselbstbild und Arbeiterfremdbild zur Zeit der Industriellen Revolution: Ein Beitrag zur Sozialgeschichte des Arbeiters in Der Deutschen Erzähl- und Memoirenliteratur um die Mitte des 19. Jahrhunderts.* Berlin: Colloquium, 1980.

Schorske, Carl E. *Fin-de-Siecle Vienna Politics and Culture.* New York: Vintage, 2012.

Schorske, Carl E. "Politics in a New Key: An Austrian Triptych." *Journal of Modern History* 39, no. 4 (1967): 344–86.

Schuster, Frank. "Die Stadt der vielen Kulturen—die Stadt der 'Lodzermenschen': Komplexe lokale Identitäten bei den Bewohnern der Industriestadt Lodz 1820–1939/1945." In *Intercultural Europe: Arenas of Difference, Communication and Mediation,* 33–60. Stuttgart: Ibidem, 2010.

Schwarz, Salomon M. *The Russian Revolution of 1905.* Translated by G. Vakar. Chicago: University of Chicago Press, 1967.

Scott, James C. *Domination and the Arts of Resistance: Hidden Transcripts.* New Haven: Yale University Press, 1990.

Scott, Joan W. "The Evidence of Experience." *Critical Inquiry* 17, no. 4 (1991): 773–97.

Scott, Joan W. "On Language, Gender, and Working-Class History." *International Labor and Working-Class History* 31 (1987): 1–13. doi:10.1017/S0147547900004063.

Sdvižkov, Denis. *Das Zeitalter der Intelligenz: Zur vergleichenden Geschichte der Gebildeten in Europa bis zum Ersten Weltkrieg.* Göttingen: Vandenhoeck & Ruprecht, 2006.

Sekura, Adrian. *Rewolucyjni Mściciele: Śmierć z browningiem w ręku.* Poznań: Wydawnictwo Poznańskiej Biblioteki Anarchistycznej Oficyna Wydawnicza "Bractwo Trojka," 2010.

Sewell, William. "Artisans, Factory Workers, and the Formation of the French Working Class, 1789–1849." In *Working-Class Formation: Nineteenth-Century Patterns in Western Europe and the United States*, 45–70. Princeton, NJ: Princeton University Press, 1986.

Sewell, William. *Logics of History: Social Theory and Social Transformation.* Chicago: University of Chicago Press, 2005.

Sewell, William. "Uneven Development, the Autonomy of Politics, and the Radicalization of Workers." In *The Industrial Revolution and Work in Nineteenth-Century Europe*, edited by Lenard R. Berlanstein, 148–62. New York: Routledge, 1992.

Sewell, William. *Work and Revolution in France: The Language of Labor from the Old Regime to 1848.* New York: Cambridge University Press, 1980.

Shanin, Teodor. *The Roots of Otherness: Russia's Turn of Century.* Basingstoke: Macmillan, 1986.

Shapely, Peter. *Charity and Power in Victorian Manchester.* Otley: Smith Settle, 2000.

Shorter, Edward, and Charles Tilly. *Strikes in France, 1830–1968.* New York: Cambridge University Press, 1974.

Shtakser, Inna. *The Making of Jewish Revolutionaries in the Pale of Settlement: Community and Identity during the Russian Revolution and Its Immediate Aftermath, 1905–1907.* New York: Palgrave Macmillan, 2014.

Siekierski, Stanisław. *Kultura szlachty polskiej: w latach 1864–2001.* Pułtusk: Wyższa Szkoła Humanistyczna Im. Aleksandra Gieysztora, 2003.

Sierakowska, Katarzyna. "Rodzina robotnicza w Królestwie Polskim w drugiej połowie XIX i pierwszej XX wieku: Ujęcie kulturowe." In *Rodzina, gospodarstwo domowe i pokrewieństwo na ziemiach polskich w perspektywie historycznej, ciągłość czy zmiana?*, edited by Cezary Kuklo, 323–41. Warsaw: Wydawnictwo DiG, 2013.

Siermiński, Michał. *Dekada przełomu: Polska lewica opozycyjna 1968–1980.* Warsaw: Książka i Prasa, 2016.

Sikorska-Kowalska, Marta. "Polskie 'Marianny': Udział kobiet w rewolucji 1905–1907 roku w świetle wydarzeń w Łodzi." In *Rewolucja 1905–1907 w Królestwie Polskim i w Rosji*, edited by Marek Przeniosło, Stanisław Wiech, and Barbara Szabat, 129–53. Kielce: Wydawnictwo Akademii Świętokrzyskiej, 2005.

Sikorska-Kowalska, Marta. *Wizerunek kobiety łódzkiej przełomu XIX i XX wieku.* Lodz: Ibidem, 2001.

Silver, Beverly J. *Forces of Labor: Workers' Movements and Globalization since 1870.* New York: Cambridge University Press, 2003.

Simmel, Georg. *Conflict/The Web of Group Affiliations.* Translated by Kurt Wolf. New York: Free Press, 1964.

Simmons, James. *Factory Lives: Four Nineteenth-Century Working-Class Autobiographies*. Orchard Park, NY: Broadview, 2007.

Skinner, Quentin. "Rhetoric and Conceptual Change." *Finnish Yearbook of Political Thought* 3 (1999): 34–63.

Skinner, Quentin. *Visions of Politics*. New York: Cambridge University Press, 2002.

Skocpol, Theda. *States and Social Revolutions: A Comparative Analysis of France, Russia, and China*. New York: Cambridge University Press, 1979.

Śliwa, Michał. "The Jewish Problem in Polish Socialist Thought." *Polin*, no. 9 (1996): 14–31.

Śliwa, Michał. "Rewolucja—przeszłość i kontynuacje." In *Z perspektywy osiemdziesięciu lat: Materiały z sesji naukowej w Wyższej Szkole Pedagogicznej w Krakowie w dniu 21 XI 1985 r., poświęconej rewolucji 1905—1907 r.*, 32–41. Cracow: Wydawnictwo Naukowe WSP, 1988.

Smele, Jon, and Anthony Heywood, eds. *The Russian Revolution of 1905: Centenary Perspectives*. New York: Routledge, 2005.

Smith, Sidonie, and Julia Watson. *Reading Autobiography: A Guide for Interpreting Life Narratives*. Minneapolis: University of Minnesota Press, 2001.

Śmiechowski, Kamil. "Hierarchia czy demokracja? Wizja stosunków społecznych w miastach Królestwa Polskiego (na podstawie dyskusji o samorządzie miejskim w trakcie rewolucji 1905 roku." *Studia z Historii Społeczno-Gospodarczej XIX i XX Wieku* 14 (2015): 103–20. doi:10.18778/2080–8313.14.08.

Śmiechowski, Kamil. *Łódzka wizja postępu: Oblicze społeczno-ideowe "Gońca Łódzkiego," "Kuriera Łódzkiego," "Nowego Kuriera Łódzkiego" w latach 1898–1914*. Lodz: Księży Młyn Dom Wydawniczy, 2014.

Śmiechowski, Kamil. "Początki prasy łódzkiej. Dziennikarze i wydawcy." *Kronika miasta Łodzi*, no. 3 (2016): 7–16.

Śmiechowski, Kamil. "Searching for a Better City: An Urban Discourse during the Revolution of 1905 in the Kingdom of Poland." *Praktyka Teoretyczna*, no. 3 (13) (2014): 71–96. doi:10.14746/pt.2014.3.4.

Śmiechowski, Kamil. "Strategie władz carskich wobec łódzkiej prasy codziennej do 1914 roku." *Klio: Czasopismo Poświęcone Dziejom Polski i Powszechnym* 28, no. 1 (2014): 63–83. doi:10.12775/KLIO.2014.004.

Śmiechowski, Kamil. "Warunki mieszkaniowe robotników na łamach 'Gońca Łódzkiego' (1898–1906)." *Studia z Historii Społeczno-Gospodarczej* 10 (2012): 105–20.

Śmiechowski, Kamil. *Z perspektywy stolicy: Łódź okiem warszawskich tygodników społeczno-kulturalnych (1881–1905)*. Lodz: Ibidem, 2012.

Śmiechowski, Kamil, Marta Sikorska-Kowalska, and Kenshi Fukumoto. *Robotnicy Łodzi drugiej połowy XIX wieku: Nowe perspektywy badawcze*. Lodz: Wydawnictwo Uniwersytetu Łódzkiego, 2016.

Snyder, Timothy. *Nationalism, Marxism, and Modern Central Europe: A Biography of Kazimierz Kelles-Krauz, 1872–1905*. Cambridge, MA: Harvard University Press, 1997.

Somers, Margaret R. *Genealogies of Citizenship: Markets, Statelessness, and the Right to Have Rights*. New York: Cambridge University Press, 2008.

Sorel, Georges. *Reflections on Violence*. Translated by T. E. Hulme and J. Roth. Dover: Courier Corporation, 2012.

Sperling, Walter. "Vom Randbegriff zum Kampfbegriff: Semantiken des Politischen im ausgehenden Zarenreich (1850–1917)." In *Politik: Situationen eines Wortgebrauchs im Europa der Neuzeit*, edited by Willibald Steinmetz. Frankfurt am Main: Campus, 2007.

Starkman, Adolf. *Łódź i łodzianie: Szkic społeczno-obyczajowy*. Warsaw, 1895.

Stedman Jones, Gareth. *An End to Poverty? A Historical Debate*. New York: Columbia University Press, 2005.

Stedman Jones, Gareth. *Languages of Class: Studies in English Working Class History, 1832–1982*. New York: Cambridge University Press, 1983.

Steenson, Gary P. *After Marx, before Lenin: Marxism and Socialist Working-Class Parties in Europe, 1884–1914*. Pittsburgh: University of Pittsburgh Press, 1991.

Stegner, Tadeusz. *Liberałowie Królestwa Polskiego 1904–1915*. Gdańsk: Nakładem autora, 1990.

Stegner, Tadeusz. "Rewolucja w opinii środowisk liberalnych Królestwa Polskiego 1905–1907." In *Rewolucja 1905–1907 w Królestwie Polskim i w Rosji*, edited by Marek Przeniosło, Stanisław Wiech, and Barbara Szabat, 21–43. Kielce: Wydawnictwo Akademii Świętokrzyskiej, 2005.

Steinberg, Marc W. *Fighting Words: Working-Class Formation, Collective Action, and Discourse in Early Nineteenth-Century England*. Ithaca, NY: Cornell University Press, 1999.

Steinberg, Mark D. *Proletarian Imagination: Self, Modernity, and the Sacred in Russia, 1910–1925*. Ithaca, NY: Cornell University Press, 2002.

Steinberg, Mark D. "Vanguard Workers and the Morality of Class." In *Making Workers Soviet: Power, Class, and Identity*, edited by Lewis H. Siegelbaum and Ronald Grigor Suny, 66–84. Ithaca, NY: Cornell University Press, 1994.

Steinmetz, George. "Reflections on the Role of Social Narratives in Working-Class Formation: Narrative Theory in the Social Sciences." *Social Science History* 16 (1992): 489–516.

Steinmetz, George. *Regulating the Social: The Welfare State and Local Politics in Imperial Germany*. Princeton, NJ.: Princeton University Press, 1993.

Steinmetz, Willibald, ed. *Political Languages in the Age of Extremes*. London: Oxford University Press, 2011.

Steinmetz, Willibald., ed. *Politik: Situationen eines Wortgebrauchs im Europa der Neuzeit*. Frankfurt am Main: Campus, 2007.

Steinmetz, Willibald. *Das Sagbare und das Machbare: Zum Wandel Politischer Handlungsspielräume. England 1780–1867*. Stuttgart: Klett-Cotta, 1993.

Steinmetz, Willibald, and Heinz-Gerhard Haupt. "Introduction." In *The Political as Communicative Space in History: The Bielefeld Approach*, edited by Willibald Steinmetz, Ingrid Gilcher-Holtey, and Heinz-Gerhard Haupt. Frankfurt am Main: Campus, 2013.

Stepnik, Krzysztof, and Monika Gabrys, eds. *Rewolucja lat 1905–1907: Literatura—publicystyka—ikonografia*. Lublin: Wydawnictwo Uniwersytetu Marii Curie-Sklodowskiej, 2005.

Stollberg-Rilinger, Barbara, ed. *Was heißt Kulturgeschichte des Politischen?* Berlin: Duncker & Humblot, 2005.

Stolleis, Michael. *Origins of the German Welfare State: Social Policy in Germany to 1945*. New York: Springer, 2013.

Strauss, Anselm L., and Juliet M. Corbin. *Basics of Qualitative Research: Techniques and Procedures for Developing Grounded Theory.* 2nd ed. Thousand Oaks, CA: SAGE, 1998.

Strobel, Georg W. *Die Partei Rosa Luxemburgs, Lenin und die SPD: Der polnische "europäische" Internationalismus in der russischen Sozialdemokratie.* Wiesbaden: Steiner, 1974.

Suny, Ronald Grigor. *The Baku Commune, 1917–1918.* New York: Columbia University Press, 1972.

Suny, Ronald Grigor. *The Making of the Georgian Nation.* 2nd ed. Bloomington: Indiana University Press, 1994.

Surh, Gerald Dennis. *1905 in St. Petersburg: Labor, Society, and Revolution.* Stanford, CA: Stanford University Press, 1989.

Suter, Andreas. "Kulturgeschichte des Politischen—Chancen und Grenzen." In *Was heißt Kulturgeschichte des Politischen?*, edited by Barbara Stollberg-Rilinger, 27–56. Berlin: Duncker & Humblot, 2005.

Swaan, A. de. *In Care of the State: Health Care, Education, and Welfare in Europe and the USA in the Modern Era.* Cambridge: Polity, 1988.

Światło, Adam. *Oświata a polski ruch robotniczy 1876–1939.* Warsaw: Książka i Wiedza, 1981.

Swietochowski, Tadeusz. *Russian Azerbaijan, 1905–1920: The Shaping of National Identity in a Muslim Community.* Cambridge: Cambridge University Press, 2002.

Szwarc, Andrzej. "Rewolucja 1905 roku na ziemiach polskich: Refleksje o historiografii i postawach inteligenckich elit." *Artes Liberales: Zeszyty Naukowe Wyższej Szkoły Humanistycznej im. Aleksandra Gieysztora* 1, no. 1 (2006): 25–36.

Szymański, Leonard. *Zarys polityki caratu wobec szkolnictwa ogólnoksztalcacego w Królestwie Polskim w latach 1815–1915.* Wroclaw: AWF, 1983.

Szyndler, Bartłomiej. *Dzieje cenzury w Polsce do 1918 roku.* Cracow: Krajowa Agencja Wydawnicza, 1993.

Taylor, Charles. *Modern Social Imaginaries.* Durham, NC: Duke University Press, 2004.

Thompson, Dorothy. *The Chartists: Popular Politics in the Industrial Revolution.* New York: Pantheon, 1984.

Thompson, Edward P. *The Making of the English Working Class.* New York: Vintage, 1963.

Tilly, Charles. *Popular Contention in Great Britain, 1758–1834.* Cambridge, MA: Harvard University Press, 1995.

Tobias, Henry Jack. *The Jewish Bund in Russia from Its Origins to 1905.* Stanford, CA: Stanford University Press, 1972.

Tomicki, Jan. *Polska Partia Socjalistyczna, 1892–1948.* Warsaw: Książka i Wiedza, 1983.

Trencsényi, Balázs, Maciej Janowski, Monika Baár, Maria Falina, and Michal Kopeček. *A History of Modern Political Thought in East Central Europe.* New York: Oxford University Press, 2016.

Upton, Anthony F. *The Finnish Revolution, 1917–1918.* Minneapolis: University of Minnesota Press, 1980.

Ury, Scott. *Barricades and Banners: The Revolution of 1905 and the Transformation of Warsaw Jewry.* Stanford, CA: Stanford University Press, 2012.

Vincent, David. *Bread, Knowledge, and Freedom: A Study of Nineteenth-Century Working Class Autobiography.* New York: Methuen, 1982.

Vincent, David. *Literacy and Popular Culture: England, 1750–1914.* New York: Cambridge University Press, 1989.

Wagner, Peter. "As Intellectual History Meets Historical Sociology." In *Handbook of Historical Sociology,* 168–79. London; Thousand Oaks, CA: SAGE, 2003.

Walczak, Jan, ed. *Dzieje robotnicze Śląska i Zagłębia Dąbrowskiego.* Katowice: Śląski Instytut Nauk, 1986.

Waldron, Peter. *Between Two Revolutions: Stolypin and the Politics of Renewal in Russia.* DeKalb: Northern Illinois University Press, 1998.

Waldron, Peter. *Governing Tsarist Russia.* New York: Palgrave Macmillan, 2007.

Walicki, Andrzej. *Philosophy and Romantic Nationalism: The Case of Poland.* Notre Dame, IN: University of Notre Dame Press, 1994.

Walicki, Andrzej. "Polish Conceptions of the Intelligentsia and Its Calling." *Slavica Lundensia* 22 (2005): 1–22.

Walicki, Andrzej. *Stanisław Brzozowski and the Polish Beginnings of "Western Marxism."* New York: Oxford University Press, 1989.

Wapiński, Roman. *Narodowa Demokracja 1893–1939: Ze studiów nad dziejami myśli nacjonalistycznej.* Warsaw: Ossolineum, 1980.

Wapiński, Roman. *Pokolenia Drugiej Rzeczypospolitej.* Warsaw: Ossolineum, 1991.

Wapiński, Roman. *Roman Dmowski.* Lublin: Wydawnictwo Lubelskie, 1989.

Warner, Michael. *Publics and Counterpublics.* New York: Zone Books, 2010.

Weeks, Theodore R. "1905 as a Watershed in Polish-Jewish Relations." In *The Revolution of 1905 and Russia's Jews,* edited by Stefani Hoffman and Ezra Mendelsohn, 128–41. Philadelphia: University of Pennsylvania Press, 2008.

Weeks, Theodore R. "Fanning the Flames: Jews in the Warsaw Press, 1905–1912." *East European Jewish Affairs* 28, no. 2 (1998): 63–81.

Weeks, Theodore R. *From Assimilation to Antisemitism: The "Jewish Question" in Poland, 1850–1914.* DeKalb: Northern Illinois University Press, 2006.

Weeks, Theodore R. *Nation and State in Late Imperial Russia: Nationalism and Russification on the Western Frontier; 1863–1914.* DeKalb: Northern Illinois Univ. Press, 2008.

Weeks, Theodore R. "Nationality and Municipality: Reforming City Government in the Kingdom of Poland." *Russian History* 21, no. 1 (1994): 23–47.

Weeks, Theodore R. "Polish 'Progressive Antisemitism,' 1905–1914." *East European Jewish Affairs* 25, no. 2 (1995): 49–68.

Weinberg, Robert. *The Revolution of 1905 in Odessa: Blood on the Steps.* Bloomington: Indiana University Press, 1993.

Weiss, Tomasz. *Przełom antypozytywistyczny w Polsce w latach 1880–1890: Przemiany postaw światopoglądowych i teorii artystycznych.* Cracow: Wydawnictwo Uniwersytetu Jagiellońskiego, 1966.

Welskopp, Thomas. *Das Banner der Brüderlichkeit: Die deutsche Sozialdemokratie vom Vormärz bis zum Sozialistengesetz.* Bonn: Dietz, 2000.

Wereszycki, Henryk. *Historia Polityczna Polski, 1864—1918*. Vol. 2. Wrocław: Zakład Narododowy im. Ossolińskich, 1990.

White, Hayden. "The Historical Text as Literary Artifact." In *The History and Narrative Reader*, edited by Geoffrey Roberts. New York: Routledge, 2001.

White, James D. "The Revolution in the Baltic Provinces." In *The Russian Revolution of 1905: Centenary Perspectives*, edited by Jon Smele and Anthony Heywood, 55–78. New York: Routledge, 2005.

Wildman, Allan K. *The Making of a Workers' Revolution: Russian Social Democracy, 1891–1903*. Chicago: University of Chicago Press, 1967.

Wimmer, Andreas, and Nina Glick Schiller. "Methodological Nationalism and beyond: Nation-State Building, Migration and the Social Sciences." *Global Networks* 2, no. 4 (2002): 301–34. https://doi.org/10.1111/1471-0374.00043.

Wolsza, Tadeusz. *Narodowa Demokracja wobec chłopów w latach 1887–1914: Programy, polityka, działalność*. Warsaw: Ludowa Spółdzielnia Wydawnicza, 1992.

Wood, Nathaniel D. *Becoming Metropolitan: Urban Selfhood and the Making of Modern Cracow*. DeKalb: Northern Illinois University Press, 2010.

Wortman, Richard. *Scenarios of Power: Myth and Ceremony in Russian Monarchy*. Princeton, NJ: Princeton University Press, 1995.

Wróbel, Piotr J. "From Conflict to Cooperation: The Bund and the Polish Socialist Party, 1897–1939." In *Jewish Politics in Eastern Europe: The Bund at 100*, edited by Jack Lester Jacobs, 155–71. Basingstoke: Palgrave, 2001.

Wróbel, Piotr J. "The Rise and Fall of Parliamentary Democracy in Interwar Poland." In *The Origins of Modern Polish Democracy*, edited by Mieczysław B. Biskupski, James S. Pula, and Piotr J. Wróbel, 110–63. Athens: Ohio University Press, 2009.

Wynn, Charters. *Workers, Strikes, and Pogroms*. Princeton, NJ: Princeton University Press, 1992.

Young, Iris Marion. "Impartiality and the Civic Public." In *Feminism as Critique: On the Politics of Gender*, edited by Seyla Benhabib and Drucilla Cornell, 96–121. Minneapolis: University of Minnesota Press, 1987.

Zahra, Tara. *The Great Departure: Mass Migration from Eastern Europe and the Making of the Free World*. New York: W. W. Norton, 2016.

Zaleska, Ilona. *Kościół a Narodowa Demokracja w Królestwie Polskim do wybuchu I wojny światowej*. Warsaw: Wydawnictwo DiG, 2014.

Zalewski, Cezary. "Świat wyszedł z zawiasów: Przemoc i jej reprezentacje w Dzieciach Bolesława Prusa." *Roczniki Humanistyczne* 59 (2011): 77–88.

Żarnowska, Anna, ed. *Dziedzictwo rewolucji 1905–1907*. Warsaw: Muzeum Niepodległości, 2007.

Żarnowska, Anna. *Geneza rozłamu w Polskiej Partii Socjalistycznej, 1904–1906*. Warsaw: Państwowe Wydawnictwo Naukowe, 1965.

Żarnowska, Anna. *Klasa robotnicza Królestwa Polskiego, 1870–1914*. Warsaw: Państwowe Wydawnictwo Naukowe, 1974.

Żarnowska, Anna. "Klasa robotnicza Królestwa Polskiego w rewolucji 1905–1907." Special issue of *Z pola walki* (1976): 61–77.

Żarnowska, Anna. "Próba analizy ruchu strajkowego w Królestwie Polskim w dobie rewolucji 1905–1907." *Przegląd Historyczny* 56, no. 3 (1956): 432–55.

Żarnowska, Anna. "Rewolucja 1905–1907 a aktywizacja polityczna klasy robotniczej Królestwa Polskiego." *Z pola walki*, no. 2 (70) (1975): 3–21.

Żarnowska, Anna. *Robotnicy Warszawy na przełomie XIX i XX wieku*. Warsaw: Państwowy Instytut Wydawniczy, 1985.

Żarnowska, Anna. "Rodowód i ruchliwość społeczna." In *Polska klasa robotnicza: Zarys dziejów*, edited by Stanisław Kalabiński. Vol. I, part 2, 70–105. Warsaw: Państwowe Wydawnictwo Naukowe, 1978.

Żarnowska, Anna. "Spojrzenie na rewolucję 1905 r. w polskiej historiografii—garść refleksji." *Kwartalnik Historyczny* 113, no. 4 (2006): 59–94.

Żarnowska, Anna. *Workers, Women, and Social Change in Poland, 1870–1939*. Burlington, VT: Ashgate, 2004.

Żarnowska, Anna. "Zasięg i wpływy PPS w przededniu rewolucji 1905 r." *Przegląd Historyczny* 67, no. 2 (1960): 351–85.

Żarnowska, Anna. "Zasięg oświaty elementarnej wśród klasy robotniczej królestwa polskiego w drugiej połowie XIX wieku." *Z pola walki*, no. 2–3 (1973): 61–77.

Żarnowska, Anna, and Stanisław Wolsza, eds. *Społeczeństwo i polityka: Dorastanie do demokracji. Kultura polityczna w Królestwie Polskim na początku XX wieku*. Warsaw: Wydawnictwo DiG, 1993.

Żarnowski, Janusz. *State, Society and Intelligentsia: Modern Poland and Its Regional Context*. Burlington, VT: Ashgate/Variorum, 2003.

Zaretskiy, Yury. "Confessing to Leviathan: The Mass Practice of Writing Autobiographies in the USSR." *Slavic Review* 76, no. 4 (2017): 1027–47. https://doi.org/10.1017/slr.2017.275.

Zarycki, Tomasz. "Class Analysis in Conditions of a Dual-Stratification Order." *East European Politics and Societies* 29, no. 3 (2015): 711–18. doi:10.1177/0888325415599199.

Zarycki, Tomasz. "Cultural Capital and the Political Role of the Intelligentsia in Poland." *Journal of Communist Studies and Transition Politics* 19, no. 4 (2003): 91–108. doi:10.1080/13523270300660030.

Zelnik, Reginald E. *Law and Disorder on the Narova River the Kreenholm Strike of 1872*. Berkeley: University of California Press, 1995.

Zelnik, Reginald E. "On the Eve: Life Histories and Identities of Some Revolutionary Workers 1870–1905." In *Making Workers Soviet: Power, Class, and Identity*, edited by Lewis H. Siegelbaum and Ronald Grigor Suny, 27–65. Ithaca, NY: Cornell University Press, 1994.

Zelnik, Reginald E. "Russian Bebels: An Introduction to the Memoirs of the Russian Workers Semen Kanatchikov and Matvei Fisher. Part I." *Russian Review* 35, no. 3 (1976): 249–89. doi:10.2307/128404.

Zelnik, Reginald E. "Russian Bebels: An Introduction to the Memoirs of the Russian Workers Semen Kanatchikov and Matvei Fisher, Part II." *Russian Review* 35, no. 4 (1976): 417–47. doi:10.2307/128439.

Zimmerman, Joshua D. *Poles, Jews, and the Politics of Nationality: The Bund and the Polish*

Socialist Party in Late Tsarist Russia, 1892–1914. Madison: University of Wisconsin Press, 2004.

Żurawicka, Janina. "Lud w ideologii 'Głosu' 1886–1894." *Kwartalnik Historyczny* 63, no. 4–5 (1956): 316–40.

Zysiak, Agata. "The Desire for Fullness: The Fantasmatic Logic of Modernization Discourses at the Turn of the 19th and 20th Century in Łódź." *Praktyka Teoretyczna*, no. 3 (13) (2014): 41–69. doi:10.14746/pt.2014.3.3.

Zysiak, Agata. *Modernizacja, socjalizm, nauka: Edukacja dla mas i budowa socjalistycznego uniwersytetu w powojennej Polsce*. Cracow: Nomos, 2016.

Zysiak, Agata. "The Polish Method—Sociology, Diary Competitions, and the Working Class's Recognition in the Twentieth Century Poland," manuscript in review.

Zysiak, Agata, Kamil Śmiechowski, Kamil Piskała, Kaja Kaźmierska, Jacek Burski, and Wiktor Marzec. *From Cotton and Smoke: Łódź—Industrial City and Discourses of Asynchronous Modernity 1897–1994*. Lodz: Wydawnictwo Uniwersytetu Łódzkiego, 2018.

Index

agricultural laborers, 141
anarchy, 69, 86, 106, 112, 171, 178–79, 202
antisemitism, 10, 62, 70–73, 102–5, 108–12, 134, 183, 201
Apukhtin, Alexander, 223
Arct's bookstore in Warsaw, 128
Arendt, Hannah, 200, 207
Austin, John L., 115
authoritarian turn, 112, 114, 205
autodidacticicsm, 125–28, 130, 136, 145

Bendix, Reinhard, 11
Bezdany, 149
biographical writing, 118–21, 129, 136, 212
Blobaum, Robert, 10
Bloody Sunday, 6, 32, 82, 84, 85, 95
Bodnar, Judit, 46
body politic, 16, 45, 182, 187, 191, 197
Bonnell, Victoria, 12
Bottici, Chiara, 17
Bottici, Chiara, 191
Bourgeoisie, 97 xxx
Brzeziński, Maksymilian

Brzozowski, Stanisław, 34
Buhle, Karol Teodor, 121

Calhoun, Craig, 207
capitalists, 89, 161, 175–79
censorship, 9, 44, 156, 168 173, 190, 251
citizenship, 11–12, 60, 63, 156, 200
clandestine education, 28–29
Crago, Laura, 104
Czerwony Sztandar (newspaper), 55
Częstochowa, 221

Dąbrowa Basin, 23
Dąbrowski, Józef (aka Grabiec), 46
democratization, 3–5, 10–11, 13–14, 68, 113, 148, 191
demographic structure, 25–27
Drzewiecki, Józef (aka Dejot), 134
Dziennik Łódzki (newspaper), 157

1863 uprising, 182
elections to the Duma, 101, 112, 230
Eley, Geoff, 11, 41
Engels, Friedrich, 11

factories as public places, 51
factory constitutionalism, 53
female militants/participation in political activism, 63–65
Finland, 198
Fraser, Nancy, 16, 206–7

Galicia, 201
general strike, 34, 85
Georgia, 198
Germans, 8, 25–26, 99, 103–4, 124, 157, 198
Geyer's factory in Lodz, 123
Golde, Estera, 73
Goniec Łódzki (newspaper), 155, 157

Habermas, Jürgen, 15, 18, 41, 205
heroism, 144, 148

industrialization, 20–23
insurrectionary tradition, 106
intelligentsia, 8, 13, 43, 208–10, 227
interpelation, 90–91

Janowski, Maciej, 181
Jastrzębski, Wincenty, 140
Jeleński, Jan, 73
Jews, 25–26, 70–72, 99–102, 109, 173, 182–86, 202
Jonsson, Stephan, 17–18

Kasprzak, Marcin, 148
Kiliński (journal), 212
Klimkiewiczówna, Michalina, 133
Kluge, Alexander, 41–42
Koselleck, Reinhart, 206, 242
Kosiorek, Michał, 132
Kossek, Władysław, 121
Kozicki, Stanisław, 71
KPP, 136, 212
Kujawa, Franciszek, 127
Kurier Codzienny (newspaper), 46

labor unions, 8, 228
land reform, 210
landed elites, 13, 20, 198
Latvia, 198
liberals, 69, 168, 201, 208
life cycle of workers, 128
living conditions of workers, 121
Lodz, 4, 23–25, 70, 81, 156
Lodz Riot of 1892, 26, 130
Lottes, Günther, 43
Luddite riot of 1861 in Lodz, 26
Luxemburg, Rosa, 55, 140

Manifesto of October 1905, 9, 46, 62
manliness, 144–48
Marx, Karl, 11
mass meeting (*masówki*), 45, 52
masses, 17
Młot (journal), 255
modernization, 161, 208

Mogilnicki, Aleksander, 181
Mulholland, Marc, 12
Müller, Jan-Werner, 18

national oppression, 124
ND, 8, 29, 59, 62, 69, 103, 106–14, 183, 201
Negt, Oskar, 41–42
NZR, 8, 29, 85, 94, 132, 230

October Revolution, 212
Okrzeja, Stefan, 148
open-air festivity (*majówka*), 48
Ostrowski, Michał, 129

Pabianice, 65
Parkot-Wójt, Stanisław, 134
Pieńkowski, Eugeniusz, 144
Piłsudski, Józef, 132, 201
Płochocki, Marian, aka Olbrzymek, 136
pogroms, 74, 94, 102
Polish-Lithuanian Commonwealth, 21
political agitation, 29, 58, 62, 79, 184
political initiation, 81, 132
political parties, 8, 29, 37
political polemics, 55–57
political representation, 17–18
political rights, 11–12
political subjectification, 61, 90

Porter-Szűcs, Brian, 8, 17, 107
Posiak, Jan, 132
PPS, 8, 29, 83, 55–57, 88, 91–92, 99–101
PPS-RF, 145, 201
professional mobility, 27, 139
proletarianization, 22
proletarian public sphere, 39–43, 52–53, 81, 152, 206–8
Proletariat (party), 148
public sphere, 15–18, 41–43, 206
PZPR, 212

Rancière, Jacques, 90
reading circles, 31
recognition, 38, 138, 187
redistribution, 209
revolution, concept of, 84
Reymont, Władysław, 69
Robotnik (newspaper), 66
Rogów, 149
Rosół (pseud.), 137, 245
Rozwój (newspaper), 157
Rudnicki, Lucjan, 125

Scheibler, Karol, 164
school system in Lodz, 27, 126, 223
Schorske, Carl, 77
SDKPiL, 8, 29, 83, 55–57, 88, 93, 99–101, 201
serfdom, 21
Sienkiewicz, Henryk, 183
Silberstein, Mieczysław, 186

Skowroński, Józef, 131
Snyder, Timothy, 16
social question, 159
socialism, concept of, 86–88
Sokolnicki, Michał, 71, 201
Sorel, George, 140
Sosnowiec, 23, 60
St. Petersburg, 6, 81
State Duma, 7, 59, 62, 78, 183, 229
Steinmetz, Willibald, 91
Stolypin, Pyotr, 254
strikes, 36–38, 139
Szapiro, Bernard, 40, 60
Śmiechowski, Kamil, 176
Świętochowski, Aleksander, 69, 181

textile workers strike of 1883 in Żyrardów, 26
terror, 146–49, 186
tsarat, 82–83, 89, 96–97, 106

Upper Silesia, 23
Ury, Scott, 10, 74

Wagner, Peter, 162
Warsaw, 4, 23, 69, 72, 81, 156

Zaretskiy, Yury, 213
Zgierz, 131